THE
POSTMODERN MOMENT

THE

POSTMODERN MOMENT

A HANDBOOK OF
CONTEMPORARY INNOVATION
IN THE ARTS

Edited, with an Introduction, by
STANLEY TRACHTENBERG

Movements in the Arts, Number 1

GREENWOOD PRESS
Westport, Connecticut • London, England

Library of Congress Cataloging in Publication Data

Main entry under title:

The Postmodern moment.

   (Movements in the arts, ISSN 8756–890X ; no. 1)
   Bibliography: p.
   Includes index.
   1. Postmodernism—Addresses, essays, lectures.
2. Arts, Modern—20th century—Addresses, essays,
lectures.   I. Trachtenberg, Stanley.   II. Series.
NX456.5.P66P66 1985   700′.9′04   85–5452
ISBN 0–313–23786–7 (lib. bdg.)

Library of Congress Catalog Card Number: 85–5452
ISBN: 0–313–23786–7
ISSN: 8756–890X

First published in 1985

Greenwood Press
A division of Congressional Information Service, Inc.
88 Post Road West
Westport, Connecticut 06881

Printed in the United States of America

The paper used in this book complies with the
Permanent Paper Standard issued by the National
Information Standards Organization (Z39.48–1984).

10 9 8 7 6 5 4 3 2 1

For Richard and Evelyn Cohen

Contents

Figures

Preface

At what moment does past become past or, more mysteriously, how does present continue to remain present? When do we recognize a new sensibility and acknowledge the development of new forms that have gathered to articulate it? One of the questions troubling any definition of postmodernism is whether it identifies a period or a style. Often a style will express more than one epoch. It may focus on the objective existence of the material world or on the shaping power of our perception of it, reflect our sense of the overpowering forces of nature or the individual response to them. It can be marked by a harmony of beliefs and unity of forms that express them and attempt to sum up the reassurances those forms and beliefs afford. Alternately, we may find ourselves dissatisfied with such interpretations and try to make our esthetic creations as unfamiliar as possible. At such times, several voices struggle to put forward their claim to describe what has changed. *The Postmodern Moment: A Handbook of Contemporary Innovation in the Arts* attempts to identify those voices.

This volume consists of original essays examining what has happened during roughly the past two decades in the fields of architecture, art, dance, film, literature and criticism, music, photography, and theatre. The essays analyze, describe, and provide an intellectual, social, and historical background as well as examine creative expression and critical thought. They attempt to show how we have first become conscious of, then tried to represent, and finally sought to assimilate recent changes in the ways we experience reality and project that understanding as art. Finally, they provide broad syntheses of critical issues and discuss representative figures and their work. Though the focus of these essays is primarily on postmodernism in the United States, it extends as well to the forms innovation in the arts has taken internationally. Included in an appendix are essays devoted to the literary expression of postmodernism in Europe and in Latin America. Additionally, a year-by-year chronology contains a listing of historical events placed alongside significant achievement in the several art forms. The chronology thus allows the parallels between the various fields to be seen at a glance and suggests something of the cultural influence on their development.

Each essay is supplemented by a comprehensive bibliography, annotating the most important items and indicating bibliographic sources. Directed at the general reader no less than the dedicated scholar, *The Postmodern Moment* is designated to make more accessible the consistently puzzling art forms of a period that seems more than at any other time to challenge continuity by not only rejecting past attempts to order experience but by making fun of its own.

Frequently movements or eras are described by an organic metaphor that refers to their birth, development, waning, and, finally, their death. It is convenient, maybe even reassuring, to think of art in terms of such parallels with life. But such a progression implies a more causal change than often is accurate, particularly at a time that sees experience as dissociative or fragmented rather than holistic or unified. The essays in this volume describe the various forms postmodernism takes, often by indicating its differences from modernism. Unlike modernism, where the work of art was a closed entity whose meanings were fixed and central and which accordingly encouraged explication or decipherment, postmodernism is dispersed. It invites collaboration. Thus it reflects a movement from symbolic representation, which proclaims the absence of what is there, to signification, which indicates the presence of an object. Where modernism cultivated ambiguity, postmodernism makes fun of it, exposing the framework that supports meaning. The work is thus pointed toward historical conditions rather than toward private meaning. Rather than an intransitive art, which constitutes an act in itself, it is transitive or purposive. For some critics, in fact, postmodernism constitutes a guerrilla action, dismantling the logic of a repressive state and the political structures and social institutions that sustain it. The representative mode of postmodernism, then, is deconstructive. It works to interrogate the audience, which is to say, causes it to reassess rather than reinforce its perception of the art object.

It is not possible, then, to speak of a postmodern tradition as it is of a tradition of modernism, for postmodernism doesn't constitute a single tendency but a number of responses. This multivalence is inclusive rather than select. It does not recognize in art the organic pattern in which elements are combined but insists on regarding each object as unique. It does not even react against the past, either to repudiate it or to acknowledge a debt. Its often remarked historicism is decorative, operating on the principle of adjacency rather than fused meaning. In contrast to modernism, which emphasized the subjective apprehension of experience, postmodernism finds itself unable to structure any ordering ideas of reality and so conceives of reality as itself unreal. To escape from the chamber of mirrors in which it thus finds itself trapped, it often adopts a strategy of irrealism, but this antimimetic impulse is not illusionistic. It is employed in an attempt to recover reality. The postmodern awareness, accordingly, concentrates on relocating the art object in the material world and so renews our perception of that object and of ourselves. It is aware, for example, of the influence of zoning ordinances on the evolution of the New York skyscraper or of reader response in determining the meaning of a text.

Postmodern art, thus, has no clearly defined boundaries; one spills into another so that it is difficult to find an appropriate term to indicate its dominant character. We have come in art, as in life, to rely on the hyphen. In short, we recognize in postmodernism the play of history and culture. In describing and analyzing postmodern art, this volume examines the innovative strategies we have adopted for engaging contemporary experience. Among them we discover not only changes in what we see but the struggle to readjust the focus of our vision. The treatment of several disciplines provides comprehensive sources for a handbook. It provides as well the foundations for a history of both the art and the culture of our time.

1

Introduction

STANLEY TRACHTENBERG

Nobody seems happy with the term "postmodernism." For one thing, there doesn't seem to be any agreement about what it is. There is some question, for example, about whether the postmodern is a reaction against earlier tendencies or merely an extension of them. Even those who maintain that it does represent a distinct way of confronting experience seldom suggest that it constitutes a movement, that is, a coherent body of work produced by a group of artists usually geographically centered and operating from at least loosely agreed upon principles. In place of any broad, ringing, social manifesto, there is Sam Shepard's justification for not inviting reviewers to attend the opening of his play *La Turista*. "It transcends time and doesn't correlate to any thesis that I had and worked out afterward," Shepard insisted, "I meant it to be a theatrical event, that's all."[1] Garry Winogrand similarly rejects the idea of meaning in his work, acknowledging that "I don't have anything to say. I photograph to find out what something will look like when photographed."[2] And John Cage, in a characteristic statement, remarks "I have nothing to say and I am saying it and that is poetry. . . ."[3] What these disclaimers indicate is that before a distinct postmodern sensibility can be identified, it will be necessary first to determine whether it makes itself known primarily as a method, a philosophy, an attitude, a tonality, a subject, a theme, or even some characteristic concerns. What questions does it ask, we might wonder, and what answers, if any, does it propose. What tactical strategies does it adopt, what risks does it take in implementing them, and what relations does it propose between esthetic structures and reality or between its own imaginative energies and those of other periods?

The term "postmodern" suggests a comparison with an era whose conventions no longer command general assent as a way of understanding our experience and making its values accessible. The conventions of any period are always somewhat fragile, and the current ones more so than most, in part because they are seemingly more exclusionary than most. The end of modernism, Craig Owens has observed, came with the exposure that our culture was not as homogenous as we liked to pretend. With the photographer Martha Rosler, Owens maintains that representational strategies, like words, have proved to be impoverished or merely diversionary. They address themselves to a controlling or mastering reality, one in which an art form pretends to speak for its subject.[4] Though Owens refers most immediately to the cultural exclusion of women, his argument is more broadly directed to Western ethnocentrism in general. It was just such a controlling vision that informed modernist aesthetics. Beginning anywhere between the last quarter of the nineteenth century and the first two decades of the twentieth, critical judgment has described modernism variously as informed by both classicism and romanticism—ironic, impersonal, and mechanical in the first instance; irrational, subjective, and intuitive in the second.[5] It is in either case animated by a fierce undercurrent of dissatisfaction, a revolution not merely in taste or even feeling, but in the direction of thought as well. Echoing Henry James, for whom reality became a way of conceiving of fiction, T. S. Eliot speaks of making the world possible for art, not the other way around. In the mythic parallels Joyce used to structure *Ulysses*, Eliot found "a way of controlling, or ordering, of giving shape and significance to the immense panorama of futility and anarchy which is contemporary history."[6] Lacking a shared sense of community formerly provided by science, religion, or even politics, modernists like Joyce and Eliot identified the distance between an earlier, ordered existence and the modern corruption of it. They adopted an ironic attitude toward the social order that led to a critical posture that finally discouraged reference to the external world. Though the modernists insisted on an objective method of representation, what they represented were states of consciousness.

The potency exerted by this approach was acknowledged even by so deliberate an artist as Thomas Mann, whose irony qualifies social values no less than the instinctive life they struggle to conceal. Mann, who called such irony "the pathos of the middle," quotes with approval Schopenhauer's belief that art subordinates the representation of outer life to the examination of the inner. "Die Kunst," Schopenhauer had written, "besteht darin, das man mit dem möglichst gerigsten Aufwand von äusserem Leben das innere in die stärkste Bewegung bringe; denn das innere is eigentlich der Gegenstand unseres Interesses."[7] Art consists in moving us most deeply with the least indication of external action, for the inner life is essentially the object of our interest. In writers ranging from Kafka and Conrad to Lawrence and Faulkner, we find the visualized forms of modernism establishing the fluid truths of that inner life.

The assertion of the irrational or underground element thus complements the impersonal concern for form just as the ahistoricism of the New Critics complemented the traditionalism of Eliot and Pound. Modernists attempted to reconcile these tensions by focusing on perception and opposing to the discredited nineteenth-century assurances their own faith—the faith in metaphor. The result, as Lionel Trilling described it, was an intensely personal literature that revealed an adversary disenchantment of the culture with culture itself. "The idea of losing oneself up to the point of self-destruction, or surrendering oneself to experience without regard to self-interest or conventional morality, of escaping wholly from society's bonds," Trilling wrote, "was an element somewhere in the mind of every modern person."[8]

Access to reality correlatively emerges in the atomized, retinal sensations of the Impressionists, the shifting planes that constitute the multiple, geometric images of cubism and the Paris School, the evocative photography of Alfred Stieglitz and the Photo Secessionists, the emotional intensity of Martha Graham's dance, the break with tonality by Debussy and, more completely, by Schönberg, in an attempt to provide an organic structure without the predictable tendencies of tonal music. The complex of feelings and attitudes I am attempting to describe may be summed up in the International Style of architecture, which, as Henry-Russell Hitchcock described it, represented a movement from mass to volume. Regularity of detail replaced axial symmetry as the ordering principle of design from which arbitrary decoration was eliminated. Load bearing walls, for example, were replaced by curtain walls, which could be fitted between the structure like screens or carried like a shell outside them. Even the glass of the windows became an integral part of that screen rather than punched into the walls as in masonry construction.[9] Following the economic and spiritual collapse of Europe after the First World War, such visionaries as Bruno Taut and Walter Gropius in Germany and Le Corbusier in France often showed little concern for the siting of their buildings or even for the fact that a technology had not yet developed that would enable them to be built. What interested them, above all, was making a fresh start. "The old forms are in ruins," Gropius remarked, "the benumbed world is shaken up, the old human spirit is invalidated and in flux toward a new form."[10] Mies van der Rohe, who succeeded Gropius as head of the Bauhaus and then followed him to the United States, continued to express this feeling when an early plan he drew for the Illinois Institute of Technology was rejected by the institute's president, Henry Heald. "They would not permit me to remove the streets until much later," Mies complained, "so I was confronted with the past."[11] Attempting to express the civilization he lived in rather than the society, Mies' structures reflected an Augustinian ideal, which looked for its truths to an ideal outside the accidents of experience. One of Mies' most important early structures, the German Pavilion for the International Exposition of 1929 in Barcelona, never housed an exhibit. The building itself was what was on display. Le Corbusier, who spoke of a house as a machine for living and was intent on incorporating machine-age materials into his utopian proposals, envisioned a skyscraper city of light suspended on *pilotis* of reinforced concrete. Mies went even further in focusing on structure rather than function. "I think structural elements are very essential elements," he remarked, "and I think pipes are not. The structure can be integrated into architecture, but I don't think that pipes can."[12]

In contrast to this attempt at an abstract, timeless statement, the postmodern aesthetic, as Mary McLeod demonstrates, looks backward; it invites imitation or reinterpretation. In place of the austere modernist abstractions, it adopts a vernacular regard for the environment. Pipes or high-tech space frames replace steel and glass cage constructions, particularly in areas requiring large spans. Unlike modernism where it is organic or inherent in form, meaning occurs only in arbitrary symbolic associations drawn from public or social contexts. This distinction informs Robert Venturi's preference for what he terms "decorated sheds" over "ducks." The decorated shed communicates its meaning through a semiotically learned or affixed meaning, the duck through an iconic identification of form and content—a donut stand built in the shape of a donut, for example, or a delivery truck whose panels resemble a shoe. The point Venturi establishes is not so much the dissociation of form and meaning or the arbitrary quality by which we arrive at communication. It is that signification must take its meaning from environment.

Unlike the consistent, unified style of Mies or Gropius, then, postmodern architecture incorporates mixed styles, whose odd angles and skewed spaces often parody the boxiness of the International Style. Along with such parodic revivalism, critics like Charles Jencks point to plural coding as characteristic of postmodernism, a preference for convention and contradiction, for ambiguity and tensions, for both-and rather than either-or.[13] Looked at another way, postmodernism advances regional suitability and contextualness that serve as a critique of the autonomous building separated from its site. Peter Eisenman's House IIa in Palo Alto, for example, contains inaccessible spaces, which make interchangeable the inside and outside of the house. The aesthetic of modernism, as Robert Hughes describes it, was utopian in nature and envisioned the power technology would control or even eliminate material scarcity.[14] The postmodern imagination questions the value of any universalizing formulation; questions even the validity of language as a means of approaching one. Quoting traditional architecture is appropriate only as a conscious allusion to historicism.

A parallel approach to quotation informs postmodern literature. Though Philip Stevick points to the enormous increase in fictional options during the past quarter century, few, if any of them, describe the progress in a hero's career that might lead to summary insight. Structure, Stevick finds, becomes additive or assembled rather than developed. Its determining principle is adjacency, governed frequently by the liberation of play. Reviewing what she described as a postcounterculture comedy of the late seventies, the critic Pauline Kael similarly noted that the characters didn't believe in anything at the beginning of the film or at the end either.[15] Critical of existing forms, postmodernism tends to substitute enactment for interpretation—a rhetorical approach for the acknowledgment of history— tends to project a two-dimensional world in which line is freed from contour; narrative movement is lateral rather than progressive; figures, even objects, are not depicted. Unlike modernism, which suggests a historical period, postmodernism describes a sensibility, a feeling for innovation, for experiment with conventional ways of framing experience so that it is at once removed from recognizable relationships and from the locations in which they exist. At the same time it is brought up close to the surface where fiction thrusts itself into the world. This movement is variously informed by a skeptical attitude toward illusion, toward a recognizable psychology of human relationships, and toward coherence of any sequence of actions. It is thus performative rather than reve- latory, superficial rather than immanent, aleatory rather than systematic, dis- persed rather than focused. Often described simply as fabulist or irrealist, it more properly adopts these strategies, among others, in a return from private to public concerns. From the problems of self and identity modernism raised, it turns its attention to the claims art makes to redefine them. The self-consciousness of the postmodern novel, as Robert Alter points out, is not preoccupied with its own artifice but with questioning its premises.[16]

Rather than observe the modernist slogan "Make It New," postmodernism thus repeats, parodies, slows things down. To the depth generated by modernism, it opposes a nonrelational uniformity of surface. A central axiom governs the difference. In modernism, art liberates us from the constructions of reality; in postmodernism, reality beckons us from the distortions of art. Andy Warhol, for example, reminds us of the difference between reality and the attempts to reproduce it in his silk-screen repetitions of celebrities, of commercial products, historical figures, or new events or in his films, in which the camera remains focused on a building or on a figure sleeping. Even in such kinetic forms as dance or music, which are dependent on temporal progression, there is a tendency both to empty the work of meaning and to reify it as an object in the world. Composers such as Steve Reich cycle their compositions on loops of spliced tape, which are then replayed over and over, while La Monte Young directs performers of his music to hold a note for a long time. Perhaps the most prominent advocate of the paradoxical centering of art in its environment while at the same time decentering its formal structure is John Cage, who, in such works as 4′33″ invites the audience to look at a piano for that period of pure silence. Cage's use of the prepared instrument on the one hand and of aleatoric performance on the other accommodate what formerly had been regarded merely as noise. Using star maps, I Ching, and various random sounds ranging from a vegetable blender to burning pine cones, Cage demonstrates that everything we hear is music. For Garry Clarke this minimalization or withdrawal in the work of such contemporary figures as Pauline Oliveros, Philip Corner, or Philip Glass, among others, results in a kind of antimusic or destruction of sound. One aspect of it is concept music, which is created not to be heard but imagined. Another, exemplified in the work of Lukas Foss or Dominick Argento, is the use of extensive quotation from earlier periods of musical history. Finally, Clarke points to performance art in which music is integrated with several other media. Silent or noisy, isolated or in combination with other forms, postmodern music announces its independence of the abstract if logical progressions of modernism that, paradoxically, dem- onstrated a renewed interest in the way music was listened to.

As towering a figure in dance as Cage is in postmodern music, Merce Cun- ningham, who collaborated with Cage on many occasions, similarly employed mixed media to open up the forms of art. Emphasizing the dissociative aspect of dance, Cunningham anticipates a movement whose overall pattern Sally Banes finds marked by "irony, playfulness, historical reference, the use of vernacular materials, the continuity of cultures, an interest in process over product, breakdowns of boundaries between the art forms and between art and life, and new relationships between artist and audience." For Banes, the permissiveness and playful rebellion found a more serious echo in the cultural upheavals of the late sixties and opened the world of dance to the broader aspects of art by shifting the locations of performance from the stage to such sites as chicken coops, parking lots, or skating rinks. At the same time, dance was marked by a foregrounding, which concentrated on the body as itself the subject rather than merely an instrument for expression. The situation of the dance became its subject rather than the relationship of the dancers. Choreographers such as Laura Dean, Trisha Brown, Lucinda Childs, or Yvonne Ranier, for example, reduce movement to a minimum, repeat it insistently with minor variations, or halt it altogether. Illusionistic effects were discouraged by wearing work clothing or sweat suits in place of classical costumes, by the minimal or repetitive movements, by an emphasis on the effort these movements required, and by what Banes identifies in the most recent stage of postmodern dance as a refusal to differentiate the dancer's body from that of the ordinary person. As part of a movement that merges high and popular traditions through historical quotation, postmodern dance invites the audience to participate in the performance rather than view it as distant spectators.

This breakdown of esthetic distance extends as well to photography, where Stanley Bowman finds in the representative work of Garry Winogrand an adaptation of the earlier documentary tradition that is, in fact, layered and disjunctive. It is a world, as Bowman describes it, in which the hierarchies of value are deliberately excluded so that while "everything is revealed nothing has meaning." This reluctance to interpret the object of vision is expressed in the democratic inclusiveness of Joe Deal, whose intention, Bowman quotes, is to make one image equal in weight or appearance to another in order to deny the uniqueness of subject matter. Marked by the increasing importance of ideas, the use of images popularized by the media, the fabrication of reality in the studio or the manipulation of the print in the darkroom, postmodern photography accommodates seemingly contrasting approaches. In the spontaneity of Winogrand or William Eggleston as well as the more highly posed images of Cindy Sherman or Ellen Brooks, however, the concern remains less the distortion of reality than what happens when the photograph attempts to capture it. The result is an antiformalism that nonetheless self-consciously calls attention to its own strategies. Gene Thornton lists a number of techniques adopted by this new photography to illustrate the peculiarities of the camera image. Among them he includes distorted scale, artificial lighting, tilted horizons, blurred or out-of-focus images, information overload as a result of congested detail, and random framing, often leaving unexplained partial glimpses of the body at the edges of the picture.[17] Combining a self-conscious awareness of photographic history with a vernacular skepticism about the degree to which a photograph can render the truth of its object, postmodern photography offers a shifting sense of where the boundaries of the photograph open into the actuality of experience.

John Paoletti identifies a parallel concern in the reversal by modern abstract art of the Renaissance denial of pictorial surface. Championed by the critic Clement Greenberg, Jackson Pollock and the Abstract Expressionists rejected recessional or volumetric space in favor of a decentralized canvas in which the entire surface was covered with forms of equal importance. Pictorial space, Greenberg argued, was no longer a dimension in which things existed or events took place. "The old masters," he maintained, "created an illusion of space in depth that one could imagine oneself walking into, but the analagous illusion created by the modernist painter can only be seen into; can be traveled through, literally or figuratively, only with the eye."[18]

Geometric, hard-edge color-field painters such as Morris Louis, Kenneth Noland, Frank Stella, or Jules Olitski took the process one step further. Using stained, rolled, or airbrushed techniques, they attempted to eliminate the presence of the artist as well as minimize the sense of illusion. In an attempt to solve the consequent relational problems, Stella, who even notched his paintings or cut holes in them to interfere with the illusion, experimented with symmetry and then color density, very much as the Impressionists had substituted color for the perspectivist geometries of the classical masters. Adopting house painter's techniques and materials, Stella emphasized the actuality of the physical properties as a means by which pictorial art could maintain the integrity of its surface. His painting, he insisted, should be regarded as an object in which only what could be seen there *was* there. "What I am trying to do," Stella insisted, "is to keep the paint as good as it was in the can."[19] This concern for surface was echoed in Jules Olitski's conviction that even edge was part of drawing rather than a boundary that separated what was on the canvas from the world in which the painting existed as an object. Working almost from within the painting toward the literalness of the picture plane, Olitski adopted a variety of materials ranging from pastel to magic marker to repeat the edge as internal frame. The picture thus contains the illusion, or rather its absence, as a separate visual object thrust toward the viewer. "What is important in painting," Olitski has remarked, "is paint. And paint becomes painting when color establishes surface."[20]

Similarly contrasting with the organic spontaneity of Abstract Expressionism are the stiffened flags or bronzed beer cans of Jasper Johns, the iconographic lipsticks, clothespins, ice bags, or toothbrushes of Claes Oldenburg, the urban junk of Red Grooms, the mummylike figures of George Segal, Wayne Thiebaud's approximations of the relations between the texture of paint and that of the subject matter, and the multiple images of movie stars, Coca-Cola bottles, or Campbell soup cans of Andy Warhol. These deliberately facsimiled constructs parody their own attempt at literalism by collapsing the distinguishing features of consumer objects into a mechanical sameness. This commercialized quality as high art representatively informs the work of Roy Lichtenstein, whose comic-strip frames of aerial dogfights, advertisements, or popular romances, along with the brushstrokes by which he parodied the gesture painting of the Abstract Expressionists, are depicted in magnified Ben Day dots, which emphasize their two dimensional plane. In contrast to the pointillism of, say, Seurat, which afforded a unified illusion when viewed from a distance, Lichtenstein's abstract style, along with the distortion that results from exaggerated scale, calls attention to its source as drawing rather than a life situation. Lichtenstein has traced this concern for composition as a subject to the early fifties when, working in Ohio, he felt cut off from what was then current painting and sculpture. "Reproduction," he has acknowledged," was really the subject of my work."[21]

The element of art as self-criticism appears as well in photo realism, where it comments on the ability of painting to draw its subject directly from experience. Often transferring likeness by projecting it on a grid, artists like Richard Estes, Robert Cottingham, Donald Eddy, Ralph Goings, Chuck Close, and Malcolm Morely, among others, remind us of life rather than create its illusion. Malcolm Morely's phone books, souvenir postcards, or travel brochures, for example, recall the images that served as his original subjects by retaining their framing borders or imperfections, while in Richard Estes' reflective surfaces what we see are not pictures of the world but of the way in which the world is reflected. Smooth flat surfaces, landscapes in which there are seldom human figures and in which almost nothing ever seems to move decline comment on the reality they approach. Unlike the selective judgments of focus that the eye makes, these paintings reproduce a photographically neutral landscape in which the camera passively records everything that falls within its perspective. This artificial quality is identified by Don Eddy, who describes his paintings as a comment on painting by establishing a tension among the outside world, the surface of the canvas, and illusionary space. In "Private Parking," Eddy paints in a fence that did not appear in the original photograph of the scene. "There was illusion behind it," he explained, "and you acknowledged the presence of that illusion, but at the same time it created a barrier."[22]

The barrier of illusion is further assaulted in minimal art, where, Paoletti suggests, rather than remaining discrete, the art object becomes congruent with that of our own world. Attributing the decline of mimesis in art to the emergence of the photographic image, the film critic Andre Bazin noted the function of the frame in emphasizing the discontinuity between the picture and the wall. "In contrast to natural space," Bazin remarks, "the space in which our active experience occurs, and bordering its outer limits [the frame] offers a space the orientation of which is inwards, a contemplative area opening solely onto the interior of the painting."[23] The frame thus exists in two dimensions, allowing each to define itself as a complete if analagous image of the other. The screen image, Bazin goes on to argue, lacks the anchoring limits provided by the frame and so in contrast to the painting depicts only a portion of reality, the whole of which extends infinitely outward. The cinematic quality projected on the screen thus dissolves the spatial boundaries not within the picture plane but between that plane and the world that lies beyond it, that is to say, between the image and the audience. This movement beyond the frame emerged during the sixties in the free standing, minimal structures of Donald Judd, Carl Andre, or Robert Morris, for whom the principle of composition is not organic and integral but dependent upon what Andre has called "anaxial symmetry." Forms are placed adjacent to one another rather than joined permanently in relation to a fixed idea of the whole. Any part, Andre explains, can replace any other part.[24] The importance of its materials as well as location distinguish this minimalism from conceptual art, with which it is often linked. Though an antiformal element runs through both, conceptualism regards the object finally as ancillary to the finished work. The difference is dramatically illustrated in a 1969 exhibition at the Whitney Museum called "Anti-Illusion: Procedures/Materials." Commenting on the work of Dan Flavin and Carl Andre, both of whom were among the twenty-two artists included in the show, Philip Leider observed that the order imposed on the materials was not intended to create the object so much as "a set of conditions which we experience as art."[25] In the work of Sol LeWitt this focus on orientation shifts to the acknowledgment of space from the necessity to take possession of it. Unemotional, illogical, purposeless, intuitive, it is, at the same time, deliberate and predetermined rather than arrived at through the process of execution or through the chance or random motion that animates minimal art. The idea, LeWitt maintains, functions as a machine that determines the result. Accordingly, he is led to the remarkable conclusion that "What a work looks like isn't too important."[26] A parallel impulse can be seen informing postmodern music. "I'm not interested in how it sounds," Pierre Boulez has remarked, "I'm interested in how it's made."[27]

LeWitt, who in 1955–56 worked in the graphics department of I. M. Pei's office and whose structures occasionally resembled some of the early buildings of the International Style (his striped table structure of 1963 is an example), nonetheless operates principally from the premises of two dimensionality. Fusing repetitive grids, concentric circles, grafittilike drawing, geometric shapes, and words or sometimes pages from a book, LeWitt imposes a personal and arbitrary order on essentially meaningless bits of information. Radiating curved or straight lines sometimes not touching alternately connect almost everything, so that nothing is joined in any way that makes one element more important than any other.[28] LeWitt's concern for the literal is echoed in the music of Philip Glass or Steve Reich or in the films of Andy Warhol, Richard Serra, or Michael Snow, which replace the illusion of duration by the actual time of performance. This minimalization, then, suggests not so much a denial of the power to move us or even of the shaping power of the artist. It is, rather, a withdrawal from the notion that art can exist independently of reality or provide some comprehensive, permanent statement about it. The result is a tension between an acute consciousness of itself as an art form and the actuality of existence, an actuality that can be arrived at only once the image of the art object is dissolved.

In this rejective art, as Lucy Lippard has termed it, representation of any sort—either of feeling or of form—is discouraged or abandoned.[29] Christo's veils conceal the objects over which they are draped; Oldenburg excavates and refills a hole in Central Park; Joseph Kosuth reproduces photostatic negatives; LeWitt's boxlike models close off visual perception or, completely buried, remain accessible only through photographic documentation. The artistic concept is thus transmitted from the artist to the viewer almost without the clumsy mediation of the object itself. This emphasis on concept even to the exclusion of form paradoxically calls attention to its own communicative strategies, isolating them as events that look to an exterior landscape rather than to a principle of internal coherence. The individual details do not combine to account for the total visual field established within the structure, to account, that is, for its imagined reality. The field serves rather as a transient bridge to the actuality of the separate elements and the viewing experience they generate. In other words, the art object establishes a surface that announces itself as part of the things of this world rather than recapitulating them and keeps from being absorbed by them not by creating or even defining an environment but by placing itself in a recognizably esthetic one.

The shift postmodernism thus indicates in our esthetic frames clearly reflects a difference in the way in which we have come to conceive of and consequently engage reality. Daniel Bell proposes an axiologic structure for a postindustrial society centered on these differences. From something that existed between man and nature, Bell contends, we have come to experience reality as existing between man and technology, and, more recently, as a projection among men. Accordingly, the problems that define our society are those that attempt to identify a change in its social structure. Though Bell acknowledges a greater degree of technical change during the nineteenth and early twentieth centuries—he points to the development of the railroad, steamship, electricity, telephone, radio, automobile, movies, airplane, and high-speed elevator—what we have lately experienced, he claims, is a sense of the increased pace and change of scale. Individuals, consequently, are cast in increasingly specialized roles that increase their sense of helplessness within a larger entity. To take one example, the benign view of corporate America during the Eisenhower administration, Bell argues, has given way to the conviction that "corporate performance has made society uglier, dirtier, trashier, more polluted, and noxious. The sense of identity between the self-interest of the corporation and the public interest has been replaced by a sense of incongruence."[30] The incongruity of the American experience and the speed with which it changed was anticipated at the turn of the century by Henry Adams, who saw the acceleration of force as a determining principle of history. Adams looked for a formula that would account for social change on the model of physical laws. Order, he maintained, was the dream of man, chaos the law of nature. Adams' dream was to impose that order by measuring the chaos. What he could not anticipate was the spread of chaos to the instruments of measurement.

Expressing the optimism generally shared in America at the end of the Second World War, *Look* Magazine confidently asserted that the prospects facing American society had never been more promising. Among the features that made up what *Look* jubilantly termed "America's new frontiers" were the modern house, the automatic washer, express highways, television, the private airplane, and quick freezing.[31] This emphasis on material well-being found a more shrill expression in the pages of *House Beautiful*, which, in 1953, felt called upon to respond to the growing authority of the doctrine that less was more. Such an idea, the editor protested in boldface type, threatened the American way of life. Among other things, it promoted "unlivability, stripped-down emptiness, lack of storage space and therefore lack of possessions."[32] The sense of promise and shared values to which these statements pointed, however, had already begun to erode. Increasingly Americans were made aware of their vulnerability to international events and their limited ability to influence the outcome. The failure of the American-backed invasion at the Bay of Pigs by Cuban exiles, the oil embargo, the seizure of the United States embassy by Iranian revolutionaries, but, most divisively, the Vietnam War dramatized those limits while irrevocably changing the nature of American society. The assassinations of John F. Kennedy, his brother Robert, and Martin Luther King, Jr., along with inner-city riots in Harlem and Watts, the shootings at Kent State University, and widespread student protests revealed a violent political climate responsive at times to the power of the media not merely to report events but to create them. In the following decade, the Watergate scandal and the resignation of the president shattered the sense of national unity. Various constituencies emerged as a result of the shift from a labor-intensive to a service-oriented economy, population shifts from the urban Northeast and Midwest to the Sunbelt, the increase in the divorce rate and the growth of single parent families. The aging of America and consequent shifting balance of retired people and the work force, the emergence of the human potential and women's awareness movements, and a concern for the environment and personal physical fitness helped to redefine cultural preoccupations and rythms. Even the image of the family changed from the wholesomeness projected in "Father Knows Best" or "Leave It to Beaver" and the comic reassurances of "Make Way for Daddy" and "I Love Lucy." Americans recognized themselves in the narrow-minded defensiveness of "All in the Family" while betraying a fascination with the venality and opulence of "Dallas," "Dynasty," and even "I, Claudius." The growth of active consumerism paralleled the indifference of private industry to the public good as manifested in overpricing, cost overruns, kickbacks, and insider transactions. Perhaps most dramatically the nation suffered a loss of confidence in the promise of technology and so of the future after the accident at the Three Mile Island nuclear reactor.

In his now classic interpretation of the American literary imagination, Richard Chase argued that "Many of the best American novels achieved their very being, their very energy and their form from the perception and acceptance not of unities but of radical disunities."[33] Writing in 1961, Philip Roth took a somewhat contrasting position. Roth found the difficulty of writing fiction in America to be the result of excesses that so embarrassed the imaginative possibilities that

writers were forced to turn from social concerns to the self as a subject.[34] Saul
Bellow was attacked for failing to locate his fiction in the social facts of experience and so willing rather than earning his affirmations. Despite Bellow's work
and that of Ralph Ellison, John Updike, and Roth himself, among others, all of
whom addressed a recognizable social reality, a sense of the discontinuity between experience and the ability to frame it within a mimetic, fictive world
seemed to be growing. The exuberance of Woodstock, of the Apollo landing on
the moon, of the celebration marked by the arrival of the Tall Ships was tempered
by the increasing perception of political divisions between extremes of a New
Left and a Radical Right and by the difficulties of the middle class in maintaining
its position between them. Equally troubling was institutionalization of the intellectual avant garde that, far from the implacable opposition to society it had
formerly voiced, now, in forms ranging from government grants, university
appointments, and foundation subsidies, looked for support to the very institutions whose values it once attacked.

These anxieties found partial expression in a poststructural or deconstructive
art in which no privileged position remained exempt from a textual surface.
Deconstruction thus challenges in one form or another the idea of a closed system
of meanings; challenges, finally, even the illusion of fictive reality or correspondence through which such meanings can be abstracted. Responsibility for
the text is shifted from an all-knowing author to a more playful auditor. Accordingly, it discourages a sense of causality, identity, unified structure, coherence, motive—discourages the fictive enterprise itself. "You have fallen into
Art," William Gass warns the reader of *Willie Masters' Lonesome Wife*, "Return
to Life."

That the meaning of language can no longer be controlled constitutes the basis
for the shift from traditional narration, which placed the reader directly in the
fictive situation. Modern narration focuses on the narrator's experience of perception. Postmodern narration deconstructs even that perceptual frame and attempts to return to the world from which the fictive details were abstracted, that
is to say, the world of the reader or auditor. For Roland Barthes, the identity
of the author is thus dissolved into a neutral space where there are no meanings.
"Everything," Barthes maintains, "is to be disentangled, nothing deciphered."
Similarly in music Barthes finds that playing ceases to exist and with it the
sympathetic identification of the listener with the performer. Replacing both the
"actor" of music as well as the interpreter, the technician abolishes even the
notion of *doing*.[35]

Unlike structuralism, which relied on linguistics as a model of cultural organization, poststructuralism discourages any closed order of signifier and signified and any pattern that would establish a connection between them. Texts
emerge not from reality but from a tradition of other texts, whose sources and
interactions are so various as to be ultimately untraceable. Even the structure of
a work becomes an interpretation and so a fiction. What deconstruction exposes,
then, is the attempt to displace the rhetorical by the referential. Put another way,

it calls attention to the illusion through which language evokes the presence of an object rather than acknowledges its absence. Fiction is thus no longer agonizingly crafted as an enabling vehicle from which the artist may view experience, even the experience of subjective perception. It becomes instead an almost self-generating invention, whose ontological condition rivals the writer's own. For critics such as Michel Foucault, it further carries the coercive force of social values inherent in language. In this way, fiction marks a shift from the modernist concern with consciousness—with ways of knowing—and reflects a self-referential strategy that insists on process and content chiefly as copy or parody. This impulse emerges both in fabulous or irrealist terms, which blur the distinction between reality and the imagination, and in a self-conscious literalism, in which the struggle of the modern hero to define himself is translated into the narrator/author's attempt to overcome the resistance of narrative form.

In either mode, action is often held in suspension, awaiting the controlling impulse of character. That impulse is seldom forthcoming. Aware of the fictive nature of the landscape in which they are called upon to exist and of the fact that they are only arbitrarily willed figures within it, characters struggle to reach the surface of narrative as though impelled toward an atmosphere that can more readily sustain life. Reflecting the range of these modalities—on the one hand a triumph of invention, on the other an escape from it—are a surprisingly disparate group of writers, whose innovative fictions combine the seemingly unposed, snapshotlike cropping of experience with the grainy distortions that remind the reader of preserved images. Synoptic rather than developmental, they are projected in the subjunctive—the conjectural—mood as frequently as in the indicative. Such fiction appears representatively in the brilliantly compressed fictions of Charles Simmons, the nightmare realities of Jonathan Baumbach, the breathless anecdotalism of Renata Adler, the spare hard tensions of Raymond Carver, the deceptively softer ones of Grace Paley, and the extravagant distortions of Donald Barthelme, Robert Coover, Don DeLillo, or Gilbert Sorrentino. What all of these fictions tells us is that the struggle with illusion, with the decreasing gap between the prosthetic and the human and the unique imagery that has evolved to express it, emerges finally as the struggle of art against itself.

This struggle takes the form of a speeded up consciousness whose attempt to make sense of life and get a historical perspective on it Saul Bellow has identified as one of the chief sources of comedy in his books.[36] The disruptive urgency of that attempt appears symptomatically in the more fragmentary fictions of Leonard Michaels. In "In the Fifties," for example, the historical events of the decade are strained through incongruous memories or impressions recorded as in a diary but without the cementing glue either of chronological sequence or a second-person address that establishes an intimate atmosphere of shared values. Sudden and inexplicable deaths or disappearances, random acts of violence, bursts of energy followed by periods of enervating lassitude all contribute to a sense of dislocation. Nothing provides any linkage. In the title story of Michaels' collection *I Would Have Saved Them if I Could*, Lord Byron's revulsion at witnessing a public execution turns to indifference at the repetition of the spectacle. Neither Byron's letter about it nor the consolation of philosophers or poets can finally affect the horror, the actuality of death as it confronts us in forms ranging from natural aging to political assassination. The narrator of yet another of Michaels' stories—"Dostoevsky"—sums up the postmodern predicament in his attempt to make sense of the chance nature of events by providing them with some ordered logic. At the last minute, Dostoevsky, standing in front of a firing squad, is reprieved by the tsar. The action is arbitrary and thus more evil than good. Nonetheless, no such random gesture saves the tsar from being killed by the Bolsheviks or, subsequently, saves Trotsky, who saw the murder of the tsar as necessary. Necessity and the attempt to structure it thus blend indistinguishably, the one unable to explain, let alone affect, the other. "It is impossible," the narrator concludes helplessly, "to live with or without fictions."

NOTES

1. Quoted in *New York Times*, March 6, 1967, sec. 2D, p. 5.

2. Quoted in Gene Thornton, "The New Photography: Turning Traditional Standards Upside Down," *Artnews* (April 1978): 76.

3. John Cage, "Lecture on Nothing," *Silence* (Middletown, Conn.: Wesleyan University Press, 1961), p. 109.

4. Craig Owens, "The Discourse of Others: Feminists and Postmodernism," in *The Anti-Aesthetic: Essays on Postmodern Culture*, ed. Hal Foster (Port Townsend, Wash.: Bay Press, 1983), pp. 68–70.

5. Among the more comprehensive discussions of modernism are Maurice Beebe, "What Modernism Was," *Journal of Modern Literature* 3, no. 5 (July 1974): 1065–84; Irving Howe, "The Culture of Modernism," *The Decline of the New* (New York: Harcourt Brace, 1970), pp. 3–33; Harry Levin, "What Was Modernism?" *Refractions: Essays in Comparative Literature* (New York: Oxford University Press, 1966), pp. 271–95; and Stephen Spender, *The Struggle of the Modern* (Berkeley: University of California Press, 1963).

6. T. S. Eliot, "*Ulysses*, Order and Myth," *Selected Prose*, ed. Frank Kermode (New York: Harcourt Brace Jovanovich, 1975), p. 177. An instructive comparison between the modernist sensibility and what came after it is suggested in Eliot's definition of the objective correlative and Robbe Grillet's description of the new novel. The only way to express emotion in the form of art, Eliot declares, is to find "a set of objects, a situation, a chain of events which shall be the formula of that *particular* emotion; such that when the external facts, which must terminate in sensory experience, are given, the emotion is immediately evoked." ("Hamlet," *Selected Prose*, p. 48). Robbe Grillet, in contrast, comments ironically on the writer's attempt to descend "into the abyss of human passions [to] send to the seemingly tranquil world (the world on the surface) triumphant messages describing the mysteries." Objects, Robbe Grillet contends, will no longer "be merely the vague reflection of the hero's vague soul, the image of his torments, the shadows of his desires. Or rather, if objects still afford a momentary prop to human passions, they will do so only provisionally, and will accept the tyranny of signification only in appearance—derisively, one might say—the better to show how alien they remain

to man." ("A Future for the Novel," *For a New Novel: Essays on Fiction* [New York: Grove Press, 1963], pp. 21–22).

7. Mann quotes this passage in "Die Kunst Des Romans," *Altes und Neues* (Frankfort: S. Fischer Verlag, 1953), p. 396. For a definitive examination of the internalization of fiction see Erich Kahler, *The Inward Turn of Narrative*, trans. Richard Winston and Clara Winston (Princeton: Princeton University Press, 1973).

8. Lionel Trilling, "On the Modern Element in Modern Literature," *Partisan Review* (January-February 1961): 9–35. Reprinted as "On the Teaching of Modern Literature," *Beyond Culture: Essays on Literature and Learning* (New York: Viking, 1961), pp. 3–30.

9. Henry-Russell Hitchcock and Philip Johnson, *The International Style* (New York: Norton, 1966), p. 19.

10. Quoted in Barbara Miller Lane, *Architecture and Politics in Germany, 1918–1945* (Cambridge, Mass.: Harvard University Press, 1968), p. 45.

11. Peter Blake, *Four Great Makers of Modern Architecture: Gropius, Le Corbusier, Mies Van der Rohe, Wright*, A verbatim record of a symposium held at the School of Architecture from March to May 1961 (New York: Columbia University, 1963; reprint ed., New York: DaCapo Press, 1970), pp. 95–96.

12. Ibid., p. 98.

13. Charles Jencks, *The Language of Post-Modern Architecture* (New York: Rizzoli, 1977).

14. Robert Hughes, *The Shock of the New* (New York: Knopf, 1981), esp. pp. 78–79, 87 passim.

15. Pauline Kael, "The Current Cinema" (Review of *Stripes*), *New Yorker*, July 13, 1981, p. 83.

16. Robert Alter, *Partial Magic: The Novel as a Self-Conscious Genre* (Berkeley: University of California Press, 1975), p. 98.

17. Thornton, "The New Photography," p. 76.

18. Clement Greenberg, "Modernist Painting," *Arts Yearbook*, 4 (1961): 106.

19. Bruce Glaser, "Questions to Stella and Judd," ed., Lucy R. Lippard, in *Minimal Art: A Critical Anthology*, ed. Gregory Battcock (New York: E. P. Dutton, 1968), p. 157.

20. Jules Olitski, "Painting in Color," *Artforum* 5 (January 1967): 20.

21. Diane Waldman, *Roy Lichtenstein* (New York: Harry N. Abrams, 1971), p. 25.

22. Nancy Foote, "The Photo Realists: 12 Interviews," *Art in America* (November-December 1972): 73–74.

23. Andre Bazin, *What Is Cinema* (Berkeley: University of California Press, 1967), p. 16.

24. Phyllis Tuchman, "An Interview with Carl Andre," *Artforum* 8 (June 1970): 57.

25. James Monte, *Anti-Illusion: Procedures/Materials* (New York: Whitney Museum, 1969), p. 10.

26. Sol LeWitt, "Paragraphs on Conceptual Art," *Artforum* 5 (Summer 1967): 80.

27. Quoted by Morton Feldman in *New York Times*, March 5, 1967, sec. D, p. 27.

28. For much of the foregoing discussion I am indebted to Robert Rosenblum's illuminating essay "Notes on Sol LeWitt," in *Sol LeWitt*, edited and introduced by Alicia Legg (New York: Museum of Modern Art, 1978), pp. 15–21.

29. Lucy Lippard, *Changing: Essays in Art Criticism* (New York: E. P. Dutton, 1971). See especially "New York Letter: Rejective Art," pp. 140–53, and "The Dematerialization of Art," pp. 255–76.

30. Daniel Bell, *The Coming of the Post Industrial Society: A Venture in Social Forecasting* (New York: Basic Books, 1973), p. 272.

31. James Gilbert, *Another Chance: Postwar America 1945–68* (New York: Knopf, 1981), p. 3.

32. Elizabeth Gordon, "The Threat to the Next America," *House Beautiful*, April 1953, p. 126.

33. Richard Chase, *The American Novel and Its Tradition* (Garden City, N.Y. Doubleday, 1957), pp. 6–7.

34. Philip Roth, "Writing American Fiction," *Commentary* 31 (March 1961): pp. 223–33.

35. Roland Barthes, "The Death of the Author," *Image Music Text*, trans. Stephen Heath (New York: Hill & Wang, 1977), p. 147. See also "Musica Practica," ibid., pp. 149–54.

36. Robert Cromie, "Saul Bellow Tells (Among Other Things) the Thinking Behind *Herzog*," *Chicago Tribune Books Today*, January 24, 1956, p. 9.

2

Architecture

MARY McLEOD

The term "postmodernism" in architecture, as in other fields, eludes easy definition. As a movement, postmodern architecture has often been much clearer about what it rejects than what it represents. Its emphasis has been on the repudiation of existing styles and beliefs rather than on the construction of a cohesive, theoretical, and formal program. In fact, as some critics have suggested, a more appropriate description might be "antimodern." The common antagonist, however, is not all modern architecture, but the architecture of the Modern Movement in Europe between the wars and its post–World War II manifestations in Europe and the United States. Specifically, this includes the designs of Ludwig Mies van der Rohe, Walter Gropius, Le Corbusier, Hannes Meyer, and Ludwig Hilberseimer, in addition to the corporate work of firms such as Skidmore, Owings, and Merrill, I. M. Pei and Partners, and the Architects' Collaborative. Advocates of postmodernism in architecture eschew both the formal and the social premises of the modern movement: its minimal, stripped-down aesthetic, including Le Corbusier's five points (strip windows, roof terraces, *pilotis* [posts], free façade, and free plan) and its accompanying ideology of structural rationalism, mass production, functionalism, and social regeneration through architecture. In short, they oppose the modern movement's messianic faith in the new; no longer, they assert, can architects naively assume that technological innovation insures a universal aesthetic and social solution.

Indeed, it is this refusal of universal models and rejection of the new as an a priori value that begins to elucidate postmodernism's more posititve attributes. In contrast to the modern architects of the twenties, postmodern architects publicly acknowledge their own objectives as pluralistic and historicist. The past is neither condemned nor ignored, but warmly embraced as a vital formal and intellectual source. All period styles, whether classical or vernacular, are considered open to imitation or reinterpretation. Like the nineteenth-century eclectics, current practitioners, such as Robert Venturi, Charles Moore, Michael Graves, Allan Greenberg, Robert Stern, and Thomas Gordon Smith, emphasize the decorative and scenographic dimensions of architecture as opposed to abstract, compositional concerns.[1] Color, texture, and profile, for instance, gain much greater prominence in their designs than in the more austere works of the twenties. To the extent that it is a self-conscious preoccupation, space is also rendered in more traditional terms. Walls, mass, and contained volumes—rooms—replace the infinite continuum implied by the modern movement grid. Similarly, the urban proposals of postmodern architects are also more traditional, recalling premodernist interpretations of the city. Streets, blocks, and monumental axes have reappeared with a vengeance, supplanting Le Corbusier's shimmering "towers in the park" with images much closer to Haussmann's Paris. Even recent graphic techniques announce a return to Beaux-Arts conventions. Postmodern architects use water-colored perspectives, shadowed elevations, and *poché* wall sections, instead of hard-lined axonometrics and plans, to convey their design ideas. And once again, the result stresses the tactile and surface properties of architecture rather than its abstract, syntactic, or structural relations.

These formal differences become clearer if we briefly compare a building of the modern movement, for example, Le Corbusier's Villa Savoye (fig. 1), with a contemporary structure, such as Michael Graves' Plocek or "Keystone" House (1977–83). Raised on concrete *pilotis*, the Villa Savoye floats as a pristine, white object above the landscape. Platonic and pure on the exterior, the formal order is complex and ambiguous in the interior. Space flows between outside and inside. The ribbon windows, sliding glass walls, driveway under the house, and surreal forms on the roof terrace all dissolve traditional boundaries of enclosure. Inside, the demarcations between zones of activity are not fixed, but implied. The column grid and asymmetrically disposed, freestanding elements create rhythms and cadences, but no explicit hierarchies. The composition denies center: first, the visitor confronts a column immediately on entry, then a ramp that occupies the central bay and shears the spatial field. Space is dispersed outward rather than inward toward one central focus as in a classical building. To the extent that the house communicates referential meanings, they are not hearth and home as we know them, but the automobile and ocean liner.

In contrast, the more overtly referential Plocek House (figs. 2–3) sits firmly on the earth. Its stucco skin, now shades of ochre and beige, no longer proclaims the innovations of the Machine Age, but recalls in its expression the classical tripartite division of basement, *piano nobile*, and attic. The "removed" keystone alludes to the fanciful conceits of Mannerist architecture and, ironically (and even more so since the project's limited execution), to an epoch of more substantial construction. Although some elements of asymmetry remain as residues of Graves' earlier cubist tendencies, the space is not continuous, but static. On entering the Plocek House, a visitor is not poised on the precipice between two worlds, as in the Villa Savoye; rather, the procession of movement is fixed firmly within the boundaries of an enclosed sequence of rooms. The central stair hall serves as a traditional focus of orientation. Plocek's axial progression echoes, in fact, Beaux-Arts interpretations of *marche*. Unlike Le Corbusier's linear axonometrics or black and white photographs, Graves' lavishly rendered colored

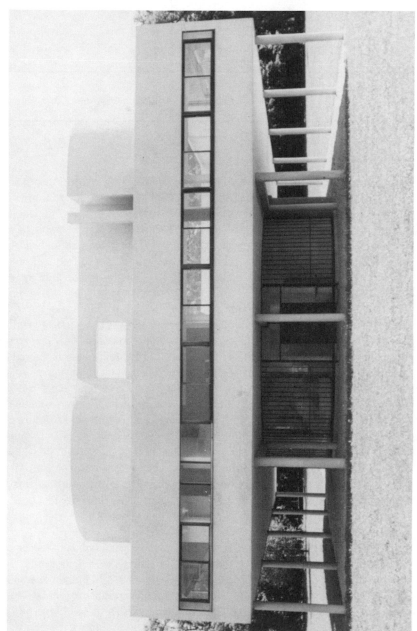

Figure 1. Le Corbusier's Villa Savoye, 1929–31.

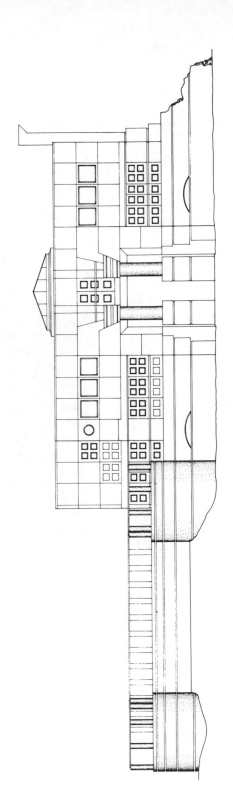

NORTH ELEVATION

Figure 2. Front elevation, Michael Graves' Plocek or "Keystone" House, Warren, N.J., 1977–83. (*Courtesy of Michael Graves.*)

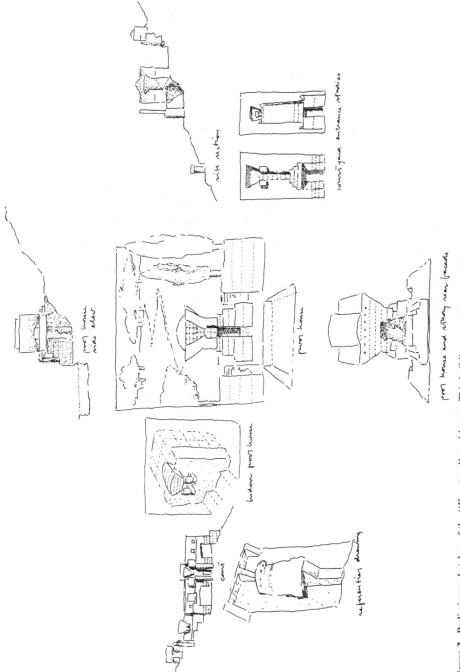

Figure 3. Preliminary sketches of the "Keystone" pool house. This building was not constructed. (*Courtesy of Michael Graves.*)

drawings present a world of opulence and classical grandeur. Instead of Savoye's requisite *objet-types*—bowler hat, laboratory vessel, golf clubs, and Thonet chairs—Plocek's proposed furnishings include silk drapery, "Empire" chairs, inlaid cabinetry, and antique statuary.

Similar points of contrast emerge if one compares the Villa Savoye to such diverse examples of postmodern architecture as Charles Moore's own residence in Los Angeles (1976–79); Robert Stern's bath house at Llewellyn Park, New Jersey (1979–81); or Allan Greenberg's recently completed house in Greenwich, Connecticut (1983–84), modeled after Mount Vernon. Each of these designs is an assemblage of historicist motifs radically at odds with the platonic forms and minimalist vocabulary of the Villa Savoye. Moore's house juxtaposes a cascading palatial staircase, corrugated metal sheeting, and a nineteenth-century pediment rescued from the wrecker's ball. Stern's pool house (fig. 4) presents an even more eclectic pastiche, incorporating references to the Roman nymphaeum, Mannerist rustication, Viennese Secession tile work, the palm tree columns in John Nash's Brighton Pavilion, and, by extension, Hans Hollein's earlier reinterpretation of Nash's structure in a travel office in Vienna. Greenberg's design, on the other hand, attempts to replicate the past literally and borrows numerous Colonial and Georgian details directly from the copybooks. In contrast to the Villa Savoye, the three projects are colorful, lavishly decorated, and ostentatious. Although Moore's house retains some of the spatial fluidity of modernist compositions, Stern's and Greenberg's primary spaces are static and symmetrical. As in the Plocek House, Le Corbusier's spatial layerings and transparencies have given way to more conventional, if monumental, interpretations of rooms and movement.

Thus, postmodernism in architecture is not, as it is in some fields, a more sophisticated and comprehensive exploration of the formal discoveries of modernism: fragmentation, dispersion, interpenetration, shear, the grid, and continuous space. Rather, it is a reaction against those very discoveries and their resultant destruction of accepted styles and compositional modes. Unlike many postmodern writers, postmodern architects ordinarily accept the canons of premodernist humanism: representation, figuration, content, and meaning. For most, this has meant an attempt to acknowledge architecture's own history, including the modern movement, through transformation and selective quotation of earlier designs in their own work. For others, however, most notably Allan Greenberg, John Blatteau, and Quinlin Terry, past architectural styles must be reestablished in toto. These revivalists view the modern movement as an unfortunate aberration in the tradition of Western architecture, one which precludes cultural continuity or social expression.

Underlying both of these reactions, and more generally the development of postmodernism in architecture in all its diverse and contradictory manifestations, is a search for meaning. As Charles Moore, one of the earliest proponents of postmodernism, explained in 1976, "It seems to me that one of the things most violently wrong with architecture in the twentieth century is that the number of

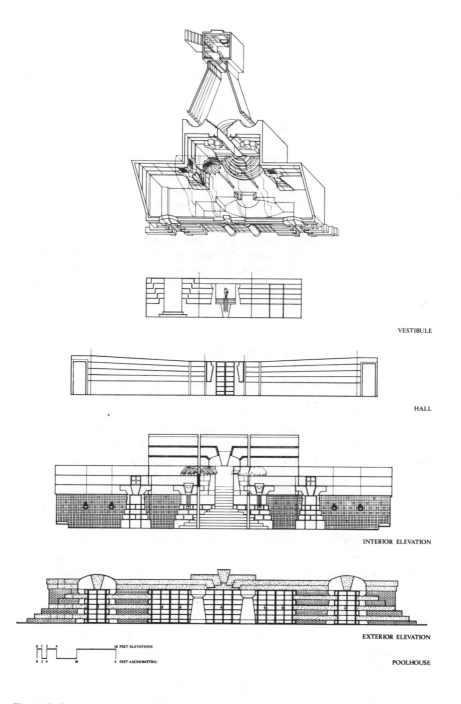

VESTIBULE

HALL

INTERIOR ELEVATION

EXTERIOR ELEVATION

POOLHOUSE

16 FEET-ELEVATIONS

3 FEET-AXONOMETRIC

Figure 4. Robert A. M. Stern, pool house addition to residence, Llewellyn Park, N.J., 1979–81. *(Courtesy of Robert A. M. Stern.)*

things that buildings have been allowed to say has shrunk so greatly that they've simply stopped being interesting to most people. . . . ''[2] Postmodern practitioners and critics tend to seek ideological justification, not in program, function, or structure, but in *meaning*. No one term has appeared more frequently in recent architectural discourse. Characteristic are statements by Robert Venturi and Robert Stern. The first, written by Venturi twenty years ago, anticipates developments to come; the second, from Stern's more contemporary manifesto, summarizes the professed objectives of what has come to be known as postmodernism:

As an architect, I try to be guided not by habit but by a conscious sense of the past, by precedent thoughtfully considered. . . . I am for richness of meaning rather than clarity of meaning, for the implicit function as well as the explicit function.

Traditional post-modernism recognizes both the discursive and expressive meaning of formal language. It recognizes the language of form as communicating sign as well as infra-referential symbol: that is to say, it deals with both physical and associational experience, with the work of art as an act of "presentation" and "representation." It rejects the idea of a single style in favor of a view that acknowledges the existence of many styles . . . each with its own meanings. . . .[3]

Charles Jencks, the most prolific populizer and apologist of postmodernism, in fact, bases his definition of a postmodern building on a dual "code of meaning." It is "one which speaks on at least two levels at once: to the architects and a concerned minority who care about specifically architectural meanings; and to the public at large, or the local inhabitants, who care about other issues concerned with comfort, traditional building, and a way of life." Similarly, the *Harvard Architectural Review* sees postmodernism as "an attempt, and an important one, to respond to the problem of meaning which was posed but never solved by the Modern Movement."[4] The return to historical styles, decoration, enclosed rooms, and traditional urban form can all be viewed as part of a larger objective to make architecture "speak." If, like modernism, postmodernism has explicit stylistic connotations, its genesis and justification can rarely be separated from the general issue of communication.

It is this issue, the idea of meaning in architecture, that must be seen as the primary concern of postmodern architects. For the architect or the critic, the most important questions to be answered are: why did this issue of meaning arise? what needs did it address? and what has been its impact on architectural practice today? In considering these questions, this discussion is divided into three parts. The first briefly situates the issue of meaning in the context of twentieth-century architectural history; the second examines the problem of the kind of meaning possible in architecture; and the third investigates contemporary examples of postmodern architecture.

The term "postmodernism" first gained widespread recognition and currency in the late 1970s. Charles Jencks' *The Language of Post-Modern Architecture*, published in 1977, is commonly credited with introducing the incipient movement to the general public.[5] The origins of postmodernism, however, can be traced to the dissatisfaction with modernism and the criticism of its precepts that took root after World War II and flourished in the 1960s. Architects and critics alike blamed the failings of post–World War II architecture on the forms and ideology of the modern movement.

As Alan Colquhoun has shown in his seminal article "Typology and Design Method" (1967), the architects of the modern movement offered two conflicting explanations for the generation of form. The first, what Colquhoun calls "bio-technical determinism," endorsed the "scientific" methods of the engineer. ("Bio" refers to the consideration of biological needs—light, space, and air—as design determinants; "technical" denotes technical issues of construction and production—structure, materials, standardization—as important criteria.) Form was, according to this positivist dogma, "merely the result of a logical process by which the operational needs and operational technique could be brought together."[6]

The second position, however, proclaimed a new freedom in formal expression and a faith in artistic intuition. The rejection of academic canons, which was necessitated in part by the new functional and structural concerns, also brought the opening of new formal possibilities. In *Towards a New Architecture* (1923), for example, Le Corbusier states that "ARCHITECTURE is a thing of art, a phenomenon of emotions, lying outside questions of construction and beyond them. . . . " And after his famous dictum, "the house is a machine for living," he immediately adds, "architecture goes beyond utilitarian needs. . . . Passion can create drama out of inert stone."[7] Perhaps the clearest example of this emphasis on artistic intuition can be found in the Bauhaus educational program. In the introductory course, the *Vorkurs*, students were instructed only in material properties and basic forms. With this knowledge they were to invent anew. Gropius considered history and design precedents as deterrents to personal creativity and eliminated them from the curriculum. As he stated in the first proclamation of the Weimar Bauhaus, he considered the artist "an exalted craftsman." It was only "in rare moments of inspiration, transcending the consciousness of his will," that "the grace of heaven may cause his work to blossom into art."[8]

Individual architects of the modern movement sometimes advocated one design approach more strongly than the other; for instance, the German architects Ludwig Hilberseimer and Hannes Meyer stressed functionalism, while the French architects Robert Mallet-Stevens and Michel Roux-Spitz placed greater emphasis on artistic freedom and personal expression. But for the most part, the leaders of the modern movement—Le Corbusier, Mies van der Rohe, and Gropius— combine, if paradoxically, these two positions.

By the early 1960s, this division was visible, not so much within the work of a single architect, but within the architectural profession as a whole. Functional determinism and personal expression became two contrary and radically opposed points of view. (Perhaps they always were, but in the early 1920s the differences were rarely consciously expressed.) On the biotechnical side, there were such forced efforts to make architectural creation scientific as Thomas Maldonado's and Max Bill's work at Ulm and Cedric Price's proposals for life support structures. In these approaches architecture was not art, but an efficient, neutral container meeting human needs. The more scientific the analysis became, the more successful the design solution was considered to be. At the other extreme were the personal statements of Eero Saarinen, Jørn Utzon, and Edward Durrell Stone. Here, there was no pretense of scientific determination, though sometimes science became part of the designer's personal rhetoric; what was significant was the architect's personal interpretation of a particular program and site. Saarinen's TWA terminal (1956) and Utzon's Sidney Opera House (1956) are two obvious examples. The sweeping forms of the terminal suggest flight; those of the opera, set against the sea, become "sails." Though paragons of impersonal and illusionless modernism, the corporate skyscrapers Lever House (1950–52) and the Seagram Building (1954–58) share certain qualities with these latter works. Their International Style forms were not conceived as resulting from technical criteria, but rather from self-conscious stylistic choices; witness Mies' exposed bronze corners or his symmetrical fountains, filled to the brim to prevent the public from sitting. In George Baird's article, "La Dimension Amoureuse in Architecture," the juxtaposition of Price's Thinkbelt project (1966) and Saarinen's CBS skyscraper (1960) effectively summarizes the growing dichotomy within the profession.[9] Whether scientifically derived or overtly expressionistic, both architectural positions avoided history and tradition. By the mid-1960s, individuals began to recognize that the possibility of making an architecture of public signification was severely limited; the false, or at least reductive, character of each approach had become all too apparent. In a field of infinite solutions, true science was an impossible objective. Personal expression appeared increasingly arbitrary and empty.

The rejection of these two approaches was closely linked to the emergence of a new critical literature reassessing modern architecture. Historical studies were among the first to be important. Early accounts of the modern movement by Siegfried Giedion, Nikolaus Pevsner, and Alberto Sartoris stressed modern architecture's aesthetic, technological, and social innovations and concomitantly its break with academic tradition. In contrast, the second generation of historical writings by Colin Rowe, Reyner Banham, and William Jordy called attention to modern architecture's links to the past. In his article, "The Mathematics of the Ideal Villa" (1947), Rowe demonstrated Le Corbusier's relation to academic composition in a convincing comparison of his villa at Garches and Palladio's Villa Malcontenta. Covering broader terrain, Jordy, in "The Symbolic Essence of Modern European Architecture of the Twenties" (1963), and Banham, in *Theory and Design in the First Machine Age* (1960), argued that the architecture of the 1920s was neither as functional nor as devoid of cultural reference as its proponents portrayed it to be. Banham's introductory chapter on the academicians Julien Guadet and Auguste Choisy showed the connections between Beaux-Arts theory and principles of the modern movement.

Architects could not so readily deny history and cultural reference once the modern movement's own unstated heritage and symbolic concerns had been exposed. Slowly, they began to express frustration with both functional determinism and the lack of expression in contemporary buildings. In the United States the most important product of this reaction was unquestionably Robert Venturi's *Complexity and Contradiction in Architecture*, published in 1966. This "gentle manifesto" condemned the minimal qualities of modern architecture and, reversing Mies' famous dictum, proclaimed, "More is not less."[10] Venturi argued that architecture should be rich, ambiguous, and complex; multiplicity of meaning, not reduction, was the appropriate goal. Historical allusion and use of precedent were essential components of architectural expression. Several other books explored related themes. Three years earlier Christian Norberg-Schulz's *Intentions in Architecture* included, in its tripartite model of architecture (task, form, and technics), cultural symbolization as part of architecture's task. "Only through cultural symbolization can architecture show that the daily life has a meaning which transcends the immediate situations, that it forms a part of a cultural and historical continuity."[11] The book also introduced semantics as an important element in architectural theory. Robert Stern's *New Dimensions in American Architecture* (1969) discussed "inclusive" and "exclusive" architecture with sympathy for the former, while Thomas Schumacher's article, "Contexturalism: Urban Ideals and Deformations" (1971), argued for a greater awareness of the traditional urban fabric. Although these texts did not yet advocate the replication of historical styles, they all rejected programmatic functionalism as the primary design objective.

In the public sphere, journalists too began to condemn modern architecture as inhuman. Jane Jacobs' best seller, *The Death and Life of Great American Cities* (1961), summarized the popular dissatisfaction with corporate skyscrapers and public housing projects, arguing forcefully that architects needed to recognize emotional and social needs as more important than Le Corbusier's famous trinity: light, space, and air. The dynamiting of the Pruit-Igoe housing project in St. Louis was, in the general press, a final symbolic indictment.[12] Destruction appeared to be the only solution for these vandalized and crime-ridden examples of the "Radiant City."

Simultaneously, in Europe, Giulio Carlo Argan's article "On the Typology of Architecture" (1962; English translation 1963) revived interest in the eighteenth-century concept of architectural typology, the consideration of building types. In its acceptance of historical forms and techniques, typology allowed contemporary architects the possibility of greater cultural reference. It also answered the apparent shortcomings of some "biotechnical" approaches. Even Thomas Maldonado, one of the most vocal advocates of "scientific" design methods, had recognized by this point that functional parameters were insufficient and that past building types might fill the void in architects' processes of decision making.[13] Aldo Rossi's *The Architecture of the City* (1966) and his subsequent urban studies gave typology an added importance for European architects and

students. These investigations shared with their American counterparts a rejection
not only of functional criteria as determinate but also in their emphasis on
collective form of the singularity of the large-scale personal gesture (Venturi's
duck) epitomized by Saarinen's TWA terminal. The architecture that has developed out of typological research—most notably the designs of Aldo Rossi,
the Krier brothers, Vittorio Gregotti, and Franco Purini—is, however, more
abstract and reductive in its vocabulary than most contemporary work emerging
in the United States. The so-called rationalists emphasize compositional principles and morphology rather than decoration and scenographic qualities. Thus,
their work remains only tangentially related to what is commonly understood as
postmodernism. Although some critics in attempts at broader categorization have
labeled it such, most architects, prone to stylistic distinctions, oppose rationalist
and postmodernist tendencies. But, in both cases, the desire for public expression
is a primary concern.

This focus on meaning can be explained in part as a return to a traditional
understanding of architecture as art. The critical literature of the 1960s, rejecting
neue sachlich principles of the modern movement, linked expression with art.
Venturi states, for example: "I speak of a complex and contradictory architecture
based on the richness and ambiguity of modern experience, including that experience which is inherent in art."[14] Venturi's validation of architecture's artistic
dimension, reiterated by such diverse practitioners as Aldo Rossi, Charles Moore,
Michael Graves, and Peter Eisenman, appears to be related to the failure of the
modern movement to generate social reform. In the 1920s, architects were willing
to accept the primacy of functional and technical parameters because they believed that efficiency and economy would produce a better environment. Le
Corbusier, Gropius, Mies van der Rohe, Andre Lurçat, Mart Stam, and Ernst
May all saw mass-produced housing as a means of solving social problems.
Their objective was not cultural expression, although the celebration of technology did not preclude that, but social and environmental reform. Architecture's
purpose transcended art to politics; as in other avant-garde movements in design
since the Enlightenment (namely, the Gothic Revival and Arts and Crafts), art
did not just express life; art transformed life.

By the 1950s, the tragedies of World War II, the tyrannies of Stalinist Russia,
and the advance of multinational capitalism had largely shattered such utopian
faith. Mass housing had created social problems, not solved them. In fact,
housing rarely existed on the scale that architects envisioned. The failures of
advocacy planning and self-help projects in the 1960s only contributed further
to the sense of political impotence. Few architects were able to sustain a belief
in their craft as a powerful social force. Meaning became an alternative means
of validation.

But such a course was also symptomatic of something missing. The conscious
identification of meaning as a problem occurred just at that moment when meaning appeared most removed from the architectural object. If the architects of the
modern movement rarely discussed meaning as an objective, they were, none-

theless, confident that they were embodying the spirit of the age, *l' esprit nouveau*, and that it was a spirit worthy of expression. The same cannot be said of the architects of the 1950s and 1960s; neither personal flamboyance—the architect's ego stamped with corporate approval—nor pseudoscientific neutrality had replaced the hope for redemption. Thus, meaning became the cry in a world seemingly devoid of content.

Yet, to view this focus on meaning as an issue internal to the history of architecture would be mistaken. If architects began to discuss communication and expression, it was partially because individuals in a variety of disciplines had already begun to do so. By the 1960s, linguistics, semiology, and structuralism had become part of general intellectual discourse, and it was not long before architects and critics recognized the relevance of these methods to their field. The semiologists Roland Barthes and Umberto Eco, following the example of Ferdinand de Saussure, frequently studied architectural elements. For architects, the systematic investigation of architecture as a system of signs served in itself to validate meaning as a design objective. From the broadest perspective, one can find parallels between the intellectual's attraction to semiology and the architect's search for meaning. In contrast to the materialism of Marxism and the subjectivity of existentialism, structuralism and semiology offered the possibility of scientific knowledge without subsuming culture in quantifiable methods of analysis. Similarly, meaning became for the architect a means to transcend both functional determinism and personal subjectivity.

In the early 1970s, several semiological studies of architecture appeared, most notably Charles Jencks' and George Baird's anthology of essays, *Meaning in Architecture*, and Mario Gandelsonas' influential article, "On Reading Architecture," an analysis of the early architecture of Michael Graves and Peter Eisenman. Semiology's popularity as an analytic approach to architecture, however, was short-lived. For many, the obscure language and somewhat contrived categories proved difficult. And for critics and theorists more sympathetic to philosophical complexity, the translation of linguistic concepts to a visual medium such as architecture became formidable. No convincing architectural equivalent, for instance, could be found for Saussure's division between *langue* and *parole*. Similarly, confusion surrounded the issue of "double articulation," or the double nature of the sign as signifier/signified. Is the building the signifier? The idea, the signified? Or is it the reverse? The idea, the signifier? The building, the signified? To explore the theoretical difficulties of developing a semiology of architecture is beyond the scope of this essay; what is significant, however, to an account of postmodernism is semiology's influence on categorizations of meaning. As a result of their association with semiology, postmodern apologists, such as Jencks and Graves, frequently use semiological terms, particularly referring to "semantic" and "syntactic" dimensions of architecture. Their interest, given the rejection of modern architecture's compositional abstraction, has focused on the former aspect of signification.

The postmodernist preoccupation with meaning raises the general question of what kind of meaning is possible in architecture today. To what extent can architecture serve as a system of visual signs expressing ideas and values?

It is clear from recent practice that architecture's role as a medium of public communication is more limited than in past epochs. As Victor Hugo stated in *Notre Dame de Paris* more than a century and a half ago, the time when architecture could be considered a "social book" has passed. The French novelist believed that the printing press would kill architecture; *ceci tuera cela*. While the book was physically more ephemeral than stone, its message, by virtue of the processes of mechanical reproduction, was both more universal and permanent. Architecture as a discipline might still exist, but in the last century we can add television, film, and photography to the list of media that have usurped architecture's role as a primary cultural statement. With these new means of communication, an increasingly small group understood established codes of architectural composition and decoration. The appearance of these codes in designs has become increasingly irrelevant.

While new means of production and social exchange may be largely responsible for architecture's diminished role, developments within the profession undoubtedly contributed to the loss of audience. Responding to the problem of nineteenth-century eclecticism, itself symptomatic of Hugo's prophecy, modern architects created a *tabula rasa*, which precluded extending any remaining literacy in classical architectural forms. Although the new vocabulary sometimes became in its own right a potent sign of the modern age (a glass curtain wall, for instance, conveyed "modern corporation" more successfully than previous classical façades), it was also, as postmodernist critics have pointed out, severely limited in its expressive range. A school looked like a factory, a house like a doctor's office. The modernists' preoccupation with new compositional strategies, such as the grid, spatial transparencies, or planar progressions, may have also made architecture less accessible. Like other artists of the period, the architects of the 1920s often focused on formal issues internal to their craft. But whether this reduction in social communication stems primarily from the increasing importance of other media or from the architect's own priorities, the result has been an architecture of diminished content. Following a common interpretation of the avant-garde, one might paraphrase Mallarmé's answer to Nietzsche's question, "Who speaks?"—"The building (the work) itself." Thus, a villa by Mies van der Rohe, such as the Tugendhat House (1930), because of its radical transformation of such traditional notions as room, symmetry, and center, is less comprehensible to the general public than a traditional house composed of elements familiar to most people. This is not to say the Tugendhat Villa does not mean, only that its meaning is increasingly about itself. It is not referential in the sense of either vernacular or classical buildings.

It would be fallacious, however, to interpret modern architecture too closely according to this model of the avant-garde. More than other artistic disciplines, architecture, because of its functional parameters, has resisted such self-conscious reflection. Although the modern movement was often preoccupied with formal explorations, it saw those explorations—however mistakenly—as intrinsically linked to the exterior world. Only in the past two decades, with the growing self-consciousness of architects, has the notion of an autonomous or pure architecture come to the fore. This idea, however, has few serious advocates besides Peter Eisenman, who opposes his work specifically to the postmodernist designs of Stern, Graves, and Moore. Eisenman has used terms such as "conceptual architecture," "post-functionalism," and most recently "de-composition" to describe his own position.[15]

Regardless of these specific contemporary developments, the nature of architecture as a largely nonrepresentational (abstract) medium makes the issue of meaning, understood in a linguistic sense, problematic. Like music, architecture does not readily lend itself to verbal explanation. It does not always mean something else if, as many semiologists assume, the concept of meaning implies the notion of reference. In other words, "double articulation," or the split between signifier and signified, becomes problematic in an abstract medium. Designation does not follow recognition; it *is* recognition. Thus, to discuss a building in terms of conveying a specific code or message of information is difficult. Even in medieval architecture, which Hugo offers as the paradigm of social communication, much of the meaning conveyed was through the sculpture and stained glass, and not the stone of the structure itself. The more architectonic dimensions of a building—structure, proportion, composition—though often evocative, rarely serve as direct vehicles of cultural communication. Their meaning is more ambiguous. With the diminished understanding and use of traditional architectural rhetoric, the problem of abstraction has become more apparent. The possibility of a clearly understood public and social meaning cannot be readily assumed.

Postmodernist architects thus confront a difficult task. Despite the limitations of architecture as an expressive medium, they seek a means for social communication, a vocabulary that is still comprehensible to a public at large—rather than accept, like Eisenman, an autonomous or silent architecture. Generally, they endorse a referential or correspondent notion of meaning: that forms can literally be read as words, that buildings can convey specific messages. Thus, their emphasis, as noted earlier, has been on architecture's semantic realm. The following descriptions of intentions are characteristic:

In the end we extended our villa as a Quattrocentro architect might have added to a real villa, two generations after it was built. . . . Our squarish gallery with its strip windows and big overhang recalls on the outside a high school gym of the 40s. . . . From the front, therefore, our complex is meant to be a succession of forms and symbols, juxtaposed and receding, a Quattrocentro monument, a decorated shed, and an enhanced loft.
—Robert Venturi, Allen Memorial Art
Museum Addition, Oberlin, Ohio, 1974

The courtyard is marked by four cypresses centering on a rather romantic stream of water which issues from the upper level of the site, organized around the auditorium forecourt pool. There is some symbolism intended in the "fall of water" from the higher level of the courtyard "ground," as we as a society tend to make referential connections between archetypal elements in nature and our invented literature. The sustenance of water in a physical sense is, of course, akin to the sustenance provided by material held within the library itself.

—Michael Graves, Public Library, San
Juan Capistrano, California, 1980

Our proposal for "La Strada Nuovissima" discusses the reality and illusion of the past— the recent past of our office's work and the distant past of architectural history. . . . The abstracted curtain/columns suggest a proscenium. . . . Noble among the players in this shadow play is the Greek temple, an abstraction of which appears as a void on the silent face of a figure standing before the curtain of history. . . . Yet the temple and overscaled moulding of the proscenium refer also to specific moments in our office's stylistic de- velopment; the former to the Best Products façade, the latter to the Lang House. . . . The threshold is a void rusticated column from Llewellyn Park which suggests the act of engaging the past in order to realize the potential richness of the present.

—Robert Stern, Biennale Façade, Venice,
Italy, 1980[16]

Venturi's ironic vernacular images, Graves' collage of Italianate and Spanish forms, and Stern's cardboard, cartoonlike caricatures of classical motifs—the vocabularies of these three architects differ considerably from each other. Yet, each stems from an attempt to appropriate a set of architectural elements as a bearer of meanings. The questions that arise are how comprehensible are these elements and, ultimately, how appropriate are they in the present context.

In consideration of these issues, it is useful to turn to two recently constructed works, heralded by critics as the most important examples of postmodern ar- chitecture to date: Philip Johnson's AT&T Building (1978–84) and Michael Graves' Portland Building (1980–82). Because they both received an enormous amount of publicity, they offer an unusual opportunity to examine the relation between the architect's intentions and public reaction.

Since its initial proposal in 1978, Philip Johnson's high-rise office tower (fig. 5) has been notorious for its "Chippendale highboy top." The structure's form, as Johnson has explained, was intended to counter the anonymity and muteness of the postwar corporate skyscraper, epitomized by his own Seagram Tower, designed in collaboration with Mies van der Rohe. In contrast to this earlier tower, AT&T is clad in granite, not steel and glass; it stands firmly at the street edge, not set back; its imagery—arches, arcade, rustication—recalls the Ren- aissance palazzo, not a machine age structure; and finally, the building is solid, not light. Johnson strove to reestablish the classical tripartite division of base, shaft, and capital, which Louis Sullivan had also endorsed in his famous essay, "The Tall Building Artistically Considered" (1897). But unlike the more aca- demically correct designs of Allan Greenberg or John Blatteau, Johnson's formal vocabulary does not exclude irony, frivolity, or "calculated shock value." To

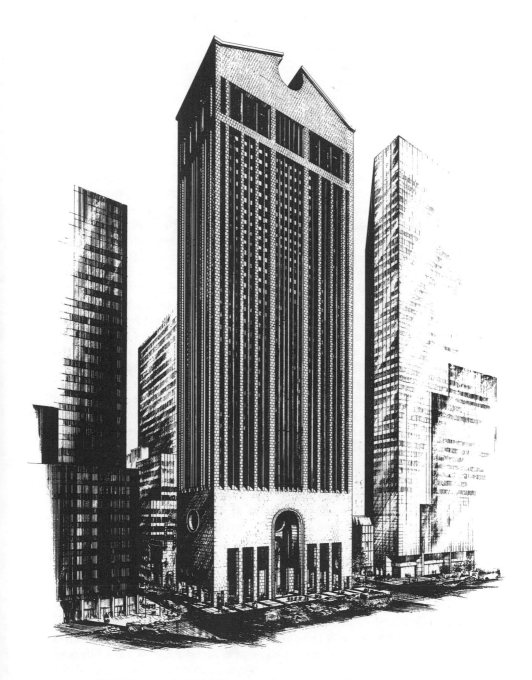

Figure 5. Philip Johnson, AT&T Building, New York, 1978–84. *(Photo by Gil Amiaga, NYC.)*

Mies' statement, "I'd rather be good than interesting," Johnson has claimed to
prefer the opposite: "I wouldn't know how to be good."[17] Nonetheless, his
objective was to create a monumental, urban architecture, which would express
once again premodern humanist values about building scale and urban life.

AT&T undoubtedly succeeds as a comment on modern architecture; irrespective of its controversy, the building's "interesting" silhouette offers an alternative to the stark forms punctuating the Manhattan skyline in recent years.
Johnson's interpretation of monumentality and Renaissance composition, however, remains unconvincing. Despite the immense expenditure on stonework and
careful detailing of joinery, the observer is immediately faced with the unfamiliar
conjuncture of a stone curtain wall veneer with a vocabulary generated out of
load-bearing construction. The building looks thin. The windows are set too
closely to the surface; the stone mullions, running the length of the glass banding,
are a mockery of Gothic tracery. The tinted glazing, heavy metal mullions, and
uninspired window pattern contribute further to the feeling of incongruence.
Instead of a convincing example of traditional monumental architecture, the
building stands as an expression of the conflict between classical language and
the economic and technical contingencies of modern skyscraper construction.
This becomes most evident in considering problems of scale. If we examine the
tower as a whole, the stones, the size of those on a four-story palazzo, seem
too small. Inversely, from the street, the arcade, proportioned according to the
structure's overall dimensions, appears too tall and counters our own historical
and anthropomorphic associations. Not only does Johnson's base surpass the
height of the lower blocks of earlier set-back towers, but it also equals in height
a classical structure further down the street. It is almost impossible to perceive
the tripartite division at once. If close, pedestrians ordinarily see the base and
window wall; if distant, they notice only the top. Efforts to proportion these
sections in accordance with each other as in a classical structure (or even one
of Sullivan's buildings) that can be perceived as a totality remain unresolved—
and perhaps are inappropriate.

Similar conflicts arise concerning the signification of Michael Graves' Portland
Building (figs. 6, 7), housing the city's municipal offices. Like Johnson, Graves
attempted in his design to address the issue of monumentality and public architecture. According to his own account, the multistoried, paired pilasters adorn
the main façades as "public portals" or gates; the large mirrored glass window,
placed in front of the city services offices, symbolizes "the collective, public
nature of the activities held within." A figurative sculpture, Portlandia, a reinterpretation of "Lady Commerce" from the city seal, stands over the entry
loggia as a further reference to the city. Garlands, a traditional symbol of welcome, embellish the side façades, and these, in turn, relate thematically to
Portlandia's wreath. As in Johnson's tower, the overall formal articulation derives
from the classical division of base, middle or body, and attic or head "in order
to reinforce the building's associative or mimetic qualities." A loggia or colon-
nade flanks the street, both to strengthen the street as a focus of urban activity

Figure 6. View of Michael Graves' Portland Building from the park, showing the service entry, Portland, Oregon, 1980–83. *(Courtesy of Michael Graves.)*

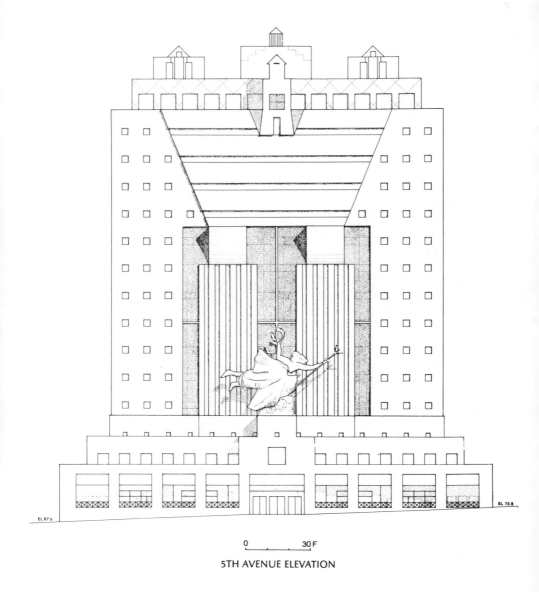

0   30 F

5TH AVENUE ELEVATION

Figure 7. Fifth Avenue (front elevation) of Michael Graves' Portland Building. *(Courtesy of Michael Graves.)*

and to refer to Portland's earlier commercial arcades. For Graves, the building's colors also possess associational value. The building's light green base relates to the ground.[18]

Other gestures are intentionally more esoteric to architecture. The inverted triangular form on the main façades serves simultaneously as a capital to the giant column formed by the paired pilasters and as a keystone. The classical village on the roof, never executed for financial reasons, alludes to a mythic past, evocative of Poussin's landscapes, Canaletto's capriccios, Rossi's analogous cities, and the roofscape of Chambord.

In its built state, the Portland Building possesses an undeniable presence. After the crushing monotony of Portland's steel and glass office blocks, the bright surfaces, unfamiliar forms, and sheer mass command attention. But its monumental character, like that of AT&T, remains qualified. Humanist intentions become ironic and ambiguous: a compromise, the more unfortunate since Graves' objectives were optimistic and reconciliatory, not critical. The meager reveals and small, square windows, set close to the surface, show the thinness—and cheapness—of the concrete membrane. Similarly, the molding sections, chopped at the corners, accentuate the planar properties of surface and exaggerate the sense of appliqué. On the park façade, a service entrance mocks the monumentality of the pilaster portal. And on the roof, the elimination of the little temples and gazebos leaves only the prosaic realities of the modern office block. The scale of the structure, while provocative in its idiosyncrasy, also compromises the classical intentions. As at AT&T, the pedestrian can rarely view the three parts of the Portland Building at once; Graves' own published photographs are taken from nearby office blocks. It is questionable whether the tripartite division even works mnemonically for most observers; the colors and unusual proportions obscure most references to classical hierarchy. Figurative references are also difficult to comprehend. Gargantuan size, unfamiliar context, and synecdochic substitutions disembody forms from their tectonic or traditional purpose. Only in the most tenuous way can the brown vertical strips sustain their role as pilasters or the wedge-shaped bars of the tenant floors convey keystone or lintel. Irrespective of the issue of public comprehension, however, the issue of appropriateness remains. Once structural functions are displaced, what is the meaning of a keystone? A reference to architecture's lost purpose?[19] Also questionable is Graves' use of garlands on the building's two side elevations. Graves has explained them as gestures of welcome, reminiscent of ancient victory wreaths. The garlands, joyful and festive in the model, emerge after the contingencies of contemporary construction as stiff parodies of their classical precedents—more vulgar than celebratory. One sardonic critic has compared them to gaudy package bows.[20] But they can also suggest less fortunate historical allusions: the funerary wreaths on Roman tombs or, as Mario Gandelsonas has suggested in an impish inversion, the crown of thorns.[21] The appropriation of classical forms appears to express the very devaluation of their original meanings.

Neither AT&T nor the Portland Building are without meaning, but the mean-

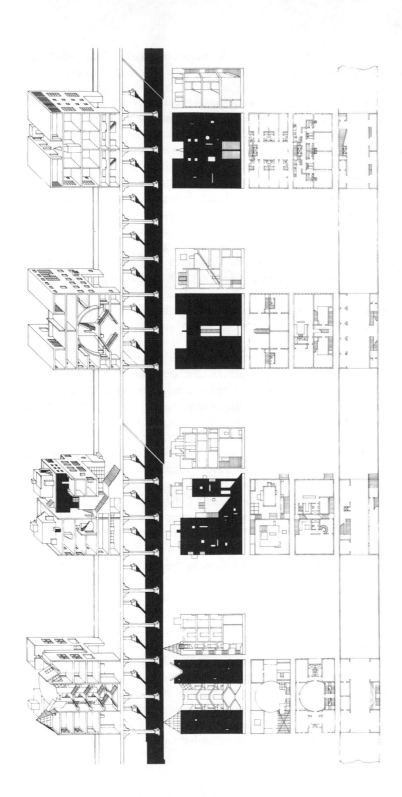

Figure 8. Steven Holl's project for Bridge of Houses, New York, 1979–82. In contrast to the postmodern work of Michael Graves or Robert A. M. Stern, Holl's work is plainer and stripped of historicist detail. (*Courtesy of Steven Holl.*)

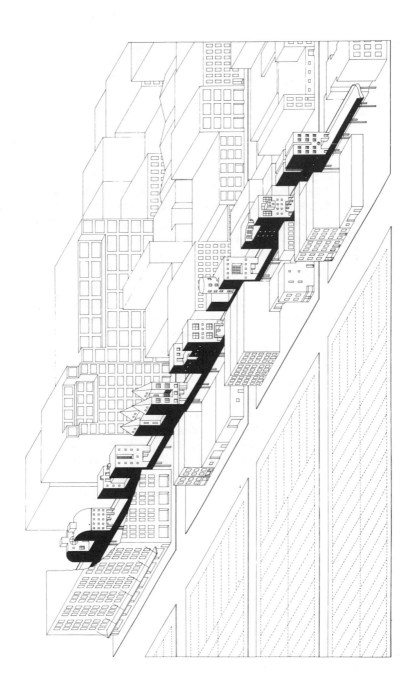

ings are not always the ones intended, nor are they generally of a specific referential nature. The Portland Building, in particular, stands as an enigmatic collage—suggestive, but without specific narrative content. In both buildings, changes in scale, the use of new materials, and the parameters of high-rise construction compromise the legibility of the classical language. In those instances where figurative gestures are understood, as in Johnson's pedimented top, the result is overstatement, what one French postmodernist termed "Disneyland Classicism." The struggle for meaning threatens to become a reduction of meaning.

This dilemma emerges most clearly in the work of more literal historicists, well represented in the recent *Chicago Tribune* competition and in the exhibition of Best Products Buildings at the Museum of Modern Art in 1979. Allan Greenberg's proposal for Best Products, a literal re-creation of a Georgian façade, for instance, seems to convey little more than "I don't like modern architecture." The relationship of past to present becomes more problematic than enriching; to the extent that the architectural gesture is understood we are left floundering between kitsch—Georgian A&P—and a nostalgia for past grandeur.

The evolution of postmodernism in architecture thus raises the question of whether the utilization of past styles has insured more meaning, or whether it is a nostalgic refusal to recognize architecture's own situation in history. In the 1930s, Clement Greenberg, writing about social realism, argued that its mechanical formulas encouraged vicarious experience, faked sensations—in fact, an inability to respond to the very values that generated it.[22] Presently, postmodernism risks a similar situation. In their duplication and exaggeration of historical forms, architects unintentionally parody that which is important to them—an architectural heritage that speaks to society. Only occasionally have postmodern architects directly confronted the ambiguity of architectural meaning, the tension between expression and silence, resulting from an abstract medium and a social situation that precludes literacy of architectural forms. Perhaps it is not accidental that a new generation of architects—Bernard Tschumi, Steven Holl (fig. 8), Rem Koolhaas, Mark Mack, Stanley Saitowitz, Lauretta Vinciarelli, Lars Lerup, and Liz Diller—who also reject functional determinism and purely intuitive approaches, have turned to a more abstract language in their pursuit of architecture's communicative power.

NOTES

1. Robert Venturi and Charles Moore are the elder spokesmen of postmodernism in architecture; Robert Stern, Michael Graves, and Allan Greenberg represent a middle generation; Thomas Gordon Smith, Peter Rose, and Wayne Berg are among the younger practitioners. Venturi and Moore are transitional figures; their theoretical work has been central to the evolution of postmodernism, but many of their earlier projects remain closely related to modernist compositional principles. Venturi's three Brant houses and

Moore's Burns House and Piazza d'Italia, however, are full-fledged examples of post-modern architecture.

The movement began as an American phenomenon, though by now it has become worldwide. The work of Ricardo Bofill in France and Hans Hollein in Austria has especially been associated with postmodernism.

My definition of postmodernism derives from common usage by architects. It is close to what Robert Stern labels "traditional post-modernism." He juxtaposes this position to that of "schismatic post-modernism," which has one representative architect, Peter Eisenman. The critics Charles Jencks and Ada Louise Huxtable also offer broader definitions of postmodernism, which include all contemporary work that rejects the principles of the modern movement. Though the term postmodernism suggests such a broad perspective, most architects use it only in reference to architecture that incorporates decoration and historical stylistic motifs.

Robert Stern, "The Doubles of Post-Modern," *The Harvard Architecture Review* 1 (Spring 1980): 75–87; Charles Jencks, *The Language of Post-Modern Architecture*, 3d ed. rev. (New York: Rizzoli, 1981); Ada Louise Huxtable, "The Troubled State of Modern Architecture," *New York Review of Books*, May 1, 1980, pp. 22–29.

2. Charles Moore, "Self Portrait," *L'Architecture d'Aujourd'hui* 184 (March 1976): xlv.

3. Robert Venturi, *Complexity and Contradiction in Architecture*, 2d ed. (New York: Museum of Modern Art, 1977), p. 16; Stern, "Doubles of Post-Modern," p. 86.

4. Jencks, *Language*, p. 6; "Beyond the Modern Movement," *The Harvard Architecture Review* 1 (Spring 1980): 4.

5. The phrase "postmodern architecture" can actually be traced back to 1945. Joseph Hudnut uses the term in his essay, "The Post-Modern House," *Architectural Record* 97 (May 1945): 70–75, reprinted in *Architecture and the Spirit of Man*, ed. Joseph Hudnut (Cambridge, Mass.: Harvard University Press, 1949), pp. 109–19. For an account of early uses of the term, see Jencks, *Language*, p. 8; also Stern, "The Doubles of Post-Modern," p. 76. Some architects and critics claim that Jencks' *The Lanugage of Post-Modern Architecture* did not just introduce the postmodern movement, but created it.

6. Alan Colquhoun, "Typology and Design Method," *Arena: Journal of the Architectural Association* 83 (June 1967); reprinted in Alan Colquhoun, *Essays in Architectural Criticism: Modern Architecture and Historical Change* (Cambridge, Mass.: MIT Press, 1981), p. 45.

7. Le Corbusier, *Towards a New Architecture*, trans. Frederick Etchells from 13th French ed. (1927; reprint ed., New York: Praeger, 1960), pp. 23, 10–11.

8. Walter Gropius, "Programme of the Staatliches Bauhaus in Weimar" (1919), in *Programmes and Manifestos on 20th-Century Art*, ed. Ulrich Conrads, trans. Michael Bullock (London: Lund Humphries, 1970), p. 49.

9. George Baird, " 'La Dimension Amoureuse' in Architecture," in *Meaning in Architecture*, ed. Charles Jencks and George Baird (New York: Braziller, 1969), pp. 79–99.

10. Robert Venturi, *Complexity*, p. 16.

11. Christian Norberg-Schulz, *Intentions in Architecture* (London: Allen and Unwin, 1963), p. 126.

12. Jencks, *Language*, p. 9, claims that the dynamiting of Pruitt-Igoe, July 15, 1972, represents the death of modern architecture.

13. Colquhoun, "Typology and Design Method," p. 43.

14. Venturi, *Complexity*, p. 16.

15. For an account of Peter Eisenman's position, see Peter Eisenman, "Notes on Conceptual Architecture," *Casabella* 25, nos. 359–60 (December 1971): 49–58; idem, *House X* (New York: Rizzoli, 1982); idem, "The Futility of Objects: Decomposition and the Process of Difference," *The Harvard Architecture Review* 3 (Winter 1984): 65–81.

16. Robert Venturi, *Allen Memorial Art Museum Bulletin* 34, no. 2 (1976–77): 83–104; Michael Graves, *Michael Graves: Buildings and Projects, 1966–1981*, ed. Karen Wheeler, Peter Arnell, and Ted Bickford (New York: Rizzoli, 1982), p. 261; Robert A. M. Stern, *Robert A. M. Stern 1965–1980: Towards a Modern Architecture after Modernism*, ed. Peter Arnell and Ted Bickford (New York: Rizzoli, 1981), p. 164.

17. Susan Doubilet, "I'd Rather Be Interesting," *Progressive Architecture*, no. 2 (February 1984): 69.

18. Graves, *Michael Graves*, p. 195.

19. With regard to the Portland Building, Alan Colquhoun has stated, "What the building is saying, with a power and intensity that are almost unique and not at all banal, is that architecture, as it has come down to us from history, is now impossible." Kurt Forster et al., "The Portland Building," *Skyline*, January 1983, p. 19. See also Kurt Forster's insightful but highly critical commentary in the same article, pp. 16–18.

20. Forster, "Portland Building," p. 18.

21. Suzanne Stephens, "At the Institute: The Portland Building Analyzed," *Skyline*, January 1983, p. 21.

22. Clement Greenberg, "The Avant-Garde and Kitsch," in *Kitsch: The World of Bad Taste*, ed. Gello Dorfles (New York: Universe Books, 1969), p. 122.

BIBLIOGRAPHICAL ESSAY

The most useful introduction to postmodernism in architecture remains Charles Jencks' seminal book, *The Language of Post-Modern Architecture*. Though sloppily written and often contradictory, the book has, more than any one text, defined the architectural movement to the public at large. The third revised edition gives an expanded account of postmodern architecture (the first edition of 1977 was anticipatory of most developments) in addition to a bibliographical account of the word's evolution. In *The Language of Post-Modern Architecture*, Jencks uses the term "postmodernism" as a catch-all for most architecture since 1970 and includes many European examples. In his recent survey, *Current Architecture*, written in collaboration with William Chaitkin, he distinguishes "postmodernism" and "late modernism" more clearly. This lavishly illustrated book includes photographs of most important postmodern buildings and a concise bibliography.

Also covering recent developments on both sides of the Atlantic are Paolo Portoghesi's two books, *After Modern Architecture* and *Postmodern: The Architect of the Postindustrial Society*. Drawing from both Daniel Bell and the Frankfurt School, Portoghesi attempts to relate postmodernism to broader social forces. His analysis, however, remains on a rather superficial plane. The first issue of *The Harvard Architecture Review* (Spring 1980), titled "Beyond the Modern Movement," is devoted to the subject of postmodernism. The editorial statement contains one of the clearest and most objective descriptions of the movement in architecture to date. Robert Stern's article in the review, "The Doubles of Post-Modern," attempts to situate architectural postmodernism in the context of other artistic currents. Although his categories are often contrived, the essay provides a useful description of "traditional postmodernism," his own architectural position. Steven Peterson's essay in the same review, "Space and Anti-Space," is one of few attempts thus far to deal with the spatial, as opposed to decorative, qualitites of postmodern architecture. Alex Tzonis and Liane LeFaivre's highly critical "The Narcissist Phase in Architecture" attempts an economic and political analysis of postmodern developments.

Other magazine issues specifically devoted to a definition and analysis of postmodern architecture include "Beyond Modernism," *Progressive Architecture*, and "The Search for a Postmodern Architecture," *CRIT: The Architectural Student Journal*. Ada Louise Huxtable's articles appearing in the *New York Review of Books* provide the general reader a good summary of the crisis in modern architecture during the 1970s. "The Troubled State of Modern Architecture" discusses some of the historical and critical literature that led to the formation of architectural postmodernism.

For a general critique of postmodern developments and their political meaning, see Jürgen Habermas' essay, "Modernity versus Postmodernity," appearing in Hal Foster's anthology *The Anti-Aesthetic*. This essay links contemporary developments in architecture and art with conservative political currents. Peter Bürger's response to Habermas in the same issue of *New German Critique* is also to be recommended. Foster's anthology includes, in addition, Kenneth Frampton's "Towards a Critical Regionalism: Six Points for an Architecture of Resistance," one of the few attempts to formulate an alternative in architecture to both modernism and postmodern historicism.

The body of publications on current postmodernist designs is vast. One of the best sources for recent developments in practice is contemporary architectural periodicals. They include *A&U* (*Architecture and Urbansim*), *Architectural Design*, *Architectural Record*, *The Architectural Review*, *L'Architecture d'Aujourd'hui*, *A.M.C.* (*Architecture Mouvement Continuité*), *Bauen und Wohnen*, *Baumeister*, *Casabella*, *The Harvard Architecture Review*, *Lotus International*, *Oppositions*, *Perspecta*, *Progressive Architecture*, and *Via*. *Architectural Monographs* devotes special issues to the work of one architect. Included in the *A&U* series are publications on Philip Johnson, Charles Moore, and Venturi, Rauch, and Scott Brown. *Architectural Monographs* has covered the work of Michael Graves and Venturi and Rauch. These issues provide good photographs and drawing documentation, but generally little text. The essays introducing the Graves publication, by Alan Colquhoun and Peter Carl, are, however, particularly insightful concerning issues of signification.

Further visual documentation can be found in the recently published monographs *Charles Moore*, by Gerald Allen; *Johnson/Burgee: Architecture*, by Nory Miller; *Robert A. M. Stern 1965–1980: Toward a Modern Architecture after Modernism*, by Robert Stern; and *Michael Graves: Buildings and Projects 1966–1981*, by Michael Graves. Published by the Institute for Architecture and Urban Studies, Kenneth Frampton's catalog *Philip Johnson, Processes: The Glass House, 1949 and the AT&T Corporate Headquarters, 1978* includes two essays discussing the shift in Johnson's work towards historicism. Frampton's description of the AT&T building is concise and informative. For an account of the initial critical reaction, see Ada Louise Huxtable's reviews in the *New York Times*, particularly the one appearing on April 16, 1978. *Skylines*, the architectural newspaper, published a number of critical assessments of the Portland Building in the January 1983 issue. Included among the commentators were the architectural historians Kurt Forster and Vincent Scully, and the architects Philip Johnson, Allan Greenberg, and Alan Colquhoun.

The work of younger practitioners still has not been widely published outside of periodicals. The more abstract designs of Stanley Saitowitz, Andrew Batey, and Mark

Mack can be seen in the exhibition catalogue *California Counterpoint*. Theoretical studies of Lars Lerup and Steve Holl appear in the *Pamphlet Architecture* series.

No bibliography on current architecture would be complete without mention of Tom Wolfe's *From Bauhaus to Our House*, which leaves virtually no architects—modernist or postmodernist—unscathed. Architects and critics have voiced a long series of objections; one of the most thoughtful critiques is by the architectural historian Rosemarie Haag Bletter, "Popshots at the Barrel House," *Art in America*, December 1981, pp. 21–23.

BIBLIOGRAPHY

The Modern Movement

Banham, Reyner. *Theory and Design in the First Machine Age*. London: Architectural Press, 1960.

Benevolo, Leonardo. *History of Modern Architecture*. Translated by H. J. Landry. 2 vols. Cambridge, Mass.: MIT Press, 1960.

Benton, Tim, Charlotte Benton, and Dennis Sharp, eds. *Architecture and Design 1980–1939*. New York: Whitney Library of Design, 1975.

Collins, Peter. *Changing Ideals in Modern Architecture; 1750–1950*. London: Faber and Faber, 1965.

Conrads, Ulrich, ed. *Programmes and Manifestos on 20th-Century Architecture*. Translated by Michael Bullock. London: Lund Humphries, 1970.

Frampton, Kenneth. *Modern Architecture: A Critical History*. New York: Oxford University Press, 1980.

Giedion, Siegfried. *Space, Time and Architecture*. Cambridge, Mass.: Harvard University Press, 1941.

Hitchcock, Henry Russell. *Architecture: Nineteenth and Twentieth Centuries*. Baltimore: Penguin Books, 1958.

Jordy, William. "The Symbolic Essence of Modern European Architecture of the Twenties and Its Continuing Influence." *Journal of the Society of Architectural Historians* 22, no. 3 (October 1963): 177–87.

Le Corbusier [Charles Edouard Jeanneret]. *Vers une architecture*. Paris: Crès, 1923. Translated from the 13th edition by Frederick Etchells as *Towards a New Architecture*. New York: Praeger, 1960.

Pevsner, Nickolaus. *Pioneers of the Modern Movement from William Morris to Walter Gropius*. Harmondsworth, Middlesex: Penguin Books, 1974.

Rowe, Colin. "The Mathematics of the Ideal Villa." *Architectural Review* 101, no. 603 (March 1947): 101–4. Reprinted in *The Mathematics of the Ideal Villa*. Cambridge, Mass.: MIT Press, 1976.

Sartoris, Alberto. *Gli Elementi dell' Architettura Funzionale*. 2d ed. Milan: U. Hoepli, 1935.

Tafuri, Manfredo, and Francesco Dalco. *Modern Architecture*. Translated by Robert Erich Wolf. New York: Abrams, 1976.

Zevi, Bruno. *Storia dell' architettura moderna*. Turin: Einaudi, 1950. Rev. ed., 1975.

Modern Architecture, 1945–65

Banham, Reyner. *The New Brutalism: Ethic or Aesthetic?* New York: Reinhold, 1966.
Drew, Philip. *The Third Generation: The Changing Meaning in Architecture.* New York and Washington, D.C.: Praeger, 1972.
Frampton, Kenneth. "Apropos Ulm: Curriculum and Critical Theory." *Oppositions* 3 (May 1974): 18–36.
Jacobus, John. *Twentieth-Century Architecture: The Middle Years, 1940–65.* New York and Washington, D.C.: Praeger, 1972.
Joedicke, Jürgen. *Architecture Since 1945: Sources and Directions.* Translated by J. C. Palmes. New York and Washington, D.C.: Praeger, 1969.
Jordy, William. *The Impact of European Modernism in the Mid-Twentieth Century.* Vol. 4, *American Buildings and Their Architects.* New York: Anchor Press, 1972.
Team 10. *Team 10 Primer.* Edited by Alison Smithson. Cambridge, Mass.: MIT Press, 1968.

Critical Reassessment

Alexander, Christopher. *Community and Privacy: Toward a New Architecture of Humanism.* Garden City, N.Y.: Doubleday, 1963.
———. *Notes on a Synthesis of Form.* Cambridge, Mass.: Harvard University Press, 1969.
Argan, Giulio Carlo. "On the Typology of Architecture." Translated by Joseph Rykwert. *Architectural Design* 33, no. 12 (December 1963): 564–65.
Blake, Peter. *Form Follows Fiasco: Why Modern Architecture Hasn't Worked.* Boston: Little, Brown, 1977.
Bloomer, Kent C., and Charles W. Moore. *Body, Memory and Architecture.* New Haven, Conn.: Yale University Press, 1977.
Colquhoun, Alan. "Typology and Design Method."*Arena: Journal of the Architectural Association* 83 (June 1967). Reprinted in Alan Colquhoun, *Essays in Architectural Criticism: Modern Architecture and Historical Change*, pp. 43–50. Cambridge, Mass.: MIT Press, 1981.
Eisenman, Peter. "Notes on Conceptual Architecture." *Casabella* 25, nos. 359–60 (December 1971): 49–58.
Eisenman, Peter, Michael Graves, Charles Gwathmey, John Hejduk, and Richard Meier. *Five Architects.* Introduction by Colin Rowe, with an essay by Kenneth Frampton. New York: Wittenborn, 1972.
Jacobs, Jane. *The Death and Life of Great American Cities.* New York: Random House, 1961.
Koolhaus, Rem. *Delirious New York: A Retroactive Manifesto for Manhattan.* New York: Oxford University Press, 1978.
Krier, Rob. *Urban Space.* London: Academy Editions, 1979.
Moore, Charles, W., and Gerald Allen. *Dimensions: Space, Shape and Scale in Architecture.* New York: Architectural Record Books, 1976.
Moore, Charles M., and Donlyn Lyndon. *The Place of Houses.* New York: Holt, Rinehart and Winston, 1974.
Norberg-Schultz, Christian. *Intentions in Architecture.* London: Allen and Unwin, 1963.

Rossi, Aldo. *L'Architettura della città*. Padua: Marsilio Editori, 1966. Translated by Diane Ghirardo and Joan Ockman as *The Architecture of the City*. Cambridge, Mass.: MIT Press, 1982.

Rowe, Colin, and Fred Koetter. *Collage City*. Cambridge, Mass.: MIT Press, 1978.

Schumacher, Tom. "Contexturalism: Urban Ideals and Deformations." *Casabella* 25, nos. 359–60 (December 1971): 49–58.

Scully, Vincent. *The Shingle Style Today or the Historian's Revenge*. New York: Braziller, 1974.

Stern, Robert A. M. *New Dimensions in American Architecture*. New York: Braziller, 1969; rev. ed. 1977.

Venturi, Robert. *Complexity and Contradiction in Architecture*. New York: Museum of Modern Art, 1966; 2d ed., 1977.

Venturi, Robert, Denise Scott Brown, and Steven Izenour. *Learning from Las Vegas*. Cambridge, Mass.: MIT Press, 1972; rev. ed., 1977.

Semiology

Barthes, Roland. *The Eiffel Tower and Other Mythologies*. Translated by Richard Howard. New York: Hill & Wang, 1979.

———. *Elements of Semiology*. Translated by Annette Lavers and Colin Smith. New York: Hill & Wang, 1968.

Broadbent, Geoffrey, Richard Bunt, and Charles Jencks, eds. *Signs, Symbols and Architecture*. New York: John Wiley and Sons, 1980.

Bryan, James, and James Sauer, eds. "Structures Implicit and Explicit." *Via: The Student Publication of the Graduate School of Fine Arts, University of Pennsylvania* 2 (1973).

Colquhoun, Alan. "Historicism and the Limits of Semiology." Reprinted in Alan Colquhoun, *Essays in Architectural Criticism: Modern Architecture and Historical Change*, pp. 129–51. Cambridge, Mass.: MIT Press, 1981.

Eco, Umberto. *A Theory of Semiotics*. Bloomington: Indiana University Press, 1976.

Gandelsonas, Mario. "On Reading Architecture." *Progressive Architecture* 53, no. 3 (March 1972): 68–88.

Guillerme, Jacques. "The Idea of Architectural Language: A Critical Inquiry." *Oppositions* 10 (Fall 1977): 21–26.

Saussure, Ferdinand de. *Course in General Linguistics*. Edited by Charles Bally and Albert Sechehaye. Translated by Wade Baskin. London: Owen, 1960.

Postmodernism: General

Baird, George. " 'La Dimension Amoureuse' in Architecture." In *Meaning in Architecture*, pp. 79–99. Edited by Charles Jencks and George Baird. New York: Braziller, 1969.

"Beyond the Modern Movement." *The Harvard Architecture Review* 1 (Spring 1980): 4–9.

Bletter, Rosemarie Haag. "Popshots at the Barrel House." *Art in America*, December 1981, pp. 21–23.

Broadbent, Geoffrey. "The Pest Strikes Back." *Royal Institute of British Architects Journal* 88, no. 11 (November 1981): 31–34.

Bruegmann, Robert. "Two Post-Modernist Visions of Urban Design: Venturi and Scott Brown and Rob Krier." *Landscape* 26, no. 2 (1982): 31–37.

Bürger, Peter. "Avant-Garde and Contemporary Aesthetics: A Reply to Jürgen Habermas." *New German Critique* 22 (Winter 1981): 19–22.

Diamonstein, Barbaralee. *American Architecture Now: Barbaralee Diamonstein with I. M. Pei (and Others)*. New York: Rizzoli, 1980.

Doubiet, Susan. "I'd Rather Be Interesting." *Progressive Architecture*, no. 2 (February 1984): pp. 65–69.

Frampton, Kenneth. "Towards a Critical Regionalism: Six Points for an Architecture of Resistance." In *The Anti-Aesthetic: Essays on Postmodern Culture*, pp. 16–30. Edited by Hal Foster. Port Townsend, Wash.: Bay Press, 1983.

Goldberger, Paul. "Now the Religion Is Anti-Modernism." *New York Times*, December 5, 1982, sec. 2, pp. 1, 36.

Groat, Linda. "Meaning in Post-Modern Architecture: An Examination Using the Multiple Sorting Task." *Journal of Environmental Psychology* 2, no. 1 (March 1982): 3–22.

Groat, Linda, and David Canter. "Does Post-Modernism Communicate? A Study of Meaning." *Progressive Architecture* 60, no. 12 (December 1979): 84–87.

Habermas, Jürgen. "Modernity versus Postmodernity." *New German Critique* 22 (Winter 1981): 3–14. Reprinted as "Modernity—An Incomplete Project." In *The Anti-Aesthetic: Essays on Postmodern Culture*, pp. 3–15. Edited by Hal Foster. Port Townsend, Wash.: Bay Press, 1983.

Huxtable, Ada Louise. "After Modern Architecture." *New York Review of Books*, December 8, 1983, pp. 29–35.

———. "Is Modern Architecture Dead?" *New York Review of Books*, July 16, 1981, pp. 17–20.

———. "Johnson's Latest Clever Tricks or True Art?" *New York Times*, April 16, 1978, pp. 26–31.

———. "Rebuilding Architecture." *New York Review of Books*, December 22, 1983, pp. 55–61.

———. "The Troubled State of Modern Architecture." *New York Review of Books*, May 1, 1980, pp. 22–29. Reprinted in *Architectural Design* 51, nos. 1–2 (1981): 81–87.

Jencks, Charles. *The Language of Post-Modern Architecture*. London: Academy Editions, 1977; New York: Rizzoli, 1978; 3d and rev. ed., 1981.

———, ed. "Free-Style Classicism." *Architectural Design* 52, nos. 1–2 (1982).

———, ed. "Post-Modern Classicism: The New Synthesis." *Architectural Design* 50, nos. 5–6 (1980). Reprint, London: Academy Editions, 1980.

———, ed. "Post-Modern History." *Architectural Design* 48, no. 1 (1978).

———, ed. "Post-Modernism." *Architectural Design* 47, no. 4 (1977).

Jencks, Charles and George Baird, eds. *Meaning in Architecture*. New York: Braziller, 1969.

Jencks, Charles, and William Chaitkin. *Current Architecture*. London: Academy Editions, 1982.

Johnson, Philip. "On Style and the International Style: On Post-Modernism: On Architecture." *Oppositions* 10 (Fall 1977): 15–19.

Kurokawa, Kishno N. "Japanese Culture and Post-Modernist Architecture." *Japan Architect* 58, no. 4 (April 1983): 4–6.

"The New Classicism." Special issue, *Progressive Architecture*, no. 10 (October 1981).

Peterson, Steven. "Space and Anti-Space." *The Harvard Architecture Review* 1 (Spring 1980): 89–113.

Pommer, Richard. "Some Architectural Ideologies after the Fall." *Art Journal* 40, nos. 1–2 (Fall/Winter 1980): 353–61.

Porphrios, Demetri, ed. "Classicism Is Not a Style." Special issue, *Architectural Design* 52, nos. 5–6 (1982).

Portoghesi, Paolo. *After Modern Architecture*. Translated by Meg Shore. New York: Rizzoli, 1982.

————. *Postmodern: The Architect of the Postindustrial Society*. New York: Rizzoli, 1983.

Portoghesi, Paolo, et al. *The Presence of the Past: First International Exhibition of Architecture—Venice Biennale, 1980*. Venice: Edizione "La Biennale di Venezia," and London: Academy Editions, 1980.

"The Presence of the Past." Special issue, *Archetype* 3, no. 1 (Spring 1982).

Safdie, Moshe. "Private Jokes in Public Places: Some Serious Questions about the Attitudinal as Well as Stylistic Demeanor of the Post-Modern Coterie of Form Givers." *Inland Architect* 25, no. 9 (November-December 1981): 20–27.

"The Search for a Postmodern Architecture." Special issue, *CRIT: The Architectural Student Journal* 4 (Fall 1978).

Searing, Helen. *Speaking a New Classicism*. Northampton, Mass.: Catalogue, Smith College Museum of Art, 1981.

Smith, C. Ray. *Supermannerism: New Attitudes in Post-Modern Architecture*. New York: E. P. Dutton, 1977.

Stern, Robert. "The Doubles of Post-Modern." *The Harvard Architecture Review* 1 (Spring 1980): 75–87.

————, ed. "American Architecture: After Modernism." *A&U* 3 (March 1981).

————, ed. [Gray architecture as post-modernism or up and down from orthodoxy]. *L'Architecture d'Aujourd'hui* 186 (August-September 1976): 83.

Tigerman, Stanley. *Chicago Tribune Tower Competition: Late Entries to the Chicago Tribune Tower Competition*. Vol. 2. New York: Rizzoli, 1980.

————. *Versus: An American Architect's Alternatives*. New York: Rizzoli, 1982.

Tzonis, Alex, and Liane LeFaivre, "The Narcissist Phase in Architecture." *The Harvard Architecture Review* 1 (Spring 1980): 53–61.

Van Eyck, Aldo. "Rats, Posts and Pests." *Royal Institute of British Architects* 88, no. 4 (April 1981): 47–50.

Wolfe, Tom. *From Bauhaus to Our House*. New York: Farrar, Straus and Giroux, 1981.

Postmodernism—Individual Architects

Allen, Gerald. *Charles Moore*. New York: Whitney Library of Design, 1980.

Cast, David. "Good, Ordinary, Classical, Modern" [discusses Allan Greenberg and Peter Kosinski Assoc., Courthouse, Manchester, Conn.]. *Progressive Architecture*, no. 10 (October 1981): 80–83.

Colquhoun, Alan. "Sign and Substance: Reflections on Complexity, Las Vegas, and Oberlin." Reprinted in Alan Colquhoun, *Essays in Architectural Criticism: Modern Architecture and Historical Change*, pp. 139–51. Cambridge, Mass.: MIT Press, 1981.

————. "From *Bricolage* to Myth, or How to Put Humpty-Dumpty Together Again." Reprinted in Alan Colquhoun, *Essays in Architectural Criticism: Modern Architecture and Historical Change*, pp. 169–89.

Coolidge, John, and Peter Cook. "Three Buildings by James Stirling, Michael Wilford and Associates." *Architectural Review* 173, no. 1033 (March 1983): 22–41.

Dunster, David. "Classical Language or Mongrel Rhetoric" [discusses Quinlan Terry]. *Architectural Review* 173, no. 1033. (March 1983): 84–87.

Eisenmann, Peter. "The Futility of Objects: Decomposition and the Process of Difference." *The Harvard Architecture Review* 3 (Winter 1984): 65–81.

————. *House X*. New York: Rizzoli, 1982.

Filler, Martin. "Charles Moore: House Vernacular." *Art in America*, October 1980, pp. 105–12.

Forster, Kurt, Arthur Drexler, Vincent Scully, Alan Colquhoun, Allan Greenberg, Philip Johnson, and John Burgee. "The Portland Building." *Skyline*, January 1983, pp. 16–19.

Frampton, Kenneth. *Philip Johnson, Processes: The Glass House, 1949, and the AT&T Corporate Headquarters, 1978*. New York: Catalogue, Institute for Architecture and Urban Studies, 1978.

Garcias, Jean-Claude. "Versailles for the People" [discusses Taller de Arquitectura]. *Architectural Review* 168, no. 1005 (November 1980): 297–300.

Graves, Michael. *Michael Graves*. Edited by David Dunster. *Architectural Monographs* 5. New York: Rizzoli, 1979.

————. *Michael Graves: Buildings and Projects, 1966–1981*. Edited by Karen Vogel Wheeler, Peter Arnell, and Ted Bickford. New York: Rizzoli, 1982.

Greenberg, Allan. "The Sense of the Past: An Architectural Perspective." *Chicago Architectural Journal* 1 (1981): 42–43.

Hollein, Hans. "Austrian Travel Agency." *A&U* 100 (January 1979): 31–46.

Johnson, Philip. *Philip Johnson*. Tokyo: *A&U*, 1979.

————. *Writings*. New York: Oxford University Press, 1979.

"Johnson and Burgee." Special issue, *Progressive Architecture* (February 1984).

Miller, Nory. *Johnson/Burgee: Architecture*. New York: Random House, 1979.

Oechslin, Werner. "New Possibilities of Distinction: The Work of Machado and Silvetti as It Reappears in Post-Modernism." *Lotus* 28 (1980): 116–35.

Smith, Thomas Gordon. "Five Projects." *A&U* 101 (February 1979): 11–14.

Stephens, Suzanne. "At the Institute: The Portland Building Analyzed." *Skyline*, January 1983, p. 21.

————. "Reconstructing Rice" [discusses James Stirling]. *Skyline*, November 1981, pp. 19–20.

Stern, Robert A. M. *Robert A. M. Stern 1965–1980: Toward a Modern Architecture after Modernism*. Edited by Peter Arnell and Ted Bickford. New York: Rizzoli, 1981.

————. *Robert Stern*. Introductory essay by Vincent Scully. London: Academy Editions, 1981.

Stirling, James. "The Monumental Tradition: Three Competition Designs by James Stirling for the Design of Modern Art Museums in Dusseldorf, Cologne and Stuttgart." *Perspecta* 16 (1980): 32–49.

Summerson, John. "Vitruvius Ludens" [discusses James Stirling]. *Architectural Review* 173, no. 1033 (March 1983): 18–21.

Taller de Arquitectura. "Les Arcades du Lac, Saint Quentin-en-Yvelines; Le Théâtre de Vallée; Studio of Taller de Arquitectura, Sant Just d'Esvern, Barcelona." *GA Document* 3 (Winter 1981): 48–67.

Terry, Quinlan. "Architectural Renaissance." *Building Design*, September 17, 1976.

Venturi, Robert. *Venturi and Rauch*. Edited by David Dunster. *Architectural Monographs* 1. London: Academy Editions, 1978.

———. *Venturi, Rauch and Scott Brown*. Tokyo: *A&U*, 1981.

———. *Venturi, Rauch and Scott Brown*. Edited by Gianni Pettena and Maurizio Vogliazzo. Milan: Electa, 1981.

Vidler, Anthony. "Reconstituting Modernism: The Architecture of James Stirling." *Skyline*, November 1981, pp. 16–19.

3

Art

JOHN T. PAOLETTI

> The aspirations of those who would isolate art from the social world are
> analogous to those of Kant's dove which dreamed of how much freer its
> flight could be if only it were released from the resistance of the air. If we
> are to learn any lesson from the history of the past fifty years of art, it is
> surely that an art unattached to the social world is free to go anywhere but
> that it has nowhere to go.
>
> Victor Burgin, "Commentary Part II," *Work and Commentary.*

Postmodernism is not a style, or, more accurately, it is not one style.[1] As a
nominative term postmodernism is as bedeviled by ambiguity and imprecision
as are most of the shorthand historical terms used to describe artistic expression.[2]
In its current usage in the visual arts, postmodernism is vaguely and myopically
used most often as a synonym for contemporary sensationalistic expressionism,
a usage that threatens the term with obsolescence as soon as the commercial
energies of the art world move to other saleable styles. Postmodernism, however,
does have value not only as a term, but as a historical construct if it is viewed,
like other period terms in the history of art (medieval or renaissance, for example,
or even modernism), as one that adequately focuses attention on a set of pervasive
and coherent core concepts regardless of the various personal or regional styles
which are employed to elaborate this unified set of ideas. Postmodernism as a
historical phenomenon, then, must be seen as cumulative rather than exclusive,
broadly historical rather than modishly expressionistic, and coherent in intention
yet varied and fluid in its means of carrying ideas; capable, in fact, of embracing
all the proscriptive and misleading terms—such as performance, body, landscape,
and conceptual—that have multiplied ad nauseum during the recent past.

Succinctly, if somewhat tautologically stated, postmodernism is an alternative
to modernism. Although arguably a successor to an earlier artistic development,
postmodernism is not a continuation and evolution of an earlier style as post-
impressionism was to impressionism, but a reaction and antithesis both to the

formalist and purist thinking of modernism and to the theoretical apologia that
critics devised to describe this style. Postmodernism could just as easily (and
perhaps more accurately) be called antimodernism.[3] As such, postmodernism
focuses attention on content, but, more specifically, on a content that is explicitly
related to the ways in which art intersects and interacts with the social system
in all of its various aspects. Postmodernism thus provides clearer insights into
the roles and presuppositions of both the art and the people within that system.[4]
The gestation period for postmodernism has been a long one; in fact, using the
inclusive mode of definition suggested here, it has been virtually as long as that
of modernism, even though the term itself is of recent coinage. Numbers of
reasons can be suggested for the eruption of a *discussion* of postmodernism, not
of postmodernism itself, in the years around 1980: the persistent and repetitive
commercialized search for novelty that had characterized the art of the previous
twenty years had worn itself out by 1980, leaving those critics engaged in the
periodic decennial exercise of trying to predict the future with little hope for a
recurrence of the phenomenal range of activity of the previous two decades;
leading modernist painters either had made radical shifts in personal style away
from the canons of modernism or produced predictable paintings as illustrations
of the canon; modernist criticism had reached a stage of incestuousness leading
to terminal torpidity; a new generation of both artists and critics appeared with
wide-ranging (academic) interdisciplinary training, thus widening the boundaries
of their expectations of the role of art; the world in which these artists and critics
lived had significantly changed, if not in actuality, at least in their perceptions
of the actualities as a result of the student protests of the sixties, the Vietnam
War, political assassinations, clandestine but pervasive international terrorist
activities, the ecology movement, the feminist movement, and numerous other
social and political causes; and entrance into the penultimate decade of the
twentieth century made a review, if not a rejection, of the past a tempting exercise
in preparation for the millennium.

    Such issues have reinvested art with a sense of content, largely ignored or
rejected by modernism, a content important not only for those making art but
for those writing about it as well. The antithetical position that postmodernism
has taken toward modernism—in style, in content, and in criticism—has created
a new awareness of art as historically matrixed with the ensuing realization that,
even if discussion of postmodernism is new, its existence is not. It is this history
of postmodernism that needs to be given at least some skeletal form.

    Postmodernism's reactive stance against its patronymic style demands some
minimal explanation of modernism itself. Modernism has had such a long history,
such strong practitioners, and such articulate critics for nearly a century that it
is not hard to understand why reaction against it has taken so long to be integrated
into critical and historical writing. Modernist painting (and modernism in the
critical literature involves virtually exclusively a discussion of painting and not
of sculpture) normally takes its inception as a style from the work of Manet in
the last four decades of the nineteenth century. Along with other painters at the

time, Manet used arbitrary pictorial devices that served to flatten out the space of his pictures and, seemingly, to deny the visual traditions of objective or veristic representation. Contrary to recent reinterpretation of Manet's work, critics contemporary to Manet—at least those who did not find the painting risible— found Manet's genius in his formal treatment of the pictorial surface. Émile Zola, for example, spoke of Manet's "broad patches of color" and his composition "in large masses"; in 1867 Zola wrote about Manet: "he has not set himself the task of representing some abstract idea or some historical episode. And it is because of this that he should neither be judged as a moralist nor as a literary man. He should be judged simply as a painter."[5] If one accepts formal analysis of pictorial events as a means of determining the painter's worth, as both Baudelaire and Zola seem to do, then it is not difficult to outline a painterly evolution during the course of the last decades of the nineteenth century to an ever more consciously flattened pictorial surface and to deliberate adjustments of form to accommodate this flattened space. The low horizon line and parallel verticals stretching from the top to the bottom of the canvas in Monet's *Poplar* paintings, the bird's eye view and arbitrary slicing of the edges of the scene in Degas' paintings of ballet dancers and bathers, the flat matte coloration and friezelike arrangement of figures in Gauguin's Tahiti paintings all seem to select compositional schema that deny traditional volumetric naturalism and insist on the manipulative aspects of the painter in transforming the visual phenomenon of the real world into the now clearly declared fictive representation on the flat pictorial surface.

Cézanne, perhaps more than any other painter coming to prominence at the end of the nineteenth century, challenged the reproductive role of art. English critics, in particular, responded to Cézanne's paintings in a decisive formalist fashion that was to help set the tone for criticism of advanced painting for the next half-century. In 1914 Clive Bell wrote that Cézanne "pushed further and further towards a complete revelation of the significance of form."[6] Bell also discussed the concept of "significant form," which he defined as "lines and colours combined in a particular way, certain forms and relations of forms [which] stir our aesthetic emotions."[7] Begging the question of just what an "aesthetic emotion" is, Bell nonetheless sought a collective descriptive quality that would allow him to discuss commonality—and quality—in "Sta. Sophia and the windows at Chartres, Mexican sculpture, a Persian bowl, Chinese carpets, Giotto's frescoes at Padua, and the masterpieces of Poussin, Piero della Francesca and Cézanne."[8] With this attempt at an inclusive formalist system for determining what art was good, what was not, and why, Bell pushed the role of the critic into that of the aesthetician. Aside from establishing formalism as the sole criterion for aesthetic quality, a formalism that supercedes the role played by representation and thus lays open the road to abstraction, Bell took the extraordinary extra step of suggesting that a painting that does not conform to his notion of significant form—and here he used William Powell Frith's *Paddington Station*—"is not a work of art; it is an interesting and amusing document."[9] Art for Bell communicates sensations to an already aesthetically refined sensibility, does so in a purely formal way, and expunges any competitive messages from the observable world.

On the face of it, the work of Picasso and Matisse, reaching maturity in the first decade of this century, fits neatly into the evolution of the reduced picture surface with juxtaposed flat planes of color and pattern where reading spatial relationships becomes an intellectual or aesthetic exercise rather than an automatic and familiar visual experience. And formalist criticism such as Bell's does offer a certain kind of accessibility to the painting, albeit only for those initiates willing to limit the discourse of the painting to one concerning the nature of art.[10]

Despite the questions raised by dada (especially by Marcel Duchamp) and surrealism, this type of critical approach continued through the early decades of the twentieth century and hardened into near gospel, in the United States particularly, with the writing of Clement Greenberg and of his followers. By 1939 Greenberg had clearly stated his belief in an artistic elite when he articulated a dichotomy between high art and low art (or kitsch); for Greenberg, the Russian painter, Repin, represented an example of debased artistic endeavor in the way that Frith had for Bell. For Greenberg, advanced, or, as he chooses to term it, avant-garde, art demands a "superior consciousness of history" in order to "keep culture moving in the midst of ideological confusion and violence."[11] Greenberg further posits that the path for the artist to follow in a period of cultural deterioration is isolation in the search for the "expression of the absolute."[12] With a faint echo of Bell's "significant form" Greenberg further states rather categorically that "content is to be dissolved so completely into form that the work of art or literature cannot be reduced in whole or in part to anything not itself."[13] The art viewing system, then, is closed and self-referential.

Although Greenberg did not write his summa, "Modernist Painting," until 1965, he had been developing his ideas about painting in an influential series of essays for the preceding twenty-five years.[14] He had developed his aesthetic position as a result of his closeness to the artists of the emerging New York School in the 1940s and as a result of his need to situate them within an accepted tradition that could be used to explain their art to an educated public. Formally the descriptive essence of Greenberg's criticism is quite simple: the paintings of artists like Jackson Pollock (of whom he was particularly fond), Mark Rothko, Franz Kline, Willem deKooning, or Barnett Newman are "all-over" paintings insofar as they have become "decentralized" canvases in which no area of the surface takes precedence over any other area. In many instances, especially in the mature work of artists like these, the canvases are large, virtually wall-size, thus encompassing a viewer's entire field of vision. Both Pollock's rivulets of paint and Newman's flat color fields—each radically different in style and temperament—emphasize a surface that is compositionally evenly textured. Even in a painting such as Pollock's *Blue Poles* (1952), where eight dancing, totemistic staffs burn through the overall web of pigment, or in Newman's *Vir Heroicus*

Sublimis (1950–51), where five thin, precise "zips" cleave the 17–foot-long expanse of red canvas, no individual unit functions as a place of focus or stasis, but rather each pulses outward to the next similar form, once again emphasizing surface activity and plane. Color, brush stroke, skeining in American abstract painting of this period stretch tautly over the surface, seemingly denying recessional or volumetric space and giving new presence to the edge of the painting, which in many instances seems to be arbitrary. Rather than the perspectival or atmospheric space of painting since the Renaissance, which denied the pictorial surface and pushed space illusionistically into the distance, abstract painting denied such visual trickery for an honestly stated exploration of the painted surface and its limits. Rather than push painting in toward the center, abstract painting pushed it out to surface and to edge and beyond.

Greenberg's ideal for modernist painting is one in which the end result is "very close to decoration."[15] From that rather straightforward verbal formulation of the visual facts of New York School painting, Greenberg then moves to construct a rather more elaborate, embracing, historical system. Advanced American painting of the 1940s and the 1950s he sees, in a voyage into historical determinism, as predicated on the paintings of the School of Paris, most particularly Picasso and cubism. American painting had merely taken the next step in a process begun by Manet toward flatness and abstraction. For Greenberg this two-dimensionality was "the guarantee of painting's independence as an art," for by eliminating all references to anything other than the support, the painting moved closer to its "unique and irreducible" purity of form.[16] Given this critical stance on what painting is (or ought to be), Greenberg had provided a measuring stick for determining what was good and what was bad painting, especially in the particularly vexed area of abstraction. What was essential for Greenberg in this system, what made painting modernist, was its "use of the characteristic methods of a discipline to criticize the discipline itself.[17] Greenberg also made the bold claim that modernism "includes almost the whole of what is truly alive in our culture."[18]

A second generation of abstract painters with a Greenberg disciple as apologist began to emerge in the early sixties. With the exhibition of *Three American Painters* organized by Michael Fried in 1965, the paintings of Kenneth Noland, Jules Olitski, and Frank Stella seemed a justification for Greenberg's position, given clear formulation by Fried in the catalogue essay.[19] More importantly, however, their painting seemed to be more directly responsive to the theoretical constructs of Greenberg's modernist criticism than it was to the painting that had gone before. Stella's compelling black paintings of 1959, for example, use the shape of the painting support to determine the inner configurations of black bands. In so doing, the uninflected geometrical pattern spreads over the surface, maintaining its flatness and dealing exclusively with what Fried called "problems intrinsic to painting itself."[20] When Stella had exhausted the simple geometric possibilities allowed by the square or the rectangular canvas, he began to make shaped paintings in which areas that were not precise duplicates or variations of the immediately adjacent bands were simply excised. These eccentric shapes, paired with a thickened support for the canvas, turned the paintings into objects, again emphasizing their self-referential role as paintings.[21]

As neat as this progressivist development of modernist painting may seem to some, it is also clear that strong dissenting voices have consistently appeared alongside the modernists. Perhaps the most articulate and forceful artist who could be termed an early antimodernist was Marcel Duchamp, who by 1913 had already developed the ready-mades—found objects, usually industrially produced, moved from their original context into an art context—in an all-out frontal attack on the aesthetic principles of style and quality that characterize discussions on modernism. Given the hermetic and apparently intensely personal content concealed in many of Duchamp's works, they nonetheless function as a coherent artistic and critical manifestation of opposition to the increasingly pervasive art-for-art's sake aesthetic by pointing out the fallacies and the limitations of the modernist system.[22] In *Tu M'* (1918), for example, the *trompe-l'oeil* tear in the canvas is really flat pictorial surface, whereas the actual shadow of the perpendicular bottle brush that pokes through the canvas, while lying on and looking like part of the painted surface, really is not, a fact especially noticeable when the painting was still in a private collection and subject to changes in lighting. In fact, rather than being completely self-enclosed and self-referential, *Tu M'* is deliberately responsive to the changes in the real world and also dependent on the viewer to complete the title, which, regardless of the verb provided, will set up a dialogue between painting and viewer. Even art that moved toward pure abstraction, like Russian suprematism, was seen by its contemporaries as content-filled and responsive to the political needs of the time. From the second decade of the century, dada and surrealism continued to argue the need for an art in which content, be it overt and political or interior and psychological, was still of dominant importance.

Modernism in the United States faced the same virtually immediate response from other artists that European modernism had faced at the hands of the dadaists and surrealists. By 1965, when second-generation modernism in America had reached maturity with artists like Stella, Morris Louis, Noland, and David Novros and when Greenberg had written his definitive essay on modernism, the modernist position had already been severely challenged for over a decade by artists such as Robert Rauschenberg and Jasper Johns and by John Cage. For a period of time, from the very early fifties to the mid-sixties, modernism and its challengers grew and developed side by side. However, by the late sixties modernist painting was obviously in a threatened position, as manifest in the dispersion of its apologists, by the attention given to new forms of art in the galleries and the museums, and by significant stylistic shifts among some of the major artists of the modernist critical canon, particularly Stella, who by the *Painted Bird* series of 1976 was painting eccentrically shaped reliefs active with spatially interpenetrating forms.

By 1951 Rauschenberg had made his first white paintings, some as large as

6 feet high, with nothing on the surfaces but evenly brushed white pigment. These paintings are mockeries of the Greenbergian all-over surfaces. While apparently accepting the modernist drive toward the flat surface, abstraction, and purism (Rauschenberg even used white), he simultaneously destroyed the demanded integrity of the painting by breaking it up into several panels, no one particularly different from any other, and by removing them from any ideology having to do with the aesthetic value or integrity of the object. Rauschenberg intended the white paintings not as pristine art objects in and of themselves, but as reflectors of the activity of the real world, that messy arena of accident that modernist painters and critics seemed determined to flee. What appeared, after all, on Rauschenberg's white paintings were the shadows of the viewers, the always changing aspects of the world exterior to the painting, not intrinsic to it. This accident was different from the programmed accident of Pollock's drip paintings insofar as the artist had nothing to do with it; the viewer, not the artist, completed the painting, thus taking the picture itself definitively out of the rarified and exclusive art context that modernist critics had been describing for half a century.[23]

The event that John Cage staged at Black Mountain College in the summer of 1952 is another focus of artistic energy providing a path totally divergent from modernism. Artists (Rauschenberg), musicians (Cage, David Tudor), dancers (Merce Cunningham), and poets (Charles Olson, Mary Caroline Richards) all participated in an event governed by chance throwing of I Ching coins, in which none of the performers knew in advance what the others would do. Rather than the intensely conscious control exerted over their paintings by artists like Pollock, Rothko, or Newman (whose own art in 1952 had just, after all, begun to receive public recognition), the Cage performance led toward dispersion of attention, to random interaction of various media and performers, and to the acceptance of ordinary events, sounds, and actions as art, as opposed to the search for the extraordinary pursued by painters of the New York School. When Rauschenberg erased a deKooning drawing in 1953, leaving only the faintest ghost image on the paper, his gesture tellingly marked the nascent drive of a new spirit to release itself from the painterly and critical constraints of modernism.

Rauschenberg's mature style, characterized by work composed of blatantly real objects like a quilt (*Bed*, 1954), or a rooster (*Odalisque*, 1955–58), or a stuffed angora goat (*Monogram*, 1955–59), accepts the accidental mating of these objects with others of a pictorial commonness (street signs, magazine and newspaper illustrations). Since none of the objects ever becomes completely subsumed within an overall scheme, they each retain their intensity as objects in the world despite their art context, thus acting in Rauschenberg's famous gap between art and life.[24]

Jasper Johns' early work, although decidedly different from Rauschenberg's in its meticulous painterly finish and in its direct single-image intensity, nonetheless shows some of the same concerns investigated by Rauschenberg and Cage. The *Flag* painting of 1954 can also be read as a parody of the modernist canon since it is an overall painting, since it is coextensive with the frame of the painting, and since the surface of the painting, with the stripes extending from one side of the image to the other, seems to be of primary concern. Yet the image is as obsessive and as common as Rauschenberg's images—both common as familiar and common as banal. While Johns' painting is carefully built up, stroke by stroke in the most refined manner, yet the blatancy of the image severely compromises our ability to read the painting merely as painting as the modernists would demand. The critical self-referential component of modernism is also vitiated by Johns' outer directed images. The *Target with Four Faces* (1955), in which Johns included partial casts of four heads above a bull's-eye target, establishes a dialogue outward toward the viewer; the four faces, their eyes ironically cut off by the upper edge of the painting, but their mouths ever so slightly different, suggesting a kaleidoscopic grin, suppose someone outside the painting—as does the target itself. Rather than being ''in the painting,'' as Pollock said he was and as Rothko and Newman implied, the Johns image gives four heads that are attached to, but decidedly outside, the painting and also seemingly responsive to activities taking place in front of the image itself.

The ready acceptance of the facts and phenomena of the haphazardly real world by Rauschenberg, Johns, and Cage was further expanded by Allan Kaprow, who made his first environment in 1958 and staged his first happening in 1959. In these theatrical events, explored yet more extensively by Claes Oldenburg, Jim Dine, and Red Grooms in 1960 and 1961, the artist provided a situation in which the boundaries of the created event were confused by the active participation of the audience. Art had moved toward theatre (anathema in the eyes of a formalist like Fried) and a celebration of the transitory, the ephemeral, the unanticipated and the ordinary, all clearly opposed to the goals of the modernist artist.[25]

Perhaps the first major threat to modernist hegemony was the explosion of pop in New York during the fall gallery season of 1962. The virtually instant acceptance of pop by the newly affluent, more urbane and more widely educated public widened the base of the antimodernist vocabulary established by Rauschenberg and Johns in the previous decade. Modernists reacted to this phenomenon with accusations of philistinism on the part of a sensation seeking and basically unintellectual public. Nonetheless Warhol's *Campbell Soup Can* (1962), an anonymous and pervasively familiar advertising image of a full-frontal tomato soup can, unmediated by the intervention of the artist and enlarged to the blatant scale of the advertising poster, or Lichtenstein's *Look Mickey* (1961), a jokey cartoon image of everybody's favorites, Mickey Mouse and Donald Duck, again originating in a collaboration of anonymous draughtsmen despite Walt Disney's ''signature,'' managed to summarize in a particularly succinct and powerful manner the experimentations of the previous decade and did so in a way that made the art accessible rather than the treasure of an inside elite. Most importantly, pop, with its commercial icons, its mass-produced and preprocessed imagery of cartoons, advertisements, and illustrations, flew in the face of that very distinction between high art and low art (or kitsch as Greenberg wrote about it) that was so central to the modernist gospel. Pop imagery was loaded with the mundane where modernist painting had sought the elevated. Pop was also sexy in the specific sense of a Wesselman *Great American Nude* displaying herself with all the hype of an advertising billboard. Rather than mythico-erotic imagery as in the 1940s paintings of Pollock and Rothko or the drawings of Barnett Newman, Wesselman's faceless nude is anonymous and undistinguished but for her familiar, pasted-on Hollywood coy red lips, erect and somewhat metalic nipples, and brushed and colorful pubic hair, a commercial product like the other products that surround her in the interior environment of the painting. Rather than the universals of abstract painting, pop gave us the tawdriness of the specific, which led even to the depiction of taboos, as in Andy Warhol films such as *Blowjob* (1963). Where access to abstract painting was a slow process of psychological and spiritual involvement, access to pop was immediate, titillating, and sensationalistic, a move from the soul to somewhere below the belt. Even the mechanical commercial techniques of the artists—the Ben Day dots of Lichtenstein, the photo silk-screens of Warhol, the collaged real elements of Wesselman, or the billboard style of Rosenquist—suggested a lack of concern with traditional painterly problems and certainly a rejection of the idea of painting discussing painting, of the self-critical stance of modernism. There was apparently—but deceptively—not a critical bone in the pop body. A comparison of pop's direct media images with Rauschenberg's ready-made images makes the earlier artist look positively arty in his pictorialism.[26]

Thus, by the early sixties all the elements for a rejection of modernism were already part of the artistic mainstream: an acceptance of commerical art and techniques; an obsessive use of image; a reference out from the painting to what was familiar in the society at large; an apparent rejection of concerns about craft and traditional modes of composition; a populist as opposed to an elite art; a reportorial rather than an interpretive art, one for which immediate impact seemed as important as eternal truths.

Two aspects in particular of sixties art deserve special attention: the evolution of sculpture as an important medium in a society where exposure to sculptural form was limited to war memorials and cemetery sculpture; and the brief and dead-ended florescence of minimalism. Sculpture, whether in the combines of Rauschenberg or the fetischistic images of Oldenburg or the tableaux of Edward Kienholz, threatened to invade the space of the viewer in an aggressive and theatrical manner. The real rooster perched atop Rauschenberg's *Odalisque* gave every indication of wanting to fly off; the food and machines of Oldenberg assumed gigantic proportions, with a concommitant Alice-in-Wonderland-like power to amaze and menace; and the inhabitants of *Roxy's* (a 1961 environment recreating a Nevada whorehouse) all invited conversation with the viewer and responded in sexually aggressive, if rewarding, ways to the viewer's touch and manipulation. None of these sculptures fits the elevated level of prescribed artistic discourse articulated by the modernists; all of them use materials or content that are directed outward toward the real world and none of them seems concerned with problems focussed on art and definition. On the contrary, they all seem intent on removing any boundary between us and the work, making the domain of the art object congruent with ours rather than unique and discrete. Where modernism had been a language for painting, these artists and others like them chose an invasive language of environment in which to act.[27]

Minimalism, on the other hand, seemed as reticent in its formal language as pop was aggressive. The hard-edged geometrical forms of Robert Morris first shown at the end of 1964 or of Donald Judd seem at first glance to be as monomaniacal in their investigation of the phenomenological aspects of the three-dimensional object as Stella had been of the two-dimensional painted surface. Morris' large, light-grey plywood structures seemed architecturally congruent with the white painted interior of the Green Gallery in which they were shown. They appeared merely to be there, both familiar and finite in their geometric simplicity. Neither his wood or later steel sculpture nor Judd's commercially manufactured metal geometrical units showed any particular point of focus; no place in the object was more privileged than any other place, even when the sculpture was composed of multiple units. Yet here again the objects, by their obsessive size, by the way in which repeated units filled up the space essentially pushing the viewer from it, set up a dialogue not within the piece itself but confrontationally between the object and the viewer, since in many cases the boundaries of the pieces or the number of repeated units seemed quite arbitrarily chosen and potentially expandable, determined essentially by the particular space in which they appeared. Although the stripped down forms and stark interplay between mass and space of this sculpture is obviously influenced by the writings and the painting of modernism, the aggressive and often humanly scaled works proved that, even when narrative content was excluded, the modernist aesthetic could not be applied to sculpture that always demands a physical exchange outward from the work to the viewer. By implication minimalist sculpture also suggested that an aesthetic system such as modernism, which operated within such a narrow range, was bound to speak to an ever diminishing audience.

Minimalist sculptures also raised the issue of the nature of the transfer of information from the art object to the viewer. By concentrating on a severely reduced body of physical phenomena, the issue became not one of subject matter, nor of how much information was contained in the piece, but the means through which the information traveled. Of course pop had been addressing this issue all along with its photo reproductive processes and with its use of already pre-coded images, but the sensationalism of the individual images often overrode the consideration of the exchange. Once again, regardless of how spartan or how sensationalistic the information may be, any art that deals in an overt way with the nature of perception or the communication of information, is by nature outwardly directed while modernist painting is self-contained. From this manner of thinking it is only a short step to certain types of conceptual art that ostensibly concentrate on ideas or information and deny the importance of the very art object itself as a thing of personal or commercial value.

LeWitt's publication of the *Paragraphs on Conceptual Art* in 1967 and the *Sentences on Conceptual Art* in 1969 provided a theoretical foundation for this extension of postmodernist thinking.[28] Although it is perhaps best now not to use "conceptualist" as an artistic term, since it seems to preclude realization of the attendant visual impact of this work, nonetheless a large number of artists became involved with new media, new modes or presentation, and extended narrative, which forced consideration not of the definition of art (painting) as modernism had done, but on the intersections of art with other various areas of our culture and on the interactions between the viewer, the art, and the culture.[29] As theoretical as some work became within the conceptualist camp, none of it sought to establish bounds for the work of art by attempting to define art; on the contrary, art in all of its possible manifestations was accepted as a given, and boundaries were consciously broken in order to allow the work of art to function outside the rarified, if not airless, realm of aesthetics. A wall drawing by LeWitt may have a different physical appearance as it is redrawn in different locations, yet while undermining the idea of the immutability of the art object, it emphasizes both the constant core of the idea as well as the transforming qualities of that idea by the place (and perhaps time) in which that idea is investigated. This linking of art to place has been one of the more fruitful explorations in recent art. It is pursued by artists such as Daniel Buren, whose stripes often call into question our predisposition toward the places in which they appear; by Hans Haacke, who has charted how the political control of museums, galleries, and government agencies affects the role of art in those places; and by Christo, whose temporary objects cause radical reinvestigation of the social, political, and environmental order of the places in which they are made.

Buren's *Within and Beyond the Frame*, shown at the John Weber Gallery in New York in October 1973, consisted of nineteen black and white striped banners of identical size, extending the length of the gallery and through the front window of the gallery to a building on the other side of West Broadway, the street on which the gallery was located. Inside the gallery space itself, knowing or merely preconditioned viewers treated the banners as a work of art, regardless of how perplexing they may have found it; outside on West Broadway, passersby interpreted the identical banners as a kind of street or festival decoration, not as art at all. Place and expectation determined interpretation. In *On Social Grease* (1975) Haacke indicated by direct quotation of public statements how trustees of major cultural institutions saw art as part of a corporate profit system, again a view biased by specific conditioning. Christo's *Running Fence* (1976) brought together farmers, lawyers, contractors, environmentalists, and students of two counties in California in planning, discussion, and execution of the temporary 28–mile fence that he had proposed; not only the final product, but the entire process from initial uncomprehending rejection, through town meetings, court hearings, and final fascination and enthusiasm constituted the work of art. In many instances such as these, therefore, discussions generated by the works of art were, more often than not, more concerned with social systems rather than with art, a situation antithetical to the modernist position.

Postmodern artists have also refused to accept the finite, bounded aspect of the art described by the modernists by expanding the object in space and in time, insuring that its completion be a process extending into a nonspecified and nonlimited time. Smithson, by far the most articulate spokesman for this mode of creation, built a spiral rock jetty at the northern end of the Great Salt Lake in Utah (*Spiral Jetty*, 1970) in which the continuing fluctuation of the depth of the water of the lake left saline deposits on the rocks, which constantly changed their coloration and appearance. Thus the jetty (at the moment completely submerged only to reappear, presumably, Atlantislike at some future date) responded to the unpredictable aspects of the natural environment and fused with the continuing process of life itself. And although any photograph of the *Spiral Jetty* may document finite aspects of its existence at specific moments in time, Smithson's predominant concern was to remove his art from any sense of closure, from the timelessness of modernism to the ever-present immediate moment.[30]

The search for an open-ended art, responsive to the accidents of life itself rather than to any preordained aesthetic system, is central to the entire concept of postmodernism and has also led artists to move away from objects altogether and to confront the viewer directly and physically through the use of their own bodies.[31] Although in some cases artists perform in a traditionally staged manner, in others they engage the audience as coparticipants or even as cocreators of the work. Thus, when Vito Acconci in his *Learning Piece* (1970) sat on the stage of the auditorium of the Wadsworth Atheneum and sang two phrases at a time of Leadbelly's *Black Betty* until he had learned the whole song, the audience, willy-nilly, also learned the song, or certainly much of it. In his *Seed-Bed* (1971) Acconci crawled below a raised platform in a New York gallery and, by means of microphone, urged visitors to the gallery space to help him masturbate by walking on the platform and following his unseen movements beneath. In examples like this the participation of the viewer is essential to the work and definitively removes the ''viewer'' (the term is no longer even valid) from passive witness to the role—willingly or not—of cocreator; thus the modernist autonomy of the art object has been breached now, not by nature, but by the witness himself.[32]

The striking content of such performances coincides with the sharply realistic (both from a visual and from a psychological point of view) aspects of a large portion of postmodernist art. Subject matter, while it may involve discussion about art in terms of the mechanics of perception (as do works by Mel Bochner, Douglas Huebler, and others), tends to have a particular, focused, and directed reference to the real world and not merely to the world enclosed by the frame.[33] Pop art, despite its veneer of dumb acceptance of whatever media image happens to catch the artist's eye, is in fact permeated with carefully selected contemporary imagery of violence and death: Warhol's *Marilyn* (1962), made after the movie star's death; his suicide, car crash, or skull paintings; his most recent series of knives, guns, and crosses (1982); Lichtenstein's war comics and pistol banner. Hardhitting and grisly explorations of violence were very much a part of the repertory of artists like Chris Burden, who used their own bodies, particularly during the politically turbulent years around 1968–70. The crass and the mundane also play a continuous role in postmodern art, from Oldenburg's greasy hamburgers, to Richard Eddy's photo-realist paintings of automobile showrooms, to Gilbert and George's mock genteel books and photomurals about drunkenness. None of these images of low life is ennobled like the peasant paintings of the LeNains or made into the ribald but moralized comic operas of Jan Steen. There is a baldness of presentation coupled with acuity of observation that insists on the presentness of the image, on the immediacy of the event, and on the fact that the event shares our world. As tawdry as the images by pop artists, photo realists, and performance artists may appear, they cannot be tamed or shunted aside as metaphors.

Political engagement by artists such as Haacke (born in Germany) and Christo (born in Bulgaria) also insists that art's role in the world is active certainly beyond any interior dialogue of what constitutes the nature of its artfulness.[34] Adrian Piper's work faces political issues with a straightforward and searing honesty while confronting the issue of what our expectations are of the art object. *Aspects of the Liberal Dilemma* (1978) presented the viewer with a photograph (22 by 22 inches) of a number of blacks descending a wide staircase and unflinchingly focusing on the camera (i.e. the viewer); simultaneously the viewer heard a six-minute tape of Piper asking direct questions about the viewer's responses to the piece. When Victor Burgin (a British artist) presented an image of a female Pakistani immigrant laborer in *St. Laurent Demands a Whole New Life Style* (1976; photograph on aluminum at the large scale of 40 by 60 inches), he set up a dialogue between the woman and her work and between the image and the accompanying text, which is an advertising copy for women's couturier clothing including passages stating that "Hips matter a lot" and that "Yves' day-time clothes . . . are a ramble through Eastern Europe." Burgin's text/image manages to oppose male/female, rich/poor, capitalist/communist tensions in a succinct summary of some of the most critical issues facing our society. Laurie Anderson in her music/performance situations also manages to insinuate volatile political issues in events that come so close to the pop music scene that she has attracted widespread audiences not normally involved with the art world. Her *O Superman* was recut and pressed into 100,000 records in England, where it made number two on the charts. This is a song that deals implicitly but unmistakably with American political and military power: " . . . when justice is gone there's always force/ And when force is gone there's always. . . . "

The strong and vital content of much of postmodern art has led some artists to dredge their own psyches in an attempt, perhaps, to find unconscious meanings that have universal reverberations. This is certainly true of many of the artists of the new expressionism. The work of the Italian painter, Francesco Clemente, for example, pulses with psycho-sexual fantasies, sometimes clothed in the Tantric language of India, where he has lived for extended periods of time. More compelling, however, are those artists who assume the mysterious role of shaman in order to bring us closer to the verities of the complex and difficult-to-decipher environments that we inhabit. Artists have assumed, through costume, through makeup, and through carefully orchestrated social activities, personae that either release the creative energies of those around them (Warhol, Beuys) or strip away the familiarity of the ordinary world to reveal the starker, unadmitted presuppositions of our activities and surroundings (Anderson and Gilbert and George). The German artist, Joseph Beuys, has carefully edited his autobiography in order to concentrate on salvific moments in his life. These he extends to his viewer in talismanic fashion through the use of fat, felt, red crosses, and mythic animals as transformative symbols. Beuys' public persona—gaunt, dressed in a vest and felt hat—has all the earmarks of ritual. The same may be said for the English sculptors Gilbert and George, whose metallic or red makeup infused the ordinariness of their very proper grey suits with a quality of magic, especially since their actions were mechanistically repeated for extended periods of time. Beuys and Gilbert and George, like Warhol before them, have no existence beyond the carefully constructed and transformative personae that they have so painstakingly created. And, shamanistically, they confront—whether they admit to this as a goal or not—aspects of our social fabric that threaten the continuation of the tribe; Warhol's suicidal car crash images (1964), Beuys' apparently innocent actions of melting blocks of fat on a small stove in *Brown Cross/Fat Corners/ Model Fat Corners* (1964) (which triggered the fury of right-wing students), and Gilbert and George's pillorying the rigidity and exclusionary social conventions of the very staid middle class by their scatology and drunkenness, all focus on the raw edges of the social order that need our communal attention if society is to be preserved. For artists such as these a search for the definition of the nature of art or philosophizing about aesthetics are empty and unrewarding exercises.

Modernism, therefore, as an artistic predisposition, may well be either a partial critical fabrication that seriously misreads or ignores the intention toward subject matter, so important in the work of Manet and Picasso, or a stylistic aberration in the history of art, important in what it tells us for a century of artistic style, but, *pace* Greenberg, one which moved progressively through its history out of the mainstream.[35] Postmodernism or antimodernism in its mature and highly inflected existence, as an international (not French or English or American) style, then, would be a deliberate and concerned attempt to maintain the traditional role of art, functioning within a society both as mirror and ritualized response to the events within that society. The content of postmodernism is unabashedly ordinary for the most part, with a scope that seems to focus in a particularly unblinking and sometimes reportorial manner on all the various areas of the social and cultural fabric that threatens to unravel, as well as on those areas of deepest psychological stress. Far from novel, postmodernism in all of its variant strains seeks to return art to its most primitive roots as a regenerative source of energy and understanding.

NOTES

1. I would like to thank Judith Rohrer for her criticism and suggestions during the writing of this essay.

2. Douglas Davis gives a good summary of recent discussions of postmodernism and indicates the amorphous concepts that the term is used to describe when he states that it "is thriving in the soft linguistic underbelly of the visual arts. . . . " ("Post Everything," *Art in America* 68 [February 1980]: 11, 13–14). Peter Schjeldahl has referred to "that rhetorical chameleon 'postmodernism'. . . . " ("Falling in Step," *Vanity Fair* 46 [March 1983]: 116.

3. The term "antimodernism" was used as early as 1971 by Marshall Cohen in "Notes on Modernist Art," *New Literary History* 3 (Autumn 1971): 215. The difficulty with this term is that it serves as a bias to describe what posmodernism isn't, rather than what it is.

4. A recent rather polemical definition for postmodernism has been given by an artist critic: " . . . 'post-Modern,' meaning simply the activity of artists searching the ruins of a discredited ideology for a renewed sense of purpose and authority. This search has typically taken the form of an investigation of text and context, of the impure situation in which art finds itself, and of the means it uses to represent itself." (Thomas Lawson, "The Dark Side of the Bright Light," *Artforum* 21 [November 1982]: 66). Lawson posits this definition in direct response to the critical attention given to recent expressionist painting in America.

5. "Une nouvelle manière en peinture: Edouard Manet," *Revue du XIX Siècle*, January 1, 1867; included in P. Courthion and P. Cailler, *Portrait of Manet by Himself and his Contemporaries* (London: Cassell, 1960), pp. 116–39; excerpted and reprinted by Francis Frascina and Charles Harrison, eds., *Modern Art and Modernism* (New York: Harper & Row, 1982), pp. 32–33. Both Baudelaire and Zola speak of "realism" in Manet's painting, and their criticism implies, when it does not categorically state, Manet's keen observation of the social realities of his own time. Théodore de Banville, writing of the Salon of 1873 in *National* for May 15, 1873, in an oblique reference to this reality, talks about Manet's "intense quality of modernity if we may use this now indispensable barbarism." (George Heard Hamilton, *Manet and His Critics* [New York: Norton, 1969], p. 172); the change in the use of "modern" and its derivatives from a reference to representations of contemporary life to painterly style has still to be charted. Curiously enough these social realities—one hesitates to say "comments"—have only recently been explicated in the paintings of artists like Manet and Degas, a historical response that coincides with the development of postmodernism; see, for example, Eunice Lipton, "The Laundress in Late Nineteenth-Century French Culture: Imagery, Ideology and Edgar Degas," *Art History* 3 (1980): 295–313, reprinted in Frascina and Harrison, *Modern Art and Modernism*, pp. 275–83; and Novelene Ross, *Manet's 'Bar at the Folies-Bergère' and the Myths of Popular Illustration* (Ann Arbor: UMI Research Press, 1982).

6. Clive Bell, "The Debt to Cézanne," first published in *Art* (London, 1914); reprinted in Frascina and Harrison, *Modern Art and Modernism*, p. 77.

7. "The Aesthetic Hypothesis," first published as the first chapter of *Art*; reprinted in Frascina and Harrison, *Modern Art and Modernism*, p. 68.

8. Ibid.

9. Ibid., p. 71.

10. This is a position taken by later modernist critics such as Michael Fried: "Roughly speaking, the history of painting from Manet through Synthetic Cubsim and Matisse may be characterized in terms of the gradual withdrawal of painting from the task of representing reality . . . in favor of an increasing preoccupation with problems intrinsic to painting itself (*Three American Painters* [Cambridge, Mass.: Harvard University Fogg Art Museum, 1965], p. 5).

11. "Avant-Garde and Kitsch," *Partisan Review* 6 (Fall 1939): 34–49; reprinted in Clement Greenberg, *Art and Culture* (Boston: Beacon Press, 1961), pp. 4–5.

12. Greenberg, *Art and Culture*, p. 5.

13. Ibid., p. 6.

14. "Modernist Painting" was first printed in *Art and Literature* 4 (Spring 1965): 193–201; reprinted in Gregory Battock, ed., *The New Art: A Critical Anthology* (New York: E. P. Dutton, 1966), pp. 100–110 and also in Frascina and Harrison, *Modern Art and Modernism*, pp. 5–10. For brief summaries of Greenberg's work during this time, see D. Ashton, *The New York School; A Cultural Reckoning* (New York: Viking, 1973), pp. 157–61 and Irving Sandler, *The Triumph of American Painting* (New York: Harper & Row, 1970), pp. 81–88, 272–74. A summary and analysis of Greenberg's work has been written by Donald Kuspit in *Clement Greenberg: Art Critic* (Madison: University of Wisconsin Press, 1979). Two critics of the modernist position articulated by Greenberg stand out above all others: Victor Burgin, "Modernism in the work of art," first presented at the Edinburgh Festival in 1976, later printed in the exhibition catalogue *Victor Burgin*, Eindhoven, Holland (Stedelijk van Abbemuseum), 1977; Casey Blake, "Aesthetic Engineering," *democracy*, October 1, 1981, pp. 37–50.

15. "The Crisis of the Easel Picture," *Partisan Review* 15 (April 1948): 481–84; reprinted in Greenberg, *Art and Culture*, p. 155.

16. Frascina and Harrison, *Modern Art and Modernism*, pp. 5, 7.

17. Ibid., p. 5.

18. Ibid.

19. See note 10.

20. Fried, *Three American Painters*, p. 5.

21. For a discussion in modernist terms of the object quality of painting see Michael Fried, "Art and Objecthood," *Artforum* 5 (June 1967): 12–23; reprinted in Gregory Battock, ed., *Minimal Art: A Critical Anthology*, pp. 116–47.

22. For an interpretation of concealed meanings in Duchamp's work see Arturo Schwarz, *The Complete Works of Marcel Duchamp* (New York: H. N. Abrams, 1970). Greenberg has also recognized Duchamp's early critique of modernism; in a recent essay, "Necessity of Formalism" (*New Literary History* 3 [Autumn 1971]: 173), he states that "Duchamp's and Dada's was the first outright assault on 'formalism,' that came from within the avant-garde, or what was nominally the avant-garde, and it stated itself immediately in a lowering of aspirations." Greenberg once again argues from the point of view of a self-defined concept of quality, the very issue that Duchamp sought to confront and deny.

23. For a view of Rauschenberg's early career, see Calvin Tomkins, *Off the Wall* (New York: Doubleday, 1980.) There is a significant difference between Rauschenberg's white paintings and those of the abstract expressionists, which were seen by some critics

like Harold Rosenberg as arenas for action. Unlike "action painting," Rauschenberg's paintings revealed nothing about the activity or the personality of the artist; moreover they "narrate" action which, far from being in the rarified self-enclosed realm of art favored by the modernists, is as common and mundane as people moving through space. It is impossible to be "in" Rauschenberg's paintings as Pollock talked about being in his; the action is all external to the art. See also note 24.

24. Max Kozloff ("The Critical Reception of Abstract Expressionism," *Arts Magazine* 40 [December 1965]: 29) has remarked on an earlier if different formulation of this search for "life" in art: Rosenberg had also used the concept in describing action painting when he said that the "apples weren't brushed off the table in order to make room for perfect relations of space and color. They had to go so that nothing would get in the way of the act of painting. . . . The new painting has broken down every distinction between art and life." ("The American Action Painters," in *The Tradition of the New* [New York: Horizon Press, 1959], pp. 23–39).

25. Fried, "Art and Objecthood."

26. Pop art, despite the obsessiveness of its media imagery, did concern itself with art and with formal qualities of painting. Warhol's paint-by-number paintings were witty and wry comments on what we choose to call art; Lichtenstein's translations of earlier masters like Monet and Picasso into the Ben Day dot technique and his studio paintings with their references to the style and to the explicit images of Matisse all give indication of the role of history and of earlier painting in the pop sensibility. Robert Rosenblum was the first critic to discuss with any clarity the formal properties of pop and their relationship to earlier styles ("Pop Art and Non-Pop Art," *Art and Literature* 5 [Summer 1964]; reprinted in John Russell and Suzi Gablik, *Pop Art Redefined* [New York: Praeger, 1969], pp. 53–56); this seminal study could well be reworked in light of the subsequent twenty years of development in the work of the artists who defined the pop aesthetic.

27. Although Greenberg has written about sculpture ("The New Sculpture," *Partisan Review* 16 [June 1949]: 637–42; reprinted in Greenberg, *Art and Culture*, pp. 139–45) and although Michael Fried has championed the work of Anthony Caro as modernist sculpture (*Anthony Caro* [London: Arts Council of Great Britain, 1969]; exhibition catalogue for the Hayward Gallery) none of the writing linking modernism and sculpture is convincing.

28. *Artforum* 5 (June 1967): 72–83; *0–9* (New York) (1969) and *Art-Language* (England) 1, no. 1 (May 1969).

29. Perhaps because Europeans were less involved with the Greenberg formulation, response to new activities in American art was more active there than here on the part of collectors like Peter Ludwig and Giuseppe Panza di Biumo and critics like Germano Celant and Rudi Fuchs, whose exhibitions of contemporary artists were always notable. In the United States Lucy Lippard is foremost among critics championing antimodernist art and Robert Pincus-Witten has been a revealing and articulate writer about art made after the mid-sixties. Neither Lippard nor Pincus-Witten have postulated an all-embracing aesthetic system comparable in scope to Greenberg. It may be that the expansion of artistic possibilities within the arts and the increased internationalism of the art world since the early sixties precludes any neat enclosed system.

In what may be seen as a development parallel to that in the visual arts, historians are now returning to narrative history, which attempts to site specific historical events or personalities within the larger cultural matrix; see Gordon Wood, "Star-Spangled His-

tory," a review of Robert Middlekauff's *The Glorious Cause: The American Revolution,
1763–1789*), *The New York Review of Books*, August 12, 1982, pp. 4–9.

30. Smithson may well be thought of as having investigated the two divergent concerns
of the New York School: the immediacy of the acted-upon, dripped paint of Pollock and
the meditative timelessness of Rothko. While Smithson's debt to earlier artists and artistic
concerns is undeniable, it is nonetheless significant that he chose a specific site for the
Spiral Jetty (and for other works as well) that cannot be bounded or domesticated by
traditional art contexts such as the gallery or the museum.

31. Similar breakdown of boundaries also exists in postmodernist theatre; Elinor Fuchs
writes about the "blurring of old distinctions between self and work, being and thing"
in "The Death of Character," *Theatre Communications* 5 (March 1983): 2.

32. One of the most stimulating investigations of performance of this nature is by
Victor Turner, "Frame, Flow and Reflection: Ritual and Drama as Public Liminality,"
which appears in a collection of essays that deserves to be better known: Michel Benamou
and Charles Caramello, eds., *Performance in Postmodern Culture* (Madison, Wis.: Coda
Press, 1977), pp. 33–55.

33. Kim Levin ("Farewell to Modernism," *Arts Magazine* 54 [October 1979], p. 91)
talks about postmodernism as "structured by time rather than form, concerned with context
instead of style. . . . " Rosalind Krauss ("John Mason and Post-Modernist Sculpture: New
Experiences, New Words," *Art in America* 67 [May-June 1979]: 121) discusses the
"outsideness of the artist to his forms," for an artist "no longer persuaded by the logic
of a conventional space he cannot inhabit."

34. Fuchs, "The Death of Character," p. 4, maintains that postmodernist theatre "is
able to mount a devastating social criticism."

35. Recent reinvestigations of subject matter were triggered by Thomas B. Hess'
compelling reading of the work of Barnett Newman in his catalogue for the Newman
retrospective at the Museum of Modern Art: *Barnett Newman* (New York, 1971); a later
exhibition catalogue for the National Gallery promised more than it delivered, but was
indicative of the growing concern during the period of the seventies of renewed interest
in content in abstract painting; E. A. Carmean, Jr., and Eliza E. Rathbone with Thomas
B. Hess, *American Art at Mid-Century: The Subjects of the Artist* (Washington, D.C.:
National Gallery of Art, 1978). This latter catalogue and subsequent articles may be yet
another historical example of the influence of contemporary art on art historical research
and writing.

BIBLIOGRAPHY

Critics and Criticism

Blake, Casey. "Aesthetic Engineering." *democracy* 1 (October 1981): 37–50. An analysis
of the historical, political, and social background of Greenberg and modernism.
Boice, Bruce. "The Scope of Michael Fried's Criticism." *The Print Collector's Newsletter* 3 (September-October 1972): 77–81. A painter reacting to second-generation
Greenbergian ideology.
Buettner, Stewart. *American Art Theory 1945–1970.* Ann Arbor: UMI Research Press,
1981. A summary of early twentieth-century theory and a history of the devel-

opment of abstract expressionism, with the curious addition of a chapter on the
happening.

Burgin, Victor. *Work and Commentary*. London: Latimer, 1973. Two essays on the
failure of modernism and the role of the artist.

———. "Modernism in the work of art." *Victor Burgin*. Eindhoven, Holland (Stedelijk
van Abbemuseum), 1977. One of the most articulate dissections of modernism,
with a particular historical and political—that is, Marxist—cast.

Cavaliere, Barbara, and Robert C. Hobbs. "Against a Newer Laöcoon." *Arts Magazine*
51 (April 1977): 110–17. Investigation of "Subjects of the Artist" school and of
content in abstract expressionism.

Collins, James. "Things and Theories." *Artforum* 11 (May 1973): 32–36. A cogent
critique of conceptualism in its narrow form and a beginning of a discussion about
meaning in art.

Davis, Douglas. *Artculture: Essays in the Post-Modern*. New York: Harper & Row,
1977. A collection of essays by an important video-artist that deal with content,
context, and what the author calls artpolitics.

———. "Post-Everything." *Art in America* 68 (February 1980): 11, 13–14. A useful
history of the use of postmodern as a term; somewhat polemical support of the
term, despite its vagueness.

Falkenheim, Jacqueline V. *Roger Fry and the Beginnings of Formalist Art Criticism*.
Ann Arbor: UMI Research Press, 1980. A close history of the beginnings of
modernism.

Foster, Hal, ed. *The Anti-Aesthetic: Essays on Postmodern Culture*. Port Townsend,
Wash., 1983. Ten searching essays seeking definitions for the postmodern in
contemporary culture.

Frascina, Francis, and Charles Harrison. *Modern Art and Modernism: A Critical Anthology*. New York: Harper & Row, 1982. A source book of essays by artists,
writers, critics, and historians.

Fried, Michael. "Art and Objecthood." *Artforum* 5 (June 1967): 12–23. A milestone of
Fried's critical writing in which he talks about sculpture as situation, shape, and
object and the concept of theatricality.

Fuller, Peter. *Aesthetics after Modernism*. London: Writers and Readers Publishing Cooperative Society Ltd., 1983. Lecture which, apart from Fuller's usual fascination
with Ruskin, suggests that aesthetics is based in biology.

———. *Beyond the Crisis in Art*. London: Writers and Readers Publishing Cooperative
Society Ltd., 1980. Collected essays by Britain's leading critic, suggesting a
beginning of a new aesthetic system.

Greenberg, Clement. *Art and Culture*. Boston: Beacon Press, 1961. A collection of
Greenberg's most influential essays, selected by the author himself.

Harrison, Charles and Fred Orton, eds. *Modernism, Criticism, Realism*. New York:
Harper & Row, 1984. A collection of twenty-four previously published essays
on such topics as aesthetics, knowledge, representation, and language.

Hertz, Richard, ed. *Theories of Contemporary Art*. Englewood Cliffs, N.J.: Prentice-
Hall, 1985. Thirty-one wide-ranging essays by artists and critics that deal with
contemporary issues in painting and performance, many of which deal with the
definition of postmodernism.

Hughes, Robert. "There's No Geist like the Zeitgeist." *The New York Review of Books*
30 (October 27, 1983): 63–68. An essay provoked by the 1982 *Zeitgeist* exhibition

in Berlin with consideration of popular responses to the figure in art and to expressionism.

Kelly, Mary. "Reviewing Modernist Criticism." *Screen* 22, no. 1 (1981): 41–62. An important critique of the theory of modernist criticism by England's leading feminist artist.

Krauss, Rosalind. "A View of Modernism." *Artforum* 11 (September 1972): pp. 48–51. An interesting apologia by a critic who began in the formalist Greenbergian vein and moved consistently farther afield.

Kuspit, Donald B. *Clement Greenberg: Art Critic.* Madison: University of Wisconsin Press, 1979. An analysis of Greenberg's theories with a complete bibliography of Greenberg's writing.

———. "Stops and Starts in Seventies Art and Criticism." *Arts Magazine* 55 (March 1981): 96–99. A review of the criticism of N. Calas, Alloway, and Pincus-Witten.

———. "The Unhappy Consciousness of Modernism." *Artforum* 19 (January 1981): 53–57. A critique of the concept of purity and transcendence.

Levin, Kim "Farewell to Modernism." *Arts Magazine* 54 (October 1979): 90–92. A provocative essay suggesting that the modern is all used up and that postmodernism involves time, not form, and content, not style.

Lippard, Lucy. *Changing: Essays in Art Criticism.* New York: E. P. Dutton, 1971. A collection of critical essays in which the author speaks against a system of criticism or fixed modes of viewing.

McEvilley, Thomas. "Doctor Lawyer Indian Chief." *Artforum* 23 (November 1984): 54–61. An incisive and thorough critique of the decontextualization of "primitive" objects in the exhibition *"Primitivism" in 20th Century Art* at the Museum of Modern Art; responses by the curators, William Rubin and Kirk Varnedoe and a sharp reply by McEvilley appeared in *Artforum* 23 (February 1985): 42–51.

———. "Heads It's Form, Tails It's Not Content." *Artforum* 21 (November 1982): 50–61. Another search for content in formalist painting, although one which the artists themselves might find foreign to their own thinking; interspersed with quotations from contemporary critics giving a mini-history of the debate.

McQuillan, Melissa. "The Art Criticism of Michael Fried." *Marsyas* 15 (1970–1972): 86–102. A serious critiquing of the philosophical underpinnings of Fried's writing.

New Literary History 3 (Autumn 1971) (issue on modernism and postmodernism).

Owens, Craig. "The Allegorical Impulse: Towards a Theory of Postmodernism." *October* 12 (Spring 1980): 67–86, and ibid. 13 (Summer 1980): 59–80. Use of allegory, references to the past, and dialogue with viewer and the past as antimodernist attributes.

Reise, Barbara. "Greenberg and the Group: A Retrospective View." *Studio International* 175 (May 1968): 254–57 and ibid. (June 1968) 175: 314–16. A brief, succinct, and reasoned review of Greenberg's development and of the vagaries of some of his followers.

Rosenberg, Harold. *The De-definition of Art.* New York, 1972. A collection of the critic's essays that tended to focus on the existential act of the artist as an alternative to Greenberg's biographically anonymous formalism.

Sontag, Susan. *Against Interpretation.* New York: Dell, 1966. A collection of this writer's essays in the lead essay of which she calls for an "erotics of art."

Postmodernism

Alloway, Lawrence, Donald B. Kuspit, Martha Rosler, and Jan van der Marck. *The Idea of the Post-Modern: Who is Teaching It?* Seattle: Henry Art Gallery, 1981. A collection of essays on the definition of postmodern art and the social and economic constraints placed on the artist.

Benamou, Michael, and Charles Caramello. *Performance in Postmodern Culture.* Madison, Wis.: Coda Press, 1977. An important collection of essays by scholars in a number of disciplines, which locates the driving energy of postmodernism in performance.

Bonito Oliva, Achille. *Europe/America: The Different Avant-Gardes.* Milan, 1976. A comparison of the different sensibilities of artists practicing on both sides of the Atlantic.

————. *The Italian Trans-avantgarde/La Transavanguardia Italiana.* Milan: Giancarlo Politi editore, 1980. A good review of the new Italian expressionism that has been at the forefront of discussion about the postmodern.

Buchloh, B.H.D. *Postmoderne–Neo-Avantgarde: Essays zur europäsche und amerikonische Kunst zwichen 1960 und 1980.* Cologne, 1984. A collection of essays by one of Europe's leading curators and critics.

Cage, John. *Silence.* Middletown, Conn.: Wesleyan University Press, 1961. A bible for artists concerned with the interpenetrations of art and life.

Celant, Germano. *Art Povera.* New York: Praeger, 1969. An early cross-section of art that eschewed finish and sought to concentrate on situation and idea.

————. *Precronistoria 1966–1969.* Florence: Centro Di, 1976. A diaristic account—see L. Lippard, *Six Years*—of new tendencies in the arts that treated minimal, conceptual, body, and environmental art as sharing some of the same convictions.

Clark, John R. "Up Against the Wall, Transavanguardia!" *Arts Magazine* 57 (December 1982): 76–81. A review of the 1982 exhibition in Rome, dealing with imagery, content, and sources for new figural art.

de Vries, Gerd, ed. *Über Kunst/On Art.* Cologne: Paul Maenz, 1974. An important collection of artists' statements, generally of a conceptualist persuasion.

Dubreuil-Blondin, Nicole. *La Fonction critique dans le Pop Art américain.* Montreal: Presses de l'Université de Montreal, 1980. A comprehensive summary of the criticism about pop and one of the first attempts to situate pop in the political turmoil of the sixties.

Dupuy, Jean, ed. *Collective Consciousness: Art Performances in the Seventies.* New York: Performing Arts Journal Publications, 1980. Photodocumentation, texts, and interviews with New York artists—a number of whom are musicians—involved with performance.

Foote, Nancy, ed. "Situation Aesthetics: Impermanent Art and the Seventies Audience," *Artforum* 18 (January 1980): 22–29. Responses by a number of artists to questions concerning their relationships to an audience.

Kozloff, Max. "The Trouble with Art-As-Idea," *Artforum* 11 (September 1972): 33–37. Important as the first critical blast from a respected writer against conceptualism, in the tenth anniversary issue of a magazine that had consistently supported the conceptual artists.

Lippard, Lucy. *Six Years: The Dematerialization of the Art Object.* . . . New York: Prae-
    ger, 1973, pp. 74–75. A critically important diary of art activity, publications,
    and exhibitions around the world whose thesis—mistakenly as it has turned out—
    was that art as material object was on the wane.
Loeffler, Carl E., and Darlene Tong, eds. *Performance Anthology: Source Book for a
    Decade of California Performance Art.* San Francisco: Contemporary Arts Press,
    1980. A chronology, like Lucy Lippard's *Six Years*, from 1970 to 1979 of artists'
    activities in performance, followed by four critical essays, two of which are
    specifically about women artists.
Masheck, Joseph. "Judy Rifka and 'Postmodernism' in Architecture." *Art in America*
    (October 1984): 148–63. Rifka's Parthenon paintings become the focus for a wide-
    ranging discussion of styles in painting and architecture.
Morris, Robert. "Anti-form." *Artforum* 6 (April 1968): 33–35. Early statement of a new
    aesthetic with roots in abstract expressionism.
Müller, Grégoire. *The New Avant-Garde: Issues for the Art of the Seventies.* New York:
    Praeger, 1972. Essentially separate essays on twelve different artists supporting
    the writer's contention that by the late sixties symbolic content had disappeared
    and art dealt with its own presence in the world.
Nosei-Weber, Annina, ed. *Discussion. The Aesthetic Logomachy.* New York: Out of
    London Press, 1983. Essays by artists—including C. Schneeman, I. Wilson, D.
    Antin, V. Burgin, R. Ashley, J. Beuys—on conversation as a basis for artistic
    activity.
Pincus-Witten, Robert. *Entries (Maximalism).* New York: Out of London Press, 1983.
    A diaristic account of the emerging expressionism of the late seventies and early
    eighties.
————. *Post-Minimalism.* New York: Out of London Press, 1977. A collection of essays
    published between 1966 and 1976 that chart a move away from formalism in the
    the arts.
Roberts, John. "Post-Modernism: Arrivals and Departures." *Art Monthly* 55 (April 1982):
    27–28. A very brief critique of Charles Harrison outlining a distinction between
    early and late modernism and containing a statement about appropriation.
Smithson, Robert. *The Writings of Robert Smithson.* New York, 1979. The collected
    writings of a seminal artist of the late sixties and early seventies.
Sondheim, Alan. *Individuals: Post-movement Art in America.* New York: E. P. Dutton,
    1977. A collection of statements and works of art by leading figures in the
    postmodern movement.
Vergine, Lea. *Il corpo come linguaggio (La Body-art e storie simili).* Milan: G. Prearo,
    1974. An important corpus of European body art and performance.

Exhibitions (arranged chronologically)

Eccentric Abstraction. Fishback Gallery, New York, 1966 (arranged by Lucy Lippard).
Funk. University Art Museum, Berkeley, 1967; catalogue by Peter Selz.
Earthworks. Dwan Gallery, New York, 1968.
Anti-Illusion: Procedures/Materials. The Whitney Museum of American Art, 1969; cat-
    alogue by Marcia Tucker.

January 5–31, 1969. Seth Siegelaub, New York, 1969.

Konzeption-conception. Stadtisches Museum, Leverkusen, 1969; catalogue edited by Rolf Wedewer and Konrad Fischer.

Op Losse Schroeven: Situaties en Cryptostructuren. Stedelijk Museum, Amsterdam, 1969; catalogue by William Beeren, Piero Gilardi, Harald Szeemann.

When Attitudes Become Form/Works-Concepts-Processes-Situations-Information. Kunsthalle, Bern, 1969; organized by Harald Szeemann; catalogue with essays by Scott Burton, Grégoire Müller and Tommaso Trini.

Conceptual Art and Conceptual Aspects. The New York Cultural Center, 1970; catalogue by Donald Karshan.

Information. The Museum of Modern Art, New York, 1970; catalogue by Kynaston L. McShine.

Sonsbeek '71. Arnhem, 1971; catalogue by William Beeren.

Documenta (5). Museum Fredericianum and Neue Galerie, Kassel, 1972; catalogue.

The New Art. The Haywood Gallery, London, 1974; catalogue by Anne Seymour.

Projekt '74: Kunst bleibt Kunst. Kunsthalle, Cologne, 1974; catalogue with introduction by Dieter Rente and texts by Evelyn Weiss, Manfred Schneckenberger, Albert Schug, Marlis Grüterich, Wolf Herzogenrath, David A. Ross.

Drawing Now. The Museum of Modern Art, New York, 1976; catalogue by Bernice Rose.

Europe in the Seventies: Aspects of Recent Art. The Art Institute of Chicago, Chicago, 1977; catalogue with introduction by A. James Speyer and Anne Rorimer and essays by Jean-Christophe Ammann, David Brown, Rudi Fuchs, and B. H. D. Buchloh.

Art of the 1970s. Albright-Knox Gallery, Buffalo, 1980; catalogue by Linda Cathcart.

Times Square Show. New York, 1980; organized in an abandoned building on 7th Avenue and 41st Street by John Ahearn, Scott and Beth B., Andrea Callard, Colen Fitzgibbon, Matthew Geller, Alan Moore, Tom Otterness, Cara Perlman, Ulli Rimkus, Mike Roddy, Mike Robinson, and Christy Rupp.

Art Allemagne Aujourd'hui. ARC/Musée d'Art Moderne de la Ville de Paris, 1981.

Avantguardia Transavantguardia. Rome, 1982; catalogue by Achille Bonito Oliva, Milan, Electa, 1982.

documenta 7. Museum Fredericianum, Orangerie, Neue Gallerie, Kassel, 1982; exhibition organized by Rudi Fuchs; catalogue (2 volumes).

Zeitgeist. Berlin, 1982; catalogue Berlin, Kunstbuch Berlin Verlagsgesellschaft, 1982.

Expressions: New Art from Germany. The Saint Louis Art Museum, 1983; catalogue by Jack Cowart.

The Critical Eye/I. Yale Center for British Art, New Haven, 1984; catalogue by John T. Paoletti.

BLAM! The Explosion of Pop, Minimalism, and Performance 1958–1964. The Whitney Museum, New York, 1984; catalogue by Barbara Haskell.

Difference: On Representation and Sexuality. The New Museum, New York, 1984; exhibition organized by Kate Linker; catalogue with essays by Craig Owens, Lisa Tickner, Jacqueline Rose, Peter Wollen, and Jane Weinstock.

Disinformation: The Manufacture of Consent. The Alternative Museum, New York, 1985; exhibition organized by Geno Rodriguez; catalogue with essays by Noam Chomsky and Edward S. Herman.

Artists (arranged alphabetically)

Acconci, Vito
> *Machineworks: Vito Acconci, Alice Aycock, Dennis Oppenheim.* Philadelphia, Institute
> of Contemporary Art, 1981; catalogue by Janet Kardon.
> *Vito Acconci: A Retrospective 1969–1980.* Chicago, Museum of Contemporary Art;
> catalogue by Judith Russi Kirshner.

Andre, Carl
> *Carl Andre: Sculpture, 1959–1977.* New York, J. Rietman, 1978; catalogue for a
> traveling exhibition, with text by David Bourdon and foreword by Barbara
> Rose.
> *12 Dialogues 1962–1963: Carl Andre, Hollis Frampton.* Edited and annotated by
> B. H. D. Buchloh, Halifax/New York: Press of the Nova Scotia College of Art
> and Design and New York University Press, 1980.

Art and Language
> *Art and Language.* Eindhoven, Holland, Van Abbemuseum, 1980.

Aycock, Alice
> *Machineworks: Vito Acconci, Alice Aycock, Dennis Oppenheim.* Philadelphia, Institute
> of Contemporary Art, 1981; catalogue by Janet Kardon.

Baldessari, John
> *John Baldessari.* New York, The New Museum, 1981; catalogue with essays by Marcia
> Tucker and Robert Pincus-Witten and an interview by Nancy Drew.

Baselitz, George
> *George Baselitz.* Venice, Biennale di Venezia, 1980; catalogue with essays by Johannes
> Gachnang, Theo Kneubühler, and Klaus Gallwitz.

Bechers, Bernd and Hilla
> *Bernd und Hilla Becher: Fotographien 1957–1975.* Bonn, Rheinisches Landesmuseum,
> 1975; catalogue by K. Honnef.

Beuys, Joseph
> *Joseph Beuys.* New York, Solomon R. Guggenheim Museum, 1979; catalogue by
> Caroline Tisdall.
> Adriani, Götz, Winfried Konnertz and Karin Thomas. *Joseph Beuys: Life and Works.*
> Woodbury, N.Y.: Barron's Educational Series, 1979.

Bochner, Mel
> Bochner, Mel. *(Toward) Axiom of Indifference.* With essay by Bruce Boice, New
> York, Sonnabend Gallery, 1974.

Borofsky, Jonathan
> *Jonathan Borofsky.* New York: Harry N. Abrams, 1984; catalogue for traveling ex-
> hibition; essays by Mark Rosenthal and Richard Marshal.

Burden, Chris
> Burden, Chris. *Chris Burden 71–73.* Los Angeles: privately printed, 1974.
> Burden, Chris. *Chris Burden 74–77.* Los Angeles: privately printed, 1978.

Buren, Daniel
> Buren, Daniel. *Limites Critiques.* Paris, Yvon Lambert, 1979.
> Buren, Daniel. *Five Texts.* New York, John Weber Gallery and London, Jack Wendler
> Gallery, 1973.

Burgin, Victor

Burgin, Victor. *Work and Commentary*, London: Latimer, 1973.

Victor Burgin. Eindhoven, Holland, Van Abbemuseum, 1977; catalogue with essays by Victor Burgin and Rudi Fuchs.

Campus, Peter

Peter Campus: Video-Installationen, Foto-Installationen, Fotos, Videobänder. Cologne, Kölnischer Kunstverein, 1979; catalogue with texts by Peter Campus, Wulf Herzogenrath and Roberta Smith.

Christo

Spies, Werner. *The Running Fence Project*. New York: H. N. Abrams, 1977.

Tomkins, Calvin. "Onward and Upward with the Arts: Running Fence." *The New Yorker*, March 28, 1977, p. 43ff.

Dibbets, Jan

Jan Dibbets. Eindhoven, Holland, Van Abbemuseum, 1980.

Gilbert and George

Gilbert and George 1968-1980. Eindhoven, Holland, Van Abbemuseum, 1980; text by Carter Ratcliff.

Gilbert and George 1974-1984. Baltimore, Baltimore Museum of Art, 1984; catalogue by Brenda Richardson.

Gilbert and George. *Dark Shadow*. London, Art for All (Nigel Greenwood Gallery), 1976.

Graves, Nancy

Nancy Graves: A Survey 1969-1980. Buffalo, Albright-Knox Art Gallery 1980; catalogue by Linda Cathcart.

Haacke, Hans

Haacke, Hans. *Framing and Being Framed*. With essays by Jack Burnham, Howard S. Becker, and Jon Walton, New York: New York University Press, 1975.

Hamilton, Richard

Richard Hamilton. London, Tate Gallery, 1970; catalogue essay by Richard Morphet.

Heizer, Michael

Michael Heizer. Essen, Museum Folkwang, 1979; catalogue by Zdenek Felix.

Hesse, Eva

Lucy Lippard. *Eva Hesse*. New York: New York University Press, 1976.

Johns, Jasper

Kozloff, Max. *Jasper Johns*. New York: H. N. Abrams, 1968.

Steinberg, Leo. "Jasper Johns." *Metro* 4/5 (May 1962): 82–109.

Jasper Johns. New York, The Whitney Museum of American Art, 1977; catalogue essay by Michael Crichton.

Judd, Donald

Judd, Don. *Complete Writings 1959-1975*. Halifax/New York, 1975.

Donald Judd. Ottawa, National Gallery of Canada, 1975.

Kawara, On.

On Kawara: Continuity/Discontinuity 1963-1979. Stockholm, Moderna Museet, 1980; catalogue with essays by Olle Granath and Peter Nilson.

Kelly, Mary

Kelly, Mary. *Post-Partum Document*. London: Routledge & Kegan Paul, 1983; American edition, 1984.

Kienholz, Edward

11 + 11. Stockholm, Moderna Museet, 1970; catalogue by K. G. Pontus Hultén and
    Katja Waldén.
LeWitt, Sol
Sol LeWitt. New York, The Museum of Modern Art, 1978; catalogue by Alicia Legg
    with essays by Lucy Lippard, Bernice Rose, and Robert Rosenblum.
Lichtenstein, Roy
Roy Lichtenstein, 1970–1980. St. Louis, St. Louis Art Museum, 1981; catalogue by
    Jack Cowart.
Long, Richard
Richard Long. Eindhoven, Holland, Van Abbemuseum, 1979.
Richard Long. Ottawa, National Gallery of Canada, 1982; Catalogue with essay by
    Jessica Bradley.
Merz, Mario
Mario Merz. Essen, Museum Folkwang, 1977; catalogue by Zdenek Felix and Germano
    Celant.
Morris, Robert
Robert Morris. New York, The Whitney Museum of American Art, 1970; catalogue
    by Marcia Tucker.
Nauman, Bruce
Bruce Nauman: Work from 1965–1972. Los Angeles, Los Angeles County Museum
    of Art, 1973; catalogue with essays by Jane Livingston and Marcia Tucker.
Oldenburg, Claes
Oldenburg, Claes. *Notes in Hand*. New York: E. P. Dutton, 1971.
Johnson, Ellen E.
Claes Oldenburg. Baltimore: Penguin Books, 1971.
Claes Oldenburg. New York, The Museum of Modern Art, 1970; catalogue by Barbara
    Rose.
Oppenheim, Dennis
Dennis Oppenheim. Paris, Musée d'Art Moderne de la Ville de Paris, 1979; catalogue
    by Suzanne Pagé, with essay by Jean-Marc Poinsot.
Machineworks: Vito Acconci, Alice Aycock, Dennis Oppenheim. Philadelphia Institute
    of Contemporary Art, 1981; catalogue by Janet Kardon.
Paik, Nam June
Nam June Paik. New York, The Whitney Museum of American Art, 1982; catalogue
    by John G. Hanhardt, with essays by Hanhardt, Dieter Ronte, Michael Nyman,
    and David A. Ross.
Rauschenberg, Robert
Tomkins, Calvin. *Off the Wall*. New York: Doubleday, 1980.
Segal, George
van der Marck, Jan. *George Segal*. New York: H. N. Abrams, 1975.
Serra, Richard
Richard Serra: Arbeiten 66–77. Tübingen, Kunsthalle, 1978.
Weyergraf, Clara. *Richard Serra: Interviews, etc. 1970–1980*. Yonkers, New York
    (Hudson River Museum), 1980.
Smithson, Robert
The Writings of Robert Smithson. Edited by Nancy Holt, New York: New York Uni-
    versity Press, 1979.

Robert Smithson. Ithaca: Cornell University Press, 1981; catalogue by Robert Hobbs, with essays by Lawrence Alloway, John Coplans, and Lucy Lippard.

Stella, Frank

Stella since 1970. Fort Worth, The Fort Worth Art Museum, 1978; catalogue by Philip Leider.

Torres, Francesc

Paoletti, John T. "Learning from Experience: Francesc Torres." *Arts Magazine* 55 (June 1981): 88–89.

Vostell, Wolf

Vostell, Wolf. *Dé-coll/age happenings*. New York, 1966.

Warhol, Andy

Warhol, Andy. *The Philosophy of Andy Warhol: from A to B and back again*. New York: Harcourt Brace Jovanovich, 1975.

Coplans, John. *Andy Warhol*. New York: New York Graphic Society, 1970.

Crone, Rainer. *Andy Warhol*. New York: Praeger, 1970.

Koch, Stephen. *Stargazer: Andy Warhol's World and his Films*. New York: Praeger, 1973.

Ratcliff, Carter. *Andy Warhol*. New York: Abbeville Press, 1983.

4

Dance

SALLY BANES

When Yvonne Rainer started using the term "postmodern" in the early 1960s to categorize the work she and her peers were doing at Judson Church and other places, she meant it in a primarily chronological sense. Theirs was the generation that came after modern dance, which was itself originally an inclusive term applied to nearly any theatrical dance that departed from ballet or popular entertainment. By the late 1950s, modern dance had refined its styles and its theories and had emerged as a recognizable dance genre. It used stylized movements and energy levels in legible structures (theme and variations, ABA, and so on) to convey feeling tones and social messages. The choreography was buttressed by expressive elements of theatre such as music, props, special lighting, and costumes.[1] Rainer, Simone Forti, Steve Paxton, and other postmodern choreographers of the sixties were not united in terms of their aesthetic. Rather, they were united by their radical approach to choreography, their urge to reconceive the medium of dance.

But by the early 1970s, a new style, with its own aesthetic canons, seems to have emerged. In 1975, Michael Kirby published an issue of *The Drama Review* devoted to postmodern dance, using the term in print for one of the first times in regard to dance and proposing a definition of the new genre:

In the theory of postmodern dance, the choreographer does not apply visual standards to the work. The view is an interior one: movement is not pre-selected for its characteristics but results from certain decisions, goals, plans, schemes, rules, concepts, or problems. Whatever actual movement occurs during the performance is acceptable as long as the limiting and controlling principles are adhered to.[2]

According to Kirby, postmodern dance rejects musicality, meaning, characterization, mood, and atmosphere; it uses costume, lighting, and objects in purely functional ways. At present, Kirby's definition seems far too limited. It refers to only one of several stages—analytic postmodern dance—in the development of postmodern dance that will be traced here.

The term "postmodern" means something different in every art form. In 1975, the same year the postmodern dance issue of *The Drama Review* appeared, Charles Jencks used the term to refer to a new trend in architecture that had also begun to emerge in the early sixties. According to Jencks, postmodernism in architecture is a doubly coded aesthetic that has popular appeal, on the one hand, and esoteric historical significance for the cognoscenti, on the other.[3] In the dance world, perhaps only Twyla Tharp could fit such a definition, but her work is not commonly considered postmodern dance. In the visual art world and in theatre, a number of critics have used the term to refer to artworks that are copies of or comments on other artworks, challenging values of originality, authenticity, and the masterpiece. This notion fits some postmodern dances, but not all. In dance, the confusion the term "postmodern" creates is further complicated by the fact that historical modern dance was never really modernist. Often it has been in the arena of postmodern dance that issues of modernism in the other arts have arisen: the acknowledgment of the medium's materials, the revealing of dance's essential qualities as an art form, the separation of formal elements, the abstraction of forms, and the elimination of external references as subjects. And yet there are also aspects of postmodern dance that do fit with postmodernist notions (in the other arts) of irony, playfulness, historical reference, the use of vernacular materials, the continuity of cultures, an interest in process over product, breakdowns of boundaries between art forms and between art and life, and new relationships between artist and audience.[4] Finally, although in dance "postmodern" began as a choreographer's term, it has become a critic's term that most choreographers now find either constricting or inexact. By now, most writers on dance use the term so loosely it can mean anything or nothing. However, since the term has been used widely for almost a decade, we should define it and use it discriminately.

THE 1960S: BREAKAWAY POSTMODERN DANCE

The early postmodern choreographers saw as their task the purging and melioration of historical modern dance, which had made certain promises in respect to the use of the body and the social and artistic function of dance that had not been fulfilled. Rather than freeing the body and making dance accessible even to the smallest children, rather than bringing about social and spiritual change, the institution of modern dance had developed into an esoteric art form for the intelligentsia, more remote from the masses than ballet. The bodily configurations modern dance drew on had ossified into various stylized vocabularies; dances had become bloated with dramatic, literary, and emotional significance; dance companies were often structured as hierarchies; young choreographers were rarely accepted into an implicit, closed guild of masters. Although Merce Cunningham had made radical departures from classical modern dance, his work remained within certain technical and contextual restraints—that is, his vocabulary remained a specialized, technical one, and he presented his dances in theatres for the most part. Cunningham is a figure who stands on the border between modern and postmodern dance. His vertical, vigorous movement style and his use of chance (which segments not only such elements as stage space, timing, and body parts, but also meaning in the dance) seem to create a bodily image of a modern intellect. In his emphasis on the formal elements of choreography, the separation of elements such as decor and music from the dancing, and the body as the sensuous medium of the art form, Cunningham's practice is modernist; his work and the theories of John Cage, his collaborator, formed an important base from which many of the ideas and actions of the postmodern choreographers sprang, either in opposition or in a spirit of extension.[5]

By breaking the rules of classical modern dance and even those of the avant-garde of the fifties (including not only Cunningham, but also such choreographers as Ann Halprin, James Waring, Merle Marsicano, and Aileen Passloff), the postmodern choreographers found new ways to foreground the medium of dance rather than its meaning.[6] Their program fit well with a cultural trend given expression in Susan Sontag's *Against Interpretation*, a book of essays written between 1962 and 1965. In the title essay, Sontag calls for a transparent art—and criticism—that will not "mean," but illuminate and open the way for experience. "What is important now," Sontag wrote, "is to recover our senses."

We must learn to *see* more, to *hear* more, to *feel* more. Our task is not to find the maximum amount of content in a work of art, much less to squeeze more content out of the work than is already there. Our task is to cut back content so that we can see the thing at all. . . . The function of criticism should be to show *how* it is what it is, even *that* it is what it is, rather than to show *what it means*.[7]

The dances by the early postmodern choreographers were not cool analyses of forms but urgent reconsiderations of the medium. The nature, history, and function of dance as well as its structures were the subjects of the postmodern inquiry. A spirit of permissiveness and playful rebellion prevailed, foreshadowing the political and cultural upheavals of the late sixties. The younger generation of choreographers showed in their dances that they departed not only from classical modern dance with its myths, heroes, and psychological metaphors, but also from the elegance of ballet and even from postmodern dance's closest influences. The breakaway period lasted roughly from 1960 to 1973. Within that time, the first eight years saw an initial bursting of forms and definitions, and several major themes of postmodern dance were set forth: references to history; new uses of space, time, and the body; problems of defining dance.

The first of these themes was, in a sense, a way of looking back, of acknowledging the heritage these choreographers had set out to repudiate. Through references to other dance traditions, often couched in ironic terms—such as Rainer's screaming fit in a pile of white tulle in *Three Seascapes* (1962), or David Gordon's instructions for how to make a successful modern dance in *Random Breakfast* (1963)—these pieces set themselves in dialogue with their own history.

   The second and third set of themes looked at the present and the future, asking
through practice what new dance could be. In works like Simone Forti's *Huddle*
(1961), in which the performers take turns crawling over the huddled group for
about ten minutes, Elaine Summers' *For Carola* (1963), which consisted of lying
down very slowly, Paxton's *Flat* (1964), which included getting dressed and
undressed in unhurried real time and striking poses, and Rainer's *Trio A* (1966),
a catalog of uninflected movements, time was flattened and detheatricalized,
stripped of the dynamics of phrasing (preparation, climax, recovery) typical of
modern dance and ballet. The use of space was explored both in terms of its
articulation in the dance (i.e., the use of architectural details in the design of
the dance or the exploration of a surface other than the floor) and in terms of
place (i.e., art gallery, church, or loft as venue, instead of a theatre with a
proscenium stage). Forti, never a member of the Judson Dance Theater, presented
her two earliest works, *Rollers* and *See-Saw* (both 1960), in an art gallery and
her evening of dance constructions (1961) in Yoko Ono's loft on Chambers
Street, where the audience walked around the relatively static dancers as if they
were sculptures. Not only was her use of space a break from the practice of
modern dance, but the particular places she used shifted the locus of her activity
from the dance world to the art world and raised the choreographer's status to
that of a serious artist. Trisha Brown danced on a chicken coop roof and in a
parking lot. Her Equipment Pieces set people walking down buildings and trees
and on walls. The members of the Judson Dance Theater performed in the
church's gym and in its sanctuary, as well as in a roller skating rink in Washington, D.C., and in the tiny Gramercy Arts Theater, which had a proscenium
stage so small that it reduced all the dances to minimum action. Paxton gave
his *Afternoon* (1963) on a farm in New Jersey, and he and Deborah Hay performed
on the grounds of a country club in Monticello, New York, in 1965. By the late
1960s, entire outdoor dance festivals were being organized by producers; the
impetus toward performing outside moved from the choreographer's aesthetic
choice to the producer's marketing tactics. By the late sixties, the galleries and
museums had become the most common venue for postmodern dance performance. This was possible partly because visual artists moved away from making
objects in the sixties, presenting performances or videotape installations, rather
than things to be stationed on the walls or on the floor. In this context, dance
events fit both aesthetically and practically into the programming of museums
and art festivals both in the United States and in Europe. Issues of the body and
its powerful social meanings were approached head on. The body itself became
the subject of the dance, rather than serving as an instrument for expressive
metaphors. An unabashed examination of the body and its functions and powers
threaded through the early postmodern dances. One form it took was relaxation,
a loosening of the control that has characterized Western dance technique. Choreographers deliberately used untrained performers in their search for the "natural" body. Another form was the release of pure energy in dances such as
Carolee Schneemann's *Lateral Splay* (1963), in which dancers hurtle through

space until they meet an object or another person, or in Brown, Forti, and Dick Levine's "violent contact" improvisations (1961). Yet another form was the use of nudity in works such as Paxton and Rainer's *Word Words* (1963) and Robert Morris' *Site* (1964) and *Waterman Switch* (1965). A number of dances involved eating onstage, and several of Paxton's works used inflatable tunnels that were reminiscent of digestive tracts. Schneemann's *Meat Joy* (1964) and Rainer's "Love" duet in *Terrain* (1963) dealt with explicitly sexual imagery in different ways.[8]

The problem of defining dance for the early postmodern choreographers was related to the inquiries into time, space, and the body, but extended beyond them, embracing the other arts and asserting propositions about the nature of dance. Games, sports, contests, the simple acts of walking or running, the gestures involved in playing music or giving a lecture, and even the motion of film and the mental action of language were presented as dances. In effect, the postmodern choreographers proposed that a dance was a dance not because of its content but because of its context—that is, simply because it was framed as a dance. This opening of the borders of dance was a break from modern dance that was qualitatively different than issues of time, space, and the body. To be nude was more extreme than to be barefoot, but it was still an action of the same sort. To call a dance a dance because of its functional relation to its context (rather than because of its internal movement qualities) was to shift the terms of dance theory.

The years 1968–73 were a transitional period in which at least three more themes were developed: politics, audience engagement, and non-Western influence. Political themes of participation, democracy, cooperation, and ecology, although often implicit in the early sixties, were now made explicit. As theatre and dance became more political, the political movements of the late sixties— antiwar, black power, student, feminist, and gay groups—used theatrical means to stage their battles. A number of choreographers mobilized large groups in their dances. Rainer's pieces of this period included *WAR*, a version of *Trio A* for the Judson Flag Show, and a street protest (all 1970). Her *Continuous Project—Altered Daily* (1970) not only examined the stages and modes of performance, but also issues of leadership and control. Paxton's *Untitled Lecture, Beautiful Lecture, Audience Performances* (all 1968), *Intravenous Lecture* (1970), *Collaboration with Wintersoldier* (1971) and *Air* (1973) were didactic works that dealt more or less overtly with issues of censorship, war, personal intervention, and civic responsibility. The Grand Union was a collective for improvisation that formed in 1970 and the following year gave a benefit performance for the Black Panthers. A women's improvisation collective, the Natural History of the American Dancer, was formed in 1971. In 1972, Paxton and others began Contact Improvisation, which has evolved not only as an alternative technique, but as an alternative social network. Contact Improvisation is concerned with physical techniques of falling, with duet situations, and with physical improvisation, but its forms have social and political connotations. Its performance seems to project a lifestyle, a model for a possible world, in which improvisation stands for freedom and adaptation, and support stands for trust and cooperation.

The influence of non-Western forms and movement philosophies, although present from the beginnings of postmodern dance through the influence of John Cage and Zen Buddhism, became more pronounced in the late sixties, as dancers forsook regular dance classes for training in such forms as Tai Chi Chuan and Aikido and, in Rainer's case, found new sources for narrative in the epic mythological dramas of India. The American fascination with Africa and the Far East, expressed not only in postmodern dance and in a resurgent black dance movement, but in cultural forms as diverse as kung-fu films, Hindu religious cults, Maoist political sects and Oriental and African fashions in clothing, reflected the changing power relations of African and Far Eastern nations and the impact of the war in Vietnam. These political crises sparked conflicts between Eastern and Western values as basic as attitudes toward time and the body. New directions in political change suggested new models for dance forms—for instance, the prospect of millions of Chinese people rising early to practice Tai Chi Chuan for health and communal spirit. For complex historical and political reasons, the aesthetic and social functions of the black dance movement of the sixties diverged sharply from the predominantly white postmodern dance movement; although African dance became an important source for black choreographers in the sixties and seventies, several postmodern choreographers were drawn to Eastern forms.[9]

THE 1970S: ANALYTIC POSTMODERN DANCE

By 1973, a wide range of basic questions about dance had been raised in the arena of postmodern choreography. A new phase of consolidation and analysis began, building on the issues that the experiments of the sixties had unearthed. A recognizable style had emerged, one that was reductive, factual, objective, and down-to-earth. It is this style to which Kirby refers. Expressive elements such as music, special lighting, costumes, props, and so forth, were stripped away from the dancing. Performers wore functional clothing—sweatpants and t-shirts or casual everyday dress—and danced in silence in plain, well-lit rooms. Structural devices such as repetition and reversal, mathematical systems, geometric forms, and comparison and contrast allowed for the perusal of pure, often simple movement. If the dances of the first phase of postmodern dance were primarily polemical in their theoretical thrust—an assortment of all kinds of rejections of the then prevailing, constraining definition of dance—then the works of analytic postmodern dance were programmatic in their theoretical thrust. That is, the analytic postmoderns were committed to the goal of redefining dance in the wake of the polemics of the sixties. And further, they had an idea of how such a definition should be pursued, that is, in terms of emphasizing choreographic structure and in terms of foregrounding movement per se. Their program was to make dance as such the locus of audience attention by making dances in which all the audience was given to see was structure and movement per se, that is, movement without expressive or illusionistic effects or reference. Lucinda Childs' *Calico Mingling* (1973), a work for four dancers composed only of forward and backward walking patterns in six-step phrases that trace semicircular or linear paths, is a paradigmatic analytic work, as are Brown's various Accumulation Pieces and Structured Pieces. Paxton's improvisatory solos of the seventies were a continuation of the analytic strand of his work present from his earliest investigations into walking in *Proxy* (1961).

In analytic postmodern dance, movement became objective as it was distanced from personal expression through the use of scores, bodily attitudes that suggested work and other ordinary movements, verbal commentaries, and tasks. Tasks were a way of producing impersonal, concentrated, real movement—goal-oriented in an immediate sense. All of these strategies had been used in the sixties, but in the seventies they became a dominant (although not exclusive) trend, and they were organized more and more programmatically. A number of choreographers continued to work in older postmodern modes (Carolee Schneemann, for instance, made performances involving issues of the female body) or moved in other directions (see, for instance, the discussion of the work of Deborah Hay and others that follows; Yvonne Rainer moved from dance to performance art to film).

The analytic dances called attention to the workings of the body in an almost scientific way. One noted the workings of the muscles in Batya Zamir's body, for instance, as she traversed her aerial sculptures. One scrutinized the particular configuration of a lift or a hold in a Contact Improvisation encounter. The anti-illusionist approach demanded close viewing and clarified the smallest unit of dance, shifting the emphasis from the phrase to the step or gesture. It combined low-key presentation and physical intelligence in a way that seemed to define a new virtuosity—a heroism of the ordinary. Analytic postmodern dance was a style and approach that was consistent with the values of minimalist sculpture. It was also consistent with the values of baring the facts and conserving means that were the legacy of a post–Watergate, post–oil-crisis society. The energy of postmodern dance was literally reduced. One of the most obvious divergences from modern dance, ballet, and the black dance movement was the rejection of musicality and rhythmic organization. But also, the analytic choreographers dispensed with principles of dramatic phrasing, contrast, and resolution. The bodies of their dancers were relaxed but ready, without the pulled-up, stretched muscle tone of the ballet or classical modern dancer.[10] The analytic postmodern dances pulled the spectator into the process of choreography, either by direct participation or by baring devices. And although these dances were not meant to have expressive meaning—for example, the psychological or literary significance of historical modern dance—they did, of course, mean something: the discovery and understanding of their forms and processes was one aspect of that meaning, and the striving toward objectivity, the down-to-earth style, the casual or cool attitude, the sense that "it is what it is" did not excise meaning, but rather, constituted a crucial aspect of the dance's import.[11] The Grand Union proposed a loose polemic in some ways resembling the earlier period of post-modern dance. Nevertheless, its performances belong to analytic dance because it was so often involved in revealing conditions of performance, ranging from choreographic structures to the display of psychological chemistry between the performers. The Grand Union demystified theatre even as the group produced it.

THE 1970S: METAPHOR AND THE METAPHYSICAL

Although the analytic mode of postmodern dance dominated the early sev-enties, another strand developed out of related sources. The spiritual aspect of the same asceticism that led to the clarification of simple movements led in its way to devotional expression. The appreciation of non-Western dance led to an interest in the spiritual, religious, healing, and social functions of dancing in other cultures. The disciplines of martial arts forms led to new metaphysical attitudes. Experiences of communal living gave rise to dance forms that expressed or even caused social bonds. Dance became a vehicle for spiritual expression. For instance, Deborah Hay's solos of the seventies included cosmic images that were reminiscent of Hindu temple dances, and Barbara Dilley's *Wonder Dances* used meditative movement explorations and explosive moments of ecstatic out-pourings in performances informed by the choreographer's interest in Tibetan Buddhism. Dance also became a vehicle for expressions of community with spiritual overtones, as in Meredith Monk's theatrical, mythic works such as *Education of the Girlchild*, a portrait of a tribe or family of heroic women. The works of Laura Dean and Andy deGroat—especially their spinning dances, resembling Sufi dances—fell somewhere between images of private and com-munal devotion. Deborah Hay's Circle Dances, dispensing with spectators, were like folk dances that were instructions for dancing with friends to popular music. Ann Halprin's "rituals" were intended for physical and psychic healing and for creating instant communities; using Esalen-type techniques, she guided large groups of dancers and nondancers to form their own structures for dancing together in individual ways. Kenneth King's use of dances as metaphors for technology, information and power systems, and the mind itself fall into this category; for instance, *The Telaxic Synapsulator* (1974), performed simultane-ously with *Dance S(p)ell* (1978), included a reading of excerpts from Marie Curie's *Radioactive Substances*, slides projecting information about the destruc-tiveness of radioactivity, dancers performing movements that seem to describe processes of breaking down chemical elements, and a marvelous machine with gleaming and spinning parts. Robert Wilson's theatre of images, often incor-porating dances by other choreographers, such as Kenneth King, Andy deGroat, Lucinda Childs, and Jim Self, also falls into this category.

Where analytic postmodern dance is exclusive of such elements, metaphoric postmodern dance is inclusive of theatrical elements such as costume, lighting, music, props, character, and mood. In this way, and in its making of expressive metaphors and representations, this strand of avant-garde dance resembles historical modern dance. But it also differs from classical modern dance in such important, basic ways that it seems more useful to include it as another category of postmodern dance than to consider it modern dance. These dances draw on postmodern processes and techiques. The key postmodern choreographic technique is radical juxtaposition. But also, these dances often use ordinary movements and objects; they propose new relationships between performer and spectator; articulate new experiences of space, time, and the body; incorporate language and film; employ structures of stillness and repetition. Metaphoric postmodern dance also counts as postmodern because it participates in the distribution system—the lofts, galleries, and other venues—that has become the arena for postmodern dance. That is, it presents itself as postmodern dance.

THE 1980S: THE REBIRTH OF CONTENT

Since 1978 or so, avant-garde dance has taken a number of new directions. Some of these directions stand apparently in direct opposition to the values of analytic postmodern dance, making the very use of the term "postmodern" problematic for current dancing. Perhaps we should reserve the term for use only in reference to the analytic mode of the 1970s, just as the strictest definition of modern dance restricts us to the late 1920s through the 1950s. Then the breakaway choreographers of the sixties could be called the forerunners of postmodern dance, just as Isadora Duncan, Loïe Fuller, and Ruth St. Denis are sometimes called the forerunners of modern dance. However, there is a strong argument for an inclusive use of the term, one that applies to the breakaway dances of the sixties, the analytic and metaphoric dances of the seventies, and the new dances of the eighties, because all of these currents are related, in large part because they set themselves apart from mainstream theatrical dance in ways that are not simply chronological. The current generation of postmodern choreographers (and the current work of the older generation) reopens some of the issues that concerned historical modern dance. Thus it seems to depart from the concerns of its immediate predecessors. But it would be ahistorical to call the current generation modern dance; we would intuitively recoil from placing the modern dance choreographers Jennifer Muller or Norman Walker in the same camp as postmoderns such as Wendy Perron, Johanna Boyce, or Bill T. Jones. The views and practices of the current generation are not simply a return to an older style or method. They build on and, in their turn, depart from the redefinitions and analyses, as well as the techniques and antitechniques, of the postmodern inquiry into the nature and function of dance.

By the end of the 1970s, the clarity and simplicity of analytic postmodern dance had served its purpose and threatened to become an exercise in empty formalism. Dance had become so shorn of meaning (other than reflexive) that for a younger generation of choreographers and spectators it was beginning to be regarded as almost meaningless. The response was an urgent search for ways to reinstall meaning in dance.

One kind of meaning in dance has always been the skills and complexities of sheer virtuosity. In the sixties, the impulse of the postmodern choreographers was to deny virtuosity and to relinquish technical polish, to literally let go of bodily constraints and inhibitions, to act freely, and also, in a spirit of democracy, to refuse to differentiate the dancer's body from an ordinary body. The level of dance technique in both ballet and modern dance had steadily risen (and continues to rise) in the United States since the thirties. As in other periods in Euro-American dance history when technique seemed all-important, the choreographers of the sixties protested. But unlike, for instance, the romantic choreographers of the 1830s and 1840s, their response was not to emphasize expression over technique; rather, they dropped out of the technical arena altogether. The notion of letting go also manifested itself metaphorically in the "one-night stand"—a refusal to hang on to dances and to store them in a repertory, an acknowledgment of dance's ephemeral nature—and, further, in the method of improvisation, in which the dance is created for the moment and instantaneously disappears. In the eighties, this impulse has reversed. The spirit is one of survival. Dances are preserved on film and videotape. One of Trisha Brown's recent works (*Opal Loop*) includes material improvised in performance by Steve Paxton that Brown's dancers Lisa Kraus and Stephen Petronio learned by watching a videotape of Paxton's performance. Now postmodern choreographers have companies—for instance, the David Gordon Pick-Up Company, the Trisha Brown Company, the Lucinda Childs Dance Company, Kenneth King and Dancers—and their companies perform works from the repertory. This is probably partly a response to economic demands set down by touring commitments and granting agencies; certainly it is also part of the process of becoming an established choreographer. Now choreography demands strength, skill, and endurance. The more a dance has in it, the more it seems worth—contra the "less is more" philosophy of analytic postmodern dance. Virtuosity becomes the subject in dances by choreographers such as Charles Moulton, whose works build on a vocabulary of athletic moves; Elizabeth Streb, whose dances quote circus acrobatics; and Molissa Fenley, whose pieces are "walls of dance" that operate at top speed and whose dancers rehearse wearing weights. These dances border on the physical feats of the athlete/gymnast, while in the world of gymnastics, figure skating, and other sports, the form has become more dancelike. Ironically, as more and more Americans take up athletic pastimes, from jogging to weight lifting, what it means to have an ordinary body has changed over the past decade. Now everyone is an athlete, and sports are no longer fun to do but, for some, a daily grind and even a source of injury. In social dancing, beginning with the disco routines of the seventies but continuing with forms such as new wave, robot dancing, breaking, and electric boogie, "doing your own thing," as in the sixties, was gradually replaced by actions of physical dexterity, complicated timing and partnering, and acrobatic embellishment. The ante has been upped for postmodern choreographers. In the virtuosic works of the eighties, the significance of the dance is the refinement of bodily skills; yet in the light of the previous generation's renunciation of bravura, the current dances also seem to establish themselves as another installment of the debate on the subject.

If in the sixties and seventies we were content to let artworks simply be rather than mean and to let criticism describe rather than interpret, in the eighties we want to find substance and order in an increasingly recalcitrant world. We can no longer afford the permissiveness of the sixties. The modest thriftiness of seventies retrenchment has given way to values in every aspect of American life more suited to the drastic economic cutbacks of Reaganism. Ours is an age of artifice, specialization, conservation, and competition. As in the thirties, the contradictions between rich and poor are great, but even those with less money to spend are willing to spend it with a vengeance on elegant clothing and entertainment, immediate pleasures that will partly compensate for inflation, debt, and unemployment. In this milieu, the current values in postmodern dance of virtuosity, elegance, and ornament are not surprising.

The current fascination with semiotics is symptomatic of our present rage for meaning and order. Scholars in every field turn to linguistic analysis and jargon in attempts to make sense of the messiness of experience. Artists, following the theorists, incorporate ready-made sign systems into their works. One method of installing meaning in dance, the most nonverbal of the arts, is to appropriate language and languagelike systems. A number of choreographers make dances based on the hand gesture, an emphasis unusual for Euro-American dance. Dana Reitz, for instance, makes improvisations in which the movements and static shapes of the hands are highlighted; the open palms or wavelike gestures, rooted in movements of Tai Chi Chuan, remind us of the powerfully emblematic use of the hands in daily life, but in the dance they do not serve as signals. Remy Charlip uses the conventional gestures of American Sign Language for the deaf, often juxtaposed to verbal texts—dreams and stories and, notably, the song "Every Little Movement (Has a Meaning All Its Own)." Jane Comfort and other younger choreographers have also used sign language translations of spoken texts, much like closed caption television, as movement vocabularies in their dances. David Gordon continues his use of often witty, punning language in his performances, showing how both verbal and nonverbal expressions change their meaning as their contexts shift. Not surprisingly, the interest in verbal language has been accompanied by a rekindling of interest in narrative structures. A "Paranarrative" series was held in 1982 at P.S. 1, featuring dances by over twenty choreographers; at a series of performances and panel discussions on new dance sponsored by the School for Movement Research at St. Mark's Church in 1982, the use of language was the subject of continual, heated debate.

As the focus on narrative suggests, another way of making dances meaningful is to make them refer to something else—plot, character, situation, emotion. Jim Self's dances, such as his 1982 solo *Lookout* in which, as the program explains, "a man watching television tries to sort the mistaken identities of two

intruders,'' or his work-in-progress, The Beehive Project, a humorous exploration of the dancing language of bees, suggest character and plot, but in oblique
ways. Judy Padow's *Complex Desires* (1981) uses certain signals of emotional
expression, but decontextualized in such a way that the emotions resist categorization, as the title suggests. Susan Rethorst's works approach descriptions
of femininity. Pooh Kaye's dances are like primitive myths that describe a
simpler, natural, animistic world. Tim Miller's works—somewhere between
dance and performance art—combine autobiography and political outcry. These
dances are different from modern dance, however, because in important ways
they present the nondance information (i.e., plot, character, situation), rather
than represent it. They are not seamless theatrical illusions, productions of fictional worlds (à la Martha Graham or Doris Humphrey). The movement vocabulary is only partially expressive; it also remains partly abstract and it resists
definitive interpretation. The emotional or narrative content remains elusive and
fragmented, and the meaning of the dance is played out on several, not always
corresponding, dimensions.

Another way to make a dance meaningful is to provide many channels of
communication. The rigor of Childs' work of the seventies has softened into an
elegant expressiveness in her recent collaborative works: *Dance* (1979; LeWitt/
Glass) and *Relative Calm* (1981; Wilson/Gibson). At the same time, she has
embellished her earlier, austere choreography with dips, rises, hops, and pi-
rouettes that recall the pulsing musicality of baroque style. Similarly, Trisha
Brown's collaborations *Glacial Decoy* (1979; Rauschenberg), *Opal Loop/Cloud
Installation #72503* (1980; Nakaya), and *Son of Gone Fishin'* (1981; Judd/
Ashley) assert the liquidity of her recent choreography on many levels: the
slipperiness of the movement as well as the water imagery of the decor and
costumes. A number of choreographers have set their dancers changing costumes
throughout a work, as though they were using a manual for the semiotic analysis
of clothing.

By the eighties, one can place oneself in the postmodern camp simply by
choosing to perform in a postmodern venue. There are six centers for postmodern
dance in New York: The Kitchen (in Soho); Dance Theater Workshop (in Chel-
sea); Danspace at St. Mark's Church, P.S. 122 (both on the Lower East Side);
P.S. 1 (in Long Island City, Queens); and the Brooklyn Academy of Music.
Although choreographers and companies are fairly mobile, switching venues
from season to season, some have become identified with one theatre or another.
For instance, the more established Childs and Brown have each appeared at
Brooklyn Academy of Music on a regular basis, and P.S. 122, the newest of
the venues, often produces very young, little-known choreographers, while The
Kitchen runs a touring program that produces Self, Moulton, Lisa Fox, and Eric
Barsness outside of New York (and in the past has produced tours for Rethorst
and Fenley); Dance Theater Workshop presents modern as well as postmodern
choreographers. These places are institutions with curators, rather than convenient places to show work (as, for instance, Judson Church had been). Thus

there is a demand for postmodern choreography by producers, and their taste partly determines who counts as postmodern. But besides these "alternative" institutions, postmodern dance is performed at countless lofts, a few churches, and also, most recently, through another distribution system: the club or cabaret. Postmodern dance, like performance art, has moved from the art world toward the music world. Visual artists have returned to making commodities that will last, and the gallery system is no longer inclined to deal in live performance. The underlying impulse of Conceptual Art—to undermine the status of the art object as a means of investment—is obviously spent; in times of economic distress, people want to buy objects rather than finance ideas or actions. With the "dematerialization of the art object" in the late sixties and seventies, the performative aspect of plastic art blossomed and (postmodern) dance and performance art became arenas in which ideas could be given temporary body.[12] Thus the result of Conceptual Art was not to diminish performance but to catalyze more of it. Further, there is definitely a relationship between the purely mental and verbal problems and systems of Conceptual Art and the rigorous intellectual structures of much of analytic postmodern dance. In the eighties, the worlds of avant-garde music, avant-garde visual art, and popular music have begun to merge, and the postmodern choreographers have joined them. The merging of the "high art" and popular traditions is one of the characteristics of postmodernism, and yet in the history of the avant-garde arts it is nothing new; vanguard artists have perennially turned to folk, popular, and exotic art as sources for breaking with mainstream values as well as for "new" materials and techiques. Perhaps what makes the current version of this practice particularly postmodern is that it is enveloped in an acute historical consciousness of its use, making quotation a laminating process across both historical periods and current geographical, social, and stylistic divisions. The music scene in New York provides a new context for postmodern dance. In the sixties, artists and dancers went out social dancing after concerts; the avant-garde of the eighties programs performance into the social scene, selling beer at intermissions or presenting art dance at discotheques and clubs in late-night performances. Thus on the one hand, postmodern dance has built its own special audiences and circuits, and on the other hand, it seeks new audiences in the wider network of popular music and dance culture.

Two changes in the choreography and the dancing itself reflect this new context. One is a new musicality, a return to the notion of "dancing to the music" that is more closely related to social dance practice than to the development of modern dance in the twentieth century, with music becoming more and more detached from the choreography. Where Isadora Duncan and Ruth St. Denis made their dances visualizations of symphonic music, Mary Wigman, a generation later, preferred to use simple percussion; Cunningham makes dances that do not correspond structurally to the music at all (except by accident); the analytic postmodern choreographers often danced in silence. Laura Dean's fusions of dancing, instrumental music, and song, inspired by various non-Western traditions, prefigured the new trend of musicality. Fenley makes dances to the polyrhythms of Afro-Caribbean music that are inspired, in part, by the ritual and social dancing of West Africa and the high energy of new wave music, but that also reflect a commitment to a search for an original movement vocabulary. The second, related change is an interest in vernacular dance itself and the presentation of social dance or fragments of social dance as art dance. Twyla Tharp's use of jazz and blues and her quotations of Afro-American dance in the early seventies foreshadowed this tendency, which now cuts across all genres of theatrical dance (e.g., in 1983, both Les Grand Ballets Canadiens and the New York City Ballet presented new dances quoting from Fred Astaire). Marta Renzi's dances, set to rock and roll, create cartoonlike images of young lovers. Karole Armitage, collaborating with new-wave composer Rhys Chatham, uses the energies, shapes, and colors of punk culture in her dances. In 1981, The Kitchen presented two programs of teenage street dancing as part of its dance series. The effect on postmodern audiences and choreographers remains to be measured; Perron, for instance, choreographed part of her *Dancing to Good Bands . . . As Revealing as Self Portraits* (1982) by using as a score a photographic contact sheet of electric boogie, shot by Paula Court at one of The Kitchen concerts.[13] Another major force in postmodern dance is the number of young black choreographers, such as Bill T. Jones, Blondell Cummings, and Ishmael Houston-Jones, who identify their work with the postmodern vein.

OUTSIDE THE UNITED STATES

For reasons that have been outlined elsewhere, postmodern dance has largely been a U.S. phenomenon.[14] However, over the past twenty years postmodern choreographers and dancers have toured Europe extensively, performing and teaching at arts festivals and in theatres all over Canada, Great Britain, and the Continent, especially in Holland, France, and Italy. More recently, European companies have commissioned dances from American postmodern choreographers. Americans Mary Fulkerson and Steve Paxton have been teaching at Dartington, in England, since the early seventies. They have contributed to a New Dance movement that has taken firm hold in England. The London Dance Umbrella has since the late seventies fostered an exchange of ideas between American postmodern choreographers and a growing community of similarly minded choreographers and dancers from Europe, with an annual festival of dance concerts, lectures, exhibitions, and workshops on music, design, and criticism. The major venues for new or postmodern dance in London are Riverside Studios and ICA. British exponents of new dance include Rosemary Butcher, Michael Clark, Laurie Booth, and Libby Dempster. In Germany, where the tradition of modern dance flowered briefly between the two world wars, the younger avant-garde choreographers seem more influenced by European avant-garde theatre than by either German or American dance. Pina Bausch and Susanne Linke are the dominant new choreographers, and both of them are expressionist rather than analytic. Various other experimental choreographers in West Germany constitute an alternative to opera-house ballet (the major form of German dance), called the Poor Dance movement. In Japan, what we might call postmodern dance is lumped together with all sorts of other kinds of dance, including Western-style ballet, as "buto," that is, dance that departs from the classical Japanese dance-theatre forms.

CRITICISM

In 1962, John Martin, the reigning dance critic at the *New York Times* and the leading advocate of historical modern dance, retired. Although Martin attended dance events "below 14th Street," he did not cover them in the *Times*. But Allen Hughes, Martin's temporary replacement (until Clive Barnes took over in 1965), was interested in writing about every aspect of dance. Many of the historic Judson Dance Theater concerts, including the first one, were reviewed by Hughes, who was more interested in describing and explaining the dances than in passing judgment on them. Better remembered for her coverage of postmodern dance in the sixties was Jill Johnston, who began writing her "Dance Journal" column for the *Village Voice* in 1959. Johnston was an avid polemicist for the Judson Dance Theater and the choreographers who emerged from it. Passionately involved in the art-world and dance-world gesture of breaking down the boundaries between art and life, she both influenced postmodern dance and was influenced by it. Her experiments in writing criticism paralleled the breakdown of artistic conventions she chronicled, both in the *Voice* and in various visual art publications. Eventually her column became a stream-of-consciousness diary, without punctuation, capital letters, or paragraph breaks, that took all of life as its beat. Her style set an example for personal journalism for which the *Voice* became well known. Her columns, some of which were collected in *Marmalade Me*, remain the most exciting account of much of the dance, art, and happenings of the sixties. During the breakaway years, most of the dance critics besides Hughes and Johnston were bewildered, if not dismayed, by the work of the postmodern choreographers.

With the dance boom of the 1970s, dance coverage expanded in the press. Partly through such organizations as the Dance Critics Association and the various training institutes for dance critics, writers themselves became more familiar with nontraditional styles. Also, although in the early seventies Clive Barnes wrote disparagingly about postmodern dance in the *New York Times*, the coverage by such critics as Marcia B. Siegel, Rob Baker, Deborah Jowitt, Laura Shapiro, Amanda Smith, and Sally Banes in such alternative papers as the *Village Voice, Soho Weekly News*, the *Boston Phoenix*, the *Real Paper* and the *Chicago Reader*, by Noël Carroll in *Artforum*, by Alan M. Kriegsman in the *Washington Post*, by Don McDonagh in the *New York Times*, and by various critics in *Dance Magazine* was much more sympathetic. By the late seventies and early eighties, Anna Kisselgoff, Jack Anderson, and Jennifer Dunning at the *New York Times* wrote about postmodern dance on a regular basis, as did Tobi Tobias in *New York* and other critics across the country. Arlene Croce, at the *New Yorker*, is less interested in postmodern dance; her article on the various camps of the genre and lines of influence sparked an angry response from a number of choreographers, but in 1983 the *New Yorker* published her lengthy profile of David Gordon and Valda Setterfield.[15]

NOTES

1. This article does not claim to analyze or describe the various styles, stages, and complexities of modern dance. For an explication of traditional modern dance structures, see the three bibles of modern dance composition: Louis Horst, *Pre-Classic Dance Forms* (New York: The Dance Observer, 1937; reprint ed., Dance Horizons, 1972); Louis Horst and Carroll Russell, *Modern Dance Forms* (San Francisco: Impulse Publications, 1961); and Doris Humphrey, *The Art of Making Dances* (New York: Rinehart, 1959; reprint ed., Grove Press, 1962); see also the many books about and reviews of modern dance.

2. Michael Kirby, "Introduction," *The Drama Review* 19 (T-65; March 1975): 3.

3. Charles Jencks, *The Language of Post-Modern Architecture* (New York: Rizzoli, 1977).

4. Since this essay was written, Roger Copeland's article "Postmodern Dance and the Repudiation of Primitivism" appeared in *Partisan Review* 50, no. 1 (1983): 101–21. Copeland argues that modern dance strove for synthesis in terms of form and unity in the audience's experience of the work. A mistrust of language underlies the primitivist longings of the modern dancers. Here and in a second recent article, "Postmodern Dance/Postmodern Architecture/Postmodernism," *Performing Arts Journal* 19 (1983): 27–43, Copeland makes some useful observations about postmodern dance. However, his definition is much more narrow than the one proposed here, although he does suggest the possibility of two different camps of postmodern dance (in "Postmodern Dance/Postmodern Architecture/Postmodernism," p. 33).

5. For descriptions and analyses of Cunningham's work, see Merce Cunningham, *Changes: Notes on Choreography*, ed. Frances Starr (New York: Something Else Press, 1968); Sally Banes, *Terpsichore in Sneakers: Post-Modern Dance* (Boston: Houghton Mifflin, 1980), pp. 5–7; Sally Banes and Noël Carroll, "Cunningham and Duchamp," *Ballet Review* 11 (Summer 1983): 73–79; Roger Copeland, "The Politics of Perception," *The New Republic*, November 17, 1979.

6. On the avant-garde of the 1950s, see Jill Johnston, "The New American Modern Dance," in *The New American Arts*, ed. Richard Kostelanetz, (New York: Collier Books, 1967), pp. 162–93; and Selma Jeanne Cohen, "Avant-Garde Choreography," *Criticism* 3 (Winter 1961): 16–35, reprinted in three parts in *Dance Magazine* 36 (June 1962): 22–24, 57; 36 (July 1962): 29–31, 58; 36 (August 1962): 45, 54–56.

7. Susan Sontag, "Against Interpretation," *Against Interpretation* (New York: Farrar, Straus and Giroux, 1966), p. 14.

8. Space does not permit a description of these dances here. However, these and many of the following dances are described in Banes, *Terpsichore in Sneakers* and in Sally Banes, *Democracy's Body: Judson Dance Theater 1962–1964* (Ann Arbor: UMI Research Press, 1983). Also, accounts of many of the dances mentioned in this essay may be found in the works by choreographers and critics listed in the bibliography.

9. On black dance in the sixties, see Lynne Fauley Emery, *Black Dance in the United States from 1619 to 1970* (Palo Alto, Calif.: National Press Books, 1972).

10. Two short films exist that show these stylistic features very clearly: Childs's *Calico Mingling* and Rainer's *Trio A*.

11. On meaning and expressiveness in postmodern dance, see Noël Carroll and Sally Banes, "Working and Dancing: A Response to Monroe Beardsley's 'What Is Going On in a Dance?' " *Dance Research Journal* 15/1 (Fall 1982): 37–41; and Noël Carroll, "Post-Modern Dance and Expression," *Philosophical Essays in Dance*, ed. Gordon Fancher and Gerald Myers (New York: Dance Horizons, 1981), pp. 95–104.

12. See Lucy Lippard, *Six Years: The Dematerialization of the Art Object from 1966 to 1972* (New York: Praeger, 1973).

13. I have written about teenage street dancing trends in several articles, including "To the Beat Y'All," *Village Voice*, April 22, 1981; "Lock Steady," *Village Voice*, October 21, 1981; "A House Is Not a Home," *Village Voice*, April 13, 1982; and "Breaking Changing," *Village Voice*, June 12, 1984.

14. In Sally Banes, "Icon and Image in New Dance," *New Dance U.S.A.* Festival Catalog (Minneapolis: Walker Art Center, 1981), pp. 7–21.

15. Arlene Croce, "Slowly Then the History of Them Comes Out," *The New Yorker*, June 30, 1980, pp. 92–95; Arlene Croce, "Profiles: Making Work," *The New Yorker*, November 29, 1982, pp. 51–107.

SELECTED BIBLIOGRAPHY

Ballet Review 1, no. 6 (1967), Judson Issue. Includes interviews and essays on Judson Dance Theater, plus a chronology that is detailed but not totally free of errors.

Banes, Sally. *Democracy's Body: Judson Dance Theater: 1962–1964*. Ann Arbor: UMI Research Press, 1983. A documentary account of Judson Dance Theater 1962–64, including descriptions of Concerts #1–16 and concerts by individual choreographers, as well as discussions of the workshop.

———. *Terpsichore in Sneakers: Post-Modern Dance*. Boston: Houghton Mifflin, 1980. Chapters on Simone Forti, Yvonne Rainer, Steve Paxton, Trisha Brown, David Gordon, Deborah Hay, Lucinda Childs, Meredith Monk, Kenneth King, Douglas Dunn, and Grand Union. Includes a chronology and an extensive bibliography (up to 1978).

Cage, John. *Silence*. Middletown, Conn.: Wesleyan University Press, 1961. A seminal book of writings by the influential composer whose ideas inspired much of early postmodern dance.

Carroll, Noël. "Post-Modern Dance and Expression." In *Philosophical Essays in Dance*, edited by Gordon Fancher and Gerald Myers, pp. 95–104. Brooklyn: Dance Horizons, 1981. Carroll argues that despite the attempt of postmodern choreographers to purge dance of emotional expressiveness, postmodern dance is expressive in a broad sense, that is, of ideas and attitudes.

———. "The Return of The Repressed: The Re-emergence of Expression in Contemporary American Dance." *Dance Theatre Journal* 2, no. 1 (1984): 16–19, 27. The author analyzes some recent aspects of expression in new dance, including allusionism, narrative, political content, infantilism, and musicality; he rejects the label "postmodern" for this stage of new dance.

Carroll, Noël and Sally Banes. "Working and Dancing: A Response to Monroe Beardsley's 'What Is Going On in a Dance?' '' *Dance Research Journal* 15/1 (Fall 1982): 37–41. In response to Beardsley's claim that dance movement is movement that is saturated with expressive meaning, the authors argue that it is context that makes movement into dance movement, using dances by Rainer, Brown, and Paxton as examples.

Cohen, Selma Jeanne. "Avant-Garde Choreography." *Criticism* 3 (Winter 1961): 16–35. Reprinted in three parts in *Dance Magazine* 36 (June 1962): 22–24, 57; 36 (July 1962): 29–31, 58; 36 (August 1962): 45, 54–56. A discussion of the older avant-garde of the 1950s, including Merce Cunningham and Paul Taylor.

Copeland, Roger. "Postmodern Dance and the Repudiation of Primitivism." *Partisan Review* 50, no. 1 (1983): 101–21. Copeland contends that modern dance strove for synthesis, with an underlying rhetoric of nostalgic primitivism, whereas postmodern dance, beginning with Cunningham, separates the elements of dance, often by using language in the performance.

———. "Postmodern Dance/Postmodern Architecture/Postmodernism." *Performing Arts Journal* 19 (1983): 27–43. The author discusses definitions of postmodern dance in relation to pedestrian movement, popular forms, and postmodern architecture.

Cunningham, Merce. *Changes: Notes on Choreography*. Edited by Frances Starr. New York: Something Else Press, 1968. Notes, sketches, and scores by the choreographer, as well as photographs of his works, in a chance-determined collage format.

Forti, Simone. *Handbook in Motion*. Halifax: Press of the Nova Scotia College of Art and Design; New York: New York University Press, 1974. An account of the choreographer's life and work, sometimes in diary form, with descriptions and photographs of dances.

Howell, John. "No to Homogenized Dancing." *Performing Arts Journal* 2 (Fall 1977): 3–12. Discusses recent works by Sara Rudner, Brown, Forti, Reitz, Overlie, and Douglas Dunn.

Jackson, George. "Naked in Its Native Beauty." *Dance Magazine* 38 (April 1964): 32–37. Article on avant-garde dance works, primarily at Judson Church, with many photographs.

Johnston, Jill. *Marmalade Me*. New York: E. P. Dutton, 1971. A selection of reviews and essays on dance, happenings, performances, and life in general by the first champion of postmodern dance. The selection chronicles the loosening of Johnston's prose style.

———. "The New American Modern Dance." In *The New American Arts*, edited by Richard Kostelanetz, pp. 162–93. New York: Collier Books, 1967. An excellent, lucid account of the breakaway years of postmodern dance, putting the work of the period in historical perspective.

Jowitt, Deborah. *Dance Beat: Selected Views and Reviews, 1967–1976*. New York: Marcel Dekker, 1977. Includes reviews of Monk, Tharp, Brown, Rainer, Childs, Dean, D. Dunn, R. Wilson, Grand Union.

Judson Dance Theater: 1962–1966. Exhibition Catalog. Organized by the Bennington College Judson Project, 1981. Essays by Jill Johnston and Sally Banes, and photographs from the exhibition.

Kirby, Michael. *The Art of Time*. New York: E. P. Dutton, 1969. Essays on the avant-garde, including "The Objective Dance."

Kostelanetz, Richard. *The Theatre of Mixed Means*. New York: The Dial Press, 1968. Interviews with various artists involved in performance, among them Ann Halprin.

Livet, Anne, ed. *Contemporary Dance*. New York: Abbeville Press, 1978. Talks, interviews, and essays by critics and choreographers, including Trisha Brown, Deborah Hay, Lucinda Childs, Michael Kirby, and Deborah Jowitt, profusely illustrated.

McDonagh, Don. *The Complete Book of Modern Dance*. Garden City, N.Y.: Doubleday, 1976. Gives short biographies and chronologies for modern and postmodern choreographers. Exhaustive, but occasionally inaccurate.

———. *The Rise and Fall and Rise of Modern Dance*. New York: New American Library, 1971. Discusses both modern and postmodern choreographers of the 1960s.

New Dance USA. Festival catalog. Walker Art Center, 1981. Essays by Sally Banes, Jill Johnston, and Allen Robertson.

Rainer, Yvonne. *Work 1961–73*. Halifax: The Press of the Nova Scotia College of Art and Design; New York: New York University Press, 1974. A thorough documentation of the choreographer's career, including scores, notes, photographs, and reprinting many of her essays.

Schneemann, Carolee. *More Than Meat Joy*. New Paltz, N.Y.: Documentext, 1979. A documentation of dance and performance works by the artist.

Siegel, Marcia B. *At the Vanishing Point*. New York: Saturday Review Press, 1973. A collection of reviews, including those of Rainer, Monk, Paxton, and Brown.

———. *Watching the Dance Go By*. Boston: Houghton Mifflin, 1977. A second collection of writings, including reviews of Brown, Dean, Childs, Grand Union, D. Dunn, William Dunas, and King.

Tomkins, Calvin. *The Bride and the Bachelors*. New York: Viking Press, 1968. Profiles, including those of Merce Cunningham, John Cage, and Robert Rauschenberg, that provide a useful context for postmodern dance and collaborations involving postmodern choreographers.

Periodicals

Artforum. Covered downtown dance regularly in the early 1970s; occasional coverage now.

Ballett International. German magazine with articles on international aspects of postmodern dance.

Ballet Review. Occasional articles on postmodern dance; regular "grading" of new works.

Contact Quarterly (formerly *Contact Newsletter*). Articles on Contact Improvisation and related body disciplines and news of events of interest to Contact Improvisers.

Dance Chronicle. Quarterly journal with occasional articles on postmodern dance.

Dance Magazine. Regular reviews and occasional articles in a monthly magazine.

The Drama Review (formerly *Tulane Drama Review*). Edited by Michael Kirby, TDR has been committed to covering postmodern dance since the early sixties. Special issues include T-30 (Winter 1965), including an interview with Halprin by Rainer and an essay by Robert Morris; T-55 (September 1972), including articles on Brown, Gordon, Grand Union, and Joan Jonas; T-65 (March 1975), the Postmodern Dance issue, with articles on Batya Zamir, Jonas, Dean, Brown, Childs, Forti, Contact Improvisation (by Paxton), and Gordon; and T-88 (December 1980), with articles on Fenley, Margaret Fisher, Reitz, Blondell Cummings, Mary Overlie, and Elaine Summers.

New York Magazine. Reviews, occasionally of postmodern dance, by Tobi Tobias.

Performing Arts Journal. A quarterly journal on theatre and dance, devoted to the avant-
    garde.
Village Voice. A weekly newspaper published in New York with regular coverage of
    avant-garde dance by Deborah Jowitt and others.
Dance Scope, eddy, Soho Weekly News, all now defunct, covered postmodern dance in
    the past.

5

Film

NOËL CARROLL

The recent history of the avant-garde film in America mirrors the general pattern of cultural experience over the last two decades. The sense of a unified oppositional movement concerned with the war in Vietnam, student protest, and opposition to racial and sexual domination gives way to a sense of the collapse of that unified energy into a range of heterogeneous projects. If in 1971, one could feel part of the cutting edge of history, that feeling is no longer available. Where in the early seventies the future seemed promising, few today have much confidence about where we are headed.

Avant-garde film of the early seventies appeared to propose, at least to many of its most vocal adherents, a privileged relation to history. It witnessed the ascendency of structural film, which asserted a decisive break not only with commercial entertainment film, but also with the previously dominant tradition of the avant-garde, which was highly expressionist in its practices and theory. At the same time structural film proposed a revolutionary break with several cinematic pasts, it also seemed to afford filmmakers with something like a paradigm for working out a project that could be expatiated endlessly into the future. In the early seventies, there was momentary euphoric agreement about the task of film and about the shape that the future of film should take. A language of criticism, quasi-theory, and appreciation took hold that invited everyone to board the train of film history and to ride into a bountiful future.

Undoubtedly the sense that structural film provided a unified project was illusory—both historically and theoretically. However, and more importantly, even the illusion of unity was short-lived. By the middle and late seventies, numerous reactions arose against the structural ethos. These took the form of the reintroduction of various of the concerns missing from the formalistically austere structural film—narrative, personal obsession, expression, reference, politics—in short, what we might loosely call ''content.'' Yet the forms of reaction to the structural film were multiple and various. Structural film was not superceded by a single movement—that is, a program like surrealism—but by a set of alternative movements, genres, and sensibilities, including the deconstructionist film, the new talkie, punk film, psychodramas, and lastly, a return to imagery that is expressive, aesthetic, elusive, and enigmatic, a kind of "new symbolism." These reactions to structural film are often quite different from each other. Nevertheless, they each bear testimony to the extreme hold that structural film exerted upon the imagination of the early seventies, insofar as each gains much of its energy from the repudiation of the structural film mystique. At the same time, these alternate movements form a rough grouping inasmuch as they are all vexed by the ostensible (rather than actual) repression of content, broadly construed, in structural film. Needless to say, each of these movements differs in the content that it wishes to restore to film. However, they do represent a loose family of movements, sensibilities, and genres that we may think of as antistructural or as poststructural.

There are several reasons I have written "poststructural" rather than "post-modern." The term "postmodern" is unsettling. It can apply to Nietzsche if we are speaking of philosophy, Venturi if the subject is architecture, Creeley if our focus is poetry, Longo and Goldstein in painting, Rainer and Paxton in dance. But what has Rainer to do with Nietzsche, or Venturi to do with Creeley? And if this could be answered by a single formula, how would that formula work for the variety of avant-garde films of the late seventies and eighties?

These rhetorical questions should signal hesitation about belief in some broad movement called "postmodernism" that manifests itself uniformly in philosophy and various artistic practices in different centuries and countries (Nietzsche and Venturi), and in different generations (Creeley and Longo). On the positive side, however, the label "postmodern" should not be ignored as a means of marking a stylistic or theoretical break within a specific ongoing discourse or art form. There is something that the term "postmodern architecture" refers to that is rather specific, just as there is something "postmodern dance" refers to. Indeed, these labels were used within certain communities of artistic practice—by actual practitioners (working artists, critics, programmers, curators, patrons, etc.)—to denominate specific historical changes of emphasis and program. "Postmodern architecture" names a style opposed to the ideal of the modern found in someone like Le Corbusier, while "postmodern dance" was antimodern dance as the latter was exemplified in the projects of Graham, Humphrey, and Limón, among others. When the scope of postmodern is appropriately limited to a particular arena of practice and to a particular time frame, and where the term is used by practitioners to highlight their differences and conflicts with their predecessors, the term "postmodern" can be found to have concrete reference and can be given a perfectly operational meaning.

However, the above considerations are exactly what gives rise to a second reservation about applying the term "postmodern" to film or, even more spe-cifically, to avant-garde film.[1] Namely, the term "postmodern" is not indigenous to film practice. The middle seventies did not witness the emergence of self-proclaimed postmodernist filmmakers nor was that label often applied by film critics. Instead, movements like punk film arose. Consequently, insofar as we speak of postmodern film, we will only, in general, be talking about film activity that is somehow analogous to activity in other arts which, in that other-art context, is already called postmodern.

In light of the preceding, antistructural film is our likeliest nominee for the title postmodern film. For the past two decades—because of the nature of the venues for avant-garde film (often museums) and because of the tendency for avant-garde filmmakers to be trained in art schools (as well as to teach in such schools)—film and fine art have been a major locus of interaction. Now, in fine art, we have witnessed the transition from modernist essentialism, whose apotheosis was minimalism, to a reaction formation called postmodernism, which reintroduced cultural content. The result was a form of politicized pop art. Similarly, in avant-garde film, the structural moment can be regarded as the celluloid correlate to painterly and sculptural minimalism. This, in turn, implies a certain loose appropriateness to employing the term "postmodernism" to the various antistructural efforts—that is, if we wish to apply it to anything at all.[2]

I prefer to speak of antistructural rather than postmodern film. For though postmodern film makes some sense homologously, it is not even as precise as the admittedly imprecise notion of antistructural film. Thus, a compromise is to write of avant-garde film in the age of postmodernism, that is, the seventies and eighties, when, in a quest for the identity of our epoch, we have become obsessed with the idea of the postmodern.

I will begin by proposing a characterization of the structural film and then proceed to chart and to describe, in some detail, major reactions to structural film, notably: deconstructionism, the new talkie, punk film, the new psychodrama, and the new symbolism.[3] These tendencies are not mutually exclusive, nor do they provide a systematic set of categories, and, lastly, they neither comprehend or exhaust the full range of contemporary avant-garde film activity.[4] After all, we are not dealing with a closed canon, like ancient Greek tragedies, and these shortcomings must be accepted by anyone who pretends to offer a historical framework for understanding the present. Also, some of these categories may at times appear overly stretched by the amount of material packed into them. Nevertheless, at present these categories provide an initially useful, albeit primitive, survey of avant-garde film.

One final caveat: By describing the field in terms of movements and genres, there is the danger of obscuring what is perhaps the most significant feature of avant-garde film in the late seventies and the eighties, namely, that the most vital and productive source of contemporary avant-garde film derives from feminism. This phenomenon transcends genre and movement classification. In each of the genres and movements discussed, women filmmakers—most often self-professed feminists—are among the leading figures. So the careful reader should take special note of the incidence of feminist activity in each of the categories. And in several categories, such as the new talkie and the psychodrama, feminism is the dominant force. Feminism cuts across the categories of contemporary film in a way that demands special attention. Moreover, there are many seminal women filmmakers whose pioneering work does not fit neatly into the fledgling taxonomy presented here.[5]

STRUCTURAL FILM

In 1969, P. Adams Sitney, the foremost chronicler of the American avant-garde (until the mid-seventies), declared "Suddenly a cinema of structure has emerged."[6] By this dramatic pronouncement, Sitney meant to call attention to a major shift with the development of the American avant-garde. From the birth of this enterprise, in the forties, through the accomplishments of Maya Deren, to the middle sixties with the work of Gregory Markopoulos, James Broughton, Harry Smith, Kenneth Anger, Sidney Peterson, and Stan Brakhage, the American avant-garde was highly expressionist, concerned with myth, dream, trance, heightened states of consciousness, and the mysteries of personality, sexuality, and metaphysics. Sitney himself referred to this dimension of the American avant-garde as "mythopoetic."[7] However, in the late sixties and early seventies a new group of filmmakers appeared, including, according to Sitney, Michael Snow, George Landow (aka Owen Land), Hollis Frampton, Paul Sharits, Tony Conrad, and Ernie Gehr. These filmmakers shared many affinities with the minimalism then emerging in fine art. And, like the minimalists in their reaction to the psychodramatic and mythic pretensions of abstract expressionism, these new filmmakers adopted strategies to depersonalize, distance, and "cool-out" their medium. Thus they came to adopt generative strategies that removed a great deal of moment-to-moment decision making, and, therefore, expressivity from their work.

These strategies came to be lumped under the label "structural." In general, two major structuring approaches were most popular. The first was to give the work a discernible, geometric shape in time. For example, Anthony McCall's *Line Describing a Cone* (1973) begins as a laserlike beam of light and, over thirty minutes, widens into a cone whose apex is at the projector lens. Similarly, Michael Snow's ←→(1969) involves repetitive lateral and then vertical camera movements. The shapes inscribed by this plan, rather than the imagery of the locale photographed, is the locus of attention. The emphasis upon highly legible, geometrical shape in these films recalls the hard-edge, linear iconography of painters like Frank Stella, though, of course, with this difference: the filmmakers' shapes evolved over time.

The second major family of strategies adopted by structural filmmakers might be called the systemic approach. Like Noland's paintings and LeWitt's sculptures, films were built on generative plans, upon repetition, repetition and variation, and upon quasi-recursive procedures. A major part of the point of such films was that the audience was supposed to grasp the underlying system that generated the imagery and, more importantly, its order. Undoubtedly artists of this period were deeply impressed by the general cultural interests in such things as generative and transformational grammar, the rise of the computer, and the pervasive talk of systems analysis. And they certainly found an iconography with which to project these preoccupations.

A strong example of the systemic approach to structural film is Hollis Frampton's *nostalgia* (1971). The film involves a parade of individual photographs, each set on a slow burning hot plate. Each shot lasts until each respective photograph turns to ash. On the sound track we hear a description of the photo we are about to see in the next shot while we watch the photo we previously heard described incinerate. The effect of this sequence of description and image is to call our attention to the difference between verbal language and pictures. None of the descriptions ever fully prepares us for the picture we later see. In this contrast, we encounter a major concern of structural filmmaking: reflexivity. Like gallery formalists, the structural filmmaker embraces the task of revealing the nature of his medium through the use of the medium itself. *Nostalgia* shows us the appropriately ineffable distinction between word and image, that is, the photographic image, as two contrasting forms of representation. At the same time, the topic of reflexivity is not restricted by the structuralist filmmaker to reflection on the medium but is also concerned to reveal the nature of our cognitive and perceptual responses to the medium. In *nostalgia*, we remark upon the way in which language primes us to look at the photos, as well as the way in which it sets up false expectations. Our visual versus our verbal capacities are set out for examination as we struggle to correlate the photo we presently view with the description we just heard. Such structural films often took on the aura of amateur, self-administered, psychological tests, providing the spectator with the opportunity to reflect apperceptively on his or her own cognitive style as well as on the forms of cognition and on memory, imagination, and expectation-formation. Of course, it is the austere restriction of interest to simple, repetitive structures that impels the spectator to such an apperceptive stance, for there is little to attend to save the process of attending.[8] Furthermore, in its concern with cognition and perception, the structural film reflects the obsession of the sixties with perception, an interest evinced as well by the drug culture and the popularization of anthropology, phenomenology, and cognitive psychology.[9]

The accomplishment of structural film is suggested in three of the masterpieces of this movement: Snow's *Wavelength* (1966), Frampton's *Zorn's Lemma* (1970), and Ernie Gehr's *Serene Velocity* (1970). Snow's film is the paradigm of the shape approach to structural film; Frampton's is the seminal systemic film; and Gehr ingeniously combines both approaches in the process of creating what looks like an animated minimalist painting.

Wavelength is a generally continuous zoom shot of a loft that takes forty-five minutes to move from a broad shot, encompassing the whole space, to a tight close-up of a photograph of waves. Though human events, such as a death, occur in the course of the film, one's attention is dominated by the forward propulsion of the camera. The film has a characterizable shape as it slowly closes on the apex of a cone, and, then, ironically, opens out again, like an hourglass, as the frame enters the perimeter of the diminutive photograph of the seascape.

For, once inside the seascape, the tiny photo effectively assumes the proportions of a long shot. This gesture makes two reflexive points about what Snow takes to be the nature of cinema. First, that cinematic space is ambiguously flat and deep—a point underscored by the photo, which is at first classified by us as a flat surface in the room but which becomes a virtual deep space when the camera "enters" it. And second, that designations such as long shot or close-up are relative insofar as, in certain senses, the shot of the photo is both.

At the same time, *Wavelength* has important implications for the notion of apperceptive reflexivity, that is, it is said to make the viewer aware of certain generic features of film perception, if not of all perception. This interpretation is set forth magisterially by Annette Michelson in her famous article "Toward Snow." Michelson notes the way in which the film captures the viewer in its trajectory and engenders a sense of anticipation about where it will stop. Will it light on the image of the seascape, or on an adjacent image of a walking woman, or will it pass through the window and out onto the street? Tension builds, revealing, Michelson believes, a basic condition of the experience of temporality, namely, narrative. She writes

And as the camera continues to move steadily forward, building a tension that grows in direct ratio to the reduction of the field, we recognize, with some surprise, those horizons as defining the contours of narrative, of that narrative form animated by distended temporality, turning upon cognition towards revelation. Waiting for an issue, we are "suspended" towards resolution. And it is as if by emptying the space of his film . . . Snow has redefined filmic space as that of action. The eye investigates the length of the loft, moves towards that conclusion which is a fixed point; in its movement toward that point, alternate conclusions and false "clues" have been eliminated, as street signs and movement and certain objects pass from view. That object is indeed another surface, a photograph of the sea. The view is held, as the sound mounts . . . [and] the photograph is re-projected in superimposition upon itself. The eye is projected through a photograph out beyond the wall and screen into a limitless space. The film is a projection of a grand reduction; its "plot" is the tracing of spatio-temporal *données*, its "action" the movement of the camera as the movement of consciousness.[10]

Frampton's *Zorn's Lemma* is the archetypal systemic film. It is divided into three sharply contrasting parts. The first introduces the theme of the alphabet as a structural device. The screen is black, but we hear a voice recite a grammar school text called *The Bay State Reader*. For each letter of the alphabet, a theologically didactic sentence is intoned whose key word corresponds to the appropriate letter of the alphabet (e.g., for "A" we hear of Adam's Fall).

The next section, lasting approximately forty minutes, is silent. It begins as block-letter images of the alphabet flash by, in their proper order, at the rate of one letter per second. These letters then give way, in a successive run, to scenes that are projected at the same, one-second-per-image pulse. Like the sentences of the first section, each of these scenes has embedded somewhere in it (e.g., in a piece of graffiti or in a sign) a word whose first letter corresponds to the letter of the alphabet whose place in the order of the shot chain the scene has taken over. We learn to assimilate the successive images as rows of alphabetic exemplifications. Then the lettered scenes are gradually replaced by ones without letters. An image of a fire substitutes for the letter "X." Over time, all the alphabetic images are replaced by unlettered scenes, by images with no writing in them.

The last section of the film is an artificially contrived long take in which we watch a man, a woman, and a dog cross a snow-covered field while six women read Grosseteste's "On Light, or the Ingression of Forms," a metaphysical generative system that proposes an account of creation not unlike the generation of words through the combinatory resources of the alphabet.

When structural film is mentioned, the first thing that comes to many people's mind is the central section of *Zorn's Lemma*. Its very title, derived from set theory, is a playful tribute to systematicity. The alphabetic structure of the image rows is immediately grasped by the spectator, who then occupies himself in a game resembling the old TV show *Concentration*. Using the alphabet as a mnemonic device, we attempt to memorize the unlettered shot chain while also anticipating the replacement of lettered scenes by unlettered ones which, in turn, leads us to anticipate the completion of the second section of the film (which we infer will come when all the alphabetic substitutions transpire). In terms of the way in which *Zorn's Lemma* engages the spectator, the second section is a field day for apperceptive reflexivity. Our responses are strongly restricted to acts of memory and anticipation, and we begin to observe apperceptively some of the ways in which these mechanisms operate.

At the same time, the film invites us to regard it as an encyclopedia of cinematic forms and as a reflection upon the nature of cinema. The second section, for example, might be interpreted as an inventory of cinematic devices. The unlettered replacement images display a differentiated battery of cinematic techniques, a kind of "vocabulary" of film, including fast motion, slow motion, superimposition, split frames, long shots, close shots, moving camera shots, and so forth. Indeed, the whole section seems to exemplify the notion of parallel editing as the alphabetic replacement series "races" to completion. Thus, the second section could be construed as a primer in cinematic technique.

The reflexive dimension of *Zorn's Lemma* is articulated not only in the inventory of devices developed in the second section, but is also worked out in the various interrelations between the film's three parts. This relies upon a dialectic of spiraling contrasts. The first section has spoken words but no images; the second part is essentially a silent film—images and written words, but no sounds—the third part has both sound and image. Moreover, the second part of the film is notably an edited film, a montage film, while the third part of *Zorn's Lemma* is a piece of long-take realism, the often privileged form of sound filmmaking, just as montage was the often privileged form of silent filmmaking. Thus, the structure of *Zorn's Lemma* alludes to a series of debates and distinctions concerning the nature of film.

The opposition of the first part to the second part, like the relation between speech and image in *nostalgia*, reminds the viewer of the difference between these forms of representation, while the stylistic opposition between the second part and the last exemplifies the alternate conceptions of film sponsored by the Soviet-surrealist tradition, on the one hand, and the Bazinian–neorealist tradition on the other. The third part might read in contrast to both of the earlier sections. If part one stands for language, and part two for film-as-language, then part three opposes both of them with what, in the context of film history, could be viewed as an aesthetic of reality. Significantly, the film ends as the snow falling on the field becomes indistinguishable from the grain of the film. Hence another vision of the nature of film is broached, the modernist idea that a film is really flat, an object in the world, like the photos that burnt up on the hot plate in *nostalgia*. That is, if the third section begins as a cinematic celebration of realism, then it ends its reductive dialectic with an affirmation of the art of the real.[11]

In many ways, Gehr's *Serene Velocity* represents the most elegant triumph of structural film. It has both a legible shape and a legible system. Like *Wavelength*, it is based upon a zoom shot. The camera moves down a greenish, institutional hallway whose spare but regular features, when flattened by the action of the zoom lens, recall the plainness and symmetricality of a minimalist painting. At the same time, the film ultimately pretends to the shape of a line as the camera pushes down the passageway to a door at the rear. But experientially this is a broken or stuttered line. This is where the element of systematicity plays its role. Sitney describes the system and its phenomenological effects thusly:

The filmmaker positioned his tripod within the corridor and then proceeded to alter his zoom lens every four frames. At first the shifts are not dramatic. He alternates four frames at 50mm with four frames at 55mm. After a considerable period the differential increases: 45mm to 60mm. Thus, the film proceeds with ever increasing optical shocks. In this system, the zoom never "moves." The illusion of movement comes about from the adjustment of the eye from one sixth of a second of a distant image to one sixth of a second of a nearer one. Although the absolute rhythm never changes, the film reaches a crescendo because of the extreme illusions of distance by the end. Furthermore, Gehr cyclically shifts the degree of exposure every frame in the phrases of four. In its overall shape *Serene Velocity* moves from a vibrating pulse within an optical depth to an accordion-like slamming and stretching of the visual field.[12]

Generated by a simple decision procedure, *Serene Velocity* evokes a series of effects that can, within the context of structural film and minimal art, be interpreted as dialectically reflexive comments on the nature of film. The hallway is initially experienced as a deep space. But at times, the juxtaposition of the four frame segments are such that they appear compressed in a single, flat frame. At one point, the image appears to constitute a large, black X, squashing the corridor in what Sitney characterizes as a slamming, accordion effect. Given the polemics of minimalism, this operation might be glossed by saying that though the film image appears deep, it is revealed to be actually flat.

Another important effect of the juxtapositions is that at times the eminently still images become alive with movement. This is an optical effect that involves our mind's imputation of movement to sequentially displayed visual arrays that are closely but not exactly aligned in regard to their figural outlines. This, of course, is the principle that makes animation possible, but also that makes all film possible. For all film movement is based upon the optical illusion of motion that results when two similar still photos are juxtaposed to each other. What Gehr has done in *Serene Velocity* is to set up a cinematic context in which the film viewer can observe for himself the origin of cinematic movement. We see the images are still; we see that certain juxtapositions result in the impression of tumultuous movement. By attending to our own perceptual response to the image, we recognize the secret of cinema. It is, in a manner of speaking, a "serene velocity—"serene" because it begins in *stillness*; "velocity" because from stillness comes quickening *movement*. Like most structural film, *Serene Velocity* addresses its audience didactically, striving to reveal the nature of cinema and the dynamics of film through elusive and elliptical "experiments."[13] The triumph of *Serene Velocity* is that it is able to allude to as many theoretical themes and to project such stark beauty by means of such a simple, that is to say minimal, initial decision procedure.

The intense didacticism of structural film is also especially apparent in the British version of the movement, which is generally referred to as structural/materialist film, whose major practitioners and proponents are Malcolm LeGrice and Peter Gidal. As the title of this movement suggests, its aim was to educate the spectator in the true, *material* nature of the medium. These filmmakers regarded representational film as illusionistic, and they sought to free the spectator from this supposed deception by adopting structures that would lead us to appreciate the real nature of the medium as a material object. Thus in LeGrice's *Dejeuner Sur L'Herbe, After Manet, Giorgione, etc.* (1974), a picnic scene is represented by four separate cameras. In terms of shape, the structure is a matter of one large square divided into four quadrants, each comprised of projections resulting from one of the initial cameras. In terms of systematicity, the structure is one of disparity, since the projectors run in and out of synchronization and since four different film stocks are employed (color, color negative, black and white, and black and white negative). The effect of these disparities, is to frustrate the enjoyment of the depiction of an anecdotal level, and is said to call our attention to the materiality of photographic representation.[14]

Initially structural/materialist film appeared to be a local variation of structural film. However, it quickly differentiated itself by contending that its commitment to revealing the ultimate materiality of film evinced a commitment to materialism in the political sense, that is, a commitment to Marxist materialism.[15] Simultaneously, proponents of structural/materialist film denounced the attempts of exegetes of structural film to claim an emancipatory role for the reflexive didacticism of the American output. Whether either or neither structural film or structural/materialist film are actually politically emancipatory or even politically significant is less important than the fact that in the shouting matches between these two competitors, the charge that American structural film was essentially formalist stuck. And this, added to other dissatisfactions with what was becoming a genre, would result in the decline of structural film in the late seventies.

Another key factor in the demise of structural film was that its early success led predictably to wide-scale imitation. This was especially the case in the area of optical printing where, through processing, images within images could be constructed in Chinese boxes of delicate games of theme and variation. In Ken Kobland's *Frame* (1976), for example, the ground of an image is a set of row houses, while the figure is an inset of the same row of houses compositionally reversed.[16] But as each new reworking of the premises of structural film appeared, audiences and commentators became increasingly disenchanted.

Since the style to a large extent relied upon seizing a simple structuring principle, it was easily imitated. And this, plus the immense volume of imitations, led to charges that the structural film was unimaginative, too facile, unchallenging, rote, and possibly trivial.[17]

In the hands of what seemed to be a horde of second-generation structural filmmakers, including Tom DeBiaso, Dana Gordon, Vincent Grenier, Peter Rose, James Benning, Joanna Kiernan, and others, the enterprise seemed to be hardening into a genre and a highly academic one at that. Strategies such as partitioned images recurred with frequency. These films were very respectable efforts and showed thorough knowledge of the tradition of avant-garde film and the other arts. But they were hardly innovative, nor did they expand greatly on the breakthroughs of first-generation structural filmmakers. The apperceptive themes of structural film—the play of memory and attention—were repeated again and again as were the reflexive, anti-illusionist comments on the nature of film.[18] These notions came to appear standardized rather than a matter of new insights. The idea that film is material became shrill with repetition, while the generic apperceptive discoveries about the operation of memory and attention were numbingly familiar even if each new film brought them to the spectator's awareness in a different way. Indeed, a constant diet of structural film, doting on the processes of one's own memory and attention, could result in a disquieting and uncomfortable sense of solipsistic monotony. This is not to deny the original accomplishment of the first structural films, nor to reject the possibility that exciting structural films can still be made—for example, Peter Greenaway's brilliant *The Falls*. However, the flood of respectable, careful but nongroundbreaking structural films left the impression that the genre was threadbare if not finally empty. And this, combined with the charges of rank formalism, routinization, and lack of imagination, led to a consensus from all sides that structural film was a dead end. Moreover, if the problem with this genre was one of barrenness, this seemed to suggest content as a line or at least a slogan of reclamation.[19]

DECONSTRUCTION

Whereas structural film can be characterized as a genre, deconstruction is more of the nature of an aim or goal that can be pursued in many ways, by many means, and across many different genres. Thus, structural/materialist films can be championed in the name of deconstruction as can found footage films, optically printed films, new talkies, and so on. Deconstruction, in short, is a catchphrase that marks the predominant sensibility of the seventies and eighties in film of the avant-garde variety, and it supplies a major source of energy for such film-making into the present.

Many readers are familiar with the term "deconstruction" from the influential writings of Jacques Derrida. There the concept, roughly speaking, denotes the isolation and explication of what are supposedly the *inevitable* contradictions of a text—that is, the collapse of any attempt to sustain the logical contrareity of such concepts as nature/culture, original/copy, speech/writing, and so on. This is *not* the way in which filmmakers and film critics use the term. Rather, for them to deconstruct is to take apart, to dismantle or, more fashionably, to subvert the dominant conventions of filmmaking. That is, this dismantling usually has a destructive connotation to it.

One deconstructs the conventions of Hollywood editing by mismatching the eyelines in a conversation scene, by failing to show the source of a striking off-screen sound, or by breaking the 180° rule in shooting an action scene. By disregarding these conventions one purportedly subverts the audience's expectations and thereby calls their attention to the putatively conventional and artificial nature of the dominant forms of filmmaking. Like the structural film, deconstruction is underwritten by a zeal for didacticism or at least a presiding metaphor of a learning situation. Furthermore, educating audiences in this way about the contrivances of dominant cinema is thought to be political because it reveals the mechanisms by which ideology is disseminated in the dominant cinema. Deconstructionism answers the call for content, supposedly, by dismantling dominant cinema through supplying spectators with the knowledge necessary to see through its artifice.[20]

Obviously the idea of deconstruction is not completely alien to the project of structural film. Artists in that vein did subvert the approach of dominant cinema in order to reveal to spectators what they thought to be the real nature of film and of the perception of film. But structural filmmakers and their proponents often spoke as if they believed that they were disclosing the *essence* of film and the *nature* of perception. It is this combination of essentialism and naturalism in the structural filmmakers' conception of reflexivity that puts them at odds with the main line of deconstruction in the late seventies and eighties. For most deconstructionists do not believe that film has an essence or that our practices of perception are natural. All is cultural and conventional.[21] Thus, structural film itself has to be deconstructed, for essentialism is politically suspect, a means of mystifying a set of conventions.

Of course, the deconstructionists' emphasis on conventions and codes marks the immense influence of semiology and poststructuralism on the imagination of the seventies and the eighties, whereas phenomenology, cognitive psychology, math, and natural science provided the preferred rhetoric of much structural film. And yet, despite these theoretical (or polemical) differences, the techniques of deconstructionists often grow out of and resemble those of structural filmmaking, though of course the deconstructionist will argue that his political perspective enables his work to avoid charges of formalism and to claim redeeming social content.

One area where deconstructionism and structural film appear close is, as might be expected, in the practice of structural/materialist film. But structural/materialist film did succeed in appropriating the vocabulary of politicized deconstruction, whereas this option was denied to structural film. The simple reason for this is probably that structural/materialists took on this rhetoric first and then refused to be convinced by proponents of structural film who attempted to do likewise.

In any case, the deconstructionist aspect of recent structural/materialist film is in place. In his *Emily—Third Party Speculation* (1979), LeGrice records adjacent off-screen sounds without cutting immediately to their source, for example, to a record player.[22] He claims that this subverts the Hollywood convention of field-reverse-field editing, thereby deconstructing and unmasking Hollywood artifice for the spectator. Whether it is true that Hollywood films always immediately cut to the source of off-screen sounds (horror films? mystery films?) and whether or not viewers of *Emily* experience the critical awakenings LeGrice claims for them is less important than the fact that the rhetoric he uses to justify his artistic choices is politicized deconstruction. For in that he exemplifies the dominant trope of contemporary avant-gardists.

To deconstruct in film is always of necessity to deconstruct something, that is, something else, something other than the deconstruction itself. That object is usually of the nature of a familiar cultural artifact—a preexisting film, genre, TV program, ad, a traditional compositional schema, traditional iconography, or even the conventions of narration. Since deconstruction always requires an object, one of the most literal-minded avenues along which to pursue the deconstructive goal is the found footage film.

A found footage film is one that is composed of old films, photographs, TV programs, or fragments thereof which are rearranged through reediting or rephotography in a way that suggests to many commentators an analogy with collage. Once images are taken out of their original context, dislodged and placed in a new and generally disjunctive setting, the image can be made to appear strange, and initially unnoticed features of it may be said to be unmasked. Imagine taking a close-up of Fay Wray screaming out of *King Kong* and juxtaposing it to an image of a Coke bottle. Displaced to this new context, we will look at this screaming in a fresh light. It will appear bizarre and its contrivance will be manifest. We may wonder how we were ever able to overlook its strangeness.

This is the method of the found footage film. Its potential usefulness for deconstructionism should be apparent; it is a ready means for reassessing and unmasking the significance of familiar iconography and narrative form.

The found footage film predates deconstructionism. It was employed in the thirties in such films as *Rose Hobart* by the surrealist Joseph Cornell, who reedited a Hollywood pot-boiler called *East of Borneo* in such a way that the narrative dissolves and his obsessive infatuation with actress Rose Hobart and her special qualities becomes central. In 1958 Bruce Conner made *A Movie*, a disjunctive compilation of movie fragments that projected a pop art vision of the madness of contemporary civilization rushing toward apocalypse. Conner has continued to work in the found footage style and has proven that the form is the avant-garde approach with the most popular appeal, undoubtedly because even audiences untutored in avant-garde aesthetics can recognize the images in such films and follow the filmmakers' subversions, parodies, and effacements of them. Found footage films can also be found in the structural film tradition in the work of Ken Jacobs whose classic *Tom, Tom the Piper's Son* (1969) involves the analytic rephotographing of a Biograph film made in 1905. *Tom, Tom . . .* and subsequent films by Jacobs, such as *The Doctor's Dream*, provide influential models for contemporary deconstructionists.[23]

Perhaps the influence of Jacobs on deconstructionists is most apparent in the work of J. Hoberman. Hoberman is not only a filmmaker but the most widely published and most influential journalistic critic of avant-garde film today. Working as a resident reviewer for the *Village Voice* in New York City, Hoberman employs the notion of deconstruction overtly in his criticism, praising those films, such as the works of Jacobs' beloved Oscar Micheaux, which appear to Hoberman to transgress the politically repressive conventions of the dominant cinema. Hoberman also brings his war with Hollywood to the editing bench. In *Broken Honeymoon #3*, he reedited an episode of *Bewitched*, a TV sitcom from the sixties. He chopped the shots of the episode into one second lengths and reordered them while taking whatever remained of the shots that were under one second and stringing them in reverse chronological sequence at the end of the film. Commenting on *Broken Honeymoon #3*, a sympathetic critic, Jonathan Buchsbaum, writes

The episode [of *Bewitched*] concerns a visit by one of the in-laws to Dick York's family, but its appeal for Hoberman lay in the sequence when Dick York attempts to show some home movies, but has difficulty with the sound synchronization. He must start the projector several times before he gets synchronization. Clearly, recutting the sitcom, with an optical track, automatically wreaks havoc on the synchronization because of the 26 frame sound advance. Since television and film build their "illusion of reality" on the base of synchronization, Hoberman has "broken" the "honeymoon" usually enjoyed by the audience of such constructions, for the audience must work at reconstituting the union of sound and image.[24]

The importance of the found footage film for aspiring deconstructionists extends beyond the fact that the genre supplies a ready modus operandi for designating the target of one's deconstruction and (literal) intertextual play. The found footage film is economical; it can be built from outtakes and discarded films. This is especially important at a time when rising film costs threaten the extinction of avant-garde film. Also, found footage films have a degree of accessibility that other avant-garde approaches may lack. Among the charges leveled at structural film was the notion that it was elitist as well as too hermetic to sustain general audience interest in avant-garde experimentation. The accessibility of the imagery of the found footage film along with its audience-pleasing parodic potentials make it immediately attractive to the avant-garde polemicist seeking to reach wider audiences. Nor has this aspect of the use of recycled imagery been lost on avant-garde video makers, such as Bruce Tovsky, whose *Invaders* (1983) deconstructs a fifties sci-fi film recorded off his TV set.

The deconstructionist who employs found footage finds his material readymade, so to speak. But one may also remount the type of narrative or genre one wishes to subvert, and in the course of that remounting, through strategies such as exaggeration, repetition, disjunction, oxymoron, and condensation, one can deconstruct as one goes along. An example of this is Manuel DeLanda's *Raw Nerves: A Lacanian Thriller* (1980) which, among other things, deconstructs the *film noir* by foregrounding the paranoid fear of women found in the genre. Jonathan Rosenbaum writes:

The ensuing paranoid plot owes a lot both to *Kiss Me Deadly* and the Mickey Spillane novel it's based on (which furnishes part of the dialogue—although the script is credited to Joan Braderman, Paul Arthur and DeLanda, among others), with iconographic (and graphic) lifts from forties and fifties *noir* as well: shadowy grill patterns on walls, colors like the inside of a fruity Fifties jukebox. In a surprise ending, the off-screen narrating voice of the hero proves to belong to a woman, who declares "Never trust a first person pronoun" before shooting him dead.[25]

Of course, the targets of the deconstructionist need not be the artifacts of popular culture but those of high culture as well. In *Misconception* (1977), Marjorie Keller offers a subversion of the child-birth film, a subgenre of the personal, avant-garde cinema made famous by Stan Brakhage. In what Keller calls "a loving critique of [Brakhage's] *Window Water Baby Moving*," she injects far more ominousness than the celebratory Brakhage in her vision of the "blessed event" via foreboding images of the demolition of a house.[26] Perhaps these anxious premonitions should be explicated as proto-feminist reservations about the male outlook that dominates the most well-known examples of the childbirth genre.

One strategy of deconstruction might be thought of as the autodestruction of the film itself through the staged collision of the elements within it. Michelle Citron's *Daughter Rite* (1978), for example, mixes documentary and fictional modes in a way that is said to call both forms of representation into question. E. A. Kaplan writes:

The use of home movies and old photographs is crucial as a device that establishes continuity through time and that reflects the fiction-making urge that, as Metz and Heath have shown, pervades even the documentary. Used as unproblematic representations, the past images function to seal individual change instead of providing evidence of the way women and their bodies are constructed by the signifying practices of both the social and the psychological institutions in which they are embedded. Interestingly enough, this construction makes a main theme in Michelle Citron's *Daughter Rite* (1978) where the slowing down of home movies enables us to see that the representations are far from an "innocent recording," that the process of making the movies itself functions to construct the place for the female child.[27]

Whether the theoretical premises that Kaplan mobilizes above are correct, of course, is not of particular significance historically, for Kaplan has accurately captured Citron's deconstructionist intentions. Those intentions, indeed, are even more explicit in the next group of avant-gardists to be reviewed—the practitioners of the new talkie.

THE NEW TALKIES

As the title of this genre implies, the new talkies are dominated by language. Indeed, as a first approximation, one might say that an identifying feature of the new talkie is that in this genre language is ultimately more important than image. Language has often been a matter of central concern to structural filmmakers—for example, Frampton's *nostalgia* and his *Poetic Justice* (1971), and Snow's *Rameau's Nephew* (1974) and his *So Is This* (1982). However, structural filmmakers appear primarily concerned with the limitations and possibilities of language (e.g., the polysemy of words and their materiality) as a form of representation as such. Practitioners of the new talkie, on the other hand, are not only preoccupied with these issues but also with using language to say something, something of political-theoretical-cultural significance. That is, key examples of the new talkie—such as Peter Wollen's and Laura Mulvey's *Riddles of the Sphinx* (1977); Anthony McCall's and Andrew Tyndall's *Argument* (1978); and McCall's, Tyndall's, Claire Pajaczkowska's and Jane Weinstock's *Sigmund Freud's Dora* (1980)—tend to espouse politicized versions of semiology and poststructuralism, that are believed to thereby become didactically available to audiences through film viewing. The goal of the majority of new talkies is to educate spectators in the role of "signifying practices" in the maintenance of political domination that is not only economic but sexual. This is what the new talkie has to tell us. Thus, unlike the structural film, the new talkie utilizes discourse—while also interrogating it—to tell us, putatively, about the content of our iives.

Another significant difference between the new talkie and the structural film regards narrative. In the main, the structural film was antinarrative or oblivious

to it. Structural film was far more concerned with the visual and cinematic
elements of films. However, in the new talkie, narrative is again center stage.
This phenomenon is yet again another example of the revolt against structural
film in the name of content. That is not to say that the new talkies are predominantly engaged in telling stories (though some of them do tell stories). Rather,
in the new talkie narration itself as a form of representation with purported social
significance is a fundamentally recurring topic. Stories are presented to be deconstructed as in the feminist film *Sigmund Freud's Dora*, which rereads Freud's
case study of the same name in order to plumb the lacunae of the original. In
this respect, the new talkie strives to be essayistic, though the topic of the essay
is often narrative. Specimen-stories are deconstructively subverted to unmask
their structural, political, and psychosexual presuppositions.

An important influence on the new talkie is the work of Jean Luc Godard. In
Godard proponents of the new talkie found a model for a cinema that is at once
intellectual, discursive, oppositional, and political. In Godard's work, such as
Le Gai Savoir (1968), the possibilities and vagaries of language and discourse
are interrogated and challenged, as they are in structural film; however, the
relations of language and signs to social reality are also subject to scrutiny and
criticism. Thus, in the jargon preferred by practitioners of new talkies, the
signifier (e.g., the word, image, and so on) is investigated by Godard, at the
same time that the signified (here best thought of first as what the signifier refers
to and then metaphorically expanded to comprehend reality, or socially constructed reality) is not forgotten and, thereby, is available for political analysis.[28]

The new talkie also derives stylistic strategies from Godard. Just as Godard
mixes documentary with fictions and facts with fancies in *Two Or Three Things
I Know About Her* (1966) and studio shooting with cinema verite style in *Passion*,
so the new talkie favors pastiche. The parents of the new talkie, Peter Wollen
and Laura Mulvey, in many of their works—including *Penthesilea* (1974), *Riddles of the Sphinx* (1977), and *Amy!* (1982)—divide the film into segments marked
by different styles and often by different media (film, video, painting, photography, theater, and so on). The effect of this pastiche is supposed to be the
dawning awareness that the audience is confronting representations whose structure is contingent rather than necessary. At the same time, these segments—
stories, lectures, documentation—do not segue into a unified discursive flow;
they are juxtapositional in a way that suggests that they are mutually inflective
or commentative. Yet, the substance of those comments must be deciphered by
an actively participating spectator. In other words, this disjunctive style, like
Godard's, functions to raise questions that the audience must wrestle with.
Moreover, this maieutic effect is, of course, what many thought to be Godard's
most salutary accomplishment.[29]

The films of Jean-Marie Straub and Daniele Huillet also provide a touchstone
for the new talkie. In films like *Moses and Aaron* (1975), an adaptation from
Schoenberg, and *Class Relations* (1983), a screen version of Kafka's *Amerika*,
Straub/Huillet evince an interest in radically remounting and, thereby, radically

reinterpreting known cultural artifacts in a way that brings the very question of interpretation to the fore insofar as Straub/Huillet's austere versions of these works subvert the expectations of viewers familiar with the earlier works. That is, radical reinterpretation is supposed to reveal the fact that received ideas about such works are also interpretations. Similarly, new talkies often play off known originals—*Penthesilea* enacts Kleist's play as a mime; *Sigmund Freud's Dora* subversively retells Freud's account with a feminist's eye for incongruities, interspersing the narrative with telling sexist TV ads and porno films and flanking the whole proceedings with feminist meditations.[30] In each case the act of radical reinterpretation is predicated on the desire to disrupt complacency toward accepted interpretations and, thereby, to reveal the interests believed to be behind those interpretations.[31]

Sally Potter's *Thriller* is arguably the most successful of the new talkies. It retells *La Boheme* as a detective story, but as the film proceeds the question of "Why did Mimi die?" demands an answer greater in scope than the identification, in the style of a "whodunit," of a single culprit. Rather, we are to understand the meaning of that death in terms of what it epitomizes about the operation of a capitalistic and sexist, psycho-sexual system. While simultaneously deconstructing the detective genre and the operatic melodrama, *Thriller* offers forays into Lacanian psychoanalysis, the privileged metaphysic of the new talkie, in order to discover a feminist explanation for Mimi's murder that accounts for both its narrative necessity in the opera and for the social significance of that very plot structure. Mimi

. . . finally understands why she had to die. Had she lived, she and Rodolfo would have borne children and she would have had to work even harder to feed them. Seen in this light motherhood is not romantic, and again, it makes the woman a subject; children activate *her* desire, and she is not able simply to be the object of male passion. She had to die because "an old seamstress would not be considered the proper subject of a love story."[32]

At present, the future of the new talkie is uncertain. Part of the reason for this may be that the new talkie did not succeed on its own terms. Politically activist proponents of the new talkie sought to reach wider audiences than the limited number of cognoscenti informed enough and willing enough to follow the refined dialectics of the gallery aesthetics of structural film. But simply trading art theory for political (content-oriented) theory—the amalgam of Lacan, Althusser, and feminism—did not make the new talkie either more accessible or more attractive to nonspecialized audiences. After all, one has to be extremely well versed in Marxist psychoanalytic theories of representation to follow these films, especially since the tenets of this philosophy were, in typical avant-garde style, only elliptically alluded to rather than coherently spelled out, with appropriate background information, in the films in question. This, of course, raises the issue of how didactically successful such films can be. But perhaps even more pressing is the possibility that didacticism, the major mode of avant-gardism since the sixties, is itself a problem for filmmakers seeking wider audiences. With this in mind, it seems that some proponents of the new talkie are headed in the direction of straight narrative feature production. Wollen and Mulvey have made *The Bad Sister* for British TV, while Bette Gordon, creator of the new talkie *Empty Suitcase*, has directed *Variety*. From dominating the avant-garde at the turn of the decade, the new talkie presently appears in danger of extinction.

A DIGRESSION: YVONNE RAINER

In the discussion of the new talkie, mention of one figure whom many may feel is the exemplar of the genre, namely, Yvonne Rainer, has been omitted. However, though Rainer's work bears affinities to the new talkie and though it was influential for and respected by practitioners of the new talkie, it is distinct. For in Rainer's work neither didacticism nor affirmation of the tenets of politicized poststructuralist theory is central. Instead, her program to date appears, broadly speaking, novelistic.

Of avant-garde filmmakers who emerged in the seventies, Rainer is the major filmmaker at work today. She came to film from a career as a choreographer, in which, during the sixties, she gained a reputation as the leading figure of the postmodern dance movement.[33] That movement, eschewing the preoccupation with the emotions found in the choreography of artists like Graham and Humphrey, was rigorously minimalist. Rainer turned from dance to film, in part, in order to find a medium that she thought would be better attuned to the exploration of the emotional life than was dance.

From an art world and a dance world background of minimalism, Rainer entered an avant-garde American film scene dominated by structural film. Yet her own films—such as *Lives of Performers* (1972), *Film About a Woman Who* . . . (1974), and *Kristina Talking Pictures* (1976)—pushed against the prevailing tide, offering narratives, albeit modernist, distanced, and disjunctive ones, of the lives of characters. Her films are narratives profuse with inner dialogue, comment, and memories, layered with quotations, observations, and contesting voices. During the seventies, Rainer was the single major American avant-garde filmmaker concerned with narrative and with the extensive use of language (spoken, written, and generally elliptical) to broach substantial issues about such things as the battle of the sexes. Rainer's allegiance to narrative and to the substantive use of language, along with the implicit feminism of her concerns with sexual power relations, inclined proponents of the new talkie to regard her as both a forerunner and a fellow traveler.

The influence of Godard also supplies a point of convergence between Rainer and the new talkie. For example, she remains particularly impressed by his Brechtian refusal to permit audiences to identify empathetically with characters. Thus, in certain of her films she will have the same character played by different performers in order to block empathy while also using printed statements or deadpan voice-over expressions of inner feelings to cool our engagement with the characters. For though Rainer wishes us to explore with her the contours of contemporary life and feeling, she wants that exploration to be detached, sober, and tough-minded, aware of complexity, conflict, and contradiction and not homogenized by strong reactive emotions.

Despite the points of tangency between Rainer and proponents of the new talkies, her work differs from theirs in its refusal to embrace and to promote a unified theory as the perspective from which to answer all the pressing moral, political, and sexual problems of contemporary life. This is apparent in her recent film *Journeys from Berlin/1971* (1980). The film can be viewed as a choir of disparate, but associatively related conversations, secondarily supported by visuals that illustrate, baldly represent or are associated with material with the discourse in the text. The voices of the conversation include an exposition of the history of the Baader-Meinhof terrorists (mostly in printed titles); selections from a morally concerned, teenage woman's diary; a stylized enactment of a psychiatric session; an offscreen discussion between a couple about revenge and terrorism; memoirs of Russian anarchists; an interview with Rainer's nephew; a videotaped "letter" from Rainer to a fictive mother. Out of this welter of material certain themes emerge about the incommensurability of private experience versus public life, about the psychiatric examination of motives and its relation to the evaluation of political action, about the fractured nature of the self and the moral significance of this. These issues are attacked from a number of perspectives— through reminiscences, dramatic enactments, lectures, and examples—in a way that suggests a protracted dialogue. The film does not resolve these problems by means of an implied theory, in the fashion of the new talkie, but rather presents an affecting tapestry of personal, moral, and political quandaries, sensitively reflective of the paralyzing knots and contradictions confronting someone who realistically yet ethically seeks to assess the significance of contemporary political life.[34]

PUNK FILM

As must already be evident, the development of avant-garde film over the past two decades is marked by a high seriousness, intellectualism, and a penchant for debate that frequently reaches academic proportions. The emergence of punk film in the late seventies is an explicit rejection of this. Many of the works of this genre are modeled on low-budget Hollywood films, signalling an interest in action rather than thought and abandoning the burdens of reflexivity in the name of entertainment.

Growing out of new wave music, punk filmmaking projected a similar view of the world, one that was sensationalist but that lacked affect or moral sensibility. The punk world combines qualities of violence and detachment. It is populated by egotistical characters, grasping, unashamed of their wants, undisturbed by the reactions their often crude frankness might elicit. They are cold and morally unresponsive. Their urban environment, often the lower East Side of Manhattan, is pictured in a way that makes it appear like a bombed-out no-man's land sometime in the future. The punk film portrays a kind of postapocalyptic state of nature where life is nasty, brutish, but immediate, and where the punk hero survives through the sort of dumb sang-froid found in a Mike Hammer. Punk heroines are often pure machismo. Other denizens of this world are hysterics wallowing in alienated, incoherent, and paralytic remorse, somnabulists, and representatives of the bourgeoisie, rendered in vicious caricature.

In 1978, the New Cinema was opened in the East Village in New York by Eric Mitchell, Becky Johnstone, and James Nares. Here films were showcased via video projection. Films were also shown in bars, clubs, and cabarets in lower Manhattan. The punk filmmakers wanted popular venues outside what they believed was the staid avant-garde circuit.

A surprising number of long films were produced very quickly, most often in the inexpensive format of super-8. Mitchell made *Kidnapped* and *Red Italy* in 1978; the married team of Beth B. and Scott B. made *G-Man* and *Black Box* in 1979 and *The Trap Door* in 1980; Becky Johnstone made *Sleepless Nights* in 1980; while Vivian Dick made *Guerillere Talks* and *She Had Her Gun Already* in 1978.

In *Black Box*, a twentyish young man, fresh from his girlfriend's arms, is kidnapped in front of an apartment building somewhere in the East Village. He is brought to a torture chamber where the minions of a secret religious organization plan to purify him using knouts, cudgels, chains, and electric shocks. The film is both a homage to sleaze and to adolescent images of evil. The villains, with thick New York accents, recall hectoring parental nagging more than the stage diction of the evil-doers of traditional B-films. Mixed with the broad shtick are sadomasochistic interludes in which the boy is beaten by his maniacal captors. The torture appears to be meant to titillate but at the same time it is comic, until finally the naked, bound, and bleeding captive is thrust into a black box, and he and the audience are assaulted at length with abrasive electric sound waves that provide an effective, horrific symbol of totalitarian repression.

The levels of irony in the film are complicated. Banality in both film and life is alternately embraced, celebrated, and satirized while the sadomasochism signals an unresolved fascination with sexual repression at the same time that such repression is derided. The sophomoric irony appears to be a disguise for a great deal of pain, which is both denied and expressed through the enactments of comic/horrific victimization.

The punk film movement was involved in a war on two fronts, rejecting mainstream Hollywood professionalism, on the one hand, and the still influential structural avant-garde, on the other. Films were originally made in the super-8 format not simply because it was inexpensive but because the primitive, amateurish look was a flag of identity belligerently flown in the face of Hollywood polish. Pariah genres, like low-budget crime films and shoe-string sci-fi, were cannibalized, their bad taste, outrageous logic, and crudity further exaggerated in such a way that the cheapness and mindlessness of these wretcheds of the film industry were intensified to the point where they could function as symbols of the punk self. At a stylistic level, the exaggerated adaptations of pulp genres stated themes of transgression of norms, of outsideness, of the valorization of the authentic, even romantically heroic, significance of bad taste. The punk filmmakers exploited the brazenly antireflective address of the genres while also expropriating the raw if rather crude energy available in their structure. At the same time the violence endemic to the Hollywood genres could be rechanneled in stories that plotted revolutionary acts against the bourgeois culture.

Like the new German cinema, punk film has an ambivalent relation to Hollywood, whose imagery it refashions into emblems of the self, projecting the signs of identity for a new generation. Often, this refashioning takes the form of parody and allusion. Like postmodernist art in other media, the punk filmmaker often gives the impression of cobbling his or her intentionally amateurish and rough hewn films out of fragments of a defunct culture—art as the practice of referring to shards and pieces of a once-vibrant civilization; art in the ruins. Into the tempos of action genres, punk filmmakers imploded long stretches of dead, hanging-around time in order to canonize the cadences of life lived outside the margins of the workaday bourgeois world.

The parodic dimension of punk recyclings of genres both resembles deconstructionism and does not. On the one hand, it is transgressive and subversive. However, this seems less a matter of teaching the audience to be aware of Hollywood conventions—though that may happen—than a means of expressing a disdain and a superiority for an established culture. The choice of action genres, as well, relates to another key punk theme: the anesthetization of feeling. Punk films seem dominated by characters who refuse to be touched emotionally or moved. By taking Hollywood genres notable for their emotionally affecting potential and their immediacy and by distancing them through low-key irony, punk filmmakers raise the theme of anesthetization to the level of style.

In opposition to the structural film, punk film aligned itself with narrative content even though the Hollywood prototypes it commandeered were subversively remodeled if not deconstructed. Moreover, the addresss of the punk film was expressive rather than reflexive, its point directed at finding objective correlatives for the textures and feelings of a certain way of being-in-the-world, the alienated ethos of the urban punk.

One of the most successful punk films is Slava Tsukerman's *Liquid Sky*, which was theatrically released in 1983. An independent film made by Soviet emigres, J. Hoberman describes it as the

. . . not unfamiliar witch's brew of decadent fashion, smacked-out club life and political terrorism. The latter, appropriately, is extraterrestial: attracted by the presence of heroin, an alien spacecraft hovers over a Lower East Side tenement, apparently drawing energy from human sexual secretions and, in any case, killing at climax the hapless lovers of the rangy, petulant model (Anne Carlisle) who lives inside.[35]

The self-consciously outlandish science fiction conceit, the apocalyptic ending, the alternately amateurish, stilted, and affectless acting and the juxtaposition of glitter and squalor mark *Liquid Sky* as pure punk as does the humor of the dialogue, which is based on a mix of parody, naivete, and ruthlessness. Most horrifying in this allegory of alienated sexuality is that survival and power are based in the "ability" not to be excited sexually, but to be anesthetized. For to have an orgasm leads to death by an intergalactic ray. Sexual lethargy, the faculty to be unmoved and untouched, to be in an emotional deep-freeze, is the closest approximation of freedom—which is equated with survival—in *Liquid Sky*. The film is composed of brutal sexual victimizers—sex as rape—on the one hand, and the victimized, emotionally anesthetized Carlisle on the other. Urban romance has rarely been envisioned as so completely and unredemptively savage.

The punk film flourished during a period in which the rediscovery of the sleazy, the grubby, and the debris of modern life was also being celebrated in the broader culture, for example, in the weekly TV program *Saturday Night Live* and in its offshoots like *The Blues Brothers*. Thus it is no surprise that, at present, the aesthetic proclivities of the punk film are, in modified form, finding their way into the broader distribution networks of commercial film. The current high visibility of *Repo Man* (1984), for example, suggests that the punk sensibility is on its way to finding mainstream expression.

THE PSYCHODRAMA

The American avant-garde film was inaugurated in the forties by films that, under the probable influence of Jean Cocteau's *Blood of a Poet*, presented themselves as dream states or as the fantasies of the protagonists. Maya Deren's *Meshes of the Afternoon* (1943) is the reverie of a young wife who envisions the death of her virgin self at the hands of her emerging sexual self, while Kenneth Anger's *Fireworks* (1947) is an imaginary testament to a homosexual's coming of age. In the psychodrama, the filmmaker creates a cinematic dream work in which, through fragmented narrative and charged imagery, anxieties and wishes are portrayed symbolically. The rise of structural film momentarily eclipsed the acceptability of psychodrama. But the yearning for a return to content, in reaction to the structural film, has predictably led young filmmakers to reassess the potentials of the psychodrama.

The mode of address of the structural film, as that of much deconstructionism and of many new talkies, is didactic. The psychodrama, on the other hand, reverts to a much more familiar mode of address, that of expression. The psychodrama presents a situation in which feeling tones, indicative of emotions, anxieties, wishes, and moods are emphasized. The audience responds by recognizing the particular emotional colorations by which the filmmaker characterizes the situation portrayed. At the very least the spectator's interest in the film is in how a certain life or a certain situation feels. Some might even claim that the spectator is moved to share whatever mood or emotion the film projects or even to be infected by it. But in the psychodrama the currency of the discourse is primarily feeling rather than theory.

In James Nares' *Waiting for the Wind* (1979) a solitary sleeper lies fitfully on a mattress on the floor of a tenement apartment. Suddenly furniture—hurled at the walls with tremendous force—flies about the room, propelled by some invisible force. It is a telekinetic spectacle of the sort one sees in films of demonic possession. But there is no Satan here to be exorcised. One interprets the violence as a dream, fantasy, or hallucinogenic state of the protagonist. The rage inscribed in the whirling furniture incongruously contrasts to the vulnerability we attribute, at first, to the sleeper. This juxtaposition projects a strong sense of the magical thinking involved in the belief in the omnipotence of the will, here appropriately situated in a context suggestive of urban loneliness, alienation, and helplessness.

The area in which psychodrama has especially come to the fore is that of feminist filmmaking. Feminists have found in the psychodrama a means of communicating the particular anxieties they suffer under patriarchal society. At the same time the genre can be used to symbolize their wishes and desires, as well as their accusations. Through the psychodrama, the feminist filmmaker can address emotional questions in their own terms rather than in the didactic, theoretical voice of the new talkie.

Discussing Su Friedrich's dreamlike journey, *Cool Hands, Warm Heart* (1979), Lindley Hanlon says that it

. . . is a defiantly feminist film, chronicling in rite after ritual the deep violence which women have accepted as part of their daily attempts to refashion their nature into a cleaned-up, pared-down image of glossy magazine mannequins. In stark, contrasty, grainy, black-and-white silent images, we watch a woman travel through a series of encounters with other women who perform daily female rituals on a raised, public platform where passers-by observe them awkwardly and curiously. In these street-performer, side-show acts a woman juggles a weapon (razor, knife or scissors) against her body or other natural entity, a piece of fruit. Out in the open, out of the bathroom closet, so to speak, for all to see, shaving legs and underarms, paring an apple, and cutting off a braid of hair look like bizarre, sado-masochistic acts that one would have to be perverse and deranged to perform.[36]

If *Cool Hands, Warm Heart* expressively reveals the latent violence and cruelty in ordinary womanly practices in patriarchy, then Leslie Thornton's *Jennifer, Where Are You?* (1981) explores the ambivalences of growing up female. The central image is of a close-up of a very young girl playing with lipstick, presumably her mother's. The film begins as a nostalgic, humorous memory. Perhaps the girl is hiding in the attic as she plays, smudging lipstick all over her face, playing at being Mommy. Offscreen, we hear a voice (her father's) calling her. As the voice repeats, it seems to become angrier and angrier. What started as a pleasant memory begins to fill with anxiety. We begin to realize that the girl's play is really preparation for the role and costuming she will have to master to succeed on male terms in modern society. The play takes on burdensome connotations. As the girl's features grow consternated, she unknowingly signals to us the ambiguity of her "harmless" play acting.

The psychodrama is a serviceable form for feminists because it can express pain and anxiety while at the same time it can allegorically accuse the social formations that give rise to that pain and anxiety. Writing of *Marasmus* (1982), by Laura Ewig and Betzy Bromberg, Paul Arthur notes

The central figure of *Marasmus* moves through a series of brightly hallucinatory spaces, alternating roughly between the insular offices of a sterile skyscraper, bleak industrial sites, and even bleaker canyon terrain. There are multiple references to and metaphors for birth, death and abortion. The protagonist's body lies near an oil pipeline covered by a clear plastic shroud, the still born of this blight or its murdered victim. The relation between industry, female reproduction, and disease is signalled by the film's title, a children's ailment found in urban slums and rural poverty areas—almost entirely in the Third World—and caused by gross malnutrition; a disease where infants acquire the blank inanition, pained movement, and wrinkled skin of the aged, with bloated bellies that grotesquely recall pregnancy. The plastic shroud, a dry bush held in front of the woman's face, and skin shown through water, all suggest an attempt to empathize with this condition of starvation.[37]

THE NEW SYMBOLISM

The options explored in the reemerging psychodrama are an element in a larger phenomenon, the revival of interest in imagery not in terms of its deconstructive significance but because of an interest in its expressive and/or aesthetic qualities. The psychodrama pursues a concern with expressive qualities, employing quasi-narrative and dreamlike structures. However, the current interest in imagery need not occur in narrative contexts, nor need the image play be notable solely in terms of the projection of expressive qualities, that is, qualities associated with human feelings, such as anger, anxiety, fearfulness, and so on. In Pat O'Neill's work, as Paul Arthur points out, there is a recurring imagistic theme in which the natural and the mechanical are conflated.[38] Through optical processing, in an O'Neill film like *Saugus Series* (1976), "natural elements such as clouds move with the speed or rhythm of mechanical objects; water is granted the colors of an industrial paint job; a potted cactus soars like an airplane."[39] Thus in O'Neill's work the viewer attends to a flow of images, remarking upon the arresting and unexpected way in which O'Neill qualitatively characterizes the objects he depicts. Water may suddenly appear metallic or a piece of paper organic. Noting these aesthetic appearances becomes, in short, the focus of the spectator's preoccupation.

This concern with image play and with the projection of expressive and aesthetic properties is a major motive for Stuart Sherman, whose twenty or so short films represent one of the most original developing bodies of filmmaking today. Sherman is a performance artist. He specializes in a form of solo that he calls "spectacles." Most often he stands behind a folding table, like a magician. On the table, he arrays small objects—toys, paper clips, pieces of paper, glasses, cards, pocket-sized souvenirs—which he manipulates, for example, grouping all the similar objects together, touching every object with every other object, or proposing visual puns. The spectator follows these spectacles by catching onto the patterns of association that underlie Sherman's manipulations of objects, his image play. At times these associations are metaphorical but they are often simply systematic, the following through of a formal plan such as changing the position of every object on the table until they are all spatially reversed.

Turning from performance art to film, Sherman continues to be concerned with image play. *Flying* (1979), a film that is only a minute long, is a strong example of his procedure. The second shot is of a metal railing—an airport bannister—that runs horizontally across the screen; on the left, a hand mysteriously holds a suitcase handle, without a suitcase. The camera moves rapidly along the railing from left to right. Then there is a cut to a shot of the plane taking off in the same direction. This shot is executed from the perspective of a passenger inside the plane. As the camera rises at a gradually expanding acute angle, the hand is superimposed on the image, the handle still without a bag. This is an elegantly elliptical symbol for travel, charged expressively by the haunting partial absence of the traveler and his belongings. The image deftly and economically makes the point that they are now elsewhere.

Sherman's films are sometimes like short poems and sometimes like riddles that call attention to the expressive qualities of objects or that urge us to encounter familiar objects in a new light—comparing ice-skating rinks with diminutive ice-cubes, for example, in *Skating* (1978). By calling attention to the qualitative dimension of the world, Sherman reacts against the structural filmmaker's preoccupation with the qualities of film (or of filmic perception). In this way, Sherman's work is concerned with the return to content, though in this context "content" does not have the political connotations found in many contemporary filmmakers. Moreover, Sherman's reliance upon the associative play of images enables him to avoid the problems of didactic address that not only tends to take an academic approach to much academic film but to alienate it from wider audiences. Sherman's films are imaginative games or puzzles, in which any sensitive viewer can take part; they afford a forum for aesthetic and interpretive play on the part of spectators. Sally Banes notes that in *Roller Coaster/Reading* (1979)

Sherman proposes, through editing and parallel camera movement, that the act of reading is exhilarating, like riding a roller coaster. The conjunction of the two actions is established in the first shot, in which Sherman gets into the car of the roller coaster without looking up from the book he is engrossed in reading. In a series of symmetrical

camera movements and compositions, a bookcase and the white wooden structure of a
roller coaster are scanned and compared, with the camera moving upward or to the right
(as if reading), or zooming in and out. The final pair of shots shows Sherman still reading,
walking into the enormous roller coaster structure (whose double doorway resembles an
open book) as the bookcase recedes.[40]

The theme of play pervades the films of Ericka Beckman, a leading figure in
the return to expressive or qualitative imagery. In *We Imitate; We Break Up*
(1978), a super-8 color, sound film, Beckman allegorically portrays the tensions
she sees in male/female relationships through juxtaposed imagery. The film
begins by cutting between the imaginary male protagonist—a pair of puppet legs
manipulated by a rope and called Mario—and a young woman, played by Beckman, dressed as a schoolgirl. At first the girl imitates all of the puppet's movements, as if she too were on a string. The schoolgirl outfit and the imitation
motif are symbols of being dominated. The man and woman play kickball, first
cooperatively, then vengefully. In the middle of this symbolic quarrel, the girl
takes the ball and comically runs away while the legs, now gigantic and threat-
ening, pursue her interminably. A male figure bowls the kickball into animated
household furniture that jumps aside into piles, literalizing the idea that the
relationship has broken up. The songs that accompany the images are repetitive,
like childish chants, while the images themselves are quite simple and easily
understood in terms of their symbolic import. Shots, for example of the girl
''running away'' are repeated endlessly so that they will be comprehended as
metaphors. But also, their obsessive recurrence expressively indicates fixations
that Beckman strives to ironize and distance through comedy and repetition. Yet
the childhood references and the clarity of exposition give the piece an overall
feeling of lightness rather than of brooding.[41]

Of course, in speaking of the return of the expressive or otherwise qualitative
use of imagery, a single genre is not being discussed, but a refocusing of interest
that can cut across genres. For example, one might make a found footage film,
in the tradition of Cornell's *Rose Hobart*, whose purpose was not deconstructive
but expressive. Conner's recent *Valse Triste* is a good example of this. Yet even
though it is not isolatable to a genre, the discussion of a renewal of interest in
expressive or qualitative imagery is not totally amorphous. For this renewal of
interest takes place against a backdrop of both structural film and cinematic
deconstructionism, which were concerned with images primarily in terms of their
functioning as signs. Images were presented and were to be viewed at an analytic
remove, like specimens under a microscope. This stance toward imagery is part
and parcel of the tendency toward didacticism that has dominated the avant-
garde imagination for two decades. The reinstatement of the image as a locus
of expressive and aesthetic properties and as a symbol to be engaged in terms
of interpretive play may supply a way out of the didactic impasse.

Diagnostically, it is helpful to note that the didacticism of structural film and
later of cinematic deconstruction corresponds to the rise of the academic approach

to film after the boom in movie connoisseurship in the sixties. Supporters of structural film and then deconstructionism were often academics involved themselves in trying to discover the nature of the medium or the symbol system about which they sought to erect a discipline. It should come as no surprise, then, that they had a special interest in films that were concerned with an enterprise similar to their own (and also, for that reason, eminently teachable). Moreover, it is easy to understand how, in this context, didactic rhetoric would be positively reinforced. Thus, even when deconstructionists claimed a political content for their work, in opposition to the supposedly contentless structural film, the preoccupation with the model of film as a lesson in the operation of symbol systems continued. Reflexive didacticism remained the presiding metaphor of avant-garde filmmaking.

But it is now quite some time since the movie boom led to the intensive study of film. We have examined the processes of filmmaking in academic writing and reflexive filmmaking for nearly twenty years. In regard to avant-garde filmmaking, it may be the case that the time for reflecting on the processes of filmmaking—even where that reflection is political—is past. The time has come again to use those processes to make images that are expressive and aesthetic, to make narratives and psychodramas, political and personal, that reflect first and foremost on life and the world rather than primarily on the medium and the sign. At present, the avant-garde film is in a state of crisis. The dominant movements of the last two decades appear to have either exhausted themselves or ground to a halt. There is no telling what will happen.

NOTES

1. Throughout I am making the assumption that to the extent that one would want to speak of postmodern film, one would want to restrict one's compass to avant-garde film. For an argument denying the label "postmodern" to commercial film, see my "The Future of Allusion: Hollywood in the Seventies (And Beyond)," *October* 20 (Spring 1982).

2. From the above, the reason should be clear as to why I want to restrict the application of "postmodernist" to films of the late seventies and eighties. For immediately prior to that period, the avant-garde film entertained a modernist aesthetic via the structural film. Obviously, the postmodernist moment could only emerge *after* the modernist interlude.

3. The reader should not assume that these labels are standard throughout the film world; they are partly borrowed and partly of my own invention.

4. For example, it does not include the efforts of autobiographical filmmakers such as Jonas Mekas or Howard Guttenplan. These have not been considered in my review primarily because their work, which is often quite striking, appears to me to be concerned with issues that predate the rise of structural film and is, therefore, not part of the dialectical narrative of antistructural film. Similarly, Brakhage, who in one sense is very antistructural and who continues to make exciting films in the wake of that movement, is not part of the story I have to tell.

5. For example, M. Duras, C. Ackerman, and C. Schneemann, among others.

6. P. Adams Sitney, "Structural Film," anthologized in *Film Culture Reader*, ed. Sitney (New York: Praeger, 1970), p. 326.

7. This is a major category in P. Adams Sitney's *Visionary Film* (New York: Oxford University Press, 1974 and 1979).

8. A third kind of approach that is often called "structural" but which emphasizes neither shape nor system involves showing long, uninterrupted takes of locales bereft of narrative or dramatic interest, for example, Andy Warhol's *Empire* (1964). I suspect that the reasons for calling such films structural are twofold. First, the decision that generates the film can certainly be called minimal while also denying the moment-to-moment expressivity of the filmmaker. And, second, the choice of such a strategy throws the spectator into an apperceptive stance, reflecting upon the way his attention is drawn when it is not guided by the interests of narrative, drama, or allegory. Thus, if such films are to be called structural, it is because they promote a kind of apperceptive reflexivity in the spectator.

Needless to say, though I have spoken of the shape, system, and single image approaches as distinct, they are not mutually exclusive, and they can all appear in a single film, for example, Ernie Gehr's *Serene Velocity* (1970).

9. In terms of psychology, I have in mind the popularity of books such as R. L. Gregory's *Eye and Brain* and *The Intelligent Eye*. One difference between the sixties and the seventies, it may be noted, is a shift from the preeminent concern with perception to a concern with language, a shift, moreover, that is reflected in the respective fortunes, with the intelligentsia, of phenomenology followed by semiotics.

10. Annette Michelson, "Toward Snow," *The Avant-Garde Film*, ed. P. Adams Sitney (New York: New York University Press, 1978), p. 175.

11. Throughout the sixties and the seventies a film like *Zorn's Lemma* would have been described as theoretical, suggesting that such a film actually proposes a theoretical argument. This notion that avant-garde films literally make theories continues into the present. I do not believe that this rhetoric, often employed by critics in the process of explicating a film, is accurate; I prefer to say that the relation of such films to theory is better characterized by saying that generally such films allude or otherwise refer to theories. My case for this approach is stated in my "Avant-garde Film and Film Theory," *Millennium Film Journal* 4/5 (Summer/Fall 1979): 135–45.

In this essay I am writing as a historian and a critic, not as a theoretician. If I present the theoretical presuppositions of film movements uncritically, it is not because I believe them but because my task here is to help the reader understand these movements in terms of what the filmmakers believed they were doing. As a theoretician I have grave reservations about all the various theories that filmmakers presupposed in the period under consideration.

12. Sitney, *Visionary Film*, p. 438.

13. Of course, it remains an open question as to how didactically viable such films really are. For it would seem that only viewers steeped in avant-garde polemics could recognize and decipher the allusions to film theory made by such films and, thereby, "learn" what the film wants to tell them. But it is not obvious that such a process is really a matter of learning insofar as the spectator must already know what he or she is supposed to be taught.

14. See Joanna Kiernan, "Two Films by Malcolm LeGrice," *Millennium Film Journal* 3 (Winter/Spring 1979): 56–71.

15. See Peter Gidal, "Theory and Definition of Structural/Materialist Film," in *Structural Film Anthology*, ed. Gidal (London: British Film Institute, 1976).

16. See Lindley Hanlon, "Collision Course: Ken Kobland's Optical Prints," *Millennium Film Journal* 7/8/9 (Fall/Winter 1980–81): 253–59.

17. The most acerbic of these criticisms can be found in Gary Doberman's "New York Cut the Crap," *CinemaNews* (Spring 1980).

18. Perhaps the reason for this was because in this genre the mode of articulation more closely resembles a rebus than an essay. This may place limitations on how specific a point it is possible to make about the nature of memory or attention. That is, general themes rather than refinements of themes may be all that can be expected in this sort of avant-garde symbol system. Refinement may require the kind of logical connectives, contrast, process of conjecture, experiment (or report of experiments), and refutation that is unsuitable to an avant-garde genre committed to an elliptical, allusive, intentionally disorienting, and initially obscure mode of presentation.

19. It is also true that the structural film was based upon certain expectations whose failure to be realized may have influenced the decline of the movement. The structural film emerged from the gallery scene connected with minimalism. Undoubtedly it was hoped that structural film would become as financially viable as minimalist painting and sculpture. However, the galleries either were unwilling or unable to turn structural film into a collectible on a par with paintings and sculpture. The reproducibility of film along with the questions of how a collector would appropriately display such an "object" were obvious problems. The growing awareness of the limitations of the economic prospects of structural film correlates with the dissipation of the energy behind the movement. Moreover, filmmakers had to turn to the academy rather than to the art world for support. And this, of course, has led some to propose economic reasons for the academic approach to structural film.

20. The most popular source for the gross misinterpretation and misunderstanding of the philosophical concept of "deconstruction" is, without a doubt, "Propositions" by Noël Burch and Jorge Dana, published in *Afterimage* 5 (Spring 1974).

21. Throughout, I refer to the theoretical prejudices of film movements in order to illuminate their practices and history. At no point should the theoretical (as opposed to critical) biases be mistaken for my own. For a statement of my own opposition to the essentialism of structural film, see my "Medium Specificity Arguments and the Self-Consciously Invented Arts: Film, Video and Photography," *Millennium Film Journal* 14/15 (Fall/Winter 1984–85): 127–54.

22. For a description of this film, see my review of LeGrice in the *Soho Weekly News*, April 12–18, 1979. It should be said that in answer to my point about affinities to structural film, LeGrice would probably retort that he is deconstructing narrative, something he conceives of as cultural and conventional, whereas the structural filmmakers attempt to disclose essential features of film as such.

23. For an account of *Tom, Tom the Piper's Son*, see Lois Mendelson's and Bill Simon's article of the same name in *Artforum*, 1971. For information concerning *The Doctor's Dream*, see Tom Gunning's "Doctor Jacobs' Dream Work," *Millennium Film Journal* 10/11 (Fall/Winter 1981–82): 210–18. Also of interest is Lindley Hanlon's interview, *Ken Jacobs* (Minneapolis: Filmmakers Filming Monographs, 1979).

24. Jonathan Buchsbaum, "Independent Film and Popular Culture: The Films of J. Hoberman," *Millennium Film Journal* 6 (Spring 1980): 111–12.

25. Jonathan Rosenbaum, *Film: The Front Line, 1983* (Denver: Arden Press, 1983), p. 76.

26. "Discussion Between Marjorie Keller and Amy Taubin," in *Idiolects* 6, parenthetical information added.

27. E. A. Kaplan, "Theories and Strategies of Feminist Documentary," *Millennium Film Journal* 12 (Fall/Winter 1982–83): 53, parentheses removed. It is also important to state that *independent* filmmakers in the seventies and eighties, in their search for a means to express content, often turned to documentary filmmaking. This is especially true of feminist filmmakers. I have not included a chronicle of this important development here because my focus is avant-garde film, not all independent film. The Kaplan article just cited is one place for the interested reader to obtain information about the state of independently produced, feminist documentaries.

28. Undoubtedly the preference for at least "equal time" devoted to the interrogation of the signifier *and* to the ramifications of its operation in the construction of (a presumably repressive) social reality is what accounts for the lack of interest of politicized post structuralists in the works of George Landow (aka Owen Land). In films such as *Remedial Reading Comprehension* (1971) and *On the Marriage Broker Joke* (1980), Landow has deconstructively subverted popular discourse—for example, ads, the jargon of institutional testing, and so forth—in order to raise questions about audience reception and interpretation. Because of its humor, his work is often accessible to wide audiences. Yet, in spite of his affinities to many of the aims and concerns of the new talkie, he does not appear to be of major interest to proponents of that genre because he does not address what for them are broader issues of reception, namely its place within a social reality that is politically, sexually, and economically oppressive.

29. The preferred format of many new talkies involves the filmmakers appearing after the film in order to answer questions and to discuss and debate issues with the audience. As with Godard's work, the new talkie is thought of as a way of initially engaging issues. It is incomplete if it does not lead to further discussion. This underscores the genre's commitment to political work and is also related to a desire for greater accessibility by these avant-gardists. It might be further connected to a more general stance by these filmmakers against the kind of "repugnant" closure found in commercial films and "aesthetic" art.

30. For an analysis of this film, see E. A. Kaplan, "Feminist Approaches to History, Psychoanalysis and Cinema in *Sigmund Freud's Dora*," *Millennium Film Journal* 7/8/9 (Fall/Winter 1980–81).

31. The intertextual preoccupations of these new talkies, rooted in a theoretical commitment to semiology and post structuralism, corresponds to the Barthesian tendencies of postmodernists in the fine arts such as Cindy Sherman. She too presents us with representations of recognizable cultural representations for the purpose of pithing their semiotic operation. The similarity between practitioners of art world postmodernism and proponents of the new talkies may suggest to some a reason to designate the latter as *the* cinematic postmodernists.

32. E. A. Kaplan, "Night at the Opera: Investigating the Heroine in Sally Potter's *Thriller*," *Millennium Film Journal* 10/11 (Fall/Winter 1981–82): 115–22.

33. See Sally Banes' article in this volume. See also Banes' chapter on Rainer in her *Terpsichore in Sneakers* (Boston: Houghton Mifflin Co., 1980).

34. For more information on *Journeys* . . . , see my "Interview With a Woman Who . . ." in *Millennium Film Journal* 7/8/9 (Fall/Winter 1980–81): 31–68. For general in-

formation about Rainer see: Annette Michelson, "Yvonne Rainer, Part One: The Dancer and the Dance," *Artforum* (January 1974)): 1157–63; Michelson, "Yvonne Rainer, Part Two: Lives of Performers," *Artforum* (February 1974): 30–35; and B. Ruby Rich, *Yvonne Rainer* (St. Paul, Minn.: Filmmakers Filming Monograph, 1981).

35. J. Hoberman, "The Divine Connection," *Village Voice*, July 26, 1983.

36. Lindley Hanlon, "Female Rage: The Films of Su Friedrich," *Millennium Film Journal* 12 (Fall/Winter 1982–83): 79–86.

37. Paul Arthur, "The Western Edge: Oil of L.A. and the Machined Image," *Millennium Film Journal* 12 (Fall/Winter 1982–83): 17–18.

38. Ibid., pp. 22–25.

39. Ibid.

40. Sally Banes, "Theatre of Operations: Stuart Sherman's Fifteen Films," *Millennium Film Journal* 10/11 (Fall/Winter 1981–82): 87–102.

41. For an account of Beckman's career, see Sally Banes, "Imagination and Play: The Films of Erica Beckman," *Millennium Film Journal* 13 (Fall/Winter 1983–84): 98–112.

BIBLIOGRAPHICAL ESSAY

There are two outstanding bibliographies of writing on the avant-garde film. The first was compiled by Caroline Angell and is printed in *The Essential Cinema*, edited by P. Adams Sitney. This is very thorough through 1973, and it is keyed to the work of filmmakers included in the canon of Anthology Film Archives. The second bibliography takes up where Angell's leaves off, expanding its survey beyond the Anthology canon and charting articles through 1981. It was compiled by Grahame Weinbren and Arlene Zeichner and is printed in *Journal of the University Film Association* 33, no. 2 (Spring 1981).

In the United States, the major journals devoted to coverage of the avant-garde cinema are *Film Culture*, *Millennium Film Journal*, and *Idiolects*. *Film Quarterly*, *Wide Angle*, and *Camera Obscura* also run articles on the avant-garde. *October* is the general-interest journal most concerned with avant-garde film. Reviews of avant-garde film can be found in *The Village Voice*. The most important British film journals devoted to the avant-garde are *Afterimage* and *Undercut*. Articles on the avant-garde film can also be found in *Framework* and *Screen*.

Sitney's *Visionary Film* is the single most useful volume for initiating oneself to the history of the American avant-garde through the mid-seventies. It is often said that this book is too partisan, and there is no denying that it has a definite viewpoint. But its very partisanship supplies it with an organizing perspective that the reader can go on to modify, expand upon, and even discard after fruitfully testing its limits. Contrary views to Sitney's can be found in LeGrice's *Abstract Film and Beyond* and in the special issue of *Studio International* devoted to film (November/December 1975).

There is no synoptic overview comparable to *Visionary Film* for avant-garde film of the last ten years. The Filmmakers Filming Monograph series, published by the Walker Art Center and Film-in-the-Cities, provides important studies and interviews concerning work produced in the late seventies and early eighties. Arden Press of Denver, Colorado, has announced its intention to publish book-length studies of contemporary avant-garde film on a yearly basis.

BIBLIOGRAPHY

Arthur, Paul. "Structural Film: Revisions, New Versions and The Artifact, Part I." *Millennium Film Journal* 2 (Spring/Summer 1978).

———. "Structural Film, Part II." *Millennium Film Journal* 4/5 (Winter/Spring 1979).

———. "The Western Edge: Oil of L.A. and the Machined Image." *Millennium Film Journal* 12 (Fall/Winter 1982–83).

Banes, Sally. "Imagination and Play: The Films of Erica Beckman." *Millennium Film Journal* 13 (Fall/Winter 1983–84).

———. "Theatre of Operations: Stuart Sherman's Fifteen Films." *Millennium Film Journal* 10/11 (Fall/Winter 1981–82).

Buchsbaum, Jonathan. "Independent Film and Popular Culture: The Films of J. Hoberman." *Millennium Film Journal* 6 (Spring 1980).

Burch, Noël, and Jorge Dana. "Propositions." *Afterimage* 5 (Spring 1974).

Camera Obscura Collective. "Yvonne Rainer: An Introduction." *Camera Obscura* 1 (Fall 1976).

Carroll, Noël. "Address to the Heathen." *October* 23 (Winter 1982).

———. "Avant-garde Film and Film Theory." *Millennium Film Journal* 4/5 (Summer/Fall 1979).

———. "The Future of Allusion: Hollywood in the Seventies (and Beyond)." *October* 20 (Spring 1982).

———. "Interview with a Woman Who. . . . " *Millennium Film Journal* 7/8/9 (Fall/Winter 1980–81).

Cornwell, Regina. *Snow Seen, The Films and Photographs of Michael Snow*. Toronto: Peter Martin Associates, 1980.

Curtis, David. *Experimental Cinema*. New York: Dell, 1971.

Doberman, Gary. "New York Cut the Crap." *CinemaNews* (Spring 1980).

Gidal, Peter. "The Anti-Narrative." *Screen* 20 (Summer 1979).

Gidal, Peter, ed. *Structural Film Anthology*. London: British Film Institute, 1976.

Gunning, Tom. "Doctor Jacobs' Dream Work." *Millennium Film Journal* 10/11 (Fall/Winter 1981–82).

Hanlon, Lindley. *Ken Jacobs*. St. Paul, Minn.: Filmmakers Filming Monograph, 1979.

———. "Recycling Cinema: *Urban Peasants* by Ken Jacobs," *Millennium Film Journal* 6 (Spring 1980).

Heath, Stephen. "Afterword." *Screen* 20 (Summer 1979).

Hoberman, J. "No Wavelength: The Para Punk Underground." *Village Voice*, May 21, 1979.

Jenkins, Bruce. "A Case Against Structural Film." *Journal of the University Film Association* (Spring 1981).

Kaplan, E. Ann. "Feminist Approaches to History, Psychoanalysis and Cinema in *Sigmund Freud's Dora*." *Millennium Film Journal* 7/8/9 (Fall/Winter 1980–81).

———. "Night at the Opera: Investigating the Heroine in Sally Potter's *Thriller*." *Millennium Film Journal*, 10/11 (Fall/Winter 1981–82).

Kiernan, Joanna. "Two Films by Malcolm LeGrice." *Millennium Film Journal* 3 (Winter/Spring 1979).

Koch, Stephen. *Stargazer: Andy Warhol's World and His Films*. New York: Praeger, 1973.

LeGrice, Malcolm. *Abstract Film and Beyond*. Cambridge, Mass.: MIT Press, 1977.

Mekas, Jonas. *Movie Journal: The Rise of a New American Cinema*. New York: Macmillan-Collier Publishers, 1972.

Mendelson, Lois, and William Simon. *"Tom, Tom, the Piper's Son."* *Artforum* (September 1971).

Michelson, Annette. "About Snow." *October* 8 (Spring 1979).

————. "Camera Lucida/Camera Obscura." *Artforum* (January 1973).

————. "Film and the Radical Aspiration." *Film Culture Reader*. New York: Praeger, 1970.

————. "Rose Hobart and Monsieur Phot: Early Films from Utopia Parkway." *Artforum* (June 1973).

————. "Toward Snow." *Artforum* (June 1971).

————. "Yvonne Rainer, Part One: The Dancer and the Dance." *Artforum* (January 1974).

————. "Yvonne Rainer, Part Two: *Lives of Performers*." *Artforum* (February 1974).

Penley, Constance. "The Avant-Garde and Its Imaginary." *Camera Obscura* 2 (Fall 1977).

Penley, Constance, and Janet Bergstrom. "The Avant-Garde: Histories and Theories." *Screen* 19 (Autumn 1978).

Renan, Sheldon. *The Underground Film*. New York: Dutton, 1967.

Rich, B. Ruby. *Yvonne Rainer*. St. Paul, Minn.: Filmmakers Filming Monograph, 1981.

Rosenbaum, Jonathan. *Film: The Front Line, 1983*. Denver: Arden Press, 1983.

Singer, Marilyn, ed. *A History of the American Avant-Garde Cinema*. New York: American Federation of the Arts, 1976.

Sitney, P. Adams. "Autobiography in Avant-Garde Film." *Millennium Film Journal* 1 (Winter 1977–78).

————. *Visionary Film: The American Avant-Garde*. New York: Oxford University Press, 1974; 2d edition, 1979.

————, ed. *The Avant-Garde Film*. New York: New York University Press, 1978.

————, ed. *The Essential Cinema*. New York: Anthology Film Archives and New York University Press, 1975.

————, ed. *Film Culture Reader*. New York: Praeger, 1970.

Wollen, Peter. " 'Ontology' and 'Materialism' in Film." *Screen* 17 (Spring 1976).

————. "The Two Avant-Gardes." *Studio International*. (November/December 1975).

Youngblood, Gene. *Expanded Cinema*. New York: Dutton, 1970.

6

Literature

PHILIP STEVICK

Although expressions of despair at the apparently waning energies of one's culture occur throughout history, it is doubtful that very many thinking persons of earlier centuries felt themselves to be at the end of an era, tentatively trying to make out the shape of the new age that had barely begun. It does become characteristic of the Western mind in the nineteenth century, however, that it organizes history into periods; and sensitive observers characteristically began to imagine themselves at the intersection of two periods. In one of his most moving and durable passages Matthew Arnold writes of the consciousness of being "between two worlds, one dead,/The other powerless to be born." In our century, that feeling of being caught between ages has been pervasive, especially in the first decade after the First World War and in the period from the mid-sixties to the present time.

It is not only subtle and introspective minds such as Arnold's that have imagined us at the end of an age and at the beginning of another. Economists have long since begun to call our period "postindustrial," observing that many of our basic industries are moribund and that our energies are increasingly given to service and high technology. Observing that fewer people take in their essential information from printed sources, drawing from the electronic media instead, sociologists and cultural critics have called us "postliterate." Our world, for good or ill, has begun to operate on principles different from those that have dominated much of the century and we tend to see ourselves as part of a culture that we may not altogether understand but which we can recognize as being "after" what we have known.

Playfully but quite seriously addressing Cervantes, Robert Coover, our contemporary, writes, "Like you, we, too, seem to be standing at the end of one age and on the threshold of another."[1] Coover restates Matthew Arnold's sense of his world but applies it to contemporary fiction. In Donald Barthelme's "The End of the Mechanical Age," two characters converse who have met a mere page before at the detergent shelf of a supermarket.

"The mechanical age is drawing to a close," I said to her.

"Or has already done so," she replied.

"It was a good age," I said. "I was comfortable in it, relatively. Probably I will not enjoy the age to come quite so much. I don't like its look."[2]

And in one of the "episodes" of Renata Adler's *Speedboat*, two of the most resonant sentences of the modernist period, by Pound and Forster, echo at the end, closing off the age that has come before us.

"Take off everything except your slip," the nurse said. "Doctor will be with you in a moment." Nobody under forty-five, in twenty years, had worn a slip, but nurses invariably gave this instruction. There they all are, however, the great dead men with their injunctions. Make it new. Only connect.[3]

The tonalities of those three passages are different but the message is the same: namely, the feeling that the authority of our dominant predecessors has severely eroded and that fiction now is obliged to be about its business in a different way.

Since we have called that body of earlier work "modernist" for so long, a growing and by now fairly widespread usage has come to label fiction that both follows and sets itself off from modernism as postmodernist. If, as a label for a movement, the epithet seems unsure of itself, it is. It does not, after all, *say* very much. When earlier cultural observers decided to name the eighteenth century the neoclassical period and the early nineteenth century the romantic period, they bestowed names on those periods that carried attributes, oversimplifying and distorting perhaps but saying something. "Postmodernist," on the other hand, seems to suggest that all that we can say of that newer body of work, at the moment, is that it "comes after" modernism. (If someone were to read a wistful melancholy into the word, his reading would not be altogether misplaced. The modernists are a hard act to follow. Consider the ease with which artists and critics earlier in the century used the phrase "avant-garde," comparing art to the forward scouts of a military expedition, and compare the stance implied by "postmodernist," the artist moving forward perhaps but with his eye cast back, over his shoulder, at the shadows of the masters.) Tentative and not very revealing, the epithet is, moreover, by no means the object of universal agreement.

Postmodernism implies a dialectical relation, or an oppositional relation, even an antagonistic relation to modernism. How we understand that opposition will obviously depend upon how we understand what modernism is, or to correct the tense, what modernism was. It will surprise no one to learn that, of that great period comprising most of the first half of our century, of prose fiction the period of Joyce, Woolf, Lawrence, Kafka, Mann, Proust, Faulkner, and a multitude of other major talents, no two observers agree precisely upon its salient features.

If we understand modernism as seeking, in Ezra Pound's phrase, to "make it new," perpetuating an unending literary radicalism (a widely shared and perfectly legitimate way of seeing modernism), then what has followed simply extends that modernist impulse, experimenting with words and forms with a motive that the great modernists would have understood. If we understand modernism as placing a special importance upon structure and design, however, insisting upon the aesthetic autonomy of the individual work, then recent works will seem to be different from that modernist norm, opposed to it perhaps, since there often appears to be a kind of willed randomness in contemporary fiction, a pleasure in the fragmentary, a sense, at times, quite the opposite of that modernist respect for the integrity of the artistic object, namely a willingness to flirt with the work's frivolity and inconsequence. If we understand modernism as expressing the position of the self in an age of crisis, projecting a shared sense of loss, exile, and alienation, or, as Ihab Hassan describes it, a pervasive negativity, a persistent reaction against culture, consciousness, and language itself, then fiction now can easily be seen as an extension of that principle of the modernist imagination since writers now hardly feel more comfortable with the world than writers of the high modernist period.[4] If, on the other hand, we understand modernist works as seeking to set up an especially rich response between surface and depth by the manipulation of symbol and mythic reference, then recent fiction will seem to be rather startlingly lacking in that modernist depth, deliberately flat, wilfully superficial, consciously nonmodernist, anti-modernist, and postmodernist.[5]

As an initial way out of such confusion, it would seem appropriate to look first to the practitioners themselves. Movements and new directions in the arts have often been accompanied by polemics, manifestos, statements of shared purpose. Most of the major figures of early modernism laid out their own programs, guided our expectations, hectored and cajoled us, made quite explicit whom they wished *not* to write like. Writers of recent experimental fiction, on the other hand, have given little of their energies to such programmatic statements and the reason is not hard to find. Legatees of an absurdist tradition, members of a generation more sensitive than any before it to dead causes, empty gestures, and hollow rhetoric, writers of postmodernist fiction can hardly surprise us by their reluctance to stake out the territory ahead. Nevertheless, two essays do exist that describe what postmodernist fiction is about, from the point of view of a writer central to the enterprise; the two of them neatly bracket the period in which postmodernism in fiction has received its initial flush of attention and analysis; and both of them are by John Barth.

Barth's "The Literature of Exhaustion" appeared in 1967. At that time, Barth was well established but other conspicuous figures—Coover and Gass, for example—were not. Everybody, in 1967, knew who Vonnegut was, and Pynchon had established his reputation with *V*. But younger figures such as Max Apple or Don DeLillo had not appeared in print. It was clearly an early moment for a statement on the new directions of fiction. In retrospect, Barth has acknowledged that the title was unfortunate. It is reminiscent of those weary debates on the death of the novel and it suggests (only the title, not the body of the essay) a group of scribblers grimly trying to dance on the grave of prose fiction. In fact, the essay is a celebration of the possibilities of fiction and the human spirit. And its argument goes like this.

At certain points in history, aesthetic conventions are used up, played out, no longer pertinent to the ways we either live in the world or exercise our imaginations. One such time is now. A writer may ignore such terminality, producing works done in the manner of fifty years ago, with, finally, not much claim on our interest. He may produce works that momentarily startle us with their formal novelty: Barth cites several curious examples of "mixed media" art. Or he may make works that take the full measure of that terminality yet move beyond it to create imaginative structures with a special pertinence for the reader now. Borges is Barth's central example, illustrating

how an artist may paradoxically turn the felt ultimacies of our time into material and means for his work—*paradoxically* because by doing so he transcends what had appeared to be his refutation, in the same way that the mystic who transcends finitude is said to be enabled to live, spiritually and physically, in the finite world.[6]

The result of such a motive, argues Barth, is likely to be parodic, often farcical, reflexive, as he describes himself and his novels *The Sot-Weed Factor* and *Giles Goat-Boy*: "Novels which imitate the form of the Novel, by an author who imitates the role of Author." If such literature seems decadent, Barth reminds us that the motives of Cervantes and Fielding were comparable.

Thirteen years later, Barth undertook a second statement, which he called "The Literature of Replenishment." By that time, 1980, postmodernism was so established as a phenomenon and "postmodernism" so established as usage that Barth was able to give a large portion of the essay to a genial and witty survey of the criticism on the subject. Late in the essay, Barth gathers together the modernist "program," those aspects of nineteenth-century realism that the modernists sought to discredit and supplant. They repudiated the nineteenth century, Barth argues, with such brilliance and passion that it hardly needs to be done again.

If the modernists, carrying the torch of romanticism, taught us that linearity, rationality, consciousness, cause and effect, naive illusionism, transparent language, innocent anecdote, and middle-class moral conventions are not the whole story, then from the perspective of these closing decades of our century we may appreciate that the contraries of these things are not the whole story either. Disjunction, simultaneity, irrationalism, anti-illusionism, self-reflexiveness, medium-as-message, political olympianism, and a moral pluralism approaching moral entropy—these are not the whole story either.[7]

The ideal postmodernist synthesizes the work of his modernist parents and his premodern grandparents, neither imitating nor repudiating but creating an art that, transcending both, is "more democratic in its appeal" than the dense and priestly art of the high modernists. It is not Borges this time who is the principal exhibit (although undoubtedly his admiration for Borges has in no way diminished) but Italo Calvino and Gabriel García Márquez. Borges, in retrospect, seems to have provided a transition between the last impulses of modernism and the energies of postmodernism. Calvino and García Márquez, on the other hand, mixing realism and magic, sophistication and directness, exemplify a literature that neither repeats nor repudiates but replenishes.

If Barth's two essays provide a programmatic frame for postmodernist fiction done by a writer within the mode, they do not exhaust such possibilities. Most of the great modernists were great talkers. And they left behind fragments of remembered conversation that have found their way into their biographies. Sustained interviews with the major figures of the first half of the twentieth century, however, are rare and when they exist are often amateur and journalistic. In the fifties, on the contrary, *The Paris Review* began a series that still continues, setting a model for a new kind of interview—substantial, highly intelligent, empathic, and trenchant. It is a mode of interviewing that has spread to other journals and book-length collections, making a body of statements on the art of fiction impressive in their candor and wit. Obliged to consult them, the reader is also obliged to be wary. Full of honesty and directness, they also abound in irony, even a kind of theatricality.[8] Meanwhile, as Barth describes in his two essays and as other writers refract in their conversations with their interviewers, critics of postmodernism have tried, by different routes, to take its measure.

In 1967, the year of Barth's "The Literature of Exhaustion," Robert Scholes published a small but arresting book called *The Fabulators*, seeking to describe certain qualities common to a species of contemporary fiction and seeking to apply those qualities to a canon of novelists. No one, describing his contemporaries, writes in stone, and readers of Scholes' book now would wish to revise it here and there. Indeed, Scholes himself has revised and extended it as *Fabulation and Metafiction* (1979). Nevertheless, the critical observations that lie behind Scholes' eccentric title seem as pertinent now as they did when they were written. By reviving that archaic word "fabulator," Scholes draws our attention to a cluster of characteristics that can serve as a ground against which further critical distinctions can follow.

A fabulator is a tale-teller. Tellers of tales enjoy their work, and it shows. There is a kind of buoyancy and pleasure of invention, in a word, joy in fabulation. Not limited by a consensual "reality," what we more or less agree upon as the contours of the experiential world, the fabulator makes stories that are unabashedly fabulous. The analogues and precursors of the fabulators are not the dogged chroniclers of the visible world or the slow, patient masters of the inner life but Rabelais, the Chaucer of the fabliaux, the Arabian Nights, the brothers Grimm, the early masters of the English eighteenth century.

"Christmas Eve, 1955, Benny Profane, wearing black levis, suede jacket, sneakers and big cowboy hat, happened to pass through Norfolk, Virginia." So begins Pynchon's *V.* That single opening sentence is enough to suggest the energies of the fabulist, implying directness, a pleasure in invention, and a zest for the vulgar in the narrative that is to follow. "I went to the bank to get my money for the day. And they had painted it yellow. Under cover of night, I shrewdly supposed.'' The beginning, this time, is from Barthelme's "Can We Talk." Barthelme is nearly everybody's favorite example of the quintessential postmodernist. And sooner or later, nearly everything that can be said about the movement can be said about him. But for the moment, what needs to be said is that the idea of a bank painting money yellow, "under cover of night," revealed in a narration at once knowing and naive, obviously initiates not a sensitive story of life in the recognizable world, done in water-color realism, but a tale, fantastic, extravagant, inventive, bizarre, "irreal," a made thing with its own delights. Drawing upon the work of such American writers as Barth, Hawkes, and Terry Southern and such English writers as Iris Murdoch, Scholes anticipates the extravagant narratives yet to appear by such writers as Coover, Stanley Elkin, Max Apple, Ishmael Reed, and dozens more, while prefiguring the American "discovery" of that brilliant group of South American novelists including Julio Cortázar, Gabriel Garcia Marquez, and Carlos Fuentes. Criticism of postmodernist fiction since Scholes has often become heavy, abstract, and full of itself. What needs to be remembered is that the single quality that most firmly unites postmodernist writers is the recovery of the pleasures of telling, cut loose from the canons of probability.

Moving beyond that fabulistic base, the criticism of postmodernist fiction, schematizing it somewhat, can be said to concern itself, first, with the self, the individual personality or its lack, consciousness, "character," and the phenomenal world the figures of such fiction respond to and in which they see themselves living. Second, it concerns itself with form, structure, continuity, the relatedness of part to part and part to whole, along, of course, with the implicit attitudes of postmodernist writers to questions of form and structure. Third, it concerns itself with the relation of such fiction to "the world," to "meaning" in the classic referential sense, to what we consensually agree to call "experience," to postmodernism's reflection, incorporation, and transmutation of culture both high and low, of history, language, ideas. It is the first of these, the nature of "character" in postmodernist fiction, that is the easiest to deal with since it is the least in dispute, in some ways the most obvious.

No one really doubts the continuing capacity of prose fiction to project human images of substance, with a full complement of wishes and fears, impulses and constraints, living in a world not very different from what we take to be our own, intended to be emblematic of the human condition at the present time. The theory of postmodernism is full of hyperbolic dismissals of the possibilities of "character." (Indeed, the impossibility of character is a persistent motif in the discussions of fiction for fifty years.) Yet it would be a strange reader who was not, sooner or later, moved and persuaded by one of the human images in the decidedly nonpostmodernist fiction of such writers as Bellow, Malamud, Maureen Howard, Paula Fox, Anne Tyler. Still, the fiction that is our subject has set about creating a structure in which the autonomy of the individual personality is reduced out of the conviction that that classic representation of selfhood is insupportable at the present time. Ronald Sukenick, in the opening lines of his story "The Death of the Novel," stakes out that position as well as anybody.

Realistic fiction presupposed chronological time as the medium of a plotted narrative, an irreducible individual psyche as the subject of its characterization, and, above all, the ultimate, concrete reality of things as the object and rationale of its description. In the world of postrealism, however, all of these absolutes have become absolutely problematic.[9]

Moved though we still may sometimes be by a developed human figure, in Sukenick's phrase, "an irreducible individual psyche," we have surely, as a culture, come to distrust the rhetoric by means of which motives are given rational intelligibility, the artifice by means of which coherence is imposed upon the fluid materials of the self, and the conventions by means of which literary characters move between certain modalities, of innocence and experience, naiveté and illumination, the immanent past and the immediate present. Responding to the problematics of the self, postmodernists have devised a method, reduced perhaps but infinitely various, in which the human image takes on a two-dimensional cast, without much depth, yet open to oddities, accident, contingency, and banality in a way that classic characters could rarely be.

Probably the most essential convention of the modernist portrayal of consciousness is the epiphany, in Joyce's word, the luminous moment in which significance, especially self-knowledge, is grasped. Implicit in postmodernist fiction is the sense that that convention of the epiphany is just that, a convention, which has served its time, and that it is, however useful to the construction of fictions, not especially true to the nature of consciousness. We seem, these days, not to punctuate our lives with luminous moments. It is Pynchon, again, who speaks the definitive word on epiphany. After some 400 pages of V, Brenda says to Benny Profane, " 'You've had all these fabulous experiences. I wish mine would show me something.' 'Why,' asks Benny."

"The experience, the experience. Haven't you learned?"

Profane didn't have to think long. "No." he said, "offhand I'd say I haven't learned a goddamn thing."

Many other novels make the point less explicitly. Charles Simmons' brilliant *Wrinkles* gathers moments from a life into a moving assemblage; yet no moment is more significant than another; there is no crisis, no climax; and no moment carries a charge of self-insight.

Modernist fiction portrays characters in touch with their own past, sensitive to their surroundings, and, at the same time, aware of the pathos of their isolation, all of which is likely to seem, to the postmodernist writer, as unusable as the epiphany. And modernist fiction presents a rhythm of traits, motifs, and symbols by means of which we are persuaded of the continuity of characters. Again, postmodernist writers are likely to feel strongly the artifice of that continuity, opting instead for images of lives less linear and whole, more improvisatory, often inscrutable, governed less by the thematics of their own composition than by the random assaults of a not very coherent world. Such figures are often named in such a way as to signal us that no full-dimensional treatment of them as characters is likely to follow: Ambrose Mensch in Barth's *Letters*, Kleinzeit and Olt, eponymous heroes of novels by Russell Hoban and Kenneth Gangemi, for that matter, Howard Johnson in Max Apple's "The Oranging of America." Commentators on Pynchon sometimes, in fact, put the word "character" in quote marks when referring to his work, as if to employ the epithet without typographic reservation were to misrepresent: Herbert Stencil and Jessica Swanlake are not characters but "characters."

So far I have argued that the human image in postmodernist fiction is as it is because consciousness is perceived as being different from consciousness perceived through the modernist conventions. A different way of understanding character is suggested by the essays, at once lyrical and philosophical, of William Gass.[10] Our traditional way of speaking of characters as if they had such amplitude and resonance that they escaped from the page and lived a separate life in our imagination and recollection of them is false both to our experience and to the nature of literature, Gass argues. Characters are made of words and the medium in which they exist is a linguistic construct. Gass means his reemphasis to apply to the whole of fiction. But it has a particular pertinence for postmodernist fiction, for at no previous time have so many writers of consequence entertained the idea, at least provisionally and intermittently, that fiction does not exist to imitate the "real world," does not even exist to abstract from or superimpose upon the world a thematic organization, but that fiction exists as a nonmimetic object, made of words, for its own sake. Insofar as fiction is informed by such a view of itself, its human images will appear minimally as characters in the classic sense, rather as elements in a composition that, if it is "about" anything, is about language. Yet it is no mere minimalization that takes place since such fiction, in abandoning, more or less, the portrayal of characters, invests the medium with a powerful life of its own.

Like its treatment of character, the postmodernists' approach to structure is no mere matter of fashion but is deeply rooted in the cultural changes that have overtaken us in the last quarter century. There are a multitude of ways of illuminating the changes in our general sense of form. But perhaps the most profitable is that body of thought generated by scores of anthropologists and psychologists, given currency by the now faded Marshall McLuhan, and now most responsibly summarized by Walter Ong.[11] Western culture, such speculation proposes, has moved through a long oral, traditional period, to a period of type and print, with the reader isolated and silent, to our present period, with its survival of print but also its increased use of the electronic media, often uniting an immense audience by speaking voices mechanically reproduced. Literature through the Renaissance and well into the eighteenth century abounds in vestiges of that older, oral culture; yet, beginning in the late Renaissance, Western culture becomes increasingly print oriented, which is to say that the entire sensorium becomes centered upon eye and space rather than upon ear and sound. The consequences of "typographic man" are a way of writing, perceiving, and forming the imagination that is causal, linear, privately conceptual rather than rhetorically disputatious, devocalized, in comparison with the possibilities open to oral man less "performative," more joyless. If we have moved beyond that stage to another one dominated by the broad transmission of oral messages by electronic means, it follows that that narration which is closely in touch with the general culture will show the erosion of that linear, causal arrangement of words, presumably as a form more fragmented, less end-directed, more playfully aware of itself. Presumably such narration will show certain affinities with earlier oral-based forms: indeed, readers of the postmodernists are less likely to be reminded of classic nineteenth-century fiction than of Rabelais, Sterne, or Smollett, early writers with a fluid, improvisatory, nonlinear, "oral" sense of form. Thus Barth writes fiction for print, tape, and voice; Elkin structures a novel upon the voice, both public and private, of a disc jockey; and Pynchon structures *Gravity's Rainbow* upon film, with heavy elements of the electronic popular culture of the forties, anticipating the spasmodic experience of television.

A section of Barthelme's "City Life" draws explicitly upon the experience of the electronic media and along the way demonstrates the formal consequences of an immersion in that experience.

Elsa and Ramona watched the Motorola television set in their pajamas.

—What else is on? Elsa asked.

Ramona looked in the newspaper.

—On 7 there's "Johnny Allegro" with George Raft and Nina Foch. On 9 "Johnny Angel" with George Raft and Claire Trevor. On 11 there's "Johnny Apollo" with Tyrone Power and Dorothy Lamour. On 13 is "Johnny Concho" with Frank Sinatra and Phyllis Kirk. On 2 is "Johnny Dark" with Tony Curtis and Piper Laurie. On 4 is "Johnny Eager" with Robert Taylor and Lana Turner. On 5 is "Johnny O'Clock" with Dick Powell and Evelyn Keyes. On 31 is "Johnny Trouble" with Stuart Whitman and Ethel Barrymore.

—What's this one we're watching?

—What time is it?

—Eleven-thirty-five.

—"Johnny Guitar" with Joan Crawford and Sterling Hayden.

Less continuous, less "whole," less coherent than we ordinarily expect fiction to be, postmodernist fiction's incoherencies take predictable routes. One is a democratization of response, in which the sensitive, reflective, self-conscious mode of so much modernist fiction is not privileged but only one of many ways of registering experience. It coexists with what would have seemed, in another age, to be the vulgar, the superficial and the ephemeral. It is an openness to

levels of experience that Joyce exploits: it is not new. Yet it does differ from
the modernist norm. When Pynchon describes a Vivaldi concerto played by a
band of kazoos, we are jolted by the shift, invited to retain our veneration for
Vivaldi while opening ourselves to the noncanonical possibilities of the kazoo,
both held in some strange equipoise, and get on with a life rather more diverse
and inclusive than the modernist classics would have had us believe possible.

The discontinuities of postmodernist fiction, of course, extend beyond local
details and principles of selection. The example of early picaresque fiction continues to provide a model both for late modernist fiction and postmodernist, the
loosely structured series of "adventures" in which no one learns, grows, or
changes, the episodes occurring in no necessary order yet presenting an oddly
disjunctive vision in their aggregate of the whole of life. The classic modes of
satire continue to energize fiction, even though the moral norms that undergird
classic satire have largely shrunk, fiction still finding it useful to adopt the free
invention based upon the puzzled observer recording the random fatuousness of
an absurd world. And recent fiction continues to respond to the model of the
subliterary media, which continually present us with models of text and advertisement, juxtapositions of texts, and variations of tone so jarring that they would
be altogether disconcerting if we had not learned to adapt to them. But most
significantly, writers of and about postmodernist fiction have sought an analogy
in the visual arts, especially collage. By now, the idea of making an artistic
construct by cutting and pasting is three-quarters of a century old and no novelty.
Converting the method to a verbal medium still startles. Collecting the debris
of our culture, scraps of conversation, names and phrases, images from the
media, manufactured items, cant phrases and ritual gestures, and pasting them
into a verbal collage accomplish many of the purposes sought by the visual artists
for all of these years.

Seen mimetically, such verbal collage "imitates" the rhythms and discontinuities of the experiential world. Seen nonmimetically, verbal collage offers a
means to accomplish aesthetic objectives by routes other than the extension of
theme, the patterning of symbol, and the fulfillment of plot. In addition, there
is a particular effect latent in verbal collage, derivative of early dada and still
useful to fiction, in which a very mysterious and complex response can be evoked
in the reader by the juxtaposition, without transition or modulation, of two words
or images totally unrelated. Responding to a question about collage, Barthelme
replies, "I'm talking about a pointillist technique, where what you get is not
adjacent dots of yellow and blue which optically merge to give you green but
merged meanings, whether from words placed side by side in seemingly arbitrary
ways or phrases similarly arrayed, bushels of them. . . . "[12] In Elkin's *The Living
End*, the central character, just dead, approaches heaven, thinking it resembles
a theme park. The raw fact of death and the idea of personal survival are suddenly
juxtaposed with the vision of Disneyland. And the reader is obliged to provide
a startled but appropriate response. Robert Coover's classic "The Babysitter"
cuts between imagined moments of "reality," desire, salaciousness, anxiety,

and fear, leaving the reader not with a "story" but with an assemblage. So it is that criticism has tried to come to terms with the discontinuities of postmodernist fiction, finding it not at all arbitrary but finding it powerfully expressive both of the spirit of our time and the extended possibilities of verbal construction.

The first thing to be said about the way in which postmodernist fiction orients itself toward the world of experience is so self-evident that criticism leaves it largely unarticulated, implicit, perfectly obvious. The main tradition of the modernists presents a world of diminished values, in which the human figures perpetually peer into the abyss, survey the wreckage, and await the end. There are, to be sure, pockets of value among the modernists. But the most pervasive sense of the world that one could derive from modernism is one of much reduced "meaning." It is a tradition that culminates in Beckett, a pivotal figure for postmodernism. Influential in innumerable matters of technique, Beckett also remains influential in his world view, a model of ways in which to make fictions of a luminous ingenuity in response to what we have called, since the fifties, "the absurd."

William Spanos has described a model of the world, positivistic, deterministic, linear; its literary theory derives from Aristotle, namely the continuing conviction of the Western mind that "stories" properly have beginnings, middles, and ends; and its corollary in the world of action is the isolation of "problems" that can always be seen to have solutions. The purest literary realization of that world view is the detective story.

Just as the form of the detective story has its source in the comforting certainty that an acute "eye," private or otherwise, can solve the crime with resounding finality by inferring causal relationships between clues which point to it (they are "leads," suggesting the primacy of rigid linear narrative sequence), so the "form" of the well-made positivistic universe is grounded in the equally comforting certainty that the scientist and-or psychoanalyst can solve the immediate problem by the inductive method, a process involving the inference of relationships between discontinuous "facts" that point to or lead straight to an explanation of the "mystery," the "crime" of contingent existence."[13]

As early as Dostoevsky, this totalizing, end-oriented view of the world begins to be rejected; and in any number of modernist works, the imperatives of plot are resisted because of the contrary pressures of a content that, suggesting disintegration, demands a disintegrative form. But it is finally with the existentialists that the view of the universe as a well-made fiction becomes understood as being not merely dubious metaphysics but a "totalitarian," specious pattern, governing art, politics, and the expectations of ordinary experience. And thus it has become the function of narrative art since the existentialists to challenge and undermine that old positivistic structure.

In the familiar language of Aristotle's *Poetics*, then, the postmodern strategy of decomposition exists to generate rather than to purge pity and terror; to disintegrate, to atomize rather than to create a community. In the more immediate language of existentialism, it exists to generate anxiety or dread: to dislodge the tranquillized individual from the "at-home of publicness," from the domesticated, the scientifically charted and organized familiarity of the totalized world."[14]

A reader of Spanos' essay who was unfamiliar with the fiction that it refers to might easily assent to the necessary death of the "detective story" as the universal plot while still remaining puzzled about the artistic consequences, which might well seem, to such a reader, merely self-indulgent, foolish, or incomprehensible. What needs to be said, extending Spanos, is that successful narrative art, confronting chaos, has had to find its own point of view toward both the nature of that chaos and the fact of confronting it, a shared point of view, characteristic of our time, distinct from that of the modernists.

Confronting its own perception of disorder, modernist narrative art ordinarily sought to impose order. T. S. Eliot's magisterial sentence on *Ulysses* is the best-known statement of such a motive. Joyce's mythic method, he writes, "is simply a way of controlling, of ordering, of giving a shape and a significance to the immense panorama of futility and anarchy which is contemporary history."[15] Metaphors of height occur easily as one tries to describe such control: the author is "above": he is Olympian. It is a mode that Alan Wilde calls "disjunctive irony."[16]

On the contrary, postmodernist fiction characteristically expresses what Wilde calls "suspensive irony." Metaphors of height give way to images of the horizontal: the author is not above but "immersed in." "Chary of comprehensive solutions, doubtful of the self's integrity, it confronts a world more chaotic (if chaos admits of gradations) than any imagined by its predecessors and, refusing the modernist dialectic, interrogating both distance and depth, opens itself to the randomness and contingency of unmediated experience."[17]

If our subject is the way criticism construes the relationship between the postmodernist fictional work and the world, then one more step is necessary to bring us full circle. Earlier, I have alluded to criticism that minimizes or argues away that relationship, the essays of William Gass, for example. It is useful here to recapitulate that position. Introducing the essays in his anthology *Surfiction*, Raymond Federman proposes a conceptual base for those essays. "To write," he argues,

is to *produce* meaning, and not to *reproduce* a pre-existing meaning. To write is to *progress*, and not *remain* subjected (by habit or reflexes) to the meaning that supposedly precedes the words. As such, fiction can no longer be reality, or a representation of reality, or an imitation, or even a recreation of reality; it can only be A REALITY—an autonomous reality whose only relation with the real world is to improve that world. To create fiction is, in fact, a way to abolish reality, and especially to abolish the notion that reality is truth.

Or, later,

The primary purpose of fiction will be to unmask its own fictionality, to expose the metaphor of its own fraudulence, and not pretend any longer to pass for reality, for truth, or for beauty. Consequently, fiction will no longer be regarded as a mirror of life, as a pseudorealistic document that informs us about life, nor will it be judged on the basis of its social, moral, psychological, metaphysical, commercial value, or whatever, but on the basis of what it is and what it does as an autonomous art form in its own right.[18]

Fiction has often struggled against its heavy mimetic tradition. Flaubert, over a century ago, expressed the wish to write a novel about nothing. The vigor of Federman's position and the fiction it reflects, by, among others, Federman himself, Ronald Sukenick, and Philippe Sollers and Jean Ricardou in France, suggest a reinvigorated wish to cut fiction loose from what seems the tyranny of resemblance, reality itself being fictive, and to establish it finally as an autotelic art, serving not the real world, whatever that is, but itself.

Such a radical skepticism about the solidity of the real world is likely to remind a reader with a nodding acquaintance with contemporary critical theory of the epistemological base of deconstructive criticism. In fact, criticism before the vogue of the deconstructionists has had a curious relationship to postmodernist fiction, even though the major theoreticians of recent years have never addressed the nature of postmodernist fiction.

The New Criticism, dominant in the fifties, looked for, and found, irony, wit, density of texture, organic form, the autonomous integrity of the individual work. It was the most potent movement in literary studies since English became a discipline, and its legacy is an attention to the text for which readers ever since will remain in its debt. In the late sixties, however, phenomenology, imported from France, established the legitimacy of looking at a work as the rendering of a mode of consciousness and the incidental result was that the integrity of the individual work was eroded, a result that had a curious corollary in the devaluation of structural integrity implicitly proposed by the postmodernists. In due course, through the work of such critics as Wolfgang Iser and Stanley Fish, a body of quite different criticism came to insist that the nature of literature was to be found in its experience in the mind of the reader—called variously affective criticism or reader-response criticism. The not so incidental result was an erosion of the idea of an explicable text, stable and autonomous, a result that had, in this case, a corollary in the tendency of postmodernist fiction to intentionally involve the reader in the production of a "meaning" not demonstrably determined by the words on the page. More recently, deconstructive criticism has argued for a total interminableness of text, based upon the imagination of a world of arbitrary signs, a "prisonhouse of language," beyond which no confirming reality exists. A corollary, in this case, is the tendency of at least some postmodernist fiction to lodge itself in a tissue of language representing nothing beyond itself.

Some writers of postmodernist fiction, Burroughs to some extent, Rudolph Wurlitzer, Barthelme here and there, have written as if influenced by the phenomenologists. Yet there is no evidence that they have read the phenomenologists or would have responded to them if they had. Other postmodernist works, the short fictions of Barth and Coover, read as if they had been in touch with reader-response criticism. Yet there is no evidence of an interest in such criticism by those writers. Similarly, Pynchon's *Gravity's Rainbow* and Gass' *Willie Masters' Lonesome Wife* read, at times, as if written under the heady spell of deconstructive criticism. Yet again, no evidence suggests such an influence. So it is that while a comparatively small body of criticism has set about describing postmodernist fiction, a large body of unignorable theory, seeking its examples often from the nineteenth century, has inadvertently constructed paradigmatic ways of thinking about literature that postmodernist fiction, also without meaning to, has concurrently exemplified.

No aspect of the criticism of postmodernist fiction is more unresolved than the canon, those writers who are postmodernist and those who are not. It is unresolved not merely because critics are irresolute and disputatious people, although they are. It is in dispute because selecting a canon involves separating writers into two categories, those who are postmodernists (or surfictionists or metafictionists, whatever one's operative category happens to be) and those who are not. A more arbitrary exercise, ultimately a more pointless exercise, is hard to imagine. American fiction in the last twenty years does not form two "traditions" or "camps" or "schools." And it does not fit into two boxes. It is, more properly, a spectrum, displaying a multitude of permutations. As a coda to the discussion, I propose the merest glance at some principles of selection, followed by a sense of where we seem to be now.

One way of facing the body of postmodernist fiction is to deny its uniqueness, to question the very notion that some kind of breakthrough has taken place from modernism to something else. Gerald Graff has argued that modernism is an extension of certain tendencies of romanticism and that what fiction in particular, literature in general, offers us now are either failed attempts at novelty or further extensions of that romantic-modernist enterprise.[19] It is an argument, of course, that runs counter to most of the present essay. Yet it is so strenuously and responsibly made that no student of contemporary fiction can afford to avoid coming to terms with it.

A less radical opposition to a clear break between late modernist and postmodernist texts is James W. Mellard's.[20] He argues that American fiction since Faulkner exhibits a variety of modes of dialectical reaction against aspects of high modernist narrative—"naive," "critical," and "sophisticated," he calls them—and that none of these constitutes a repudiation of modernism or the emergence of something new. Mellard's book is as densely and subtly argued as Graff's. And the two of them serve as a warning against extravagance to those of us who do think that postmodernist fiction does, in certain respects, break with tradition.

If, unlike Graff and Mellard, one assumes that something decisive *has* taken place with the art of fiction in the last two decades, then one is obliged to decide who the exemplary figures are. The most obvious way of beginning to form such a canon is to gather those writers who seem unusual or unconventional; the more rigorous epithets are "experimental" or "postrealistic." The point of contrast is not the modernist masters of the early century but American fiction of mid-century, a body of fiction with its surreal aspects, to be sure, but still largely realist in its presentational conventions. Against such a background—Salinger, Cozzens, James Jones, early Mailer, early Styron, early Bellow—writers since can be seen to break into two groups, those who perpetuate that largely realist tradition and those who do not. It is the method of *The Harvard Guide to Contemporary Writing*, for example, which contains an excellent essay on "Realists, Naturalists, and Novelists of Manners" and another essay on "Experimental Fiction." There are difficulties with such a division. One difficulty is that "experimental" is, finally, so broad and amorphous a category that one is left with a large and invariably disparate group of writers. (Josephine Hendin, in her essay in the *Harvard Guide*, includes William Burroughs, Flannery O'Connor, Kurt Vonnegut, and John Gardner, for example, a group for whom very few common principles can be found.) Another difficulty is that writers now often move among modes with a peculiar fluidity. Roth is, in one book, a social realist, in another a post-Kafkan fantasist. The novels of Joyce Carol Oates and Gail Godwin are largely realist but many of their short stories are startlingly unconventional.

Implicit in that attempt to sort out a group of writers who began to seem experimental in the sixties is another method, the historical. Forming a canon, one would wish to know where its representatives came from and when; and one would wish to know how the contours of that body of writing have changed in the last twenty years. It seems likely that we will need more distance than we now have to write such a history; none exists now. What can be said is that the beginnings of postmodernist fiction are diffuse, with no manifesto, no commanding journal or publishing house, no charismatic figure but rather some shared traits, displayed in writers of divergent backgrounds, coherent enough to be tentatively discussed by 1965, two years after Pynchon's *V*, one year after Barthelme's *Come Back, Dr. Calligari*, and five years after Barth's *The Sot-Weed Factor*. The shifting aesthetics of that growing body of fiction can be derived from the exchanges and symposia that punctuate the period.[21] But it is too early to expect that literary history can instruct us wisely on the shape of postmodernist fiction, in history, or on the canon of its exemplars.

Our only promising way of making a canon at the present time is to attempt to gather a body of writers who not only share certain unconventional traits of style, organization, and deviation from a literalist, verisimilar norm, or a modernist, symbolist norm, but who share a sense of tactic and ideology, whether one wishes to call it postmodernist or something else. Such a group of writers makes not only a list of names but, one would hope, a gestalt.

Barth, in the two essays cited earlier, gathers a group of writers with whom he feels a common bond of sensibility and method. Robert Scholes has made a working canon, first of "fabulists," subsequently of "metafictionists." Albert

Guerard has made a working canon of the "antirealists," as opposed, of course, to the realists.[22] Mas'ud Zavaradeh's operative category is "supermodernism," by means of which he forms a canon distinguished from those implicit in "antimodernism" and "paramodernism."[23] And Jerome Klinkowitz has gathered a group of qualities and exemplary writers under the rubric "postcontemporary."[24]

It all seems confusing. Yet it is not. Consensus will elude us for the present time. Meanwhile, what we have is the general agreement that fiction of the last twenty years has radically altered both its relation to the tradition from which it comes and to the world of experience. It is possible to argue against such a change. But one had better be prepared to argue mightily. As for the canon, critics of the period are in general agreement that Borges, Beckett, and Nabokov bear heavily on what has happend to fiction since them, however we choose to characterize those three. There is general agreement that the work of the "magic realists" in Latin America, especially the work of Gabriel García Márquez, bears unignorable affinities with postmodernism in America. There is general agreement that the postmodernist imagination eludes or baffles the English so that, except for occasional work by John Fowles and Anthony Burgess, it is a direction not congenial to the English sensibility. There is general agreement that postwar German fiction bears powerful resemblances to American postmodernism, with older figures such as Günter Grass and younger figures such as Peter Handke. There is no agreement at all concerning the French: some theorists of, and practitioners of, the American postmodernist mode will maintain that the work of such French writers as Robert Pinget, Claude Simon, and Philippe Sollers is inseparable from postmodernism in the United States; others will maintain that the work of the French has been both insular and incomprehensible for twenty years. There is universal agreement that any formulation of the principles of American postmodernism that does not apply to the work of Italo Calvino is useless.

In reformulating the American canon, the first difficulty is that the audience is multilayered and fragmented. One segment of that public that reads unconventional fiction will find a given author central; another segment will find him peripheral; and another will not have heard of him at all. Of course those problems of definition that have formed the center of this essay affect considerably one's sense of who is central and who is not. Still, it would be an eccentric sense of the canon that did not place these figures at its center: John Barth, Donald Barthelme, Robert Coover, Kurt Vonnegut, William Gass, Stanley Elkin, and Thomas Pynchon. A number of figures may, in the long run, seem just as central. At the present time, either their reputations are less firmly established or they seem to speak less powerfully to the aesthetic impulses of postmodernism than the first group. They are Max Apple, Richard Brautigan, Harry Mathews, Gilbert Sorrentino, William Gaddis, Jonathan Baumbach, Don DeLillo, Ishmael Reed, Guy Davenport, Ron Sukenick, Charles Simmons, Rudolph Wurlitzer, Walter Abish, Ursule Molinaro, and Russell Banks. There are figures, John Hawkes,

Jerzy Kosinski, E. L. Doctorow, Thomas Berger, dozens more, who share affinities with the writers listed and the tendencies described.

There will always be readers who long for a return to a period of conventionality in fiction, in which any new novel can be responded to and measured against some fairly stable and self-perpetuating norms, although there are good reasons for arguing that such a period of stability and continuity in fiction has never existed. There will always be other readers, however, for whom a period like ours is a particularly exciting time to be alive and reading, a transitional period, full of irreverence and audacity, with infinite amounts of imaginative energy, yet with the nature of the collective enterprise that postmodernist fiction makes not completely defined or fully understood.

NOTES

1. Robert Coover, *Pricksongs & Descants* (New York: Dutton, 1969), p. 78.

2. Donald Barthelme, *Amateurs* (New York: Farrar, Straus and Giroux, 1976), p. 176.

3. Renata Adler, *Speedboat* (New York: Random House, 1976), p. 73.

4. Ihab Hassan, *The Dismemberment of Orpheus: Toward a Postmodern Literature* (New York: Oxford University Press, 1971).

5. Perhaps the best single source for the nature of modernism is Irving Howe, ed., *Literary Modernism* (New York: Fawcett, 1967).

6. John Barth, "The Literature of Exhaustion," *Surfiction: Fiction Now . . . And Tomorrow*, ed. Raymond Federman (Chicago: Swallow Press, 1975), p. 27.

7. John Barth, "The Literature of Replenishment" *Atlantic Monthly* 245 (January 1980): 70.

8. The best recent collections of interviews with contemporary American writers are Joe David Bellamy, *The New Fiction: Interviews with Innovative American Writers* (Champaign: University of Illinois Press, 1974); and Tom LeClair and Larry McCaffery, *Anything Can Happen: Interviews with Contemporary American Novelists* (Champaign: University of Illinois Press, 1983).

9. Robert Sukenick, *The Death of the Novel and Other Stories* (New York: Dial Press, 1969), p. 41.

10. See "The Concept of Character in Fiction" and "In Terms of the Toenail: Fiction and the Figures of Life," in William H. Gass, *Fiction and the Figures of Life* (New York: Alfred A. Knopf, 1970).

11. Walter J. Ong, *The Presence of the Word* (New Haven, Conn.: Yale University Press, 1967).

12. J. D. O'Hara, "Donald Barthelme: The Art of Fiction LXVI," *The Paris Review* 80 (1981): 192.

13. William J. Spanos, "The Detective and the Boundary: Some Notes on the Postmodern Literary Imagination," *Boundary 2* 1 (Fall 1972): 150.

14. Ibid., p. 155.

15. "*Ulysses*, Order, and Myth," in *Selected Prose*, ed. Frank Kermode (New York: Harcourt Brace Jovanovich, 1975), p. 177.

16. Alan Wilde, *Horizons of Assent: Modernism, Postmodernism, and the Ironic Imagination* (Baltimore: Johns Hopkins University Press, 1981), p. 10 and passim.

17. Ibid., p. 129.

18. Raymond Federman, "Introduction" to *Surfiction: Fiction Now . . . and Tomorrow*, p. 8.

19. Gerald Graff, *Literature Against Itself: Literary Ideas in Modern Society* (Chicago: University of Chicago Press, 1979).

20. James M. Mellard, *The Exploded Form: The Modernist Novel in America* (Urbana: University of Illinois Press, 1980).

21. For two lively examples, see "A Symposium of Fiction: Donald Barthelme, William Gass, Grace Paley, Walker Percy," *Shenandoah* 27 (Winter 1976): 3–31; and James McKenzie, ed., "Pole-Vaulting in Top Hats: A Public Conversation with John Barth, William Gass, and Ishmael Reed," *Modern Fiction Studies* 22 (1977): 131–51.

22. Mas'ud Zavarzadeh, *The Mythopoeic Reality: The Postwar American Nonfiction Novel* (Urbana: University of Illinois Press, 1976), p. 3.

24. Jerome Klinkowitz, *Literary Disruptions: The Making of a Post-Contemporary American Fiction* (Urbana: University of Illinois Press, 1975).

BIBLIOGRAPHY

Alter, Robert. "The New American Novel." *Commentary* 60 (November 1975): 44–51.

———. *Partial Magic: The Novel as a Self-Conscious Genre*. Berkeley: University of California Press, 1975. On reflexivism in fiction from Cervantes to the present. See the last chapter, "The Inexhaustible Genre."

———. "The Self-Conscious Moment: Reflections on the Aftermath of Modernism." *TriQuarterly* 33 (Spring 1975): 209–30.

Altieri, Charles. *Enlarging the Temple: New Directions in American Poetry during the 1960's*. Lewisburg, Pa.: Bucknell University Press, 1979. For a reader interested in the quite different sense in which "postmodernism" is applied to poetry as opposed to fiction, this is an essential book.

Barth, John. "The Literature of Exhaustion." *Atlantic Monthly* 220 (August 1967): 29–43.

———. "The Literature of Replenishment: Postmodernist Fiction." *Atlantic Monthly* 245 (January 1980): 65–71.

Barthelme, Donald, William Gass, Grace Paley, Walker Percy. "A Symposium on Fiction." *Shenandoah* 27 (Winter 1976): 3–31.

Beebe, Maurice. "What Modernism Was." *Journal of Modern Literature* 3 (July 1974): 1065–84.

Bellamy, Joe David. *The New Fiction: Interviews with Innovative American Writers*. Champaign: University of Illinois Press, 1974. Interviews with, among others, Barth, Gass, Sukenick, Barthelme, Ishmael Reed.

———. *Superfiction, or The American Story Transformed*. New York: Vintage Books, 1975. An anthology of short fiction; see the introduction.

Bergonzi, Bernard. *The Situation of the Novel*. London: Macmillan, 1970. An urbane speculation on the fiction, English and American, of mid-century. See especially chapter 4, "America: The Incredible Reality."

Bradbury, Malcolm, ed. *The Novel Today: Contemporary Writers on Modern Fiction*. Glasgow: Fontana/Collins, 1977. Previously published essays; see the introduction.

Brooke-Rose, Christine. "Eximplosions." *Genre* 14 (Spring 1981): 9–21.

Caramello, Charles. "Fleshing Out *Willie Masters' Lonesome Wife.*" *Sub-stance* 27 (1980): 56–69.

———. "Performing Self as Performance: James, Joyce, and the Postmodern Turn." *Southern Humanities Review* 15 (1981): 301–5.

Dickstein, Morris. *Gates of Eden: American Culture in the Sixties.* New York: Basic Books, 1977. See chapter 8, "Fiction at the Crossroads: Dilemmas of the Experimental Writer," for a bracing account of fiction in the sociopolitical context of the sixties.

Durand, Regis. "On Conversing: In/on Writing." *Sub-Stance* 27 (1980): 47–51.

Federman, Raymond, ed. *Surfiction: Fiction Now . . . And Tomorrow.* Chicago: Swallow Press, 1975. A rich collection of essays set in a conceptual framework by Federman.

———. "What Are Experimental Novels and Why Are There So Many Left Unread?" *Genre* 14 (Spring 1981): 23–31.

Fogel, Stanley. " 'And All the Little Typtopies': Notes on Language Theory in the Contemporary Experimental Novel." *Modern Fiction Studies* 20 (Autumn 1974): 328–36.

Gardner, John. *On Moral Fiction.* New York: Basic Books, 1978. A rather heavy-handed polemic that seeks to demolish the subject of this bibliography.

Gass, William H. *Fiction and the Figures of Life.* New York: Knopf, 1970. An essential collection of essays, both theoretical and applied, which advances a nonmimetic position toward fiction with wit and philosophical rigor.

———. *The World Within the Word.* New York: Knopf, 1978. A rich and stylish collection of essays, mainly on modern fiction, less polemical than *Fiction and the Figures of Life.*

Gilman, Richard. *The Confusion of Realms.* New York: Vintage Books, 1970. Stimulating essays on Barthelme and Gass.

Graff, Gerald. *Literature Against Itself: Literary Ideas in Modern Society.* Chicago: University of Chicago Press, 1979. A brilliant polemic. See especially the chapters "Babbitt at the Abyss" and "The Myth of the Postmodernist Breakthrough," in which Graff argues that "postmodern literature extends rather than overturns the premises of romanticism and modernism."

Green, Geoffrey. "Relativism and the Multiple Contexts for Contemporary Fiction." *Genre* 14 (Spring 1981): 33–44.

Greenman, Myron. "Understanding New Fiction." *Modern Fiction Studies* 20 (1974): 307–16.

Guerard, Albert J. "Notes on the Rhetoric of Anti-Realist Fiction." *TriQuarterly* 30 (Spring 1974): 3–50.

Hafrey, Leigh. "The Gilded Cage: Postmodernism and After." *TriQuarterly* 56 (1983): 126–36.

Hansen, Arlen J. "The Celebration of Solipsism: A New Trend in American Fiction." *Modern Fiction Studies* 19 (1973): 5–16.

Harris, Charles B. *Contemporary American Novelists of the Absurd.* New Haven, Conn.: College and University Press, 1971. On Heller, Vonnegut, Pynchon, Barth.

Hassan, Ihab. *The Dismemberment of Orpheus: Toward a Postmodern Literature.* New York: Oxford University Press, 1971. A meditation on the impulse toward silence and disintegration since the symbolists. See especially the last chapter, "Postlude: The Vanishing Form."

154   The Postmodern Moment

———. "Joyce, Beckett, and the Postmodern Imagination."*TriQuarterly* 34 (Fall 1976): 179–200.

———. *Paracriticisms: Seven Speculations on the Times*. Champaign: University of Illinois Press, 1975. See especially chapter 2, "POSTmodernISM: A Paracritical Bibliography."

Hayman, David. "Double-Distancing: An Attribute of the Post-Modern *Avant-Garde*." *Novel* 12 (Fall 1978): 33–47. An important essay on distance; the illustrations are largely from European contemporaries but there are important applications to the American postmodernists.

Heckard, Margaret. "Robert Coover, Metafiction, and Freedom." *Twentieth Century Literature* 22 (May 1976): 210–27.

Hendin, Josephine. "Experimental Fiction." In *Harvard Guide to Contemporary American Writing*, ed. Daniel Hoffman. Cambridge, Mass.: Harvard University Press, 1979. Largely a revision of her *Vulnerable People*.

———. *Vulnerable People: A View of American Fiction Since 1945*. New York: Oxford University Press, 1978. A thematic survey with commentary on the more prominent postmodernists: Barth, Barthelme, Pynchon, Vonnegut.

Henkle, Roger. "Wrestling (American Style) with Proteus." *Novel* 3 (Spring 1970): 197–207. Portions of a stimulating symposium on contemporary fiction.

Johnson, R. E., Jr. " 'Bees Barking in the Night': The End and Beginning of Donald Barthelme's Narrative." *Boundary 2* 5 (1976): 71–89.

Kazin, Alfred. *Bright Book of Life: American Novelists and Storytellers from Hemingway to Mailer*. Boston: Little, Brown, 1973. A nontheoretical but lucid and intelligent survey of recent fiction with commentary on the more prominent postmodernists.

Kennard, Jean. *Number and Nightmare: Forms of Fantasy in Contemporary Literature*. Hamden, Conn.: Archon/Shoe String Press, 1975. Some excellent stylistic analysis.

Klinkowitz, Jerome. "Avant-garde and After." *Sub-Stance* 27 (1980): 125–37.

———. *The Life of Fiction*. Champaign: University of Illinois Press, 1977. Contains discussions of some postmodernist writers not widely discussed elsewhere: Gilbert Sorrentino, Michael Stephens, Walter Abish, Clarence Major, Steve Katz, Jonathan Baumbach.

———. *Literary Disruptions: The Making of a Post-Contemporary American Fiction*. Champaign: University of Illinois Press, 1975. Despite a conceptual scheme that will strike some readers as unnecessarily divisive, Klinkowitz offers perceptive commentary on Sukenick, Federman, Sorrentino, Barthelme, Vonnegut, among others.

Lauzen, Sarah E. "Men Wearing Macintoshes, the Macguffin in the Carpet, (Aunt Martha—*still*?—on the Stair)." *Chicago Review* 33 (Winter 1983): 57–77.

LeClair, Thomas. "Avant-garde Mastery." *TriQuarterly* 53 (Winter 1982): pp. 259–67. On the relation between certain large postmodernist novels. Gaddis's *J.R.* and Barth's *Letters* for example, and systems theory.

LeClair, Tom, and Larry McCaffery. *Anything Can Happen: Interviews with Contemporary American Novelists*. Champaign: University of Illinois Press, 1983. Barth, Barthelme, Rosellen Brown, Coover, Doctorow, DeLillo, Elkin, Federman, Gardner, Gass, Hawkes, Irving, Diane Johnson, Steve Katz, Joseph McElroy, Tony Morrison, Tim O'Brien, Ron Sukenick.

Levin, Harry. "What Was Modernism?" In his *Refractions*. New York: Oxford University Press, 1966.

McCaffery, Larry. *"Literary Disruptions*: Fiction in a 'Post-Contemporary' Age.*"Boundary 2* 5 (1976): 137–51. An important review essay.
——. *The Metafictional Muse.* Pittsburgh: University of Pittsburgh Press, 1982. Both theoretical and applied; an essential book.
McConnell, Frank. "The Corpse of the Dragon: Notes on Postromantic Fiction." *TriQuarterly* 33 (Spring 1975): 273–303.
McKenzie, James, ed. "Pole-Vaulting in Top Hats: A Public Conversation with John Barth, William Gass, and Ishmael Reed." *Modern Fiction Studies* 22 (1977): 131–51.
Marcotte, Edward. "Intersticed Prose." *Chicago Review* 26 (1975): 31–36. On fiction organized into "short, paragraph-like segments, separated by space."
Martin, Richard. "Clio Bemused: The Uses of History in Contemporary American Fiction."*Sub-Stance* 27 (1980): 13–24.
Mella, John. "On Innovative Writing." *Chicago Review* 33 (1982): 13–27.
Mellard, James M. *The Exploded Form: The Modernist Novel in America.* Urbana: University of Illinois Press, 1980.
Noel, Daniel C. "Tales of Fictive Power: Dreaming and Imagination in Ronald Sukenick's Postmodern Fiction." *Boundary 2* 5 (1976): 117–35.
Olderman, Raymond. *Beyond the Wasteland: The American Novel in the Nineteen Sixties.* New Haven, Conn.: Yale University Press, 1972. A stimulating survey of the major novelists of the decade, seeking coherence in their common response to certain mythic possibilities.
Porlish, David. "Technology and Postmodernism: Cybernetic Fiction." *Sub-Stance* 27 (1980): 92–100.
Rother, James. "Parafiction: The Adjacent Universe of Barth, Barthelme, Pynchon, and Nabokov." *Boundary 2* 5 (1976): 21–44.
Russell, Charles. "Individual Voice in the Collective Discourse: Literary Innovation in Postmodern American Fiction." *Sub-Stance* 27 (1980): 28–39.
Ryf, Robert S. "Character and Imagination in the Experimental Novel." *Modern Fiction Studies* 20 (Autumn 1974): 317–27.
Said, Edward W. "Contemporary Fiction and Criticism." *TriQuarterly* 33 (Spring 1975): 231–56.
Samet, Tom. "Rickie's Cow: Makers and Shapers in Contemporary Fiction." *Novel* 9 (Fall 1975): 66–73. A stimulating review essay on Bellamy's *The New Fiction.*
Schmitz, Neil. "Robert Coover and the Hazards of Metafiction." *Novel* 7 (Spring 1974): 210–19.
Scholes, Robert. *Fabulation and Metafiction.* Urbana: University of Illinois Press, 1979. An expansion of the earlier *The Fabulators.*
——. *The Fabulators.* New York: Oxford University Press, 1967.
Spanos, William V. "The Detective and the Boundary: Some Notes on the Postmodern Literary Imagination." *Boundary 2* 1 (Fall 1972): 147–68. An important essay on the philosophical orientation of postmodernist fiction.
Stevick, Philip. *Alternative Pleasures: Postrealist Fiction and the Tradition.* Urbana: University of Illinois Press, 1981.
——. *Anti-Story: An Anthology of Experimental Fiction.* New York: Free Press, 1971. An anthology of short fiction; see the introduction.
Sukenick, Ronald. *The Death of the Novel and Other Stories.* New York: Dial Press,

1969. A collection of fictions that incorporate, here and there, statements of the author's aesthetic position.

————. "The New Tradition." *Partisan Review* 39 (Fall 1972): 580–89.

————. "Thirteen Digressions." *Partisan Review* 43 (1976): 90–101.

Tanner, Tony. *City of Words: American Fiction, 1950–1970.* New York: Harper & Row, 1971. A brilliant survey of the fiction of the period with perceptive commentary on the early postmodernists.

————. "Games American Writers Play: Ceremony, Contestation, and Carnival." *Salmagundi* 35 (Fall 1976): 110–40. A important examination of the metaphor of fiction as game.

Vidal, Gore. "American Plastic: The Matter of Fiction." In his *Matters of Fact and Fiction.* New York: Random House, 1977. An unsympathetic view of the mode of fiction treated here.

Wasson, Richard. "Notes on a New Sensibility." *Partisan Review* 36 (1969): 460–77. A brilliant early essay on the transformations of mind and art in the late sixties.

Werner, Craig Hansen. *Paradoxical Resolutions: American Fiction Since James Joyce.* Urbana: University of Illinois Press, 1982. Of the several treatments of the influence of Joyce, this one is the most pertinent to the American postmodernists.

Wilde, Alan. *Horizons of Assent: Modernism, Postmodernism, and the Ironic Imagination.* Baltimore: Johns Hopkins University Press, 1981. A highly sophisticated study of the development of the characteristic posture of postmodernist fiction to experience.

Zavarzadeh, Mas'ud. *The Mythopoeic Reality: The Postwar American Nonfiction Novel.* Urbana: University of Illinois Press, 1976. More than a book on the "nonfiction novel," a rich speculation on fiction and contemporary culture.

7

Music

GARRY E. CLARKE

How, we might ask initially, are the labels "modern" and "postmodern" employed when describing music? The first part of the question is not difficult to answer. The word "modern" is normally used when recently composed music—contemporary music—is being discussed. Often there is a negative connotation in the use of the term. G. M. Artusi's work of 1600, " . . . *Delle imperfezioni della moderna musica*," and Henry Pleasants' *The Agony of Modern Music* (1955) are representative and demonstrate that modern music is often music that is difficult to comprehend.[1] The label also describes works composed in previous generations that are still not dated in any significant way. Monteverdi's madrigals, which Artusi was attacking, are modern even in the 1980s. At this writing, the label "postmodern" is not commonly used in musical analysis. Most musicians, in fact, will admit to confusion when asked for a definition of the term in reference to their art.

In this essay, a general discussion of cultivated music of the past three decades is followed by an analysis of a number of works, mostly American, that might logically be called musical examples of postmodernism. Let us, as a point of departure, gain a perspective on the recent past by considering two works that were first played in the fall of 1962 for the opening of Philharmonic (now Avery Fisher) Hall at Lincoln Center for the Performing Arts in New York. Aaron Copland's *Connotations* is a moving, austere composition based on serial procedures. This kind of writing, so far removed from the "popular" Copland of *Appalachian Spring* and *Rodeo* fame, and much misunderstood by audiences because it is abstract rather than folksy, nevertheless represents one of the composer's important statements. Its beginnings may be found as early as 1930, when Copland produced his Piano Variations; indeed, a serious and even severe side of Copland has appeared from time to time in his music over the years. In the program notes written for the first performances of *Connotations*, the composer stated that the piece's "primary meaning" is summarized in the three four-voiced chords heard at the beginning of the work. The harmonic and melodic implications of the material are defined by Copland as the piece proceeds through a number of sections that are ingenious developments of the opening material. Just as the creation of Lincoln Center represented an important step for culture in America, this composition, by a man who for forty years had produced works that would easily label him as one of the finest of America's musical creators, demonstrated the writing of a mature American composer at his best.

A second work commissioned for the opening of Lincoln Center was a piano concerto by Samuel Barber. Here was a brilliant virtuoso piece by a composer whose works had been widely performed since the late 1930s. As an accessible concerto very much in the romantic tradition, it has been played by a number of pianists and has enjoyed success with audiences during the past two decades. There is a first movement following traditional formal lines (a lyrical, haunting "second theme" in the oboe and a cadenza reminiscent of the nineteenth-century piano concerto); a poignant *canzona* for a second movement; and an "ostinato" finale, with passages that could almost be mistaken for Prokofiev, Rachmaninoff, and Ravel, which brings the work to a brilliant conclusion. These two compositions represent a kind of continuum—a continuing tradition in music by well-established composers—and they also are indicative of something else. For by the 1960s, Barber and Copland, as well as most of their contemporaries, were "out" as far as many of the younger, progressive intellectuals (the "ultramodernists" as they have sometimes been called) were concerned. If such compositions are solid musical achievements, they also represent ideas that were viewed as old fashioned at the time they were written.[2]

Who was considered progressive? During this period, two schools of musical thinkers, of which John Cage and Milton Babbitt are representative, demonstrate what has been termed the "experimental" and the "scientific" approaches to music composition.[3] Cage, beginning in the late 1930s, pioneered many important new musical concepts—from the prepared piano (in which metal, wood, and rubber objects are inserted between the piano strings) to aleatoric events and chance operations, from the idea of experiencing music in its environment to the philosophy of viewing music itself as life and as silence. Cage's notable career continued in the 1960s and 1970s as the composer created new works and happenings, guided by star maps and his own concept that everything we do is music. Among his numerous achievements of the past two decades is *O' O''* (1962), which the composer performed in the mid-1960s by preparing and slicing vegetables, placing them in a blender, then blending and drinking the juice. The sounds of these activities were amplified and became the musical work. In 1971, Cage wrote *Sixty-Two Mesostics re Merce Cunningham* for "unaccompanied voice using Microphone." The *Etudes Australes* (1974–75), thirty-two pieces for piano, were composed employing chance operations with the help of the *I Ching* and a book of star maps. They emerge as abstract and difficult études that might be mistaken for serial compositions. *Apartment House 1776* (1976) is a mixed media event, which contains music from the American Revolution, while *Child of Tree* (1975) and *Branches* (1976) are verbal scores written for such vegetable instruments as amplified cactus. A related work is

Inlets (1977), for four conch players, which includes the sound of burning pine cones. This music sometimes presented problems in the hearing, and boredom was a factor often noted by audiences. The importance of the philosophies behind much of it could hardly be denied, however, since what in the past had been called noises became sound sources for Cage's music.

Milton Babbitt's total serialization of a work, where every aspect of a composition from pitches to rhythms and dynamics is chosen according to elaborate organizational procedures that can be traced to Schoenberg, is a method that has resulted in some of the most complex and difficult music ever conceived. Babbitt's *Philomel* (1964) for soprano, electronically altered vocal sounds, and synthesized sound is a moving and brilliant concert piece whose virtuostic gestures recall Liszt and whose sensuous and lyric qualities are above all intensely musical. His often humorous *All Set* for jazz ensemble (1957), with its singing lines, and the String Quartet No. 4 (1976), with its formidable and varied rhythms and textures, are representative; they speak of a man who has used his intricate methods to construct works that are always admirable and often beautiful. The pianist Alan Feinberg, playing three of Babbitt's miniatures as a set in New York in March 1983 (*Partitions* [1957], *My Compliments to Roger* [Sessions] [1978], and *Playing for Time* [1977]), noted that "as with the Chopin études, one can never play them too well: these Babbitt works have all the exhilaration of virtuoso études together with a kind of Dixieland freshness." Andrew Porter, writing in the *New Yorker*, saw the pieces as "jewelled constructions intricately wrought; airy towers of delight seven octaves high; a world of fantasy, swift emotion, and orderly wit."[4] Babbitt's many honors include a special Pulitzer citation awarded in 1982 for "his life's work as a distinguished and seminal American composer."[5] His compositions constitute an important statement by a mature artist.

In the case of Cage, Babbitt, and their contemporaries, there are countless sound possibilities for a musical work—far more than those available to composers of a previous generation. Cage's philosophy makes anything a proper choice for a musical sound source—from brake drums and amplified typewriters, to electronic sources, to conventional instruments. Babbitt himself was instrumental in the development of electronic music and was a founder, in 1959, of the Columbia-Princeton Electronic Music Center. These sound options, together with those afforded by the computer, began what appeared to be a revolution in music. Indeed, in the 1960s, the existence of so many possibilities made a work for conventional orchestra (even if based on serial procedures) and a piano concerto in the manner of Barber seem especially outdated in instrumentation as well as in design.

The influence of Cage and of Babbitt has been far-reaching. Many composers embraced the ideas of Cage, among them such unlikely individuals as the Polish composer Witold Lutoslawski, who in 1960 heard part of Cage's Piano Concerto on the radio: "Those few minutes were to change my life decisively. . . . While listening to it, I suddenly realized that I could compose music differently from that of my past. . . . I could start out from the chaos and create order in it, gradually."[6] Lutoslawski's *Venetian Games* (1961), which contains elements of chance, is an example of a work in which Cage's influence may be found. The American composer, Earle Brown, wrote his *Novara* in 1962 for the Tanglewood Festival. The work consists of twenty composed "sound elements" that give the piece its identity and which can be freely sequenced, juxtaposed, and combined by the conductor. The players each perform a fixed element as the conductor chooses them in an open, "mobile" way. Brown notes that the "action-painting" techniques of Jackson Pollock in the 1940s originally inspired the concept of a work that is formed while it is being conducted. The mobiles of Alexander Calder, which have fascinated and influenced Brown, were also a factor in the creation of *Novara*. In a sense, in the cases of both Brown and Calder, the works have a fixed content, but as they are heard or viewed, the elements move and are perceived in different lights.[7] In fact, structural indeterminacy is a trait common to many compositions of the 1950s and 1960s.

Babbitt's influence also may be seen through his students, who studied and taught the art of combinatoriality and related serial procedures. Since most had not the ability of their mentor, the results were usually not significant. Of those few who had an originality of their own, Peter Westergaard employed serial procedures in his own individual way, producing notable results in the process.

It is obvious that the work of Cage and Babbitt gives only a partial view of musical creativity in America. Babbitt's teacher, Roger Sessions, born in 1896, a towering and uncompromising figure writing difficult and complicated serial compositions, continued to produce important works such as the cantata, *When Lilacs Last in the Dooryard Bloom'd* (first performed in 1971), and the Pulitzer Prize winning Concerto for Orchestra, first played in Boston in 1981. Elliott Carter, whose compositions are firmly rooted in the art music of the European tradition yet display a firm and unmistakable personal style, has maintained a masterful and meticulous control over the elements that comprise his works. The neoclassical traits of his youth (he was born in 1908) have not been lost, but the continuing development of a distinctiveness in his music has made such compositions as the Piano Concerto (1964–65) and *A Symphony of Three Orchestras* (1976) major and complex accomplishments. Carter's *A Mirror on Which to Dwell* (1975), six settings of poems by Elizabeth Bishop, reveals another side of the composer, a simplicity and accessibility aided by a clear and careful setting of texts. Each work Carter produces is a unique achievement developing out of his own aesthetic rather than from the experimentation of Cage or from the serial procedures of the university.

Some of America's accomplishments are described by these examples, and Europe has its counterparts. Karlheinz Stockhausen's use of electronic sources and serial and chance procedures, which produced such notable works as *Gesang der Jünglinge* (1955–56) and the *Klavierstücke*, gave way to the composer's fascination with ritual, meditation, and mysticism. *Stimmung* (1968) consists of a single harmony, to be sustained for seventy-five minutes. *Mantra* (1970) for two pianists is a long work based on a single melodic formula that is developed in numerous ways and which shows the composer's interest in the culture of the Far East. Stockhausen has considered new uses of physical space in music. *Sternklang* (1971), which the composer describes as "sacred music," is a large piece to be performed in the open air by several groups spaced around a park, "reading" their music from the constellations in the evening sky. The composer states that *Sternklang* is "based on five harmonic chords, each with eight notes, tuned as overtones in *pure* tuning. All have one note in common." The music's purpose is described as follows: "*Sternklang* is music for concentrated listening in meditation, for the sinking of the individual into the cosmic whole. It is intended as a preparation for beings from other stars and for the day of their arrival."[8]

Lutoslawski's and Krzysztof Penderecki's spectacular essays for orchestra (the latter's famous *Threnody for the Victims of Hiroshima* (1960) for fifty-two strings is an example) demonstrate the virtuostic writing of the 1960s. Pierre Boulez's serial compositions, formidable and highly complex creations of the early 1950s, were followed by works employing chance procedures (which can be noted as early as the Piano Sonata No. 3 of 1956–57). The scientific and mystical essays and music of Iannis Xenakis attempted to draw art and science together.[9] Lucanio Berio's work with electronic music, serialism, and aleatoric processes gave way to an eclectic approach—uses of already existing material, both of the composer and of others; varied uses of the human voice; combinations of live and prerecorded sound; and the concept of the never-concluded "work in progress." Often these pieces taxed performers, for they were formidable in their difficulties. Composers, too, were taxed, finding it necessary to invent new methods of notation to communicate their ideas.

Another progressive composer, Bruno Maderna, made use of some of these techniques, including serial and aleatoric devices. In the foreword to the score of his *Quadrivium per 4 esecutori di percussione e 4 gruppi d'orchestra* (1969), the composer wrote that his music was intended "to interest and entertain the audience...."[10] This statement evidenced a concern for the listener, which critics of the ultramodernists claimed was too seldom the case in many creations of the 1950s and 1960s. Babbitt, in his article, "Who Cares If You Listen?" had presented one point of view in 1958, although the provocative title does not present a complete summary of Babbitt's thinking.[11] But the crisis in music, in essence, became the issue of communication. Works hopelessly abstract, needlessly complicated, sometimes exploiting the new simply for the sake of novelty, would not endure if they did not also demonstrate a profound and logical musical sensibility.

Yet Babbitt, Carter and others composed pieces in which the technique proved to be secondary to the music, while Copland, also, through his *Inscape* for orchestra of 1967 and the *Duo* for flute and piano (1970–71), continued his tradition of writing significant compositions, both severe and simple; thus works of substance—and works that communicated—were being produced in many

ways and with differing viewpoints. Modern music need not be what a critic
writing in the 1950s had termed "the noise made by deluded speculators picking
through the slagpile."[12] A feeling existed by the late 1960s and early 1970s that
experiments and science could go only so far. Much of what had been produced
by the progressive schools could hardly be termed any more musical than the
countless hack works being churned out for high school bands and parish choirs.
The worlds of abstraction and unrelenting dissonance and the lack of the human
element (if a computer or electronic means were employed) helped to bring
about, essentially, a swing of the pendulum that came to constitute the new
music of the last fifteen years.

If the term "postmodern" is to be used in describing this music, it is necessary
to ask what the music goes beyond. An answer might be this: Babbitt at his
most organized; Cage at his least organized. In quite a number of works, there
was a move from complexity to simplicity. Sounds that were hardly tolerated
in the 1960s (consonant chords and tonality, for example) were once again
embraced by a number of serious composers. The simplicity was often deceptive
but was, nevertheless, a logical reaction to the overriding complexity that could
make modern music such an agonizing experience for musicians and the public
alike. Composers made *communication* an important priority and did care if the
audience listened.

Minimalism, one of these movements to a supposed simplicity, is a case in
point. The term, much in evidence during the past decade and itself somewhat
problematic, may be used to describe music in which a minimal number of
materials is employed.[13] The works may be long—very long—but the Western
practice of a variety of structural elements continuously developed is abandoned
for something outwardly more simple. Experimental music had no limits, but
this music could be limited even to a single entity. The concept owes much to
minimal art. There is also a relationship with serialism in music, since stasis (a
pitch class that always sounds in the same octave during a work, for example)
is an integral part of some serial pieces, just as it is a concept in minimal music.

An early musical effort that relates to minimalism, Cage's *4'33"* (1952), is
a piece where the performer or performers remain silent for the amount of time
prescribed by the work's title. Yet this deceptively simple composition—it is
nothing, in essence—shows that pure silence does not exist. The sounds of the
audience, the inadvertent noises made by the performers, the fact that no human
environment itself can be free of sound, can contribute to what is actually a
complex composition. A number of La Monte Young's compositions in the
1960s exemplify what for obvious reasons has been called "trance music."
These include *The Tortoise, His Dreams and Journeys*, a short piece, repeated,
reworked, and embellished every day, perhaps for many years or even for the
lifetime of the composer. Another work consists, in its entirety, of two pitches,
"to be held for a long time." Yet another contains a single instruction: "Draw
a straight line and follow it." These ideas are not strictly new and can be traced
to Eric Satie and his *Vexations* (ca. 1893–95), a short piece that is to be performed

840 times in succession. A well-known and related example from the 1960s, Terry Riley's *In C*, consists of fifty-three musical fragments, repeated in a specific order. The players may perform a fragment once or many times before moving on. A performance issued on Columbia Records takes forty-three minutes and emerges as a multifaceted monolith.[14]

Tom Johnson's *The Four Note Opera* (1971) is described by the composer as "part absurdist, part minimalistic, part satiric and part simply comedy."[15] Using only the pitch classes A, B, D, and E, Johnson has written a forty-five-minute one-act work that is a spoof on opera and its singers and conventions. The limiting of sounds available for use has helped the composer produce an opera that achieves singularity because only four pitches are involved. Pauline Oliveros, playing improvisational dinner music in November 1983, "engage[d] in a process called emptiness." In the words of a critic, "this was largely static music: Miss Oliveros . . . began with a sustained note, which she gradually allowed to turn into a chord, which eventually shifted into another chord, then another. At the end of the hour, everything died away peacefully."[16] Of course, works need not be as long as an opera, a dinner hour, or a lifetime. Philip Corner's *One Note Once* is exactly what the title suggests.

One of the leading composers of minimal music, Philip Glass, received a traditional training (Peabody Conservatory, The University of Chicago, Juilliard, and Nadia Boulanger all figure in his background), and his early compositions reflect his musical upbringing. But an exposure to Indian music, the development of a philosophical understanding of it, and the realization that there were methods beyond those strictly Western (not only in the development of materials but in the notion that tension and release are essential in such matters as rhythm and in the handling of consonance and dissonance) led him to minimalism and its meditational possibilities. The static simplicity of the harmonic language often hides a complexity of rhythm and texture. In the words of one critic, describing a New York City Ballet performance of "Glass Pieces," the composer's music in a ballet choreographed by Jerome Robbins, "it is an absolute victory of complex simplicity."[17]

This victory can be seen in short works (the pieces in the album "Glassworks"—worlds unto themselves—are examples).[18] It is also evident in the four-act, five-hour *Einstein on the Beach* (1976), an opera without a conventional plot and with concepts of minimalism extended until the music emerges as endlessly static yet constantly changing sounds in time suspended. Here is the problem with the term "minimal," for the course of the long work, a gradual process with meditative implications, is actually a many-faceted world emerging from deceptively simple sources.

Glass is not the only composer to work in an attempt to, if not synthesize, at least somehow bring the Far East and the West together. Some of the efforts of Lou Harrison and Cage come to mind as earlier prototypes. And Glass' contemporary, Steve Reich, has also disregarded the traditional formulaic devices of Western music. There is always the hope that somehow a true synthesis—even of Western, Oriental, and African musics—will take place. And there is the thought that music need not offer a constant variety in order to communicate. Should musical memory always function as it does when a work with a conventional series of events is perceived? Must a listener always think of the transformations of materials to come in a work and anticipate their arrival? One answer to these questions is a simple no.

Antimusic, in essence the destruction of sound, the search for the ultimate paradox, relates to minimalism. Examples can be seen as early as the 1930s in I. A. MacKenzie's *Wind Sound Sculptures*, pieces of sculpture played by the wind, placed where human ears will not hear the music. Self-destructing works, such as a piece composed with disappearing ink, are a form of antimusic as is "danger" music. Dick Higgins' *One Antipersonnel Type CBU Bomb Will Be Thrown into the Audience* is one obvious and frightening example of the latter.

"Concept music," pieces conceived by the mind for the mind, also relate to these processes. Some of Pauline Oliveros' *Sonic Meditations*, a number of works in verbal notation, are examples, as is Steve Reich's *Slow Motion Sound* (1967), which, according to the composer, "has remained a concept on paper because it was technologically impossible to realize. The basic idea was to take a loop, probably of speech, and ever so gradually slow it down to enormous length *without lowering its pitch*."[19] Reich describes a concept—one that has many possibilities—but for the mind alone.

Another general tendency has been to view the past not as a matter of embarrassment, but as a source of inspiration for the present and future. The earlier notion that anything of the past was by definition old-fashioned and to be avoided gave way to the thinking that the artifacts of history were invaluable to the present. One example of a work in which this philosophy is evident is the *Baroque Variations* (1967) of Lukas Foss. The movements, the composer notes, are "dreams" about three familiar Baroque pieces, all in the key of E Major (a movement of a Handel concerto grosso, a Scarlatti sonata, and the Prelude from Bach's Partita in E for solo violin). Although the texts of the original works are left for the most part intact, Foss achieves transformations and a good deal of humor through various musical additions and amplifications. The observation that Baroque style characteristics as well as actual uses of other composers' works have found their ways into a number of works by twentieth-century composers (Stravinsky, for example, whose *Pulcinella* bears a relationship to the *Baroque Variations*) is not to undermine Foss' achievement in transforming already existing materials into a new work.

Dominick Argento's *Postcard from Morocco*, an opera first produced in 1971, unfolds as a series of dreamlike sequences that take place in a train station in Morocco. One of the episodes, an instrumental divertimento entitled "Souvenirs de Bayreuth," is a resurrection of the nineteenth-century practice of pasting together a string of "memories" of a certain locale (Gottschalk's *Souvenirs d'Andalousie* [1851] is a period example). Argento's remembrances contain a number of Wagnerian staples, potpourri fashion, including portions of the "Evening Star" from *Tannhauser* and the "Spinning Song" from *The Flying Dutch-man*, strains of *Lohengrin* (the "Bridal Chorus" and a fragment of the "Prelude" to Act III), and some allusions to the *Ring* cycle. Argento's piece is really a fox-trot, a nostalgic 1970s view of 1914 (when the opera takes place and when Wagner's popularity was such that his music could, indeed, have been heard in a Moroccan railway station).

George Crumb has embraced tonality in some of his work (the G-flat Major "Song of Reconciliation," a part of *Music for a Summer Evening* (1974) is an example). He also quotes from other composers, the borrowed material emerging as an integral part of his compositional process. *Black Angels* (1970) for electric string quartet contains tonal passages quoting music of Schubert (*Death and the Maiden*) and Tartini (*The Devil's Trill*) as well as the modal *Dies Irae*. "Thirteen Images from the Dark Land," the work's subtitle, describes in part its program. The composer intends *Black Angels* to be a commentary or parable on the contemporary world. In writing his statement, he has not avoided the concepts and works of previous generations of composers.

Some composers used the past by exhuming actual materials and requoting or reworking them while others embraced a general philosophical association with it.[20] From the late 1960s, various earlier periods of music history have been unashamedly consulted for inspiration. Romantic thinking and musical materials have characterized the work of a number of composers in recent years. Schoen-berg's statement, "romanticism is dead, long live the new romanticism," has been quoted to describe not only the essence of new works, but to serve as a reminder that the romantic impulse has existed often in music history and in one form or another during most stylistic periods.[21]

A man whose music demonstrates these characteristics is David Del Tredici, yet another composer who came from a background of serial training (at Prince-ton, with Sessions) and whose work of the 1960s is reflective of his early musical upbringing. In 1968, however, Del Tredici embarked on a series of works that are settings of sections of Lewis Carroll's *Alice in Wonderland*. *Pop-Pourri* (1968, revised 1970), for soprano, rock group, chorus, and orchestra, employs texts from *Alice*, from Carroll's *Through the Looking Glass*, from the *Liber Usualis* ("The Litany of the Blessed Virgin Mary"), as well as a chorale from a Bach cantata. An *Alice Symphony* occupied the composer off and on between 1969 and 1972. *Vintage Alice* dates from 1972, *Adventures Underground* from 1975. *Final Alice* (1976) is a sixty-five-minute "cantata" for amplified soprano-narrator, soprano saxophones, mandolin, tenor banjo, accordion, and a very large orchestra. Its linking of symphonic forces with a group of folk instruments, of the operatic gesture with elements of popular music, and its sheer length (recalling the late nineteenth century) results in an eclectic and new experience despite the music itself, which often hearkens to another era and to the world of tonality. The sensuality of the music, its nostalgic qualities (an obvious aspect of works that evoke the past), the size of the forces required for performance of the composition, so far-removed from the economy of means that often characterizes music of the 1950s and 1960s, all speak to a revival of a certain romantic sensibility, if not to a new romanticism itself. Del Tredici's further adventures with Alice have produced the evening-long, four-part *Child Alice: In Memory of a Summer Day* (winner of a 1980 Pulitzer Prize), *Quaint Events*, *Happy Voices*, and *All in the Golden Afternoon*, another series of essays for amplified soprano and large orchestra in the tradition of the grand tone painters Mahler and Richard Strauss.

An indication of the importance of this school of musical thinking may be seen in a series of concerts given in June 1983 by the New York Philharmonic. "A New Romanticism?" asked a promotional brochure, explaining that Jacob Druckman, the artistic director for the festival and himself a distinguished composer, argues that a new romanticism has indeed arrived. Some of the works programmed (Foss' *Baroque Variations*, Del Tredici's *All in the Golden Afternoon*, George Rochberg's *Imago Mundi*) sustained the premise admirably. Others, at best, were questionable. John Rockwell, writing in the *New York Times* after one of the concerts, observed that if the promotional materials had not reminded the audience of a "new romanticism," the "concert would have sounded like a perfectly ordinary contemporary music concert of the sort we have been encountering for the past couple of decades."[22] Donald Martino's *Triple Concerto* (1977) for soprano clarinet, bass clarinet, contra-bass clarinet, and chamber orchestra was in one sense a questionable example of a new romanticism, and this is not surprising. Martino, a student of Babbitt (to whom the score is dedicated) and a Pulitzer Prize winner in 1974 for his *Notturno*, represents a musician whose works can be inordinately complex in their serial constructions, fiendishly difficult in their rhythmic structures, and aurally abstruse. The *Triple Concerto*, which reminded Mr. Rockwell of "a particularly New York extension of Central European Expressionism," is intense and emotional—common traits in Martino's work and themselves romantic characteristics. But to observe the body of Martino's work is to find that the *Triple Concerto* represents only one side of a multifaceted musical personality. He, like Westergaard, represents a Babbitt prodigy who has used his training to help in the evolution of his own individual style. Like Copland, with his simple and severe styles, Martino has his easily accessible moments. The *Seven Pious Pieces* for a chorus of mixed voices (1971) demonstrates that a serial composition can sound tonal. These are warm and intimate works whose gestures recall the great romantic choral tradition of the nineteenth and early twentieth centuries. Martino's *Augenmusik*, a "satirical vignette" of 1972 "for Actress Danseuse, or Uninhibited Female Percussionist," and the *Paradiso Choruses* for soloists, chorus, orchestra, and tape (1974) also abandon the often uncompromising austerity of serialism. These pieces are a reminder that there is both an Apollonian and Dionysian aspect of most composers' creative thinking. If Martino's aesthetic does not really represent a new romanticism, it does show a willingness to experiment with different styles.

Does this thinking in general demonstrate a conservative reaction or a return to the old for lack of the new? In some cases, the answers to these questions are affirmative. Yet in others, in most of the works cited previously, in fact, the past is used productively. Something innovative and profound emerges as the new is integrated with the old.

Other developments of the last few years may be observed in what has become the common crossing of media boundaries. Harry Partch, the inventor of wonderful new instruments and an octave divided into forty-three microtones, had produced a music-theatre piece, *Delusion of the Fury—A Ritual of Dream and Delusion* (1963–66) drawing on the cultures of the Far East and Africa for sounds and for imagery. Glass, too, could write a music-theatre piece. *The Photographer*, based on the life and works of Eadweard Muybridge (1830–1904), and first performed in May and June of 1982 in Amsterdam, is an example. This three-part work is a play with incidental music, a concert with violin solo (with Muybridge's photographs developed and projected at the rear of the stage), and a dance. Other composers, including Robert Ashley and Pauline Oliveros, have experimented with mixed media. Roger Reynolds, another composer whose exposure to the Far East has influenced his work, has explored the symbolic, technical, and ritualistic implications as well as the psychology of multimedia works. Laurie Spiegel has worked with "visual music" and has investigated the possibilities of color video. And Laurie Anderson, a "performance artist," combines art-rock, poetry, and theatre in her work. Her four-part, two-evening *United States*, first given a complete performance in February 1983, integrates visual-art and multimedia aspects of performance art. Anderson's abilities as a composer, artist (she is a fine sculptor and photographer), and performer (as violinist, keyboard artist, and singer/speaker) combine to help her produce works that transcend boundaries—"O Superman," a song from *United States*, reached second place on the British popularity charts when it was released in England by Warner Brothers Records in 1980. The term "performance art" is still debated by critics, but a helpful definition might simply be works whose components simultaneously fall into several realms of art and of performance.

A healthy and long-awaited integration of the arts is an outcome of these efforts. Music itself today may build on the technologies of the modern age, and if the past few years have seen the demise of a rugged adherence to serial procedures in most circles and a decline in the production of electronic music, they have also seen these procedures as available resources, to be used if required.[23] If the equivalents of a *Connotations* of Copland or a piano concerto of Barber were given premieres today, they would be accepted on their own terms. If today a Babbitt creation and an essay in minimalism can exist side by side and both be lauded, music's diversity, always evident, seems to be especially pronounced. If punk and new wave rather than minimal music have the necessary immediacy for the 1980s, as one writer suggests, the ever-present and continuing process of change is evident today—as it has always been.[24]

Perhaps one of music's most vital purposes, one of its central functions, is being pursued with success in this eclectic period. Steve Reich's thought that "obviously music should put all within listening range into a state of ecstasy," speaks to communication on an exalted level.[25] Music has continued to do this during the past two decades with endless diversity from countless perspectives.

NOTES

1. Cf. G. M. Artusi, "... *Delle imperfezioni della moderna musica*," a portion of which is reprinted in Oliver Strunk, ed., *Source Readings in Music History* (New York: W. W. Norton & Co., 1950), pp. 393–404; Henry Pleasants, *The Agony of Modern Music* (New York: Simon and Schuster, 1955).

2. Similar thoughts were expressed at a contemporary music conference in New York in 1981, where the low opinion of the Barbers, Hansons, and Brittens during this period was blamed on narrow thinking as well as on intimidation and pressures of the ultra-modernists, in this case the "academic musical establishment." Cf. Walter Simmons, "Contemporary Music: A Weekend of Reflections," *Fanfare* 4 (May-June 1981): 22–23.

3. Cf. Garry E. Clarke, *Essays in American Music* (Westport, Conn.: Greenwood Press, 1977), pp. 179–92. In an endnote, the use of these terms is explained: "The author does not wish to imply that writers who were for the most part traditionalists [in this case, in the early 1960s, a Copland or a Barber] did not experiment or did not employ a 'scientific' approach to their music. Nor does he mean that the 'scientific' way is devoid of any traditional qualities or any experimentation. The ... categories are simply convenient generalizations that point to the music of a [generally conservative composer], a Babbitt, and a Cage." (p. 230)

4. Andrew Porter, "All American," *New Yorker*, March 21, 1983, p. 102. Feinberg is quoted in this review.

5. That Babbitt's ability has long been recognized is further demonstrated by a laudatory telegram that was read at a concert celebrating Babbitt's fiftieth birthday in the spring of 1966. Its author: Igor Stravinsky.

6. Steven Stucky, *Lutoslawski and His Music* (Cambridge: Cambridge University Press, 1981), p. 84.

7. Earle Brown, "Directions for Performance," *Novara* (London: Universal Edition, 1979).

8. Karlheinz Stockhausen, *Sternklang* (Kürten, West Germany: Stockhausen Verlag, 1977), p. 23.

9. An essay of Xenakis, "The Way of Research and Questioning: Formalization and Axiomatization of Music," was distributed with a recording of three of his compositions (*Metastasis*, *Pithoprakta*, and *Eonta*), on Vanguard Records VCS-10030.

10. Bruno Maderna, "Instructions for the Performance of *Quadrivium*," *Quadrivium per 4 esecutori di percussione e 4 gruppi d'orchestra* (Milan: G. Ricordi, 1969).

11. Milton Babbitt, "Who Cares If You Listen?" *High Fidelity* 8 (February 1958): 38–40, 126–27. The article is reprinted in Elliott Schwartz and Barney Childs, eds., *Contemporary Composers on Contemporary Music* (New York: Holt, Rinehart and Winston, 1967) and in Richard Kostelanetz, ed., *Esthetics Contemporary* (Buffalo: Prometheus Books, 1978) under the title that Babbitt had originally intended: "The Composer as Specialist."

12. Pleasants, *The Agony of Modern Music*, p. 3.

13. Minimal music has also been labeled "systematic" music. Cf. Paul Griffiths, "System (ii)" in *The New Grove Dictionary of Music and Musicians*, vol. 18, ed. Stanley Sadie (London: Macmillan Publishers, 1980), p. 481.

14. Columbia recording MS 71778. The score is reprinted on the record jacket and in Joscelyn Godwin, ed., *Schirmer Scores: A Repertory of Western Music* (New York: Schirmer Books, 1975), pp. 1060–61.

15. Tom Johnson, *The Four Note Opera* (New York and London: Associated Music Publishers, 1973), p. iii.

16. Tim Page, "Accordion: Pauline Oliveros," *New York Times*, November 13, 1983, p. 76.

17. Nancy Goldner, "Music by Glass Meets Dance Steps by Robbins—and It's a Draw," *Christian Science Monitor*, June 10, 1983, p. 16.

18. Cf. Philip Glass, "Glassworks," CBS Recording 37265.

19. Steve Reich, *Writings About Music* (Halifax and New York: The Press of the Nova Scotia College of Art and Design and New York University Press, 1974), p. 15.

20. Elsewhere, I have termed this general trend a "New Eclecticism," and have cited as examples works of George Rochberg, George Crumb, Robert Morris, and James Drew. Clarke, *Essays*, pp. 192–213.

21. The program notes accompanying Isaac Stern and the Pittsburgh Symphony's performances of George Rochberg's Violin Concerto in the spring of 1975 quote Schoenberg. The concerto itself is an example of what could very well be termed a "new romanticism."

22. John Rockwell, "Philharmonic: Festival of New Music," *New York Times*, June 5, 1983, p. 54.

23. It is interesting to note two of Steve Reich's "Predictions (1970) about the Future of Music": "Electronic music as such will gradually die and be absorbed into the ongoing music of people singing and playing instruments," and "the pulse and the concept of clear tonal center will re-emerge as basic sources of new music." Reich, *Writings*, p. 28.

24. Peter Wetzler, "Minimal Music," *Ear Magazine East* 6 (June-July-August 1981): 6.

25. Reich, *Writings*, p. 44.

BIBLIOGRAPHICAL ESSAY

The sources listed here offer views on the various kinds of music that are discussed in the preceding essay. A specific text on postmodern music is nowhere to be found in the bibliography. As stated in the essay, the term "postmodern" has not been applied to music in any significant way. One could speculate that here is another instance of terminology employed later in the field of music than in other arts.

One may wonder about the inclusion of volumes on such subjects as electronic music in the bibliography, which would appear to be a kind of music typical of a modern rather than a postmodern era. But electronic sound sources are important to many composers working today, and reading about the subject is helpful for anyone who wishes to understand current compositional practice. Indeed, although the bibliography may at first glance appear to be somewhat eclectic, each of the suggested readings relates to the subject at hand and in some way illuminates the work of composers currently at work.

Of the books listed, Salzman's *Twentieth-Century Music: An Introduction*, although published in a second edition a decade ago, remains a vital, comprehensive source, by an important musician. John Rockwell's *All American Music* (1983) discusses current trends in a series of twenty excellent, stimulating, and often opinionated essays. The representative sampling of articles from other sources should be amplified by a general comment on three periodicals that can be helpful, presenting as they do views on the current state of music from some rather different perspectives. *Ear Magazine East*, a new music and literary journal published by New Wilderness Foundation, Inc. (365 West End Avenue, New York, New York 10024), celebrated its tenth anniversary of continuous publication in February 1983. It explores new music with enthusiasm from a worldwide perspective. First published in 1962 by Princeton University Press and now produced at Bard College and at the University of Washington, *Perspectives of New Music*, in almost every issue, presents valuable material dealing with the current state of music and the work of contemporary composers. Sometimes an issue is centered on the work of a specific composer: much of the Spring-Summer/Fall-Winter 1976 issue (14–15), for example, is devoted to Milton Babbitt. Some of the articles are highly technical, while others are of a more general nature. *Soundings*, which first appeared in 1977, publishes works of unknown composers as well as pieces by well-known composers who have been ignored by commercial publishing houses. Many important artists have been represented over the years. *Soundings* is essentially the work of one man, Peter Garland, and may be ordered from him at 948 Canyon Road, Santa Fe, New Mexico 87501.

ANNOTATED BIBLIOGRAPHY

Books, Dictionaries, Encyclopedias, and Anthologies

Appleton, John H., and Ronald C. Perera, eds. *The Development and Practice of Electronic Music*. Englewood Cliffs, N.J.: Prentice-Hall, 1975. This is a helpful series of essays by a number of important musicians including Otto Luening, Gordon Mumma, and A. Wayne Slawson. The book is appropriate for students and musicians, as well as the layman.

Battcock, Gregory, ed. *Breaking the Sound Barrier: A Critical Anthology of the New Music*. New York: E. P. Dutton, 1981. This anthology contains a number of interesting essays reprinted from such sources as the *Musical Quarterly*, *Perspectives of New Music*, *Current Musicology*, and *The Village Voice* relating to an eclectic assortment of subjects and composers.

Boretz, Benjamin, and Edward T. Cone, eds. *Perspectives on American Composers*. New York: W. W. Norton & Co., 1971. These essays, reprinted from issues of *Perspectives of New Music* and often quite technical, may not be especially helpful, although the work of such composers as Copland, Carter, and Sessions is mentioned.

Boulez, Pierre. *Boulez on Music Today*. Translated by Susan Bradshaw and Richard Rodney Bennett. Cambridge, Mass.: Harvard University Press, 1971. This is a difficult but important book, and some of the general considerations on musical technique are well worth studying.

Brindle, Reginald Smith. *The New Music: The Avant-Garde Since 1945*. London: Oxford University Press, 1975. A wide variety of topics is covered, from serialism and electronic music to jazz and the Orient. Notation, the theatre, and music and society are among the other considerations.

Cage, John. *Empty Words: Writings '73-'78*. Middletown, Conn.: Wesleyan University Press, 1981.

————. *For the Birds: John Cage in Conversation with Daniel Charles*. Boston and London: Marion Boyars, 1982.

————. *M: Writings '67-'72*. Middletown, Conn.: Wesleyan University Press, 1973.

————. *Silence: Lectures and Writings*, Middletown, Conn.: Wesleyan University Press, 1961.

————. *Themes & Variations*. Barrytown, N.Y.: Station Hill Press, 1982.

————. *A Year from Monday: New Lectures and Writings*. Middletown, Conn.: Wesleyan University Press, 1967. Cage's anthologies and other writings, listed here in alphabetical order, present a fascinating view of the musician, his work, and his philosophies. *Themes & Variations* consists of mesostics on the names of fifteen people who have been important in Cage's life.

Cope, David. *New Directions in Music*. Dubuque, Iowa: Wm. C. Brown Company Publishers, 1976. There is much in this volume that is crucial for an understanding of current compositional practices.

————. *New Music Composition*. New York: Schirmer Books, 1977. Compositional techniques of the entire twentieth century are covered, but there is an emphasis on the last forty years. The book offers clear explanations of often difficult concepts as well as excellent musical examples.

Cott, Jonathan. *Stockhausen: Conversations with the Composer*. New York: Simon and Schuster, 1973. These conversations offer important thoughts on music, the creative process, and human experience as seen through the eyes of one of the century's most important composers.

Delone, Richard, and Vernon Kliewer, Horace Reisberg, Mary Wennerstrom, Allan Winold, Gary E. Wittich (coord. ed.). *Aspects of Twentieth-Century Music*. Englewood Cliffs, N.J.: Prentice-Hall, 1975. Topics covering such areas as form, timbre and texture, rhythm, melody, harmony, and serial procedures often relate to the first years of the twentieth century, although the recent past is also discussed. Many terms and concepts that are often confusing—serialism, for example—are explained effectively.

Edwards, Allen. *Flawed Words and Stubborn Sounds: A Conversation with Elliott Carter*. New York: W. W. Norton & Co., 1971. This is a source, covering many topics and revealing various aspects of Carter's philosophies.

Gagne, Cole, and Tracy Caras. *Soundpieces: Interviews with American Composers*. Metuchen, N.J.: Scarecrow Press, 1982. Twenty-four American composers, including Copland, Cage, Babbitt, Carter, Sessions, Reich, and Glass, are interviewed. There are also listings of composers' works.

Gena, Peter, and Jonathan Brent. *A John Cage Reader: In Celebration of His 70th Birthday*. New York: C. F. Peters Corporation, 1982. This fascinating collection covers many aspects of Cage's art and is accompanied by a series of reproductions of the composer's scores.

Grayson, John, ed. *Sound Sculpture: A Collection of Essays by Artists Surveying the Techniques; Applications; and Future Directions of Sound Sculpture*. Vancouver, British Columbia: A. R. C. Publications, 1975. The work of many artists is discussed in this volume that covers experimental efforts in sound sculpture. There are illustrations of both art works and of innovative new musical instruments.

Griffiths, Paul. *Cage*. London: Oxford University Press, 1981. This volume, from the

Oxford Studies of Composers series, provides a succinct yet penetrating analysis of Cage's work.

————. *Modern Music: The Avant Garde Since 1945.* New York: George Braziller, 1981. The volume presents an excellent history of developments in music since World War II.

Hamm, Charles. *Music in the New World.* New York: W. W. Norton & Co., 1983. Among the material covered in this book is a helpful chapter on "The American Avant-Garde."

Harvey, Jonathan. *The Music of Stockhausen.* Berkeley and Los Angeles: University of California Press, 1975. This book follows the career and analyzes the works of Stockhausen through the mid-1970s.

Hays, William, ed. *Twentieth-Century Views of Music History.* New York: Charles Scribner's Sons, 1972. The final chapters of this work contain studies on twelve-tone composition, electronic music, and aleatoric music, as well as a 1969 essay by Eric Salzman, "The Revolution in Music."

Henze, Hans Werner. *Collected Writings 1953–81.* Translated by Peter Labanyi. Ithaca, N.Y.: Cornell University Press, 1982. This series of writings by an important German composer covers a variety of interesting topics.

Hitchcock, H. Wiley. *Music in the United States: A Historical Introduction.* Englewood Cliffs, N.J.: Prentice-Hall, 1974. The discussions of current musical practices in America (to 1974, when the second edition was published) are comprehensive and excellent.

Johnson, Roger, ed. *Scores: An Anthology of New Music.* New York: Schirmer Books, 1981. This is a fascinating collection of the scores of mostly recent works by American composers. It is divided into sections by medium and provides first-hand examples of the various kinds of music currently being composed.

Lipman, Samuel. *Music after Modernism.* New York: Basic Books, 1979. Despite the title, very little of this book relates to the subject of postmodernism. One chapter, however, "Yesterday's New Music," contains a perceptive discussion of music after World War II and a review of a series of recordings of new music issued by Deutsche Grammophon between 1968 and 1970.

Maconie, Robin. *The Works of Karlheinz Stockhausen.* London: Oxford University Press, 1976. This analysis of Stockhausen's work contains copious musical examples and an introduction by Stockhausen.

Meyer, Leonard, B. *Music, the Arts and Ideas: Patterns and Predictions in Twentieth-Century Culture.* Chicago: University of Chicago Press, 1967. This superb book describes musical culture in a manner that is helpful to an understanding of music in the 1980s.

Nyman, Michael. *Experimental Music: Cage and Beyond.* New York: Schirmer Books, 1974. Although such topics as minimal music are covered and opinions are often interesting and thought-provoking, this volume sometimes seems dated. The author is more successful in speaking of Britain and experimental music there than in analyzing music in America.

Oja, Carol, ed. *American Music Recordings: A Discography of Twentieth-Century U.S. Composers.* Brooklyn: Institute for Studies in American Music [Brooklyn College], 1982. This discography is a valuable source for locating recordings of American works composed in this century.

Perle, George. *Serial Composition and Atonality.* Berkeley: University of California Press,

1972. Although the book is quite technical and centers on the works of Schoenberg, Berg, and Webern, it is an invaluable text for those wishing to learn the intricacies of serial composition.

Porter, Andrew. *Music of Three Seasons: 1974–1977*. New York: Farrar, Straus and Giroux, 1978.

———. *Music of Three More Seasons: 1977–1980*. New York: Alfred A. Knopf, 1981. Porter's essays for the *New Yorker*, some of which are reprinted in these two volumes (listed here chronologically) offer intelligent, thorough, and thoughtful responses to recent performances of new music, as well as to performances of standard works of other periods.

Reich, Steve. *Writings About Music*. Halifax and New York: The Press of the Nova Scotia College of Art and Design and New York University Press, 1974. Reich's essays are thought-provoking, and the musical examples and photographs are interesting and helpful.

Reynolds, Roger. *Mind Models: New Forms of Musical Experience*. New York: Praeger Publishers, 1975.

Rockwell, John. *All American Music*. New York: Alfred A. Knopf, 1983. These twenty essays, discussing such musicians as Ernest Krenek, Milton Babbitt, Elliott Carter, John Cage, David Del Tredici, Philip Glass, Laurie Anderson, Keith Jarrett, Ornette Coleman, Stephen Sondheim, and Neil Young, present thoughtful opinions on music in the 1980s.

Sadie, Stanley, ed. *The New Grove Dictionary of Music and Musicians*. 20 vols. London: Macmillan Publishers, 1980. There are many specific as well as general articles that are useful in the *New Grove Dictionary*. It is an invaluable standard reference.

Salzman, Eric. *Twentieth-Century Music: An Introduction*. Englewood Cliffs, N.J.: Prentice-Hall, 1974. The latter chapters (part five) of this important study are especially helpful for an understanding of recent music (to 1974).

Schafer, R. Murray. *The Tuning of the World: Toward a Theory of Soundscape Design*. Philadelphia: University of Pennsylvania Press, 1980. Schafer analyzes the sonic environment: its past, present, and possible future in this important book.

Schwartz, Elliott. *Electronic Music: A Listener's Guide*. New York: Praeger Publishers, 1973. This is an excellent source for beginners.

Schwartz, Elliott, and Barney Childs, eds. *Contemporary Composers on Contemporary Music*. New York: Holt, Rinehart and Winston, 1967. The second part of this book, "Experimental Music and Recent American Developments," is a fascinating collection of articles and interviews, still vibrant despite the publication date of 1967.

Vinton, John, ed. *Dictionary of Contemporary Music*. New York: E. P. Dutton, 1974. There are many biographical as well as general articles in this important, though somewhat dated, source. (Reich is discussed in a biographical sketch, for example, but not Glass.) The work is a standard reference book, however, and is often helpful and illuminating.

von Gunden, Heidi. *The Music of Pauline Oliveros*. Metuchen, N.J.: Scarecrow Press, 1983. For the most part an excellent introduction to the works of the composer. The book's subtitle describes well these stimulating essays that address time, notation, sound, and change, as well as such topics as "The States of Art" and "Morphology in Music."

Whittall, Arnold. *Music since the First World War*. New York: St. Martin's Press, 1977.

One of the book's sections, "The Spread of Serialism," discusses such composers as Sessions and Babbitt. The third section of the volume, "From Past to Future," considers such topics as "The Radical Aesthetic" (including Cage) and the work of "Seven Europeans" (Lutoslawski, Xenakis, Ligeti, Berio, Boulez, Henze, and Stockhausen).

Yates, Peter. *Twentieth-Century Music*. New York: Pantheon Books, 1967. This volume contains valuable essays on the experimental tradition and on the work of John Cage.

Young, La Monte, and Marian Zazeela. *Selected Writings*. Munich: Heiner Friedrich, 1969. These writings and "scores" illuminate the work of La Monte Young.

Zimmerman, Walter. *Desert Plants: Conversations with 23 American Musicians*. Vancouver, British Columbia: Walter Zimmerman and A.R.C. Publications, 1976. The work of a German writer, these personal and telephone interviews with such composers as Cage, Glass, Reich, Philip Corner, and Robert Ashley are often unconventional yet helpful, and sometimes of questionable value (cf., for example, the section on La Monte Young).

Other Sources

Amirkhanian, Charles. "Steve Reich." *Ear [West]* 7 (March-April 1979): 1, 4–5. This is an interview from September 1978. Influences on Reich's music are discussed as well as some of his works.

Ballantine, Christopher. "Towards an Aesthetic of Experimental Music." *Musical Quarterly* 63 (April 1977): 224–46. This article places the theory and practice of experimental work in music within the framework of arguments of Walter Benjamin, Bertold Brecht, and Theodor Adorno.

Cage, John, and Roger Reynolds. "John Cage and Roger Reynolds: A Conversation." *Musical Quarterly* 65 (October 1979): 573–94. These excerpts from a conversation that took place on August 28, 1977, cover a wide variety of topics.

Childs, Barney. "Time and Music: A Composer's View." *Perspectives of New Music* 15 (Spring-Summer 1977): 194–219. The demise of the "dramatic curve" in twentieth-century music is discussed. Peculiarities of time and melody are two other subjects that are explored.

Cormier, Ramona. "Indeterminacy and Aesthetic Theory." *Journal of Aesthetics and Art Criticism* 33 (Spring 1975): 285–92. Theories of indeterminacy are discussed, and the author offers a defense for employing indeterminacy in the arts.

De Lio, Thomas. "Structural Pluralism: Some Observations on the Nature of Open Structures in the Music and Visual Arts of the Twentieth Century." *Musical Quarterly* 67 (October 1981): 527–43. The author offers an essay on structure and how recent concepts of structure have expanded upon traditional notions on the subject. An analysis of Robert Ashley's *in memoriam . . . Esteban Gomez* is included in the article.

Dennis, Brian. "Repetitive and Systematic Music." *The Musical Times* 115 (December 1974): 1036–38. "Multi-repetition" in music is analyzed from a number of perspectives. Musical examples from the work of several composers including Steve Reich, Terry Riley, Alec Hill, and John White are included in the article.

Foss, Lukas, and others. "Contemporary Music: Observations from Those Who Create It." *Music and Artists* 5 (June-July 1972): 11–23. There are comments by twenty-eight contemporary composers from a number of countries. Among those represented are David Del Tredici, Lukas Foss, and George Rochberg.

Gillmor, Alan. "Interview with John Cage." *Contact* 14 (Autumn 1976): 18–25. This conversation, which covers a number of topics, dates from July 1973.

Klein, Lothar. "Twentieth-Century Analysis: Essays in Miniature. John Cage." *Music Educators Journal* 54 (May 1968): 57–60. The importance of Cage is analyzed. The author offers the view that it was inevitable that such a composer would emerge after World War II.

Kramer, Jonathan D. "Moment Form in Twentieth Century Music." *Musical Quarterly* 64 (April 1978): 177–94. Discontinuity, the compositional idea of endlessness, and the perception of durational propositions are among the topics that are analyzed.

Moore, F. Richard. "The Futures of Music." *Perspectives of New Music* 19 (Fall-Winter 1980/Spring-Summer 1981): 212–26. There are views of music history as well as speculations concerning current aspects of the art and its future.

O'Grady, Terence J. "Aesthetic Value in Indeterminate Music." *Musical Quarterly* 67 (July 1981): 366–81. A number of works (by Cage, Riley, and Reich) are described, and problems that pieces with indeterminate factors present to a listener are noted and explained.

Osterreich, Norbert. "Music with Roots in the Aether." *Perspectives of New Music* 16 (Fall-Winter 1977): 214–28. Osterreich summarizes his reactions to "Music with Roots in the Aether," in fourteen taped video segments concerning a number of contemporary composers including Robert Ashley, Philip Glass, Pauline Oliveros, and Terry Riley. The tapes include interviews as well as performances of the composers' works.

Page, Tim. "The New Romance with Tonality." *New York Times Magazine*, May 29, 1983, pp. 22–25, 28. Although the main subject of this article is David Del Tredici, George Rochberg is also interviewed, and there is a general discussion of composers' uses of tonality in the 1970s and 1980s.

Parsons, Michael. "The Music of Howard Skempton." *Contact* 21 (Autumn 1980): 12–16. The work of Skempton, a composer of minimal music that is often a model of clarity and simplicity, is analyzed. The article contains a number of helpful musical examples.

———. "Systems in Art and Music." *The Musical Times* 117 (October 1976): 815–18. The relationship between systematic (minimal) composers and visual artists in England is explored.

Potter, Keith, and Dave Smith. "Interview with Philip Glass." *Contact* 13 (Spring 1976): 25–30. Although some of the conversation relates to a tour of England by Glass and his ensemble, a number of the composer's compositions are discussed and analyzed.

"Prophets, Seers and Sages: An MM Guide to the Major Movements in Avant-Garde Music." *Melody Maker* 51 (April 24, 1976): 26–27. The article begins with Satie and Ives, discusses such movements as serialism and a number of composers including Cage, then proceeds to an analysis of miminalists and their music.

Reise, Jay. "Rochberg the Progressive." *Perspectives of New Music* 19 (Fall-Winter 1980/Spring-Summer 1981): 395–407. There is a specific analysis of late romantic influences on a contemporary composer in the article: The relationship of Rochberg's Third String Quartet and Mahler's Ninth Symphony.

Rochberg, George. "Indeterminacy in the New Music." *Score* 26 (1969): 9–19. Serialism and indeterminacy are discussed, the author stating a preference for indeterminacy as a return to subjectivity.

————. "Reflections on the Renewal of Music." *Current Musicology* 13 (1972): 75–82. This penetrating essay, by a composer who has reached into the past for inspiration after establishing a career as a serial composer, makes a number of points, including the argument that gestures of the twentieth century do not invalidate those of earlier periods.

Salzman, Eric. "The *New York Times* Was Supposed to Print This But Didn't." *Ear Magazine East* 5 (November-December 1979): 6–7. The "dominant forces" of the "new" American music, minimalism and conceptualism, are discussed using the festival of June 8–17, 1979, at the Kitchen in New York's Soho as a point of departure.

Schwartz, Elliott. "Electronic Music: A Thirty-Year Retrospective." *Music Educators Journal* 64 (March 1978): 36–41. This is an excellent guide to electronic literature, and a helpful discography is an integral part of the article.

Schwarz, Robert K. "Steve Reich: Music as a Gradual Process" (part 1). *Perspectives of New Music* 19 (Fall-Winter 1980/Spring-Summer 1981): 373–92; (part 2): 20 (Fall-Winter 1981/Spring-Summer 1982): 225–86. This is a lengthy analysis with musical examples of Reich's philosophy and his work.

Shewey, Don. "The Performing Artistry of Laurie Anderson." *New York Times Magazine*, February 6, 1983, pp. 26–27, 46–47, 55, 59. Performance art and the work of Laurie Anderson are covered in this article.

Smith, Dave. "Following a Straight Line: La Monte Young." *Contact* 18 (Winter 1977–78): 4–9. Young's philosophies and his compositions are discussed with musical examples, and his influence on other musicians is documented.

————. "The Music of Phil Glass." *Contact* 11 (Summer 1975): 27–29, 30–32. Glass' work is described and several of his compositions are analyzed with musical examples.

Summerfield, Jackie. "Laurie Anderson." *Ear [West]* 8 (January-February 1980): 1, 10. A brief discussion of Anderson and her work is followed by an interview with Anderson, conducted by Summerfield and Kathy Sheehy.

Wasserman, Emily. "An Interview with Composer Steve Reich." *Artform* 10 (May 1972): 44–48. This interview covers a number of topics and is illustrated.

Wetzler, Peter. "Minimal Music." *Ear Magazine East* 6 (June-July-August 1981): 6. The author presents a brief discussion of the term "minimal" and its various connotations.

Yalkut, Jud. "Philip Glass and Jon Gibson." *Ear [West]* 19 (Summer 1981): 4–5. This interview with Glass and his colleague, Jon Gibson, dates from September 1980.

8

Photography

STANLEY J. BOWMAN

Despite photography's current acceptance in museums and galleries, the debate continues over whether photography legitimately belongs in the art world. One consequence of this sideline position is that photography has also remained largely outside the mainstream of postmodernism. Thus, while the works of some artists, notably Sherrie Levine, Cindy Sherman, Richard Prince, and Laurie Simons, do contend with the postmodernist struggle, many others reflect a healthy diversity of intentions and explorations.

Unlike the traditional art media, in which, through a clever and suspect cooptation, radical artists are absorbed into the art world and their new and unusual work granted immediate acceptance, photography has retained a true avant-garde. Many photographers exist outside of the mainstream because galleries and museums play it safe, displaying and collecting works more closely related to tradition, such as landscapes or portraits. Those who experiment with process or image translations find a few enthusiasts outside their own ranks and very few buyers. Protected from the ravages of the art market and from pressures that could blunt their inventiveness, these photographers have successfully retained their separate identities and creative edge.

Today photography stands at the edge of the modern art world. Perhaps one explanation for its position is to be found in its rather brief and separate historical existence. Photography's origins stretch back less than two centuries and are rooted as much in scientific invention as in artistic evolution. Practitioners have needed to be knowledgeable in physics and chemistry as well as in aesthetics and sometimes were skilled only in the former. Photography was allowed grudgingly into the art world at the turn of this century, and, today, its validity is still questioned. Despite and very possibly because of its isolation, photography has avoided many of the twentieth-century art world's swings of mood and style.

In one respect photography has avoided much of the postmodern malaise because it has never been fully modern. Photography cannot escape its representational nature. If one accepts the notion that a lenticular image is prerequisite for photography, then all photographs have linkages to the external world. Regardless of the manner in which a photographer artist renders an image, whether it is reproduced in a straightforward manner or pushed into an extraordinary translation, we are aware that at some moment in time there were objects in front of the lens and that these objects have actuality in our real, practical, experiential world. A photographer may try but will never quite escape the unconscious or preconscious associations that overlie an image and link it to the external world.

Remaining relatively separate from the modern or postmodern art world, photography has also undergone its own unique sense of evolution. Research and development of materials and equipment have altered working methods; its acceptance into a radical twentieth century art world has modified the aesthetic standards for the medium; and the multifaceted roles of photography in a culture of accelerating change have made practitioners think about photography in new terms.

However, photography, in the twentieth century, has also assimilated modernist aesthetics. The major reason for this transition has been photography's partial assimilation into the art world and its appearance in galleries and museums both in America and abroad. Alfred Stieglitz is generally regarded as the father of twentieth century art photography. In 1905, Stieglitz and his following of creative photographers introduced photography as art through impressive exhibitions in important galleries and museums in the eastern United States, at his own galleries in New York City, and through his amazing publication called *Camera Work*. Perhaps of greatest significance is the fact that Stieglitz exhibited photography on an equal footing with modern painting and sculpture with artists like Matisse, Picasso, Braque, Brancusi.

At the turn of the century the popular notion was that photography was intended for descriptive purposes, to record important historical events, or to fix human likenesses. Stieglitz, however, thought photography could do more than render detailed information about the external world; it could also be expressive through its composition, organization of shape, line, texture, and lighting. Speaking about his 1907 photograph, *The Steerage*, taken on the deck of a ship bound for Europe, marked by clear focus and exceptional detail, he saw "A round straw hat, the funnel leaning left, the stairway leaning right, the white drawbridge . . . white suspenders . . . round shapes of iron machinery . . . a mast cutting the sky, making a triangular shape . . . and underlying that the feeling I had about life."[1] With this photograph and others like it, photography became modern and adopted aesthetic standards still of concern to most twentieth-century photographers.

Although Stieglitz is considered the pivotal figure in the development of contemporary photography, Paul Strand and Edward Weston explicated its modernist expression. In 1916 Strand made and exhibited *The White Fence*, showing that some of the abstract qualities of modern art were now also in photography. All attention seems directed at the shape of the fence, its location and importance in the picture frame. In the background soft shapes of buildings play against it.

Light and tonality convey a strong mood, yet serve compositional demands. The impact of this photograph is to be found in its visual appearance, not in its descriptive or associative meanings. Furthermore, its title identifies the object we see, not its location or context.

On the West Coast of the United States Edward Weston set the clearest standards yet for modern art photography. After a brief affair with abstraction, he turned to the faithful representation of an image previsualized at the moment of exposure. Writing about his preference for "significant presentation—not interpretation," Weston said "to see the *Thing Itself* is essential . . . without the fog of impressionism. . . . "[2] This aesthetic became the norm for modern and postmodern photography in the twentieth century.

Weston's photographs at Point Lobos provide a clear expression of his modern aesthetic. In *China Cove*, 1940, one experiences the full merger of his powers as an artist to describe and to transcend. The water reflects the intensity of late afternoon sun in the distance, kelp glows out of the dark water in the foreground. A nearby rock on the lower right secures the viewer, allowing one a point of reference. The ocean is brightest, but it is the kelp flowing out of the darkness that commands attention. Weston the photographer presents *China Cove* in meticulous detail, but Weston the artist also presents a powerful pictorial vision of lines, shapes, and textures.

The apex of the modern photographic aesthetic at mid-century is to be found in three persons, Minor White, Aaron Siskind, Harry Callahan. Although Minor White began the serious study of photography in 1937, it was not until the late 1940s that he reached his full creative powers. Expanding on the notions of equivalence and sequence gained from study with Stieglitz and influenced by the formal structures in the work of Weston, he began to create his own unique pictorial vocabulary, relying on conscious, meticulous attention to clear focus and sharp detail, careful organization and rendition of shape, line, and texture, and appreciation of the evocative qualities of light and shadow. White brings a new dimension; the photograph as equivalent. He says, "the talisman paradox for unique photography is to 'work the mirror with a memory' as if it were a mirage, and the camera a metamorphosing machine, and the photograph as if it were a metaphor. . . . "[3] One of the earliest sequences of photographs by Minor White characterizes his work through the 1950s and beyond. *Song Without Words*, a group of fifteen images made on the California coast in the fall of 1947, were expressions of his feelings as he thought about a friend still in the war on the other side of the Pacific. While all the photographs are clear and sharply focused, some, like *Black Cliff & Waves, Surf Vertical*, and *Sun in Rock*, become abstractions of shapes composed of the most specific details. Others conform to more traditional presentational modes of landscape. All are straightforward single images that rely on the formal organizational, tonal, and light qualities so clearly articulated by Stieglitz, Strand, Weston, and others. But these abstractions are also puzzles with hidden meanings, pregnant with emotions. Moreover, for White these aspects are not in the photographs, but between images. Sequencing allows an expression of ideas and feelings not available through single imagery, but through juxtaposition. As the result, by mid-century modern photography is concerned with faithful representation, pictorial presentation, and metaphoric or symbolic statement.

In the late 1940s and early 1950s Aaron Siskind and Harry Callahan emerged as major figures in modern art photography. Siskind, in his early years, created documentary studies in New York City. Then, in 1942, in Gloucester, Massachusetts, he initiated a series of photographic still lifes of fish heads, rope, and other commonplace objects. It became clear that subject matter was now secondary, and abstraction most important. In the late fifties he began to photograph walls and surfaces with peeling paint and papers. *Chicago, 1957* is a highly detailed, straightforward rendition of a wall covered with peeling posters, a half moon darkened shape emerging in the center. There is a direct correspondence with abstract expressionist painting of that period, yet we are completely aware that this is a photograph. Apparent is the strong influence toward abstraction of the Institute of Design with which he was associated in 1951.

Harry Callahan met Lázló Moholy-Nagy in 1946 and this led to his association with the Institute of Design. Like Siskind, he became aware of the structural and formal properties of an image. Perhaps the most interesting aspect of his photography is its variety within the bounds of a consistent set of parameters. In 1948 he began a series of photographs of his wife, Eleanor. Later he made pictures of water and weeds around Detroit (1940), sunlight on water (1949), multiple images and patterns on building walls in Chicago (1950s), collaged images (1957), street photographs of people (1960), classical street facades (early 1970s), New York skyline and Cape Cod (mid-1970s). His overriding concern has always been the organization of the image, shapes, textures, and line.

While strides were being made in art photography, another tradition, documentary and reportage, found its way into the art world and provided a different course. At the same time that photography was being introduced into the art world, it was also being recognized as a forceful tool to examine and document the real world. Beginning with its use by Mathew Brady, who recorded the Civil War with unprecedented realism, and then by others to show the western American landscape, this tradition matured after the turn of the century with Lewis Hine, Walker Evans, Dorothea Lange, and other 1930s Farm Security Administration photographers. Their work reflected Strand and Weston's formal qualities of directness, attention to detail and clarity, full tonal rendition, concern with light, and a stillness that is characteristic of large format imagery.

Lewis Hine, a sociologist by education, began using the camera to record immigrants arriving at Ellis Island and then to study their assimilation into American culture. Although his initial impetus was documentary, he also recognized the formal, pictorial qualities of his images. *Child Labor-Breakerboys* (ca. 1911) was intended to address a serious national problem, and it does so by faithfulness to the straight tradition of photography. But it also reflects attention to spatial organization, light, tone quality, and evocative impact. The round faces of children glow out of the dark interior of the cavelike building. A lone ceiling light illuminates the unsmiling children nearest the camera, allowing others to vanish into the darkness. Two small windows at the upper left suggest escape, but the window mullions seem like bars of a prison. The drama of the image, its careful structuring, detail, and obscurity, these are aspects that place the image in the twentieth-century modern tradition. Yet, to Hine, a picture has no value in itself. It is worthwhile because of its contribution to the presentation and correction of a pressing social problem.

Walker Evans epitomizes the documentary tradition. A contemporary of Weston and Strand, his career covered more than forty years. His work gains force from its uncompromising direction and attention to detail. It never wavers from the immediate presence of the scene in front of the camera. Often Evans would spend hours composing a scene before making an exposure. During his brief association with the Farm Security Administration documentary project, his photographs continued to have the same personal qualities that marked all his work. A catalogue of his work published by the New York Museum of Modern Art in 1971 shows his clear and single-minded vision. Titles always refer to location and time. *Tuscaloosa Wrecking Company, Alabama, 1936* has the camera slightly left of front of the building, with cars in the parking lot in the foreground and a tree to the left. It is a brilliant photograph in terms of camera location, balance of pictorial elements, and relationships to the frame edge. *Interior Near Copake, New York, 1933* gives dramatic attention to light and movement through an interior space. Yet Evans' photography serves broader purposes than description of time and place. Photographic realism is most important to Evans.

Dorothea Lange, also associated with the FSA project, worked independently, like Evans. She concentrated on the people she met and the catastrophic forces that afflicted them during the disastrous depression years. Working primarily in the western United States, she began photographing migrants arriving in California in the mid-1930s. In *Migrant Mother, Nipomi, California, 1936*, one of her most famous images, the camera is close, framing children and mother whose drawn, wrinkled face clearly reflects worry and anxiety. The two children press in on either side but with backs turned, as if they cannot or will not face the frightening reality at which the mother stares directly and intensely. Field notes by Lange explain this scene as a thirty-two-year-old mother with two children who had just sold the tires on their car to buy food. Lange uses a traditional pictorial and formal approach to speak about a very real social condition. The visual language is modern, but it serves deeper concerns.

The most radical change of direction in this century was brought about by a technical innovation, the introduction of the 35 mm camera. With fast shutter and ease of winding, suddenly a whole new range of picture-making possibilities opened up for photographers, especially in documentary photography. Henri Cartier-Bresson was one of the first to exploit the potential of the small camera. Realizing the possibility afforded by rapid advance and sequencing, Bresson developed a style that he later called "decisive moment," the moment and camera place wherein the essence of the scene becomes clarified. One of his most famous photographs is of a man leaping a puddle of water. The picture is dramatic, structured, yet rooted in a particular moment of time. Bresson espouses the same aesthetic standards of modern documentary photography but brings to it a new dimension, the issue of time.

Reportage has followed a path very similar to that of the modernist documentary, but with variations. Beginning with Brady, it has primarily concerned itself with the occurrence of significant historical events. The FSA photographers, Lange, Russell Lee, Arthur Rothstein, Marion Post Wolcott, John Vachon, Ben Shahn, all responded to their perception of the historical moment and the broad changes in American society. In Europe photographers like Bresson joined with others like Werner Bischof, Earnst Haas, René Burri, Marc Riboud, Brassaï and André Kertész, followed similar impulses, and produced work that was both exciting, innovative, and definitely modern. Whether American or European, these photographers worked broadly with the social fabric of contemporary culture until major events would intrude and direct picture-taking activities. During the Second World War photographers like David Seymour, Robert Capa, and W. Eugene Smith brought a new dimension to the portrayal of war and its affect upon people the world over. For the most part, these photographers remained faithful to formal picture-making traditions of the nineteenth century yet actively used the drama of light, tonality, and spatial organization to convey their messages.

At mid-century, documentary and reportage began to be accepted into the art world alongside Weston and Minor White. Perhaps it took historians and critics time and emotional distance from specific events before they could recognize the pictorial and formal strengths of this tradition of imagery. Whatever the reason, photographers like Cartier-Bresson, Kertész, and Brassaï came into their own in the art world. But it was Robert Frank in the 1950s who generated the most interest in the American photographic art world with the publication *The Americans*. This harshly critical, highly personal book laid the seeds for a new tradition in documentary photography that would invade the art world in the 1960s. Frank's vision is uncompromisingly direct and frighteningly honest, and his style breaks traditions. Images are sometimes out of focus, picture planes titled with the frame edge arbitrarily cutting the scene into a momentary glance. The sense of immediacy is overpowering. *San Francisco* shows a couple lying on a hillside park overlooking the city with the bay in the distance. The picture is unusual in that the frame cuts off the lower portion of these people in the foreground. Both have turned around to stare at us or at the photographer. The street and skyline in the distance are tilted and hazy. This photograph seems to have been "shot from the hip," to use current terminology. It appears rushed, without proper framing—a disjointed piece out of a larger fabric. The concerns are documentary, but the approach and style are new. Gone is the studied framing of Evans, the sense of drama with the use of light and tonality. The image is brash, jarring, yet seemingly well suited to express the sensation of a new time in history and a new way of seeing, one that builds upon the emerging modernist documentary aesthetic.

In 1962 Robert Frank and Harry Callahan held a joint exhibition at the Museum of Modern Art in New York City. For the first time these two heretofore separate traditions of photography were publicly recognized as part of a single art tradition. Callahan, one one hand, represented the impulse to make forceful images that stand on their own formal qualities apart from the subject or scene photographed. Frank, on the other, embodied the attitude that photography should serve the occasion and moment of picture-taking and be enhanced and made evocative by stylistic attention. Both displayed in their work the modernist impulses toward abstraction and formal manipulation yet within the historic imagery based on a unique personal vision that cannot easily be copied. At the same time Callahan and Frank, along with Minor White, stand as foils for the younger practitioners who emerge in the postmodern period of art after 1960.

If one conducts an overview of the last twenty years of photography, several aspects are apparent. Historically, the medium is like a small stream flowing downhill, which becomes wider, deeper, and swifter until it becomes a raging torrent. To trace the history of photography up to 1960 is relatively easy, perhaps because of the dominance of the single straight image. But in the early 1960s photographers like Jerry Uelsmann, Robert Heinecken, and Bea Nettles broke with the preciousness of the tradition and proposed that images are "made" in the darkroom, printshop, and so forth, rather than "taken." Furthermore, in the 1970s, simplified colored photographic processes propelled photographers into new issues of the medium. As a result, the last twenty years of photography, its postmodern period, if you will, has been its most rich and exciting time. It is also the hardest period to describe not only because of the enormous number of practitioners and breadth of works created, but also because it has seen the progressive blurring of distinctions between photography and other media.

Perhaps more than any other recent artist, Frank has affected several generations of photographers. In December of 1966 *Contemporary Photographers: Towards a Social Landscape* opened at George Eastman House in Rochester, New York. Clearly indebted to the genius and inspiration of Frank, the exhibition included the work of Bruce Davidson, Lee Friedlander, Garry Winogrand, and Danny Lyon, all of whom would become major photographers. In its catalogue curator Nathan Lyons says, "What I am suggesting, however, is that our concept of environment and landscape expand . . . to deal with the greater interrelatedness of things."[4]

Lee Friedlander's style and approach in the *Social Landscape* show seems most in debt to Frank. Dramatic cuts of the frame edge, layering of information, and concern with cultural symbols also characterize his approach. In one photograph, *New York, 1962*, we look into a telephone booth. In front of us is the blurring telephone box and behind, through the glass, a dark colored automobile, its grillwork gleaming in sunlight on the right. To the left we see a parking meter, and nearby a small portion of a trash can. A reflection on the lower left tells us that we are looking through the glass. Overlays of information project into the frame yet we can only guess at their meaning. The object, a telephone, is not startling, but the way in which it is shown arrests our attention. Never have we seen it pictured in this way.

Garry Winogrand also established his basic approach to image-making in the *Social Landscape* exhibition. In *Los Angeles, 1964,* we look down on a man and woman in the foreground in a car moving along the street. A car in the background is blurred, in motion. The arresting aspect of the image is a white bandage on the man's nose. The woman passenger, hair piled high on her head, stares straight ahead. It is an arrested instant in time, and we see this as a harsh, fractured moment, much in the same way we viewed Frank's San Francisco photograph.

There is no doubt that Winogrand uses the standards that characterize documentary photography in the postmodern era. His style has clear, subjective overtones. Winogrand's 1970s photographs often have a characteristic tilt of the picture plane that produces a sense of imbalance, a contradiction of gravity. People frequently seem strange, awkwardly placed, all rendered in a moment where nothing makes sense, all is out of sync. Images seem to be transitory moments where everything is revealed, but nothing has meaning. It is a world of anomie, charged, but fractured, layered, disjointed.

Danny Lyon became involved in photography in the early 1960s, and his work in the *Social Landscape* show reflected his growing concern with social issues. In *Jack from "The Bikeriders," 1965,* and *Sparky and Cowboy* and in *Gary Rogues,* both from *"The Bikeriders," 1965,* one finds the elements that characterize Lyon's photography. The former photograph shows a gang member leaning with back to camera on the counter of a diner restaurant. The latter picture is a direct frontal portrait of two members of the gang. The former shows context, the latter the individuals. In *Conversations with the Dead*, a book first produced in 1969, Lyon uses the same approach, context and person. In the picture *Hoe Sharpener and the Line* we see a man in the center foreground on one knee, working on a tool and in the distance up a hillside a long line of white-suited inmates working the ground with hoes. A mounted officer is just visible beyond the line of men. In *Inmates Outside Warden's Office* we see a convict in white clothing, manacles on his feet, against a wood-paneled wall of a room. He stands formally, cigarette in one hand. A small plant in a pot is on the right, and above is a formal portrait of George Washington. Lyon also identifies several men in particular and prints their rap sheet with numbered photographs. The impact is intense, as we learn more about these men as individuals and more strongly feel the isolation, loneliness and terror of incarceration within a prison.

Some of Bruce Davidson's photographs were the result of a project on youth in America done in the early 1960s. There were also images of a middle-aged couple in a bare living room with worn, aging furniture; a young, lonely woman sitting on a bench at Coney Island; boaters standing on debris along a river in

New Jersey; a campground in Yosemite with unsmiling people of many ages seated in aluminum folding chairs outside of camp trailers. The exhibition established Davidson's reputation, but it was in his 1970 project on East 100th Street that his work fully matured. For two years, Davidson resided and photographed the people who lived on this ghetto street in East Harlem, New York. His photographs are classical in style with studied compositions, highly posed, sharp detail, the result of his use of a large format camera. There are also intense, personal, sympathetic portraits of ghetto inhabitants. In one photograph of a room interior, on the right foreground, a young black mother, partially clothed, sits up in bed, blankets covering her lower body. She stares at the camera with a blank expression, mouth slightly open as if to say something, but unable. In the left background near a window, a young black child stands, one arm raised, looking down to the floor with a blank expression that matches that of her mother. Flowered window curtains are pinned together as if to keep out a hostile world. Just in front of the woman, in the foreground, on the bed, is a newspaper advertisement that says, with a sense of irony, "SALES AT GIMBELS."

Diane Arbus also came into prominence as a photographer in the 1960s, and her work is both documentary and highly individualistic. People, her most frequent subject, appear as tortured individuals. Photographs of a giant man, transvestites, and midgets show a fascination with freaks. Yet other portraits also have the same character and feeling. Arbus saw her world as imperfect and people as highly flawed. *A Retired Man and His Wife at Home in a Nudist Camp One Morning, N.J., 1963*, shows a middle-class living room with an older couple seated on either side of a TV set. The fact that they are nude gives the scene a surreal, disjointed atmosphere. One finds a perverse fascination with the image, but also a growing sympathy for this rather pathetic couple. Her photographs are clearly documentary but the mood is both personal and devastating.

In her book, *On Photography*, published in 1978, Susan Sontag develops a lengthy critique emphasizing what she sees as the antihumanist message of Arbus' imagery. Moreover, Sontag believes that for Arbus and all other photographers "The camera is a kind of passport that annihilates moral boundaries and social responsibility toward the people photographed. The whole point of photographing people is that you are not intervening in their lives, only visiting them."[5] Also, she says "The person who intervenes cannot record; the person who is recording cannot intervene."[6] Sontag's voyeuristic notion elicited a storm of angry protest and disagreement in the late 1970s from many photographers who knew from firsthand experience that it is quite possible to both record and intervene because a photographer does not, by necessity, withdraw from participation when making a photographic record. Arbus revealed her involvement, respect, and empathy for the people she photographed when she said, "they made me feel a mixture of shame and awe. . . . Freaks were born with their trauma. They've already passed their test in life. They're aristocrats. . . . "[7] The act of photographing can be and, in the case of Arbus, is an act of intervention. Moreover, it is the intensity of her involvement that makes Arbus' photographs compelling.

Fascination with the dark side of urban culture seems to be a strong interest of some photographers in the postmodern era. Larry Fink, indebted to Arbus, made a series of untitled photographs in 1978. One depicts an interior scene from an unknown social event. A couple, the woman with her back turned, and the man facing us, stand in front of an open folding door that leads into a darkened interior. We see, partly lit, and partly in shadow, a table, glasses, people. Over the door a small sign says "He Who Enters Here is A Stranger But Once." The man's face is an immobile mask as he glances unsmilingly, eyes vacant, to our left. Several buttons on his shirt are open, and he wears a sport coat and slacks. We see only the back of the woman, low cut evening gown, glowing blond hair, her right arm reaching out to almost touch the man, but not quite. The light, coming from the upper left, is like a spotlight that partly illuminates this dark scene where people, empty stereotypes, carry on strange ritualistic social customs. Unlike Arbus, these people are comic and familiar. Moreover, Fink makes them seem to have chosen their lifestyle while Arbus made her people seem ordained to their existence.

Since 1960 not all social documentary has tended to be dark in mood. In *Suburbia*, published in 1973, Bill Owens treats stereotypical suburbanites with humor and affection, but also with mockery and some derision. One might laugh with both amusement and scorn when looking at the photograph of a boy climbing a tree picking off fall leaves, captioned "My dad thinks its a good idea to take all the leaves off the tree and rake up the yard. I think he's crazy."[8] We also feel pathos and sympathy as we encounter this ritualized and rather restrictive lifestyle of the suburbs.

Emmet Gowin, as a documentarian, leads us to rural Virginia, to a world of people who are warm, loving, and dignified. Published in 1976, his monograph shows us a tender vision of his wife's family, "a family freshly different from my own." He says "I admired their simplicity and generosity, and thought of the pictures I made as agreements."[9] Edith, his wife, is his most frequent subject. One picture, *Edith. Danville, Virginia, 1967*, appears opposite another, *Ruth, Danville, Virginia, 1968*. She is Edith's sister. Both women fill the center of the frame, and both are treated with kindness. Ruth, outdoors, looks to our right, toward the ground, the wind blowing her hair out over her shoulders. On the opposite page Edith is inside a house, a fireplace left, a doorway on the right leading to a kitchen. She stares straight at the camera. Both women have faint smiles. The light is soft, the mood transcendent. Although classically documentary, Gowin's photographs are clearly and decisively his own interior reality.

In 1974 the Museum of Fine Arts in Boston organized an exhibition called *Private Realities*, its first major exhibition of contemporary photography. The show contained the work of ten photographers, including Gowin. In the catalogue introduction curator Clifford Ackley said that the title was chosen "to indicate that, although all of the works in this exhibition make use of objective realism, they are primarily concerned with the recording of subjective states of feeling. Those works are not so much documentary as surreal, fantastic, autobiographies, profoundly personal.''[10] Perhaps this exhibition, in its time, clearly declared the emerging tendency for contemporary documentary photography to be subjective.

Another exhibition, *Mirrors & Windows*, 1978, also contained work by Gowin and made the same observation. Curated by John Szarkowski, director of the Department of Photography at the Museum of Art in New York, this show looked at photography since 1960 and spoke of the inadequacy of traditional terms like ''straight'' and ''manipulated'' to describe contemporary photography. Szarkowski illustrates their deficiencies by referring to the work of Minor White and Robert Frank. White worked with the notion of photographs as ''equivalents,'' metaphors for the emotions of the photographer artist, whereas Frank was involved with the rhetoric of the image, the form and language used to express one's perception of the external world. However, both were ''straight'' in that neither used any manipulative devices in the process of producing an image. He contends that ''mirrors'' and ''windows'' are better terms. Mirrors point one back at the photographer and, as such, tend toward autobiography or autoanalysis. Windows, however, appear to direct attention at what is seen so that ''one might better know the world.''[11] Szarkowski is certainly correct in his criticism of traditional terms, but one wonders if his substitutions are any less problematic. Mirrors and windows appear as opposites, denying the possibility that photography can, paradoxically, be both about the world and about the image maker. Moreover, contemporary documentary photography seems to rest squarely on this paradox.

In 1975, three years before the *Mirrors and Windows* show, another form of documentary photography appeared and began to demand attention. An exhibition at George Eastman House in Rochester, called *New Topographics: Photographs of a Man-Altered Landscape*, included works by Robert Adams, Lewis Baltz, Bernd and Hilla Becher, Joe Deal, Frank Gohlke, Nicholas Nixon, John Schott, Stephen Shore, Henry Wessel, Jr., all of whom were new arrivals to the photographic art world. In the introduction, curator William Jenkins states ''There is little doubt that the problem at the center of this exhibition is one of style.''[12] Jenkins chose these photographs because their work addresses the issue of making a photograph rather than what the photograph is about, that is, what is in front of the lens.

Bernd and Hilla Becher used photography to create taxonomies. Starting in the mid-1970s they began producing typologies of man-made structures, clear examples of an impulse toward classifications. Their inspiration seems to derive from the 1920s work of August Sander, who attempted to picture the German people in terms of social and occupational classes. The Bechers, however, concentrate on more neutral subject matter such as industrial buildings and houses. In one series of photographs their camera circles around a *House near Kutztown, Pennsylvania*, to straightforwardly record eight images, each from a different point of view. There is an enigmatic quality in this activity that is absent in Sander. The photographs of the German people clearly explain themselves and declare Sander's motives. They are social documents. The Bechers' photographs are a puzzle as regards purpose or message. On one hand, the strong realism and multiple points of view allow one to think we learn something from the vast amount of detailed information. But then we realize this knowledge is of little value because it is presented without context. We also realize the deficiencies of mere appearance in any quest for knowledge. Finally we are led to the conclusion that any real knowledge is about the nature of photography and not about the subject matter.

This show was also concerned with the issue of objectivity. Nicholas Nixon believes that "the world is infinitely more interesting than any of my opinions concerning it."[13] The role of the photographer is to present fact and evidence regarding the existence of the external world without reference to oneself. The photographer, hence, becomes transparent. In the picture *View of Boston from Commercial Wharf, 1975*, we look down on the city at dusk. The wide-angle lens shows a mass of buildings, tall and short, some with lighted windows. It is a complicated, detailed fabric of urban skyline. However, the picture is not about Boston or a personal opinion of cities. It is about picture-making and is a statement of facts without conclusions.

Perhaps an even more telling statement about objectivity is made by Lewis Baltz, who says,

To function as documents at all they (photographs) must first persuade us that they describe their subject accurately and objectively: in fact, their initial task is to convince their audience that they are truly documents, that the photographer has fully exercised his powers of observation and description and has set aside his imaginings and prejudices. The ideal photographic document would appear to be without an author or art.[14]

One might then conclude that Baltz rejects the adoption of a style in order to remain anonymous. But, to the contrary, he chooses a style that we can clearly and easily recognize, one with which we are familiar, so that style will cease to be an issue, giving way to factual statement. Baltz is classical in approach, adopting the rhetoric of nineteenth-century landscape photography, the formal coherence of Weston and Walker Evans. Yet he renders the image with a precision and tonal quality that can only be obtained with contemporary lenses, film, paper, and chemicals. When one examines Baltz's series on industrial parks, his attitude is evident. In *South Wall Mazda Motors, 2121 East Main Street, Irvine, 1974*, he shows us the building in sharp, full detail. Little is obscured. All is organized in a carefully controlled frontal arrangement so that we see the information with clarity. Baltz employs a straightforward formalism. A column sits dead center, horizontal bands of tone and texture move from top to bottom of the images, and a rock on the left balances with a doorway on the right. Yet, none of this information is weighted. We are left to draw our own conclusions, make our own judgments, provide our best guess. Moreover, he has taken buildings from a rather mundane scene and made them the subjects for a monumental, formalist, manifesto that in no way explains anything or draws conclusions.

In the *New Topographics* exhibition Joe Deal presents what one critic has labeled an "optical democracy."[15] The entire field of vision is rendered from edge to edge in sharp detail. The wide landscape of *Untitled View (Albuquerque, 1973)* contains no horizon because the camera points down sufficiently to eliminate the sky. One can see both nearby objects and distant buildings, from ten feet to perhaps five miles away, all with perfect clarity. A white house sits in the center of the picture, yet does not command more importance than the rocks in the foreground or trees that are miles away. Speaking of this work, he says his intention was to make a series of photographs "in which one image is equal in weight or appearances to another. Many of the conscious decisions . . . had to do with denying the uniqueness in subject matter . . . with a minimum of interference by the photographer."[16]

Frank Gohlke expresses the same attitude when he says, "Making pictures is a way of creating worlds within the frame that provide almost the same richness and pleasure as direct experience of the world—yet the world itself is never quite so clear as a good photograph."[17] Gohlke, however, admits that a photograph is an altered perception of limited and organized information. In another series of photographs made in Texas in 1978, he offers a viewer magnificently detailed and ordered views of houses and landscape, the place of his origins. One photograph, *House—Waxahachie, Texas, 1978*, shows an older building with peeling paint, heavily curtained windows, a barren bush in the foreground, dry grass and a broken concrete walkway to the front porch. Sunlight is slightly diffused, gentle, giving the scene a dated, nostalgic atmosphere. Although Gohlke uses the strict accuracy of large format, he comments that "the Texas pictures seem more and more like dreams to me."[18]

Beginning in the early 1960s, color photography burst upon the art world. Although it was not a new process, color offered the photographer artist both a new range of creative possibilities and presented intriguing aesthetic questions. The last two decades have seen what heretofore were complicated laboratory multistep processes become simple two- or three-step procedures that can easily be accomplished in the home darkroom. Dramatic decreases in cost coupled with increases in availability of materials have made color nearly as popular among amateur photographic enthusiasts as black and white.

Color photographs have frequently been considered more descriptive and hence real because they provide a more complete picture of the world we see with our eyes, a world of color. Joel Meyerowitz, in the late 1970s, discussed this notion in his book, *Cape Light*. When asked why he turned to color, he replied, "Because it describes more things. . . . I don't only mean mere fact and the cold accounting of things in the frame. I really mean the sensation I get from things— their surface and color. . . . Color plays itself out along a richer band of feelings— more wavelengths, more radiance, more sensation."[19] Speaking about the comparison of color to black and white photography, Meyerowitz adds: "Black and white photography translates color into form, whereas color photography can convey significance from the very roots of the act of vision itself, from a place where you respond to primal kinds of things.''[20] Meyerowitz asserts that black and white photography is about rendition of intensity of light whereas color is also concerned with hue. As such, it more fully informs us about the visual world, and it can make us feel a wider range of emotions.

In *Cape Light* Meyerowitz shows us a world that includes, on one hand, rather straightforward photographs of people on the beach at social gatherings and impressive panoramic views of the coast. Although the images are quite believable, the viewer is forced to become hypersensitive to the colors of things in the image, thus deflecting attention from the social context of the scene. The intense blue of the sky and rich ochre of the sand are obsessively demanding. In *Bay/Sky, Provincetown, 1977*, we look out from some unknown height onto the beach and ocean. The brownish yellow foreground gradually changes into an intense blue ocean and a bluish purple skyline. A band of yellow sand protrudes up through the water in the middle ground, on which a sunbather, very small in size, lies. Two people, also shown small, work on a sailboat in the foreground. But this is not a picture about the ocean, boating, or people. It is about color and emotion.

In *Cape Light* Meyerowitz also introduces the viewer to another aspect of color photography: its capacity to translate and transform our familiar visual world into a dramatically different impression. Color films are balanced for particular color temperatures (typically daylight or tungsten light) and their use in situations where the existing light comes from a variety of natural and artificial sources produces some very strange and exotic transformations. In particular, night scenes are rendered in a visual mode quite unlike the way we see things with our eyes. In *Red Interior, Provincetown, 1977*, Meyerowitz shows an intense bluish purple sky over seashore cabins where the one that is closest has a slightly pinkish wall and a pale green wall when mentally we know them to be painted white walls. On the right is a car whose doors are open to us, revealing a glowing red interior. A green street lamp, the moon, and a mysterious yellow light on the left foreground complete the rendition of this bizarre nighttime aberration. This is a Cape Cod world that we have never before seen.

In the mid-1970s William Eggleston had an exhibition of color photographs at the Museum of Modern Art in New York, the subject of which seemed to be Memphis, Tennessee, and parts of Mississippi. Yet, of this work, John Szarkowski says ''we see uncompromising private experience described in a manner that is restrained, austere, and public. Eggleston's subjects are 'simply present' . . . or so the photographs would have us believe . . . they serve Eggleston's interests.''[21] Quite rightly, Szarkowski identifies the hidden subjective undercurrent that becomes apparent with the knowledge that Eggleston has chosen to visually describe a particular region of the United States, a region of his own personal origins. Like snapshots, we encounter people of many generations, all unexpected and unexplained. Yet we sense the intensity of the picture maker, although we cannot precisely identify his emotions.

Eggleston, like Meyerowitz, recognizes the dichotomous character of color photography. In *Jackson Mississippi* a woman sits outside on a stationary, rusty metal swing. Brown leaves cover the foreground, and a white grilllike trellis sits walllike, behind. All attention is on the woman, frail, older, with glasses, smoking a cigarette, but clothed in a dress with an intense red and blue pattern. Furthermore, the seat and back of the swing have a brightly multicolored flower pattern providing dramatic contrast for her dress. It is the variation and conflict of color that command our scrutiny, as well as the posture and expression of the woman. Much is implied about age, decay, change.

However, Eggleston also includes in his book another picture called *Greenwood, Mississippi*. The image is extraordinary in that the lone, bare light bulb in the right foreground of a room bathes everything in a rich red glow. A naked man stands in the center of the picture, next to a bed with rumpled sheets, his right arm is raised scratching his head as he stares at the floor on the right. Above his head, on the wall, the word "GOD" has been spray painted along with "Tally Ho" and other words. It is an absolutely bizarre scene rendered even more strange by color film's ability to translate tungsten light into unnatural hues of orange and red.

In 1981 Sally Eauclaire authored a book called *The New Color Photography* in which she examined the work of forty-eight contemporary photographers. Included in a chapter on color photographic formalism are Stephen Shore, Meyerowitz, and Eggleston. Shore, in *U.S. 10, Post Falls, Idaho, August 25, 1974*, shows boxes and bags of vegetables piled in front of a business establishment, perhaps a restaurant. On the left is a portion of a truck with door open, on the right the open back portion of another truck out of which the boxes of fruit have been unloaded. A car with open doors sits in front of the building above which hangs a neon sign, "The Falls." The bottom of the frame cuts off a pile of bags of onions and corn stalks. The open car and truck doors and the stacks of fruit and vegetables give a sense of immediacy, of a moment in time. Yet all elements are precisely arranged in the rectangular frame in a manner not unlike Walker Evans. The scene is 1970s but the pictorial approach is traditional. With regard to compositional concerns, Shore has said, "I had decided that every time I took a photograph I would consciously decide where the edges were going to be before I took it. . . . I worked on keeping all four edges alive. Then I started to examine the spaces between things in the whole picture."[22]

Pushing the boundaries of color formalism, John Pfahl transforms his color photographs by introducing elements that cause a viewer to question scale and proportion. In *Triangle, Bermuda, August 1975*, from a recent series intended to play visual tricks, one sees the ocean, sand in foreground, blue skyline in the distance with a large rock emerging from the ocean. Of major intrigue are lengths of string attached to pegs in the sand, extending horizontally left to right in the foreground and out into the ocean toward the distant rock. But if one looks at the picture two dimensionally, it is apparent that the string creates a perfect triangle, hence the Bermuda Triangle. It is a fascinating puzzle reminding us of the dual nature of pictorial imagery, illusion and object. It is also a reminder of the hidden mythic character of visual perception and experience.

Eauclaire's book also includes the work of several artists who create elaborate arrangements to be photographed. Historically, such imagery has been considered contrived, heavy handed, and lacking in authenticity. Recently the photographic world has undergone an almost total about-face, shifting from disapproval to applause. This change is due, in no small measure, to the efforts of Duane Michals, who published *Sequences* in 1969 and *Take One and See Mt. Fujiyama* in 1976. Both contain several precisely structured series of single images that are clearly contrived and intended to communicate ideas that are abstract and metaphorical. In *The Spirit Leaves the Body*, Michals deals with notions about death and afterlife. A succession of eight images, all taken in the same barren room, from the same camera location, shows a single window, which provides illumination, and a bed on which reclines a nude male. Through double exposure it would seem that the spirit, in human form, rises from the body and walks from the room. The whole scene is clearly staged and the double exposure technique is obvious, even to an amateur. Michals cares about the idea more than the sense of believability. In fact, he allows the viewer to be sure of the artificiality of the scene so that one does not become involved with the issue of authenticity.

In the second book Michals becomes more narrative and adds text. We no longer have a series of images taken from one location, but a sequence of photographs made at different places and times. In *The Pleasures of the Glove* Michals weaves a curious fantasy where a glove becomes animated, propelled through a series of psychological and sexual encounters. The photographs are straightforwardly real, but the narrative is a provocative and fanciful daydream. The viewer knows each image has been staged but disregards the visual falsehood of the scenes in favor of the poetic fascination of the story.

In 1974 the work of Ralph Eugene Meatyard was published in an *Aperture Magazine* monograph. His imagery had some of the same narrative and fanciful implications as Michals', yet without the strict sequencing. Meatyard, however, deals less with ideas and more with the evocation of emotion. In the monograph some of his photographs are clearly staged, others seem carefully arranged, and a few, very few, appear natural. All photographs are untitled. One shows an interior, a weathered door to the right, a partially covered window, perhaps with torn shade, to the left. A face is seen just emerging from the darkness, and it is like a death mask, weathered, immobile, mysterious. In another photograph, also taken in a decayed building, a person holds, with both hands, a pure white mask in front of his or her face. The mask is bland, without eye or hair definition. Clearly staged, it is a disturbing dark image. Yet another photograph shows four young children sitting on the weathered wooden steps of what may be a grandstand. The strangeness of the picture is in the masks worn by the children, giving them enlarged grotesque facial appearances. Although a bit amusing, the total effect is dark, mysterious, and frightening. The viewer sees consistantly in Meatyard a world of his construction, one that is obviously staged, but one that is powerfully evocative. Meatyard seems able to bring to the surface our mythic and fearsome unconscious inner life.

Les Krims is another photographer artist who creates staged and narrative imagery. In the early 1970s he produced several limited edition folios such as *The Deerslayers* and *The Little People of America*. Seemingly rooted in the documentary tradition, the first offers a visual essay showing mostly grotesque portraits of deer hunters; the latter is concerned with picturing people who attended a national meeting of this organization, portrayed as Americans in everything but physical size. Both present a rather bizarre and satiric vision of subcultures, yet they are images that are clearly personal and idiosyncratic. In another two series, *The Incredible Case of the Stack O'Wheats Murders* and *Making Chicken Soup*, done in 1972, Krims resorts to imagery that is both staged and narrative. The former series, both ludicrous and humorous, is based upon studies of unsolved murders, and it shows nude females sprawled on the floor in puzzling interior scenes, covered with chocolate syrup, a substitute for blood, with a large stack of pancakes on a plate nearby. In the latter series Krims uses his mother, a middle-aged matronly Jewish woman, dressed only in panties, to straightforwardly describe how to make chicken soup. The bizarre surrealism of both series lies in their contrast: pancakes next to a staged murder, and his almost naked mother making a typically Jewish dish. Moreover, the obviousness of the structuring of the scenes allows the viewer to dismiss the reality and authenticity of the images while experiencing the implications that each suggests about the real world.

Other aspects of this work are the apparent conceptual implications. Krims, like Michals and Meatyard, forces the viewer to consider the question of verisimilitude and admit to the inherent fictional character of photographs. Once taken onto this level, all photographs are suspect and linked to both the mind and intentions of the image maker as well as the viewer.

During the 1970s Robert Cumming and John Baldessari raised similar questions about the conceptual framework of photography. Cumming's work tends to provoke a viewer to consider the ideas that produce the image rather than the image itself. In a show at the Houston Museum in 1977 he exhibited a work called *Farm Fence Metaphor*, 1975–76. There are two images in the piece, and the upper one identifies a person, Bradley Hindson, holding a long horizontal high-contrast photograph of a fence that seems Oriental in mood. Below is the actual fence in a rural farm area. The typewritten message on the upper photograph superimposes a thought process and announces its message. It is a puzzle to decipher, not by looking, but by thinking. The image is amusing by virtue of the comparison, and it seems almost tongue in cheek. At the same time the viewer is challenged to rethink the nature of the visual experience and the informational character of photography. Yet no answers are given, only questions. Moreover, these questions allow the viewer a glimpse of the issues that are of interest to Cumming.

John Baldessari shares many of Cumming's concerns. In the same 1977 Houston exhibition Baldessari exhibited a work called *Repair/Retouch Series: An Allegory About Wholeness (Plate and Hand), 1976,* which is a triptych. On the left are two pictures: above a plate broken in pieces and, below, a hand broken at the wrist with what appears as deep wounds. In the center both plate and hand move toward being mended. Above right is the whole plate, cracks gone, and the whole hand below it with only one faint scar remaining. It is a metaphor, yet it also is a lecture on visual perception, reminding the viewer of the power of the photograph to obscure and restructure ocular reality. As a photograph it raises doubts about both itself and photographic representation.

Both Cumming and Baldessari employ structuring and staging to deal with personal interests and conceptual ideas. One might describe the operational strategy of this approach in terms of the careful fabrication of a scene so that it might be photographed. Before making further reference to photographers who employ this methodology, it is important to look at the debt that is owed to Frederick Sommer who, in the early 1950s, began producing images that derived from deliberate fabrications.

In 1930 Sommer made one of his first collaged images, *Untitled, Negative #66 (Chicken Parts).* The photograph shows the grisly pieces of a chicken arranged on what is possibly snow. Loose in formal structure, the image may have resulted less from intentional impulse and more from accidental discovery. The arrangement is casual, but highly provocative.

More than ten years later Sommer created *Young Explorer, 1951,* photographed from a carefully constructed formal collage. Every inch of the image has rich detail with studied attention paid to shape and structure. In the center is a strong, simple abstract shape, resembling both language and musical symbols. Also in the center is a young male figure overlaid by the abstract shape. Sommer, the photographer, gives us a delight of fine detail, rich tonality, and metaphoric meaning, evocation of concerns about time, change, and evolution. But equally as strong is Sommer, the artist, who carefully creates a formal symphony of line, texture, shape, and spatial depth.

To some extent the work of Olivia Parker, in the 1970s, derives from the same impulse that motivated Sommer, yet her work seems more delicate. Initially trained as a painter, Parker turned to photography and imbues her imagery with a special sensuous character. In a series of selenium toned black and white prints reproduced in a 1978 monograph, *Signs of Life,* she demonstrates her painterly concern for careful formal organization of objects to be photographed. Parker uses fabrics, shells, and feathers because she is a collector of found objects. These images have a beauty that is based upon a sensitivity to exquisite texture, tone, and pattern. But they are also to be seen metaphorically as concerned with transition through life to death, as the title of her monograph indicates.

Parker's color work also evolves out of the same theme, only the addition of hues adds a further dimension to the metaphor. As a colorist, Parker confines her palette to a selection of hues of low intensity and a carefully selected narrow range. In *Untitled, 1979*, a polaroid color, eight-by-ten print reproduced in the Sally Eauclaire book, one sees flowers on a shelf glowing out of a rich dark background. Underneath on another shelf is a skull, partially wrapped in paper and string. The skull and paper have multiple delicate pastel tones and also emerge out of a brown darkness. The lighting of objects is carefully conceived, and the color is enormously effective, both visually and evocatively. Moreover the natural disparity between skull and flowers is lessened by the translation into rich polaroid color, making possible a metaphorical statement on life and death. As a painter Parker has constructed a scene that she then translates, as a photographer, into a powerful visual and symbolic image.

Lucas Samaras also came to photography with a broad background as an artist. However, unlike others, he continues to be prolific and enormously creative in many media including photography, drawing, painting, sculpture, and printmaking. Samaras also organizes and constructs scenes for photographs. *Untitled Still Life, October 24, 1978*, in Eauclaire's book, shows a collection of objects lying on a flat interior desk surface in front of a wall. Objects include reproductions of historical Greek or Roman figures, playing cards, pencils, books, a radio on the right, a desk lamp illuminating the wall, and many, many other ordinary and strange objects. Like Parker, Samaras seems to be a collector and appears interested in literary connections. But it is the intense and varied color of light that transforms the scene to render it unique. The foreground on the left is red and blue on the right from unseen illumination. The rear wall has green on the left and right and is blue and white in the center. It is a surreal rendition, packed with objects that fascinate and puzzle the viewer. As a colorist Samaras shows a love of intense and varied hue, as well as its concomitant range of visual and symbolic associations.

In 1979 Van Deren Coke, curator of photography at the San Francisco Museum of Modern Art, initiated an exhibition called *Fabricated to Be Photographed*, which included the work of ten photographers who employ related approaches to image making. In the catalogue introduction Coke says

All of the fabricators have thoroughly thought out their photographs from a formal as well as ideational standpoint. Their approaches represent a major shift away from offhand photography and photography that depends upon being at the right place at the right time. The photographers have learned how to mold reality to suit their purposes rather than wait for or search out the moment that will best convey their ideas.[23]

It might also be said that these photographers, by virtue of their process, both align themselves with the synthetic approach of painters and also sever connection with the tradition of photography that values recording of unaltered reality. Yet all make straight, clear, sharp focus photographs that are unaltered in process or darkroom and therefore follow a tradition back to the origins of photography.

Despite similarities, there exists extraordinary variety among artists in this show. Ellen Brooks has fabricated doll-house sets showing room interiors with male and female figures in melodramatic stage sets. Stephan Collins incorporates pieces of glass, cut in different shapes, that are partially spray painted in bright colors, hence avoiding the referential or narrative aspects of Brooks. Robert Cumming, continuing his conceptual interests, shows a pair of view camera photographs that picture, in black and white, a metal pail and wooden chair suspended between two posts, at night, spotlit. Les Krims has toned silver prints, one showing a schoolroom interior, a blackboard with two female nudes on either side standing on chairs, and cardboard cutouts of letters and simple representational objects on the blackboard. Victor Schrager, alluding to his literary interests and to photography's representational ambiguities, has color photographs that are oblique views of a collage of books, magazines, reproductions, photographs, lying on a rug. The range of imagery is enormous, and many of these artists have been or will be discussed here in terms of other directions in contemporary photography. All share the aspect of preconception, prefabrication, and previsualization of imagery. Yet only the last of these three concerns— previsualization—has been a dominant shared aspect in the history of photography.

One result of the infusion of artists into photography is a greater concern with formal aspects of the image. This is apparent in the work of Parker, Samaras, Brooks, and Cumming. Yet other photographers whose backgrounds were limited to photography also contributed to a contemporary attention to formalism. Following the foundation laid by Callahan and Siskind at the Institute of Design in Chicago, Ray Metzker employs formal arrangements that create patterns. *PCA, 1965*, is a work of approximately fifty-by-forty-five inches and contains numerous single black and white images of walking silhouette people, arranged tightly in eleven horizontal rows. Another, *Juniper St., 1966–67*, shows twenty-five images, five across, five down with no separation. Each is a black and white photograph of the same scene, in which one or more persons are walking through a patch of sunlight on an urban street. Both are repetitions yet both employ series of individually unique images. They are formal arrangements creating patterns when viewed at a distance and individual encounters when the viewer is next to the works. It is, for its time, a unique and unexpected vision of a photograph. And, despite its formalism, or perhaps because of it, these works suggest metaphorical statements on urban life, of anonymity and repetitious boredom mixed with unexpected visual encounter and excitement.

Jan Groover also employs a strong formalism in her work. Coming from a painting background like Parker, Groover made, in 1978, a series of color images of kitchen utensils, knives, forks, spatulas, and so forth. Carefully arranged close-ups focused attention on color and shape, reflecting Groover's formal artistic training. About these images, she says, "In the real world, these forks and kitchen implements can have many associations and functions; in the photographs, it doesn't matter. Formalism is everything."[24] *Tybee Forks and Starts (J) 1978* is typical of this series. Objects intrude diagonally into the rectangular picture space, reflections of the fork on the shiny metal surface of the start, strong blue, green, and brown hues, all demonstrate her straightforward concern for formal organization.

In the photographic world the strictly formal image is not aways praised. Emotional and symbolic content, frequently associated with subject matter, is often more highly valued. Groover's images have been referred to as playful formal manipulations without content. Yet the larger art world knows of the suggestive and contextual potential of such formalist studies and is more likely to given an enthusiastic response to this kind of imagery. Kitchen utensils are still to be read as such and carry associations. Knives are sharp for cutting as are spatulalike utensils with saw teeth. One might imagine these as implements from a hospital operating room as well as from a kitchen. Shapes, shadows, textures, and identification of objects all make it possible for the imagination to work with a variety of intellectual ideas and emotions.

Barbara Kasten, another painter turned photographer, also emphasizes formal considerations. Using a view camera and polaroid twenty-by-twenty-four film, Kasten creates purely abstract images as in two works published in the April 1983 issue of *Polaroid Close Up*. In *Construct LB/2, 1982*, the straight edges of mirrors are reflected in multiple horizontal bands with subtle gradations of gray and white and with a modestly red triangle in the center. On the opposite page *Construct NYC-8, 1983* also mirrors, has triangular and rectangular shapes and numerous intense colors. Kasten's images seem conceptually similar to those of Lázló Moholy-Nagy, who referred to photography as the "manipulation of light." The work also bears distant relationships to twentieth-century constructivism and cubism. Yet there is also a very strong and enticing abstract vision that can only be explained as the vision of Barbara Kasten.

Since 1960 photographers can be viewed, for the most part, as modernists working in the postmodernist era. Several postmodernist critics such as Thomas Lawson and Douglas Crimp refer frequently to a small group of photographers when they discuss the contemporary dilemma in art. Lawson mentions Cindy Sherman, Sherrie Levine, and Richard Prince as he considers photography's potential to subvert art and dislodge normalized perception, only to assert its failure to be truly deconstructive and reconstructive.[25] Crimp, however, takes a more positive stance by arguing photography's ability to subvert by showing that the "aura" of an art object is only a copy, not an original.[26] For Crimp, Sherrie Levine and Cindy Sherman are two artists who most forcefully deal with photography as "copy of a copy."

In 1983, in the catalogue to her exhibition at the University of Pennsylvania which included the work of "postmodernist" photographers, Paula Marincola, says: "*Image Scavengers Photography* focuses on nine photographers who appropriate their imagery, or their imagemaking strategies, from media sources— TV, films, newspapers, magazines, books. . . . They reproduce the 'look' of certain formats—the movie still, for example, soap opera scenario, or fashion and product advertisement."[27]

These photographers are interested in the process of "recontextualization" whereby the imagery of mass culture is decoded so that one can understand the implications of signs and posture. In the process images are set adrift from their meaning and allowed to drift into allegory.

Cindy Sherman has become preeminent among those postmodernist photographers included in the Pennsylvania exhibition. In a series of photographs between 1976 and 1980, called *Untitled Film Stills*, she uses postwar Hollywood stills into which she inserts herself. In *Untitled Film Still (#35) 1979* Sherman stands next to a door, scuffed and dirty, wearing a patterned old dress, bandana, and an apron. She faces into the room corner where coats hang loosely on the wall, and she looks over her shoulder at something outside our view of vision. Hand on hip, she seems dejected, resigned. Yet it is clearly a film cliche of an unhappy heroine of a fifties or sixties B movie.

The image can be seen simultaneously as a revealing self-portrait and as fiction, clearly describing the ambiguous and paradoxical nature of both photography and self-portraiture. That which is shown assumes the aspect of reality, yet is false. By inserting herself into well-known movie stills she makes the viewer aware of popular feminine stereotypes that have come to us and been mediated by photography. In so doing, Sherman brings about the total effacement of herself as a person. Although she is there, she is not. She is only a copy of the copy.

Another photographer to receive attention by postmodernists is Laurie Simmons who, like Ellen Brooks, first used doll-house sets to deal with female stereotypes. In the *Image Scavengers* show Simmons displayed *Under the Sea (Diagonal Diver), 1979*, a photograph based upon the popular Lloyd Bridges TV drama, "Seahunt." For this Simmons used a fish tank and a toy skindiver who is pointed downward, descending ever deeper. The scene is a real-life drama, yet it is trivialized by the use of toys and sets. At the same time Simmons makes the viewer aware of the stereotype that produces the picture and the power of stereotypes to control and direct our perceptions of self and world.

Richard Prince appropriates his images directly from mass advertising media sources. His method consists of photographing an original ad in black and white, which is then converted to a transparency, given an extra dot screen, and collaged with other images. *Untitled 1982* pictures a man, blurred, on the right, and a woman, left, with arms on his shoulders. She is leaning backward, and her head is outside the frame edge. The woman's image in large dot screen on the left gradually fades into smoothness on the right. There is strangeness, unreality, yet the unmistakable reference to mass media imagery. It is a question mark, provoking the viewer to question what is shown and thus what mass media shows.

Appropriation of mass-media imagery is not new to postmodernist artists. In the 1920s and 1930s John Heartfield in Germany created montages with available imagery to denounce the Nazi regime. In the 1960s photographer artists appropriated photographs from magazines and newspapers to make art that challenged traditional concepts of single imagery and that also blurred distinctions between photography and other media. In postmodernism appropriation is being used to recontextualize images and meanings. In the 1960s appropriation was a strategy because it was an easy and convenient source of imagery and because of its impact and immediacy.

One of the most intriguing aspects of this earlier appropriation was the corresponding discovery or assertion that the single image need not be the end of the process, but could be the beginning. This led to the notion of taking apart and restructuring an image, perhaps with other images. By the early 1970s Jerry Uelsmann had produced a body of work that defined this attitude for the next generation of emerging photographers. He called his approach "postvisualization." The moment of creation is in the darkroom rather than at the moment of exposure. Using a group of enlargers, Uelsmann created multiple images that contain numerous moments in time. In one sense Uelsmann is a traditionalist in the way that he prints the image on a single piece of photographic paper. On the other hand his restructuring creates images that, like those of Michals, deny the sense of reality which is found in straight photographs. Uelsmann's images are mythic, symbolic, and metaphoric in a directly obvious sense. By means of their structure they declare that they are to be interpreted as well as experienced. In *Strawberry Day 1967* Uelsmann uses several negatives to make one single image that shows dense trees on the left, a strawberry in the middle and a woman, hands to her face, on the right. All is symbolic, but the symbols are open, unspecific, evocative of multiple meanings.

Robert Heinecken, like Uelsmann, adopted a process that employs multiple images. Unlike Uelsmann, however, he also freely translates photographic imagery from silver paper into other media. In some of his work he has created lithographic translations of multiple photographic images. In other pieces he has worked upon traditional photographic papers with stains, dyes, tray cleaner, pastels, and other materials. Cutting up photographs, he has pieced them back together in new configurations. Magazine pages are used to make photograms. Provocative images are randomly printed over the pages of magazines. Photograms of food are translated into lithographs. The sources for Heinecken's art are also images from mass media—magazines, newspapers, and TV. Heinecken's art often causes critics to refrain from referring to him as a photographer. Even he prefers to call himself an artist. Yet his imagery is overwhelmingly photographic, which clearly links him to twentieth-century photography.

In 1973 the Hudson River Museum mounted what they described as a "comprehensive exhibition of contemporary images in photography" that was "intended to emphasize the wide diversity of approaches used by photographers, many of whom are incorporating old and new techniques in creating works of art with startling visual impact."[28] In all, forty-three artists were involved, including such prominent figures as Robert Heinecken, Jerry Uelsmann, Emmet Gowin, Van Deren Coke, Thomas Barrow, William Larson, Todd Walker, Betty Hah, Keith Smith, Ellen Brooks, and Robert Fichter.

Perhaps the most unusual aspect of this show was the presentation of ''contemporary photography'' as a multiple, translated, or staged imagery. For the most part, there were few straight, traditional silver photographic images. One could assume quite easily that photography had merged, quite creatively, with other media and no longer felt constrained by its pure aesthetic traditions.

Photographs by Todd Walker showed solarized and flashed images of a female nude in the landscape. Keith Smith sewed strips of photographs together. Douglas Prince sandwiched film between sheets of clear acrylic to create three dimensional ''boxes.'' Naomi Savage etched photographic images on copper plates. Catherine Jensen made a soft sculpture bedroom with photographic images on objects applied through cyanotype. In all, the show was indicative of the wide creative variations in photography at that time.

It does give one cause to question the scope of this show when we realize that the *New Topographics* exhibition at George Eastman House originated only two years later in 1975. This may be solid evidence for the proposition that, for any trend, there is a countertrend. On the other hand, I would assert that this supports my contention that photography is an ever-widening and swiftly moving river of creative exploration in which certain attitudes and imagery come in and out of the spotlight. It is not at all unusual to find simultaneous shows on new color, postmodernism, traditional documentary, and so forth. It is only a question of which at any one time is receiving the most attention by critics, galleries, and museum directors, or the artists themselves.

NOTES

1. In Beaumont Newhall, *The History of Photography* (New York: Museum of Modern Art, 1964), p. 111.

2. Nancy Newhall, ed., *The Daybooks of Edward Weston, Volume 2, California* (Millerton, N.Y.: Aperture, 1973), p. 154.

3. Newhall, *The History of Photography*, p. 198.

4. Nathan Lyons, ed., *Contemporary Photographers: Towards a Social Landscape* (Rochester, N.Y.: Horizon Press, 1966), introduction.

5. Susan Sontag, *On Photography* (New York: Farrar, Straus and Giroux, 1977), pp. 41–42.

6. Ibid., p. 12.

7. Diane Arbus, *Diane Arbus*, An Aperture Monograph (Millerton, N.Y.: Aperture Press, 1972), p. 3.

8. Bill Owens, *Suburbia* (San Francisco: Straight Arrow Books, 1972).

9. Emmet Gowin, *Emmet Gowin Photographs* (New York: Alfred A. Knopf, 1976), p. 100.

10. Clifford Ackley, ed., *Private Realities* (Boston: Museum of Fine Arts, 1974), introduction.

11. John Szarkowski, *Mirrors and Windows: American Photography since 1960* (New York: Museum of Modern Art, 1978), p. 25.

12. William Jenkins, ed., *New Topographics* (Rochester, N.Y.: International Museum of Photography, 1975), p. 5.

13. Ibid.

14. Ibid., p. 6.

15. T. Barrow, S. Armitage, W. E. Tydeman, eds., *Reading into Photography: Selected Essays, 1959–1980* (Albuquerque: University of New Mexico Press, 1982), pp. 201–7.

16. Jenkins, *New Topographics*, p. 6.

17. Renato Danese, ed., *American Images: New Work by Twenty Contemporary Photographers* (New York: McGraw-Hill, 1979), p. 110.

18. Ibid.

19. Joel Meyerowitz, *Cape Light: Color Photographs by Joel Meyerowitz* (Boston: New York Graphic Society, 1978), introduction.

20. Ibid.

21. John Szarkowski, *William Eggleston's Guide* (New York: Museum of Modern Art, 1976), p. 11.

22. Tony Hiss, *American Photographer* 11, no. 2 (February 1979): 35.

23. *Fabricated to Be Photographed* (San Francisco: San Francisco Museum of Modern Art, 1979), p. 12.

24. Danese, *American Images*, p. 140.

25. Thomas Lawson, "Last Exit: Painting," *Artforum* (October 1981): 45.

26. Douglas Crimp, "The Photographic Activity of Postmodernism," *October* 15 (Winter 1980): 94.

27. Paula Marincola, ed., *Image Scavengers: Photography* (College Park: University of Pennsylvania, 1982), p. 5.

28. Donald L. Werner, ed., *Light and Lens: Methods of Photography* (Dobbs Ferry, N.Y.: Morgan and Morgan Inc., 1973), foreword.

BIBLIOGRAPHICAL ESSAY

Photography in the twentieth century is, in large part, both critically and historically understood through Beaumont Newhall's seminal works, *The History of Photography, from 1839 to the Present Day*, and *Photography: Essays & Images*. These books by the former curator of photography at the Museum of Modern Art in New York are among the most complete and definitive texts available, yet they fail to contend adequately with one of the richest periods of photographic activity, the postmodern era since 1970. Other excellent books such as Nathan Lyons' *Photographers on Photography* and Arnold Gassan's *A Chronology of Photography* have enjoyed wide popularity but have their own particular character. Gassan's book is more of a critical survey than a historical text, looking at the development of photography according to subject areas (i.e., the portrait, the cityscape, the social landscape, the nude, etc.). Lyons' book is a widely used critical anthology of writings by major photographers since the turn of the century and represents one of the first serious attempts to collect important writings on photography. Its major weakness now, however, is that it was published in 1966 and therefore contains little concerning the postmodern period.

Of more recent vintage are *American Photography* by Jonathan Green, *Reading into Photography: Selected Essays, 1959–1980*, by Thomas Barrow, Shelley Armitage, and William Tydeman, *The Camera Viewed: A Critical Anthology of Writings on Photography* by Peninah R. Petruck, and *Classic Essays on Photography* by Alan Trachtenberg. Jonathan Green's new book is an interesting and articulate survey of the history of

American photography since 1945, and despite rather affected chapter titles such as
"Surrogate Reality" and "The New American Luminism," there are excellent critiques
of individual photographers. Green's book is well worth reading as the only existing
survey of contemporary photography. The other books are excellent anthologies of writings by critics and photographer artists and constitute the best source of knowledge we
have about contemporary ideas and attitudes.

Monographs are another means by which one can examine the work of twentieth century
photographer artists. Comprehensive books on some major modernist photographers are
Alfred Stieglitz: An American Seer by Dorothy Norman, *Paul Strand: Sixty Years of
Photographs, Ansel Adams, Images: 1923–1974,* and *Edward Weston: His Life and
Photographs* by Ben Maddow. *The Daybooks of Edward Weston,* volume 1, Mexico,
and volume 2, California, are fascinating to read and provide extraordinary insight into
the thoughts of one of the major photographers of this century. Photographs and biogra-
phies on significant documentary and reportage photographers are found in monographs
such as *Walker Evans* by John Szarkowski, *Dorothea Lange: Photographs of a Lifetime,*
Robert Frank's *The Americans, Henry Cartier-Bresson, Photographer, Alfred Eisenstaedt: Germany,* Andre Kertész's *A Lifetime of Perception,* and *W. Eugene Smith,* an
Aperture Monograph. Four books on important mid-century photographer artists include
(Harry) *Callahan* by John Szarkowski, *Aaron Siskind, Photographer,* Minor White's
Mirrors Messages Manifestations, and *Diane Arbus,* an Aperture Monograph.

Works by a few artists in the postmodern era are to be found in monographs such as
Bruce Davidson's *East 100th Street, Lee Friedlander: Photographs, Sequences/Duane
Michals,* and *Jerry N. Uelsmann, Twenty-Five Years. A Retrospective.* Contemporary
color photography in postmodernism is best represented in *The New Color Photography*
by Sally Eauclaire. Also, more examples of color works by individual artists can be found
in monographs such as *William Eggleston's Guide, Cape Light: Color Photographs by
Joel Meyerowitz,* or Stephen Shore's *Uncommon Places.*

Exhibition catalogues may be the best source for understanding a broader range of
contemporary photography. Of major importance is the book that resulted from the show,
Mirrors & Windows: American Photography since 1960 that was curated by John Szarkowski at the Museum of Modern Art in New York in 1978. Although ambitious in
scope, the exhibition exclusively used works from the museum collecction, works that
seem to be mostly oriented toward realism. As counterpoint one might look at the
catalogues for the shows *The Persistence of Vision* curated by Nathan Lyons in 1967 at
the George Eastman House and *Light and Lens: Methods of Photography* organized at
the Hudson River Museum in 1973 by Donald Werner. Both present examples of nontraditional process manipulated work that constituted such a strong current in photography
in the 1960s and 1970s.

Contemporary American Photographic Works, organized by Lewis Baltz at the Museum
of Fine Arts at Houston in 1977, and *American Images: New Work by Twenty Contemporary Photographers* are important because they feature some of the better known
contemporary photographers but also seem heavily directed toward the realist impulses
of the last ten years. The show *Fabricated to Be Photographed* curated by Van Deren
Coke at the San Francisco Museum of Modern Art in 1979 is refreshing in that it presented
both some of those artists who still work with less conventional methods and also represents new interests. Finally, *Image Scavengers: Photography,* a catalogue of a show
curated at the University of Pennsylvania in 1982 by Paula Marincola, makes direct
reference to postmodern photography, both in terms of reproductions and texts. It is a

highly interesting treatise, well worth the effort of reading, but also leads one to believe that the works of nine artists comprise the photographic activity of the postmodern era. Simply stated, this is not the case, and in this sense the catalogue can be misleading.

It is in periodicals that one finds the majority of current discussion of postmodern photography. Michael Starenko, in "What's An Artist To Do? A Short History of Postmodernism and Photography," *Afterimage* (January 1983), wrote an excellent review of the issues, critics, and artists who have come to the attention of the art world in postmodern photography. Starenko makes reference in his article to about a half dozen photographers such as Cindy Sherman, Sherrie Levine, and Richard Prince. Douglas Crimp also concerned himself with many of the same artists when he wrote "The Photographic Activity of Postmodernism," *October* 15 (Winter 1980), in which he discussed the issue of postmodernism in the context of Walter Benjamin and those aspects of photography that have to do with reproduction of copies. The thrust of his argument is that postmodern photography is about showing that "aura" or any claims for originality are fiction because they use images that are already seen, appropriated images. Thomas Lawson in "Last Exit: Painting," *Artforum* (October 1981), discusses the strategic use of photography to subvert conventional thought and art forms, but challenges its ability to be an effective tool in a deconstruction process because of photography's sideline position. Painting, says Lawson, is the best tool because of its still dominant position in the contemporary art world.

Other recent articles also refer to postmodernism but list a different group of photographer artists than does Starenko, Crimp, or Lawson. Gene Thornton wrote "Postmodern Photography: It Doesn't Look Modern at All," *Artnews* (April 1979), in which he looks at recent practitioners in the medium such as Duane Michals, Jan Groover, Garry Winogrand, and Joel Meyerowitz and concludes that photography today is alive and flourishing because photographers have never been expected to be as radical as painters. In "The New Photography: Turning Traditional Standards Upside Down," *Artnews* (April 1978), Thornton looks at and discusses the work of contemporary photographers such as William Eggleston, Winogrand, Lee Friedlander, Emmet Gowin, Mark Cohen, and Stephen Shore. He scrutinizes their images in terms of a new formalism in contemporary photography that then places this work in the wider context of twentieth-century art. Perhaps the most curious aspect of Thornton's articles is that his survey of contemporary photographers in a postmodern era makes no reference to any of the artists mentioned by Starenko, Crimp, or Lawson. It would appear that in current photographic criticism one tends to find at least two separate intepretations about what constitutes postmodern photography. Perhaps, with time, other points of view will appear. In sum, this supports the contention that postmodern photography is much too pluralistic and varied to be easily summarized by any one critic or historian.

BIBLIOGRAPHY

Books and Anthologies

Barrow, Thomas F., Shelley Armitage, William E. Tydeman, eds. *Reading into Photography: Selected Essays, 1959–1980*. Albuquerque: University of New Mexico Press, 1982.

Capa, Cornell, ed. *The Concerned Photographer*. New York: Grossman Publishers, 1968.

Coleman, A. D. *Light Readings: A Photography Critic's Writings 1968–1978*. New York: Oxford University Press, 1981.

Eauclaire, Sally. *The New Color Photography*. New York: Abbeville Press, 1981.

Gassan, Arnold. *A Chronology of Photography*. Athens, Ohio: Handbook Company, 1972.

Gidal, Tim. *Modern Photojournalism*. New York: Macmillan Publishing Co., 1972.

Green, Jonathan. *American Photography*. New York: Abrams, 1984.

Lyons, Nathan, ed. *Photographers on Photography*. Englewood Cliffs, N.J.: Prentice-Hall Inc., 1966.

Malcolm, Janet. *Diane and Nikon: Essays on the Aesthetic of Photography*. Boston: David R. Godine Publisher, 1980.

Newhall, Beaumont. *The History of Photography, from 1939 to the Present Day*. 5th ed. New York: Museum of Modern Art, 1982.

———. *Photography: Essays and Images*. Boston: New York Graphic Society, 1981.

Sontag, Susan. *On Photography*. New York: Farrar, Straus and Giroux, 1977.

Petruck, Peninah R. *The Camera Viewed*. Vols. 1 and 2. New York: E. P. Dutton, 1979.

Szarkowski, John. *Looking at Photographs: 100 Pictures from the Collection of the Museum of Modern Art*. New York: Museum of Modern Art, 1973.

Trachtenberg, Alan. *Classic Essays on Photography*. New Haven, Conn.: Leete's Island Books, 1980.

Monographs

Adams, Ansel. *Ansel Adams, Images: 1923–1974*. Boston: New York Graphic Society, 1972.

Arbus, Diane. *Diane Arbus*. Millerton, N.Y.: Aperture, 1972.

Bry, Doris. *Afred Stieglitz: Photographer*. Boston: Museum of Fine Arts, 1965.

Cartier-Bresson, Henri. *Henry Cartier-Bresson, Photographer*. New York: International Center of Photography, 1979.

Coleo, Robert, ed. *Dorothea Lange: Photographs of a Lifetime*. Millerton, N.Y.: Aperture, 1982.

Cumming, Robert. *Cumming Photographs*. Edited with an essay by James Alinder. Carmel, Calif.: The Friends of Photography, 1979.

Cunningham, Imogen. *Imogen Cunningham: Photographs*. Introduction by Margery Mann. Seattle: University of Washington Press, 1970.

Davidson, Bruce. *East 100th Street*. Cambridge, Mass.: Harvard University Press, 1970.

Eggleston, William. *William Eggleston's Guide*. Essay by John Szarkowski. New York: Museum of Modern Art, 1976.

Eisenstaedt, Alfred. *Alfred Eisenstaedt: Germany*. Edited by Gregory A. Vitiello. New York: Abrams, 1981.

Frank, Robert. *The Americans*. Millerton, N.Y.: Aperture Press, 1978.

Friedlander, Lee. *Lee Friedlander: Photographs*. New City, N.Y.: Haywire Press, 1978.

Gowin, Emmet. *Emmet Gowin: Photographs*. New York: Alfred A. Knopf, 1976.

Heinecken, Robert. *Heinecken*. Edited by James Enyeart. New York: The Friends of Photography in association with Light Gallery, 1980.

Kertész, André. *A Lifetime of Perception*. New York: Abrams, 1982.

Kostelanetz, Richard, ed. *Moholy-Nagy*. New York: Praeger, 1970.

Krims, Les. *The Little People of America, 1971*. Buffalo, N.Y.: Les Krims, 1972.
————. *Making Chicken Soup*. Buffalo, N.Y.: Humphry Press, 1972.
Lyon, Danny. *The Bikeriders*. New York: Macmillan, 1968.
————. *Conversations with the Dead*. New York: Holt, Rinehart and Winston, 1971.
Lyons, Nathan. *Notations in Passing*. Cambridge, Mass.: MIT Press, 1974.
Maddow, Ben. *Edward Weston: Fifty Years*. Millerton, N.Y.: Aperture, 1973. New
    expanded edition reissued as *Edward Weston: His Life and Photographs*. Miller-
    ton, N.Y.: Aperture, 1979.
Meyerowitz, Joel. *Cape Light: Color Photographs by Joel Meyerowitz*. Boston: New
    York Graphic Society, 1979.
————. *St. Louis & The Arch*. Boston: New York Graphic Society, 1980.
————. *Wild Flowers*. Boston: New York Graphic Society, 1983.
Michals, Duane. *Sequences/Duane Michals*. New York: Doubleday, 1969.
Newhall, Nancy, ed. *The Daybooks of Edward Weston, Volume I, Mexico*. Millerton,
    N.Y.: Aperture Press, 1973.
————, ed. *The Daybooks of Edward Weston, Volume II, California*. Millerton, N.Y.:
    Aperture, 1973.
Norman, Dorothy. *Alfred Stieglitz: An American Seer*. New York: Random House, 1973
    and Millerton, N.Y.: Aperture, 1973.
Owens, Bill. *Suburbia*. San Francisco: Straight Arrow Books, 1972.
Shore, Stephen. *Uncommon Places*. Millerton, N.Y.: Aperture Press, 1982.
Siskind, Aaron. *Aaron Siskind: Photographer*. Edited with an introduction by Nathan
    Lyons. Essays by Henry Holmes Smith and Thomas B. Hess. Rochester, N.Y.:
    George Eastman House, 1965.
Smith, W. Eugene. *W. Eugene Smith*. Millerton, N.Y.: Aperture Press, 1969.
Strand, Paul. *Paul Strand: Sixty Years of Photographs*. Millerton, N.Y.: Aperture Press,
    1976.
Szarkowski, John. *Callahan*. New York: Museum of Modern Art, 1976.
————. *Walker Evans*. New York: Museum of Modern Art, 1971.
Uelsmann, Jerry N. *Twenty-Five Years. A Retrospective*. Boston: New York Graphic
    Society, 1982.
White, Minor. *Mirrors Messages Manifestations*. Millerton, N.Y.: Aperture, 1969.
————, ed. *Ralph Eugene Meatyard*. Millerton, N.Y.: Aperture, 1974.
Winogrand, Garry. *The Animals*. Afterword by John Szarkowski. New York: Museum
    of Modern Art, 1969.
————. *Public Relations*. Introduction by Tod Papageorge. New York: Museum of
    Modern Art, 1977.
————. *Stock Photographs: The Fort Worth Fat Stock Show and Rodeo*. Austin: Uni-
    versity of Texas Press, 1980.

Exhibition Catalogues and Books

Ackley, Clifford, ed. *Private Realities: Recent American Photography*. Boston: Museum
    of Fine Arts, 1974.
Baltz, Lewis, ed., *Contemporary American Photographic Works*. Houston: Museum of
    Fine Arts, 1977.
Bowman, Stanley J., ed. *Translations: Photographic Images with New Forms*. Ithaca,
    N.Y.: Herbert F. Johnson Museum of Art, 1979.

Coke, Van Deren, ed. *Fabricated to Be Photographed*. San Francisco: San Francisco Museum of Modern Art, 1979.

Danese, Renato, ed. *American Images: New Work by Twenty Contemporary Photographers*. New York: McGraw Hill, 1979.

Glenn, Constance, and Jane Bledsoe, eds. *Frederick Sommer*. Long Beach: California State University, Long Beach, 1980.

Gore, Arnold, ed. *Metzker*. Milwaukee: Arrow Press, 1970.

Jenkins, William, ed. *New Topographics*. Rochester, N.Y.: International Museum of Photography, 1975.

Lyons, Nathan, ed. *The Persistence of Vision*. Rochester, N.Y.: George Eastman House, 1967.

Marincola, Paula, ed. *Image Scavengers: Photography*. College Park: University of Pennsylvania, 1982.

Szarkowski, John. *Mirrors & Windows: American Photography since 1960*. New York: Museum of Modern Art, 1978.

Werner, Donald, ed. *Light and Lens: Methods of Photography*. Dobbs Ferry, N.Y.: Morgan and Morgan, Inc., 1973.

Zeitlin, Marilyn, ed. *Presences: The Figures and Manmade Environments*. Reading, Pa.: Albright College, 1980.

Articles

Becker, Howard. "Do Photographs Tell the Truth?" *Afterimage* (February 1978): 9–13.

Crimp, Douglas. "The Photographic Activity of Postmodernism." *October* 15 (Winter 1980): 91–101.

Foster, Hal. "The Problem of Pluralism." *Art in America* (January 1982): 9–15.

Greenberg, Clement. "Modern and Post-Modern." *Arts Magazine* (February 1980): 64–66.

Grundberg, Andy. "John Berger and Photography." *The New Criterion* (March 1983): 43–47.

———. "Towards a Critical Pluralism." *Afterimage* (October 1980): 5.

Hagan, Charles. "Photographs and Time." *Afterimage* (April 1980): 6–7.

Kramer, Hilton. "Postmodern: Art and Culture in the 1980's." *The New Criterion* (September 1982): 26–42.

Kuspit, Donald. "Postmodernism, Plurality and the Urgency of the Given." *The Idea: At the Henry* 2 (April 1981): 13–24.

———. "The Unhappy Consciousness of Modernism." *Artforum* (January 1981): 53–57.

Lawson, Thomas. "Last Exit: Painting." *Artforum* (October 1981): 40–45.

Lonier, Michael. "Summing up the '70's." *Afterimage* (March 1979): 14.

Rossler, Martha. "The System of the Postmodern in the Decade of the Seventies." *The Idea: At the Henry* 2 (April 1981): 25–48.

Starenko, Michael. "Modernism, Melting on a Troubled Culture Wave." *The New Art Examiner* (January 1980): 1, 7.

———. "What's An Artist To Do? A Short History of Postmodernism and Photography." *Afterimage* (January 1983): 4–5.

Thornton, Gene. "The New Photography: Turning Traditional Standards Upside Down." *Artnews* (April 1978): 74–78.

————. "Postmodern Photography: It Doesn't Look Modern at All." *Artnews* (April 1979): 64–68.

Trachtenberg, Alan. "Reflections on Art in Photography." *Afterimage* (April 1980): 10–11.

Wartofsky, Max. "Cameras Can't See: Representation, Photography, and Human Vision." *Afterimage* (April 1980): 8–9.

9

Theatre

JUNE SCHLUETER

Some thirty years ago, Joseph Wood Krutch, newly retired from his post at Columbia, gathered his observations about "modernism" in modern drama in a monograph by that title.[1] Focusing on what is now commonly thought of as the first phase of modern drama, from Ibsen through Pirandello, roughly from 1880 to 1920, Krutch argued a moralist's position, asserting that a cavernous gap lay between the values of previous centuries and the values of our own. Those few who clung to the remnants of tradition could only admit, like the despairing old carpenter in Friedrich Hebbel's *Maria Magdalena* (1844), "I do not understand the world anymore." As Krutch points out, the questioning of convention that characterizes the middle period of Ibsen's work culminates in Pirandello's dramatization of "the most inclusive denial of all, namely, the denial that the persistent and more or less consistent character or personality which we attribute to each individual human being, and especially to ourselves, really exists at all." Krutch sees the continuous self as the assumption upon which "all moral systems must rest, since obviously no one can be good or bad, guilty or innocent, unless he exists as some sort of continuous unity."[2]

Such a vision of the twentieth century as fundamentally different from and alien to all previous human history became an assumption of both modernism and, later, postmodernism, though its assimilation into the national character of America, and hence of that country's art, was somewhat delayed. After discussing those European playwrights who commonly receive accolades as the progenitors of modern drama, Krutch attaches a postscript to these four early decades of dramatic activity that canonized no American playwrights. Asking "How Modern Is the Modern American Drama?" he suggests that in the 1920s American drama was only beginning to come of age, with Eugene O'Neill and Maxwell Anderson in large part responsible for its passage out of childhood and at least into adolescence, if not maturity. By this time, of course, Ibsen, Chekhov, and Strindberg were dead, and Shaw's major work was done. So the American dramatist hardly needed to argue "the theses of modernism." He had only to assume them.

The logical direction of modern American drama, then, should have been away from the drama as a forum for moral investigation, created to observe, advocate, lament, or change the moral life of modern man, toward a more formally experimental drama that itself reflected the prevailing relativity of values and fragmentation of experience and of self. Indeed, in the next three decades, several playwrights began extending the boundaries of dramatic form in ways that both imitated and anticipated such European experiments as surrealism, dadaism, expressionism, and epic theatre. O'Neill's use of episodic form, expressionistic techniques, and masks (*The Hairy Ape*, 1922, and *The Great God Brown*, 1926) contributed notably to new dramatic structure, as did Thornton Wilder's fluid treatments of time (*Our Town*, 1938, and *The Skin of Our Teeth*, 1942), Tennessee Williams' memory devices and slide screens (*Glass Menagerie*, 1945-44), and Arthur Miller's cinematic flashbacks (*Death of a Salesman*, 1949).[3] But, for the most part, American drama in the period between Pirandello and Beckett, roughly from 1920 to the mid-1950s, slipped into the comfortable model of the realistic social play.

To employ this model, however, American playwrights had, in effect, to ignore even modernism, to reinstate the law of cause-and-effect that even Ibsen had sought to repeal. For decades critics have characterized the predominant realistic-social-psychological-moral tendencies of American drama as "Ibsenian," pointing particularly to the retrospective exposition of Miller's *All My Sons* (1947) as exemplary of the dramatic cycle that moves from excavation to revelation to expiation of guilt. But, as Robert Brustein observes, it was, after all, not the crack in the chimney flue that Solness had refused to repair that caused the fatal fire in *The Master Builder* (1892–93); the flames began, rather, in a closet, inexplicably.[4] Were American playwrights truly Ibsenian, they would have pursued the Norwegian's questioning of cause-and-effect relationships into the vision of the arbitrary nature of life that so intrigued their European counterparts. But, instead, they reestablished faith in causality and its attendant moral claims, returning drama to the fundamental premise of realistic form.

In Europe, meanwhile, the period during and after World War I was rich in experiment, particularly in Germany and in France. The Weimar culture that produced expressionist artists Wassily Kandinsky, Emil Nolde, and Ernst Ludwig Kirchner and the artists and architects associated with the Bauhaus inspired expressionism in drama as well. Playwrights such as Walter Hasenclever (*The Son*, 1916), Georg Kaiser (*Gas, I and II*, 1918, and 1920), and Ernst Toller (*Man and the Masses*, 1920) collectively created an accommodating form that at once reflected the unconscious, often bestial life of the human being, the intrusiveness of mechanization, the growing breach between generations, and the horror of war. A drama of passion, aggression, and violence, German expressionism created visual and aural correlatives through bizarre stage lighting and garish sets, grotesque masks, and fragmented dialogue that made possible the staged equivalents of Edvard Munch's *The Scream*.

Somewhat later, Bertolt Brecht, whose earliest play, *Baal* (1922), reflected the turbulence of expressionism, developed his own aesthetic of theatre, which remains the most influential of Germany's contributions to modern drama. Using alienation techniques such as narrative, placards, and episodic structure, Brecht created an epic theatre that served his didactic purpose, enabling him, at least theoretically, to disseminate his Marxism without the identification that mimetic theatre involved. *Mother Courage and Her Children* (1949), though not successful in emotionally distancing the audience, became a symbol of Germany's history of war and a preliminary blueprint for the actor/audience relationship as collaborative process.

In the 1960s, Peter Weiss and Peter Handke continued Brecht's experiments with form, contributing to the internationalizing of German drama. Set in an insane asylum, Weiss' *Marat/Sade* (1964) stages a debate about revolution, engaged in by Jean-Paul Marat and the Marquis de Sade, author of the play the inmates are performing about the assassination of Marat. A highly theatrical play-within-a-play, *Marat/Sade* combines styles as diverse as realism, expressionism, and epic theatre, creating an incredibly sensuous drama of hysteria and violence. Handke's theatre pieces aggressively attack the assumptions of drama that even the expressionists and Brecht preserved. Eliminating even the function of actor, Handke's earliest "speech play," *Offending the Audience* (1966), involves a sustained address to an audience that must endure verbal abuse until it understands that it, not the speakers, is the subject of the play. In *Kaspar* (1968), Handke questions the value and function of language through a character who has been isolated from human contact all his life but who, under the tutelage of the Prompters, learns to speak. In *The Ride Across Lake Constance* (1971), there is no progression of events, no resolution, no characterization, and no coincidence between behavior and language. Through relentless scrutiny of the semiotics of language and experience, Handke demolishes even the remnants of mimesis on stage.

In France, the disillusionment that was the legacy of the First World War, combined with a disgust among the intellectual elite for artistic pretension, inspired a formal revolution in drama that found expression in the pocket theatres of Paris. Animated by Alfred Jarry's schoolboy spoof, *King Ubu* (1896), and by the dadaist movement begun in 1916 in Zurich by Tristan Tzara, the French avant-garde, led by Guillaume Apollinaire, André Breton, Antonin Artaud, and others, produced performance pieces that, while inaccessible as mimetic drama, remain powerful spiritual and artistic documents of the time. The anarchistic precepts of dadaism and surrealism spilled over into the genre, as avant-garde dramatists approached art not as representation but as an act of creation, an expression of psychic experience. Avant-garde art reaffirmed the artist's faith in human potential to master the universe and in the artist's own divinity. As in surrealistic art, uncommon juxtapositions defied the phenomenal world, divesting familiar objects of conventional value and creating a dreamlike world unwilling to submit to causal law. Hence Apollinaire's *The Breasts of Tiresias* (1918-17) presents the feminist Theresa, who loses her breasts, sprouts a beard, and becomes Tiresias, and a man who gives birth to 40,049 children in a day; Tzara's *The Gas Heart* (1920) hosts characters named Eye, Mouth, Nose, Ear, Neck, and Eyebrow, who spit out words in unlikely combinations and comment non-chalantly on the lagging conversation; Jean Cocteau's *The Eiffel Tower Wedding Party* (1921) features disembodied voices, a dialogue between phonographs, an ostrich emerging from a camera, and a dance of telegrams; and Artaud's *Jet of Blood* (1925) creates a shower of human body parts, mingled with scorpions, a frog, and a beetle, following its affirmation of young love.

At the same time that the French avant-garde was pursuing its revolution, Luigi Pirandello's *Six Characters in Search of an Author* (1921) invaded the Paris stage, causing so pervasive a reaction that, within the next few years, the Pirandellian symphony resounded through the major capitals of Europe. Play after play stated and restated, embellished, and varied the single theme of reality and illusion. With *Six Characters*, Pirandello ingeniously disrupted the comfortable frame of drama by inventing a family who claims to be abandoned characters from a play their author did not fully conceive. As they intrude upon a stage rehearsal and insist on telling and acting their story, the line between what is real and what is fiction becomes increasingly fluid, even as the possibility of a fixed identity dissolves. The Italian playwright had such an impact on both the French and the international stage that the phrase "after Pirandello" became—and remains—a critical commonplace.

Throughout the period between the wars, while American dramatists contented themselves with producing and reproducing realistic social plays, drawing their characters and their plots with indelible ink, European playwrights were erasing the frame, refusing to accept even the most fundamental premises of language and form. German expressionism, Pirandello, French avant-garde drama, and the less radical but influential plays of Paul Claudel, Jean Giraudoux, Jean Anouilh, Jean-Paul Sartre, and Albert Camus were all part of the line of development that led to the postwar phenomenon Martin Esslin has called the "theatre of the absurd," plays characterized by a shared vision of the world as one of nagging despair, reflecting a breakdown in the constructs and patterns once assumed inviolable. In England, the menacing undercurrents of Harold Pinter's *The Room* (1957) and *The Homecoming* (1965), created through a spareness of language, an abundance of punctuating pauses, and a refusal to articulate motivation, best exemplifies one strain of the genre, while in France the self-conscious artificiality of Jean Genet's *The Maids* (1947) and *The Balcony* (1957), the linguistic ridicule of Eugene Ionesco's *The Bald Soprano* (1958), and the spare style of Samuel Beckett's *Waiting for Godot* (1952-53) suggest ways in which absurdist drama yielded its boundaries in order to accommodate a persistent and pervasive postwar vision of contemporary life.

It was, in fact, the 1956 New York production of *Waiting for Godot* that finally roused American playwrights from their lethargy and reminded them of what they themselves might have been attempting for decades. That landmark play economically portrays the empty hope of humankind through the excruciatingly painful yet comic insistence of two vagabonds on waiting, despite all odds, for Godot, on waiting for whatever it is that gives significance to the human experience. Using a spare, metaphoric style that reduces language, time, and action to a minimum and turns back on itself in repetition, Beckett punctuates the games of Vladimir and Estragon with self-congratulation and then silence, as the two contemplate what they will do next "to give us the impression that we exist."[5] Theirs is a world of contingency, a world in which the systems that validate and sustain human experience have disintegrated, leaving the incoherent Lucky as their spokesman and the decadent Pozzo to pronounce benediction: "They give birth astride a grave, the light gleams an instant, then it's night once more."[6]

Clearly American audiences were not ready for such a despairing vision of contemporary life or such a radical deconstruction of dramatic form: taxi drivers queued outside the theatre at intermission, anticipating fares from those unwilling to sit through a second repetitive act in which "nothing happens" and "there's nothing to show." But those who wrote plays could no longer ignore the discrepancy between European drama and their own. After 1956, mainstream dramatists Lillian Hellman, William Inge, Arthur Miller, and Tennessee Williams were compelled to yield their positions to a new generation of American playwrights, a generation that felt obliged to chisel away at the solidified boundaries of the realistic form that had so long defined their art. Beckett's *Waiting for Godot* made postmodern drama in America possible.

Among the first to react to the Beckett production were Jack Gelber and Edward Albee, who took the lead in redefining American drama. Gelber's *The Connection* (1959) drew both thematically and structurally from the Beckett play, through the portrayal of a drug culture equivalent to the circumstance of Beckett's expectant tramps. In the American play, a group of heroin addicts, allegedly collected from the streets of New York and asked simply to improvise while they were being filmed, wait for Cowboy, their contact with the connection, who will provide their fix. Like Vladimir and Estragon, the junkies engage in a variety of interim activities but consistently direct their energies toward the arrival of that which enables them to endure. Their presumed improvisations find a complement in the jazz that accompanies the play, conveying the flux and the intensity of those needing the fix. Acutely conscious of itself as theatre, as was the Beckett play, *The Connection* functions on several levels of illusion, recalling Pirandello's earlier concern with the interplay between the fictive and the real and endorsing that continuing inquiry as central to the contemporary stage. During the intermission, characters from Gelber's play—the street junkies, who may or may not be genuine—ask audience members for handouts, disregarding conventional barriers between spectators and stage.

Some months later, Edward Albee's *The Zoo Story* appeared, first on the Berlin stage (1959) and then in New York (1960), to be followed by *The American Dream* (1961). The earlier play constructs story within story told by a painfully lonely New Yorker whose park-bench efforts at communication culminate in suicide; the later play is a ruthless, relentlessly comic attack on American values and dramatic form that celebrates through imitation the antitheatre of Ionesco. Unlike Gelber, whose subsequent plays—*The Apple* (1961), *Square in the Eye* (1965), *The Cuban Thing* (1968)—received little critical attention, Albee remained a significant figure in American drama and may well be credited with establishing postmodern American drama.

Albee's vision, in both *The Zoo Story* and *The American Dream*, departs from Beckett's more philosophic analysis of contemporary life in assuming the sterility that Beckett questions. His drama acknowledges the forms of the values that have sustained American culture but refuses either to lament their demise or to endorse their recovery. Though critics trained in moral interpretation claim Albee's plays hint at the possibility of restoration, both *The Zoo Story* and *The American Dream* presage the posthumanist mode and vision of Sam Shepard. Grandma, after all, in packing bogus lunches and entering baking contests with day-old cakes, is just as unconscionable as her opportunist daughter, who lets Daddy "bump his uglies" in order to earn her inheritance. And this representative of earlier times is hardly shocked by the commercialism of Mommy and Daddy, who complain of their defective adopted child and chop it to pieces in protest. Nor does Jerry in *The Zoo Story* have any hope of filling his empty picture frame or of establishing contact with Peter; he is looking instead to communicate through the technology of the evening news, where he will become an electronic image in homes across the nation. His park-bench improvisations are carefully designed to culminate in the suicide that he has been planning, through indirection, all day.

Albee's first major full-length play, *Who's Afraid of Virginia Woolf?* (1962), though more nostalgically humanistic, is also a sophisticated foray into the nature of illusion, posing questions of an epistemological nature and encouraging the kind of poststructuralist criticism that Shepard's work also invites. Unfortunately, critics reacted violently—and parochially—to Martha's venomous tongue, paying little attention to the more fascinating questions raised by George, who may or may not be responsible for the deaths of his parents and who is clearly responsible for the death of the couple's imaginary son—just as "The Story of Jerry and the Dog" may or may not be true.

Even more unfortunately, the play appeared on Broadway, where it was applauded as a model of realism, and where it could not have the impact it might have had had it been staged at the Caffe Cino or La Mama's or any of the lofts, garages, churches, or other spaces that were coming into their own in the 1960s and being referred to collectively as off-Broadway.[7] As varsity theatre, Albee's play joined the privileged American mainstream, claiming the advantages that Broadway offered America's playwrights that New York's alternative theatre could not.

But by the 1960s, playwrights—and the public—were already associating Broadway with commercialism, and a number were refusing to take their places on the gravy train. William Gibson, who achieved modest fame through the

Broadway production of *Two for the Seesaw* (1958), referred to his success as a hollow achievement, complaining that the contemporary American theatre (meaning the commercial theatre, or Broadway) was primarily a place not to be serious but to be likeable. In the 1960s, the price of a living wage was accession to popular taste, and a generation of playwrights was opting for an alternative stage. As a consequence, off-Broadway over the next two decades became the forum for such playwrights as Jean-Claude Van Itallie, Arthur Kopit, Israel Horovitz, Amiri Baraka, Ed Bullins, Lanford Wilson, John Guare, David Mamet, David Rabe, Christopher Durang, Ntozake Shange, Megan Terry, a host of feminist and ethnic playwrights, and, surely most notably, Sam Shepard, the one writer who has done more than any other American in defining postmodern drama.[8]

A southern California transplant, for whom rock music, hallucinogenics, pop culture, and high tech are a way of life, the Who and the Stones heroes, and John Cage mentor, Shepard emerged in the 1960s as America's most brilliant and most exciting contemporary playwright, an electronic greyhound who continues to set the pace for New York's alternative theatre. Shepard's subject is contemporary America, created through a mixture of the plastic artifacts of popular culture and the hallowed remnants of the legendary West. His is an unrelenting vision of distortion, of an America that perpetuates the forms of its myths without connecting with their essence. The Cowboy becomes Shepard's symbol for the death of the American West, which has been replaced by freeways and shopping centers and the Hollywood mystique. In *True West* (1980), Hollywood writer confronts desert bum in a modern-day battle that ends not in the victory of one brother's value system over the other's but in a reversal of roles. The Gangster, the Rock Star, the Millionaire, all part of the contemporary American fabric, weave freely in and out of Shepard's plays—most notably *The Tooth of Crime* (1972)—creating a sense of surface and vacancy yet curiously celebrating the persistence of an American mythology. As *Suicide in B Flat* (1977) insists, myths cannot be killed; they continue surfacing in Shepard's drama, if not through the language of rational expression, then through the unconscious.

With mythographer Joseph Campbell, Shepard maintains that when a culture loses contact with the truth of its mythology, it degenerates. In *Buried Child* (1978), Shelly, expecting apple pie, turkey, and a Norman Rockwell setting, encounters the diseased remnants of a family, who years earlier murdered what may have been an incestuous child. During the course of the play, Shepard evokes—and subverts—several crosscultural myths, including those of the Fisher King and the Corn King; Tilden ceremonially buries the wounded King Dodge, the family's decrepit, impotent, alcoholic head, and later exhumes the muddied corpse of the buried child. Shepard stops short of implying healing, however, balancing textual signs of redemption—Halie's sighting of the cornfields, for example—with theatrical signs—fading lights, silence—that fight against them.

Indeed, such subversive unpredictability typifies the progress of Shepard's plays, which use paradox, discordancy, and grating juxtapositions, connecting and disconnecting fragmentary moments in a seemingly arbitrary, even capricious design that respects neither consistency nor reason. As Bonnie Marranca remarks in "Alphabetical Shepard," Shepard's drama "captures a reality that disregards realism's supposition of the rational." It converts the causal structure that so long dominated American drama into "explosions and contradictions," "disruption," "simultaneity," "anomalies."[9] In Shepard's drama, the crack in the chimney becomes a textual superfluity; the fire in the closet is assumed.

Nor do Shepard's irreverence and innovation limit themselves to dramatic structure. With names like Galactic Jack, Star-Man, Sloe Gin Martin, Spiderlady, and Hoss, Shepard's characters are at once familiar figures of pop culture but dramatically strange, assaulting as they do the consistency of character that Krutch claimed essential for the attribution of moral responsibility. The playwright's note to actors in *Angel City* (1976) indicates the extent to which he repudiates the concept of character on which realistic drama depends:

Instead of the idea of a "whole character" with logical motives behind his behavior which the actor submerges himself into, he should consider instead a fractured whole with bits and pieces of characters flying off the central scheme. Collage construction, jazz improvisation. Music or painting in space.[10]

These collage characters are accretions not of recognizably real people but of billboard faces, *People Magazine* smiles, and Hollywood celluloid, of surfaces without substance, of repetitive vacuity. Pirandello's teasing foray into the nature of identity, his bold "dissolution of the ego," clearly anticipates the ravaged remnants of character in a Shepard play. With Shepard, American drama finally could be compared productively with the work of Beckett, Ionesco, Pinter, Handke, and other Europeans for whom causal construction and consistency of character were anachronisms.

Shepard's plays stand as précis of postmodern drama, embodying the indeterminacies—"ambiguity, discontinuity, heterodoxy, pluralism, randomness, revolt, perversion, deformation"—and the deformations—"decreation, disintegration, deconstruction, decenterment, displacement, difference, discontinuity, disjunction, disappearance, decomposition, de-definition"—that Ihab Hassan has identified as central to postmodernism.[11] So also do they occupy a central position in that period of immensely vital theatrical activity that began with the Cage-Cunningham performance at Black Mountain College in 1952 and found its most exciting expression in the off-Broadway theatre of the 1960s and 1970s.[12] As Richard Gilman observes of Shepard's plays, the relationship between art and life "shows itself as a rambunctious reciprocity in which the theatrical, as a mode of behavior, takes a special wayward urgency from life, while the living—spontaneous, unorganized and unpredictable—keeps breaking into the artificial, composed world of the stage.[13]

Gilman's observation is instructive in that it identifies as a fundamental characteristic of postmodern texts and performance, the celebration of art as artifice and theatre as process. In such a theatre, fidelity to text, that sacred tenet that had so long governed performance, becomes irrelevant, as postmodernism, both as critical inquiry and as theatre, begins to challenge whether any text is authoritative, whether, indeed, a dramatic text can be anything more than performance script; whether the play even exists before it is staged. In *Blooded Thought*, Herbert Blau concedes that "so far as performance goes, the Text remains our best evidence *after* the fact, like the quartos and folios of the Elizabethan stage." But what, he asks, is "the nature of the Text *before* the fact?" "The *idea* of performance," he suggests, "has become the mediating, often subversive third term in the on-again off-again marriage of drama and theatre.[14]

Blau's remark takes us back to the cafés, the lofts, the garages, the churches of off-Broadway, to the generation of playwrights that Shepard best represents, but also to the Caffe Cino, La Mama, the Happening, the Living Theatre, the Open Theatre, the Theatre of the Ridiculous, Bread and Puppet Theatre, guerrilla theatre, environmental theatre, poor theatre, Jerzy Grotowski, Joseph Chaikin, Peter Brook, and a host of performance groups and directors who brought vitality to theatre not through innovation in text but through performance. It takes us back to the twenty-seven-year period, from 1952 to 1979, from Cage-Cunningham to the closing of Richard Foreman's environmental theatre, that Richard Schechner assesses as a preservable moment in theatrical history, to be included alongside the sixty-seven years that produced all the extant Greek tragedies and the thirty-five years of the Golden Age of Renaissance Drama.[15] And it takes us back to the 1960s and 1970s, when the off-Broadway child who had shown signs of infant life in the late 1950s not only learned to walk but proceeded to run, cartwheel, and somersault its way through two decades of one of the Western world's most exciting theatrical spectaculars—a spectacular which, Schechner notwithstanding, still glows.

The nonliterary nature of the earlier years of the off-Broadway movement was its single most disturbing characteristic. In the 1960s, performance scripts were regularly replacing literary texts, and performances were occurring that were intended to occur only once. The notion of the primacy of the text and authorial authority deferred to directorial and acting impulses, making the created event a collaboration quite independent of text. As a consequence (or perhaps this new perception was a cause), the play-life metaphor so prevalent in Shakespeare and, later, in Pirandello, expanded into the recognition that if all life is performance, no event in a performance space may be said to be imitative. Hamlet's mirror shattered, the theatre recognized theatricality as a primary human activity: "It is not a mirror, but something basic in itself. Theatricality doesn't imitate or derive from other human social behavior, but exists side-by-side with them [sic] in a weave.[16]

Out of this new spirit of theatrical primacy there developed "A Bunch of Experimental Theatres"—as the organization Schechner headed called itself—

and a bunch of theories and theatres outside that organization, each riding its own hobbyhorse through the sacred gates of the Thespian city.

Among the earliest, most applauded, and most maligned of the avant-garde groups was the Living Theatre, whose production of *The Connection* (1959) and *The Brig* (1963) proved seminal in the experimental theatre movement. The Living's politically radical, pacifist leaders, Julian Beck and Judith Malina, found a theatrical counterpart for their political anarchy in a form of production that insisted on the continuity of theatre and life; that celebrated nudity, sex, and freedom; and that employed provocation, intimidation, seduction, and shock. Its 1968–69 productions of *Mysteries—and Smaller Pieces*, *Frankenstein*, *Antigone*, and *Paradise Now* reflected a demolition of conventional forms too irreverent for contemporary critics to endure. The Living thrived on a physical and a verbal freedom so thorough that it was years after the staging of *Paradise Now* before the public knew that amid the riot of theatrical sex witnessed and participated in by the audience, Malina was raped.[17] The event, ironically, perfectly embodied the absorption of life into theatre, symbolically, though unholily, consummated the marriage between life and art. Even more ironically, the aggression inherent in rape became an operating principle for the experimental theatre, which intruded upon its audience's personal space through verbal and physical assault.

Intent on achieving an audience participation that would obliterate the line dividing theatre and life, the experimental theatre of the 1960s and 1970s created performance spaces in places where no one suspected theatre could take place and repealed the law of audience passivity. The Happening, which had its genesis in the plastic arts with Allan Kaprow and soon became theatrically ubiquitous, provided minimal scripts, necessitating abundant improvisation, and freely, sometimes shamelessly, mixed theatre and life. Jean-Jacques Lebel staged such a Happening in 1960 in Venice by inviting friends to a black-tie party that turned into a mock funeral for a sculptured corpse, though it was not until sometime after *Funeral Ceremony of the Anti-Process* ended that the guests knew the corpse had never breathed Venetian air.

In the Open Theatre, established in 1963 in New York, Joseph Chaikin and Peter Feldman were developing an aesthetic through which they could present dream, myth, and ritual on stage, while breaking out of the rational dictates of mimetic theatre. In *The Presence of the Actor* (1972), Chaikin speaks of encounters between actors and audience and urges a theory of acting as abstraction and illusion, as well as collective creativity. Feldman, in his notes, speaks of releasing the actor's unconscious "through non-rational, spontaneous action celebrating the actor's own perceptions about modern life.[18] The Open Theatre worked through meditation, developing a non-verbal stage language of gesture, rhythm, sound, and silence that functioned more through instinct than training and that, unlike the work of other groups, reflected passivity, not aggression. Jean-Claude Van Itallie and Megan Terry, among the several writers working with the Open, refined the group's early improvisations and transformation exercises into productions, the best known being *Viet Rock*, a collage piece created in Terry's acting workshop and staged in 1966 by La Mama, and Van Itallie's *America Hurrah* (1966). In 1973, after ten years of commitment, the Open Theatre disbanded, leaving as its legacy a provocative design for a new acting style and a new theatre.

In the late 1960s and 1970s, Richard Schechner and Richard Foreman were redefining theatrical space through selecting and designing environments in which to perform the primitive rituals best exemplified by the Performance Group's *Dionysus in 69* (1968). Begun in 1968, Schechner's Performance Group dedicated itself to reacquiring ritual through a celebratory event involving actors, audience, and the free definition of theatrical space. *Dionysus in 69*, based on Euripides' *The Bacchae*, proved an orgiastic rendition of the life cycle, beginning with the ritual birth of Dionysus through the simulated birth passage created by naked actors. Freely sexual, the production invited spectators to partake in the orgy and to help create the portions of the event that did not rely on the Greek text. Though Schechner left after two years to work on his own, directing, in 1979, a stunning collage production of Genet's *The Balcony*, the Performance Group, reformed as the Wooster Group, continued with Foreman for a decade.

At the same time, Peter Schumann's Bread and Puppet Theatre was engaging audiences in the Christian ritual of communion, beginning each of its productions with a bread-breaking ceremony before presenting its New Left activism. John Vaccaro and Charles Ludlam were developing their savagely nihilistic Theatre of the Ridiculous. Robert Wilson was staging his three-hour speechless epic, *Deafman Glance* (1971) in Paris, creating a Theatre of Silence. And Peter Brook was experimenting with nonproscenium staging and "the empty space," most notably in his productions of *Marat/Sade* (1964) and *A Midsummer Night's Dream* (1970). In the Shakespeare play, the bare stage offered only a whirligig of circus trapezes, conceived not as props but as extensions of the actors' bodies and voices, encouraging contemporary interpretations of the classics, which stripped the stage of theatrical cliché, but at the same time respected the text.

Together, these and other movements and moments in the avant-garde pursued a readiness to take risks with theatrical form such as the American theatre had collectively not known before. And together they paid homage to European theoreticians Antonin Artaud and Jerzy Grotowski, who, in celebrating not text but the irrational or transrational experience of engagement through performance, were both highly influential in this period of theatrical experiment. Artaud's *The Theatre and Its Double* (1938) accepts theatre as an alternate reality that stands in a dialectic rather than a mimetic relationship with life. In "The Theatre as Plague," Artaud speak of the "infective" power of performance, and in "The Theatre of Cruelty" he speaks of converting impulses into action, all in the service of a cathartic effect for both actor and audience. Ultimately, Artaud moves toward the "empty space," described by Timothy J. Wiles as "an unused state of potentiality which is *restored* through the violent activity in the other realm, restored because that activity does not impinge upon it. . . . This restoration results in a purification of the space itself, and of our selves by bestowing its potentiality upon us.''[19] The resulting "empty space," which precedes theatre and which makes theatre possible, became an operating assumption of Grotowski's Polish Laboratory Théâtre and of America's avant-garde.

As early as 1959, in Poland, Grotowski was developing his concept of "poor theatre": to be poor in the biblical sense is to abandon all externals; to be poor in the theatrical sense is to reject artifice. *Apocalypse cum figuris* (1968) took place in an empty, windowless, dark-walled room, a space that actors filled with body movements and voices, extending Stanislavsky's psychological method into a psychophysical one. The Polish director trained his actors to strip the artifice from a text and to cultivate a communion with its essential ideas. Or, as with *Apocalypse cum figuris*, he engaged his actors in communal creation, producing a script only after rehearsals determined the movement and expression appropriate to the pieces of biblical and literary texts and liturgical chants that comprised the piece's Second Coming theme. Grotowski's theatre was a theatre of myth that sought to reestablish connections with enduring cultural structures and celebrated the primacy of the naked spirit. Margaret Croyden describes his theatre as a "microcosm of metaphysical man's search for self-definition and modern man's search for moral imperatives":

Formalized with exquisite skill in wails, chants, laments and liturgies; in fits, beatings, and the fluttering of muscles; in spasms, leaps, and writhings; in images of crucifixions, crematoriums, and inquisitions, [its] agony is a metaphor for the actors' lives. It is they who define the Grotowski theatre; it is their scream we hear: a primitive, modern, Hebrew, Catholic, Polish, American howl. To see all this is to see the fusion of religious art and modern cruelty in a totally new form, and to apprehend the phenomenon of Grotowski.[20]

In 1968, the Polish Laboratory Théâtre staged *Akropolis* at the Edinburgh Festival, bringing Grotowski's vision and method to the English-speaking world for the first time. The group toured internationally for ten years, their work encouraging American directors to reevaluate their own.

For the off-Broadway theatre of the 1960s and 1970s, mainstream theatre became historical subtext, the framework for frustrated expectation. The dramatic text that remained no longer demanded fidelity but served as impetus for a range of performance that found fullest expression in the context of the tradition against which it revolted. No longer representative of sustained segments of quotidian experience, theatre became insults hurled at an audience, a recitation of aphorisms, the amplified breathing of a man masturbating, the sounds of a woman walking in a room or rocking in a chair. In the other arts, meanwhile, Claes Oldenburg was digging a hole in Central Park, Christo Javacheff was erecting a twenty-four-mile nylon fence in California, John Cage was giving a four-minute, thirty-three-second piano performance in silence. And John Simon was asking, "when . . . is any so-called work of art not a work of art but a piece of trickery, a hoax, a nonsensical game, a fraud?''[21]

If the cry of narcissism was shrill in the plastic arts, in theatre it was deafening. Playwrights, directors, actors, plays, and performances were being accused of self-absorption, and those who had felt themselves a part of the community of performers that the Happening and improvised performance had created left theatres feeling not integration but distance. Memories, of course, tend to be short, and that generation of playgoers may have forgotten the mass exodus American audiences made from the 1956 *Waiting for Godot*.

If *Godot* managed to survive the uncertainties of public reaction, though, and become a permanent part of the dramatic repertoire, many plays of the experimental theatre movement of the 1960s and 1970s did not, and for good cause. The fact is that the theatre's commitment to nonliterary performance proved, not surprisingly, to be self-defeating: after the performance, no text remained, and recreation, even if it were desirable, was unlikely. The experimental theatre's material legacy consisted of only a few scattered scripts and the memories of those who had participated and who have since moved on to other (paycheck-bearing) ventures, often outside the theatre. In *The End of Humanism*, Schechner analyzes the self-destructive patterns inherent in the movement—including the primacy of the performance text and the abundance of solo performances—as well as other causes for its demise: shortage of money, stupid journalism, and the end to societal activism.[22] His observation on the state of theatre, from the perspective of 1982, sounds the death knell for the era of experimental theatre:

The Living Theatre is living in Italy . . . the Bread and Puppet, which once performed with regularity on the New York City streets, now visits there only occasionally . . . the Open disbanded in the early '70s . . . Foreman's theatre is closed and his work in America is mostly directing other people's scripts. The Manhattan Project, Pageant Players, Judson Poets' and Judson Dancers' Theatres, Grand Union, New Lafayette, Caffe Cino, Theatre Genesis, Play-House of the Ridiculous—all are gone. . . . the heart of the movement is stopped.[23]

Yet despite Schechner's lament, experiment in American theatre is far from moribund. Ellen Stewart remains the indomitable earth mother of La Mama, nurturing new and provocative American playwrights and importing groups, directors, and works from countries as diverse as Portugal and Japan. Productions of Beckett and Pinter directed by the late Alan Schneider continue to thrive, as do Andrei Serban's interpretations of Chekhov. For some time now, Joseph Papp has devoted his talents not to Lincoln Center's more conventional Vivian Beaumont Theatre but to The Public, where he hosts The Mabou Mines. And even the Beaumont's conventionality yielded recently to Peter Brook's *Carmen*. Brook has remained spiritually and, for the most part, physically apart from the commercial theatre since his staging of *A Midsummer Night's Dream*. Indeed, the American theatre of the 1980s is a theatre in which all things are possible. As Schechner observes in *The End of Humanism*, the activity of the 1960s and 1970s redefined "what a performance was, where it could take place, who it involved, how it could be constructed, who or what could generate it." As a consequence, "the field remains permanently enlarged."[24]

New York's alternate theatre today has become the measure of contemporary American theatre, inviting as it does participation by ethnic and gender groups, by blacks, Hispanics, Jews, homosexuals, and feminists. The New York theatregoer may choose from nearly a hundred off-Broadway productions on any weekend night, and he or she is bound to have among his or her choices work by Americans Shepard, Rabe, Mamet, Lanford Wilson, and Guare, and by Europeans Beckett, Pinter, and often Handke, as well as contemporary interpretations of Shakespeare and the classics. Occasionally, innovative dramatic texts are staged on Broadway—most recently Tom Stoppard's *The Real Thing*, Arthur Kopit's *The End of the World*, and David Mamet's *Glengarry, Glen Ross*—but as Broadway ticket prices continue to rise and commercial tastes fossilize, the off-Broadway theatre remains responsive to those who reject realism as an accommodating form and commercialism as a prevailing mode.

Collectively, these playwrights, directors, and actors see theatre as a chimera, fragmented and whole, formidable and seductive, an unreal creature of the imagination that can be neither harnessed nor tamed. The chimera lives not only in New York, which has traditionally defined American theatre, but in regional houses across the country, in pockets of America's major cities, in black boxes within its universities. All of those theatres are looking to the generation of playwrights since *Waiting for Godot*, particularly to Shepard and to the legacy of the nonliterary experiments of the 1960s and 1970s, which have with some certainty identified those characteristics of drama and theatre—fragmentation, indeterminacy, spontaneity, theatricality, pluralism, paradox, performance—that urge us toward a definition of the postmodern.

NOTES

1. Joseph Wood Krutch, *"Modernism" in Modern Drama: A Definition and an Estimate* (Ithaca, N.Y.: Cornell University Press, 1953).

2. Ibid., pp. 77, 78.

3. When two dates are given parenthetically, the first refers to publication, the second to production.

4. Robert Brustein, "The Crack in the Chimney: Reflections on Contemporary American Playwriting," *Theatre* 9, no. 2 (Spring 1978): 21–29.

5. Samuel Beckett, *Waiting for Godot* (New York: Grove Press, 1954), p. 44.

6. Ibid., p. 58.

7. Theatre in New York falls into three categories: Broadway, off-Broadway, and off-off-Broadway, but when a New Yorker says "off-Broadway," chances are good that he means "off-off Broadway." Both off-Broadway and off-off-Broadway theatres are literally *off* Broadway, or out of the Broadway commercial theatre district in mid-town Manhattan. The theatre that is properly designated off-Broadway constitutes only a small section of the New York theatre and, for the most part, offers commercial theatre on a smaller scale and smaller budget than its Broadway cousin. It is the off-off-Broadway

theatre that has provided the forum for experimental work and about which I am speaking in this essay, though I refer to it as off-Broadway.

8. I am indebted to two colleagues, Suzanne Westfall (Lafayette College) and Una Chaudhuri (New York University) for a number of the observations about Shepard's work that follow.

9. Bonnie Marranca, "Alphabetical Shepard: The Play of Words," in *American Dreams: The Imagination of Sam Shepard*, ed. Bonnie Marranca (New York: Performing Arts Journal Publications, 1981), p. 15.

10. Quoted in Richard Gilman, Introduction to Sam Shepard, *Seven Plays* (New York: Bantam Books, 1981), p. xiv.

11. Ihab Hassan, "POSTFACE 1982: Toward Postmodernism," in *The Dismemberment of Orpheus: Toward a Postmodern Literature* (New York: Oxford University Press, 1971), p. 269.

12. At Black Mountain College, John Cage lectured on Meister Eckhart, and Merce Cunningham danced, while others played piano, played records, showed a film, and commented on the lecture, creating an antiart event.

13. Gilman, *Seven Plays*, p. xvi.

14. Herbert Blau, *Blooded Thought: Occasions of Theatre* (New York: Performing Arts Journal Publications, 1982), p. 37.

15. Richard Schechner, *The End of Humanism: Writings on Performance* (New York: Performing Arts Journal Publications, 1982), p. 21.

16. Ibid, p. 72.

17. Ross Wetzsteon, "The Living Theatre at the Pittsburgh Station," *Village Voice*, April 21, 1975, pp. 1, 73–75.

18. Quoted in Margaret Croyden, *Lunatics, Lovers and Poets: The Contemporary Experimental Theatre* (New York: Dell Publishing, 1974), p. 175.

19. Timothy J. Wiles, *The Theater Event: Modern Theories of Performance* (Chicago: University of Chicago Press, 1980), p. 137.

20. Croyden, *Lunatics, Lovers and Poets*, p. 136.

21. John Simon, *Uneasy Stages: A Chronicle of the New York Theatre, 1968–1973* (New York: Random House, 1975), pp. 366–67.

22. Schechner, *The End of Humanism*, pp. 29–70.

23. Ibid., p. 23.

24. Ibid., pp. 23–25.

BIBLIOGRAPHICAL ESSAY

In drama and theatre, "postmodernism" is less clearly defined than in the other arts, in part because of the distinction between literary text and performance. In the foregoing essay, I attempt to assess the phenomenon both in drama and in theatre of the past twenty-five years, though theoretical books on the subject focus almost exclusively on performance. The best books on postmodern theatre (as opposed to drama) are Richard Schechner's *The End of Humanism: Writings on Performance*, Herbert Blau's *Blooded Thought: Occasions of Theatre*, and Blau's *Take Up the Bodies: Theatre at the Vanishing Point*. Both Schechner and Blau were personally involved in the theatre movement of the 1960s and 1970s as directors of experimental productions and have recorded their observations and speculations in these volumes.

Blau's *Blooded Thought* contains six indispensable essays, including "The Thought

224 The Postmodern Moment

of Performance: Value, Vanishing, Dream, and Brain Damage," "The Remission of
Play," "Look What The Memory Cannot Contain," "Precipitations of Theatre: Words,
Presence, Time Out of Mind," "Theatre and Cinema: the Scopic Drive, the Detestable
Screen, and More of the Same," and "Flights of Angels, Scattered Seeds." The author
describes his book as "theory . . . activated by occasions," "concerned with what incites
the theatre at its most subliminal levels." *Take Up the Bodies* continues and extends this
discourse in a more speculative mode and a larger postmodern artistic context. Schechner's
book contains essays on "The Decline and Fall of the (American) Avant-Garde," "The
Natural/Artificial Controversy Renewed," "The End of Humanism," and "The Crash
of Performative Circumstances: A Modernist Discourse on Postmodernism." Though a
touch too nostalgic and far too willing to function as a postmortem, the book intelligently
and immediately assesses the experiment of the 1960s and 1970s in comparison with that
of today's theatre and hopes for a union of form and content that will integrate socially
and politically informed texts and new forms of theatre.

Margaret Croyden's *Lunatics, Lovers and Poets: The Contemporary Experimental
Theatre* is an exceptionally informative study of these two decades of theatrical innovation.
The book presents an overview and analyses of several of the major forces in the American
experimental theatre, including the Happening, the Living Theatre, Jerzy Grotowski's
poor theatre, Joseph Chaikin's Open Theatre, Schechner's environmental theatre, and
Peter Brook. Pierre Biner's *The Living Theatre: A History Without Myths* provides valuable
information on Julian Beck and Judith Malina's performance group, which redefined the
relationship between actors and audience and the limitations of the playing space. Michael
Kirby's edited collection, *The New Theatre: Performance Documentation*, contains essays
that record and evaluate a number of experimental productions throughout the world from
1968 (Grotowski's *Apocalypsis cum figuris*) through 1974, arranged in three categories:
dramatic pieces with acting and characterization, performances that do not make use of
acting, and the new dance. About half of the twenty-four essays in the collection are
devoted to performances in the United States. James Schevill's *Break Out: In Search of
New Theatrical Environments* and James Roose-Evans' *Experimental Theatre from Stanislavsky to Today* also document some of the efforts and achievements of the experimental
theatre movement. Gerald M. Berkowitz's *New Broadways: Theatre across America
1950–1980* offers an informative account of thirty years of alternative theatre in America.

In drama, as opposed to theatre, the term "postmodernism" has not yet acquired
currency. Ruby Cohn's *New American Dramatists: 1960–1980* identifies playwrights and
plays of the past twenty years and discusses their contributions to American drama.
Hedwig Bock and Albert Wertheim's edited collection, *Essays on Contemporary American Drama*, includes pieces on playwrights from Tennessee Williams to David Mamet
and Lanford Wilson but makes no claim to postmodernism. Bonnie Marranca and Gautam
Dasgupta's *American Playwrights: A Critical Survey* treats only recent playwrights, surveying their work but seeking no unifying principles. Ronald Hayman's *Theatre and
Anti-Theatre* offers a useful survey of European and American drama that attempts to
give unity to contemporary reactions against realism but makes no attempt at defining
postmodernism.

Those interested in postmodern drama might do better to read Sam Shepard. In his
excellent introduction to Sam Shepard's *Seven Plays*, Richard Gilman identifies the
characteristics common to text and performance that Shepard's plays reflect. Bonnie
Marranca's *American Dreams: The Imagination of Sam Shepard* collects essays on Shepard's work by critics, playwrights, directors, actors, and Shepard himself, all of which

identify him as a contemporary playwright who has intelligently integrated text and performance and promised a postmodern drama.

A number of directors who were active in postmodern theatre have recorded their observations and approaches in books that give valuable insight into the theatrical context of those two decades. These include Peter Brook's *The Empty Space*, Joseph Chaikin's *The Presence of the Actor: Notes on the Open Theatre, Disguises, Acting, and Repression*, and Jerzy Grotowski's *Toward a Poor Theatre*.

Several studies dealing with a specific aspect of postmodern theatre, that is, theatrical self-consciousness, which still characterizes recent work in the theatre, are also useful in understanding postmodernism. These include Lionel Abel's *Metatheatre: A New View of Dramatic Form*, which identifies examples of theatrical self-consciousness in plays from the Greeks through Shakespeare through Beckett; Elizabeth Burns' *Theatricality: A Study of Convention in the Theatre and in Social Life*, which examines the relationship between sociology and theatre and the prevalence in life of the theatrical metaphor; Ruby Cohn's *Currents in Contemporary Drama*, particularly her chapter on "The Role and the Real," which further explores the world-stage metaphor; and June Schlueter's *Metafictional Characters in Modern Drama*, which focuses on the inherently dual nature of the actor/character and the ways in which modern plays examine this dichotomy.

Useful reviews and assessments of contemporary plays and the contemporary theatre, which make no attempt to define postmodernism but do suggest characteristics and trends, are Robert Brustein's *The Third Theatre*, a collection of polemics, opinions, and observations on the theatre from 1957 to 1968, and his "The Crack in the Chimney: Reflections on Contemporary American Playwriting," an especially astute piece that looks at recent American plays in terms of causality and the Ibsenian model; Harold Clurman's "The New Theatre," which suggests the diversity of avant-garde theatre; and Jan Kott's "Can the Theatre Survive without Drama?" which questions the evaporation of text in the contemporary theatre; and, most importantly, Richard Schechner's *Public Domain: Essays on the Theatre*, a collection of pieces that appeared in a number of drama and theatre journals in the 1960s. Patrice Pavis' *Languages of the Stage: Essays in the Semiology of the Theatre* reflects the contemporary linguistic and performance theory being applied to classical and contemporary texts, as does Keir Elam's *The Semiotics of Theatre*. Richard Schechner and Mary Schuman's *Ritual, Play, and Performance: Readings in the Social Sciences/Theatre* and Victor Turner's *From Ritual to Theatre: The Human Seriousness of Play* approach performance from an anthropological perspective, emphasizing the relationship between ritual and theatre.

Important related studies of postmodern literature are those by Ihab Hassan: *The Dismemberment of Orpheus: Toward a Post-modern Literature*; *Paracriticisms: Seven Speculations of the Times*, which includes, among others, essays on "Frontiers of Criticism: 1963, 1969, 1972," "POSTmodernISM: A Paracritical Bibliography," and "The New Gnosticism: Speculations on an Aspect of the Postmodern Mind"; and "Culture, Indeterminacy, and Immanence: Margins of the (Postmodern) Age." All include analyses of the distinctions between modernism and postmodernism as well as speculations on postmodern theatre.

Particularly valuable background readings are Robert Martin Adams' "What Was Modernism?" Joseph Wood Krutch's *"Modernism" in Modern Drama: A Definition and an Estimate*, and Romano Guardini's *The End of the Modern World: A Search for Orientation*, which attempt to articulate the experience of postmodernism's predecessor period, modernism. Adams does this through an assessment of innovations in art forms occurring within ten years of Virginia Woolf's famous transitional date of December 1910, Krutch through a look at the major figures in modern drama from Ibsen to Pirandello, and Guardini from a religious-philosophical perspective.

There are a number of studies of the movements preceding postmodernism that help place postmodernism in context. J. M. Ritchie's *German Expressionist Drama* analyzes the phenomenon of expressionism, and Walter H. Sokel collects some of the major texts in *An Anthology of German Expressionist Drama*. Michael Patterson's *The Revolution in German Theatre 1900–1933* studies theatrical experiment in the context of its intellectual and political origins. Analyses of the modern French theatre may be found in Leonard Cabell Pronko's *Avant-Garde*, Wallace Fowlie's *Dionysus in Paris*, and Jacques Guicharnaud's *Modern French Theatre from Giraudoux to Genet*. Martin Esslin's *The Theatre of the Absurd* remains an excellent analysis of the work of Beckett, Adamov, Ionesco, Genet, and others whose vision and style served as a prelude to the postmodern. Books on individual playwrights from Pirandello to Beckett to Handke are, of course, abundant and too readily discoverable to be listed here.

Background reading on the performance theory that has influenced the American theatre may be found in Timothy J. Wiles' *The Theatre Event: Modern Theories of Performance*. Wiles discusses the principles of Stanislavski, Brecht, Artaud, Grotowski, and Handke, handling his material with ease and offering sophisticated analyses of distinctives and connections. Primary comments by those most influential in defining a postmodern aesthetic of these theatre theoreticians may be found in Bertolt Brecht's *Brecht on Theatre: The Development of an Aesthetic*, Antonin Artaud's *The Theatre and Its Double*, and Jerzy Grotowski's *Toward a Poor Theatre*.

Drama and theatre journals that regularly contain articles of both an analytical and theoretical nature on contemporary drama and theatre include *Comparative Drama*, *The Drama Review*, *Modern Drama*, *Performing Arts Journal*, *Theater*, and *Theater Journal*. The daily *New York Times* and the Sunday Arts and Leisure section as well as *The Village Voice* are the best sources of reviews of New York productions and of commentary on the contemporary theatre. Performing Arts Journal Publications in New York has been particularly energetic in publishing seminal works on postmodern theory and theatre.

SELECTED BIBLIOGRAPHY

Abel, Lionel. *Metatheatre: A New View of Dramatic Form*. New York: Hill & Wang, 1963.

Adams, Robert Martin. "What Was Modernism?" *Hudson Review* 31, no. 1 (Spring 1978): 19–33.

Artaud, Antonin. *The Theatre and Its Double*. Translated by Mary Caroline Richards. New York: Grove Press, 1958.

Benedikt, Michael, and George E. Wellwarth. *Modern French Theatre: The Avant-Garde, Dada, and Surrealism*. New York: E. P. Dutton, 1964.

Berkowitz, Gerald M. *New Broadways: Theatre across America 1950–1980*. Totowa, N.J.: Rowman and Littlefield, 1982.

Biner, Pierre. *The Living Theatre: A History Without Myths*. Translated by Robert Meister. New York: Avon Books, 1972.

Blau, Herbert. *Blooded Thought: Occasions of Theatre*. New York: Performing Arts Journal Publications, 1982.

————. *Take Up the Bodies: Theatre at the Vanishing Point*. Urbana: University of Illinois Press, 1982.

Bock, Hedwig, and Albert Wertheim, eds. *Essays on Contemporary American Drama*. Munich: Max Hueber Verlag, 1981.

Brecht, Bertolt. *Brecht on Theatre: The Development of an Aesthetic*. Translated by John Willett. New York: Hill & Wang, 1964.

Brook, Peter. *The Empty Space*. New York: Avon Books, 1968.

Brustein, Robert. "The Crack in the Chimney: Reflections on Contemporary American Playwriting." *Theatre* 9, no. 2 (Spring 1978): 21–29.

————. *The Third Theatre*. New York: Simon and Schuster, 1969.

Burns, Elizabeth. *Theatricality: A Study of Convention in the Theatre and in Social Life*. New York: Harper & Row, 1972.

Chaikin, Joseph. *The Presence of the Actor: Notes on the Open Theatre, Disguises, Acting, and Repression*. New York: Atheneum, 1972.

Clurman, Harold. "The New Theatre." *Dialogue* 5, no. 2 (1972): 57–68.

Cohn, Ruby. *New American Dramatists: 1960–1980*. New York: Grove Press, 1982.

————. *Currents in Contemporary Drama*. Bloomington: Indiana University Press, 1969.

Croyden, Margaret. *Lunatics, Lovers and Poets: The Contemporary Experimental Theater*. New York: Dell Publishing, 1974.

Elam, Keir. *The Semiotics of Theatre and Drama*. London: Methuen, 1980.

Esslin, Martin. *The Theatre of the Absurd*. 3d ed. New York: Penguin Books, 1980.

Fowlie, Wallace. *Dionysus in Paris: A Guide to Contemporary French Theatre*. New York: Meridian Books, 1960.

Gilman, Richard. "Introduction." In Sam Shepard, *In Seven Plays*. New York: Bantam Books, 1981, pp. ix-xxv.

Grotowski, Jerzy. *Toward a Poor Theatre*. New York: Simon and Schuster, 1969.

Guardini, Romano. *The End of the Modern World: A Search for Orientation*. Translated by Joseph Theman and Herbert Burke. Edited by Frederick D. Wilhelmsen. London: Sheed and Ward, 1957.

Guicharnaud, Jacques, with June Guicharnaud. *Modern French Theatre from Giraudoux to Genet*. Rev. ed. New Haven, Conn.: Yale University Press, 1967.

Hassan, Ihab. "Culture, Indeterminacy, and Immanence: Margins of the (Postmodern) Age." *Humanities in Society* 1, no. 1 (Winter 1978): 51-85.

————. *The Dismemberment of Orpheus: Toward a Postmodern Literature*. London: Oxford University Press, 1971.

————. *Paracriticisms: Seven Speculations of the Times*. Urbana: University of Illinois Press, 1967.

Hayman, Ronald. *Theatre and Anti-Theatre*. New York: Oxford University Press, 1979.

Kirby, Michael, ed. *The New Theatre*. New York: New York University Press, 1974.

Kott, Jan. "Can the Theatre Survive Without Drama?" *The New Republic*, November 30, 1974, pp. 21–24.

Krutch, Joseph Wood. *"Modernism" in Modern Drama: A Definition and an Estimate*. Ithaca, N.Y.: Cornell University Press, 1953.

Marranca, Bonnie, ed. *American Dreams: The Imagination of Sam Shepard*. New York: Performing Arts Journal Publications, 1981.

————, ed. *The Theatre of Images*. New York: Drama Book Specialists, 1977.

Marranca, Bonnie, and Gautam Dasgupta, eds. *American Playwrights: A Critical Survey*. New York: Drama Book Specialists, 1981.

Patterson, Michael. *The Revolution in German Theatre 1900–1933*. Boston: Routledge and Kegan Paul, 1981.

Pavis, Patrice. *Languages of the Stage: Essays in the Semiology of the Theatre*. New York: Performing Arts Journal Publications, 1982.

Poirier, Richard. *The Performing Self: Compositions and Decompositions in the Languages of Contemporary Life*. London: Oxford University Press, 1971.

Pronko, Leonard Cabell. *Avant-Garde: The Experimental Theater in France*. Berkeley: University of California Press, 1966.

Ritchie, J. M. *German Expressionist Drama*. Boston: Twayne Publishers, 1976.

Roose-Evans, James. *Experimental Theatre from Stanislavsky to Today*. New York: Avon Books, 1970.

Schechner, Richard. *The End of Humanism: Writings on Performance*. New York: Performing Arts Journal Publications, 1982.

———. *Public Domain: Essays on the Theatre*. Indianapolis: Bobbs-Merrill, 1969.

Schechner, Richard, and Mary Schuman. *Ritual, Play, and Performance*. New York: The Seabury Press, 1976.

Schevill, James. *Break Out: In Search of New Theatrical Environments*. Chicago: Swallow Press, 1973.

Schlueter, June. *Metafictional Characters in Modern Drama*. New York: Columbia University Press, 1979.

Sokel, Walter H., ed. *An Anthology of German Expressionist Drama: A Prelude to the Absurd*. Garden City, N.Y.: Doubleday and Co., 1963.

Turner, Victor. *From Ritual to Theatre: The Human Seriousness of Play*. New York: Performing Arts Journal Publications, 1982.

Wiles, Timothy J. *The Theater Event: Modern Theories of Performance*. Chicago: University of Chicago Press, 1980.

Periodicals with regular items on theatre and drama:

Comparative Drama (Western Michigan University)
The Drama Review (formerly *Tulane Drama Review*) (New York University)
Modern Drama (University of Toronto)
New York Times (daily and Sunday Arts and Leisure Section)
Performing Arts Journal (New York)
Theater (formerly *Yale/Theatre*) (Yale University)
Theatre Journal (formerly *Educational Theatre Journal*) (American Theatre Association, Washington, D.C.)
The Village Voice (New York)

Appendix I

Postmodernism in Europe: On Recent German Writing

DAVID E. WELLBERY

To cut a very large and complex subject—postmodernism in Europe—down to manageable size, some rather brutal selections had to be made. This account is restricted to recent German literary production, with several side glances toward the theoretical work of the so-called French poststructuralists. The inclusion of the French is, albeit brief, by no means arbitrary. The fact is that, in the absence of any widespread use of the term "postmodern" as an identificational tag in Germany, French influence, either direct or by cultural osmosis, provides a useful criterion for sorting out those contemporary German writers who might legitimately qualify as postmodernists. A second choice here was not to attempt the kind of narrative account common to historical surveys, and this was for two reasons: first of all because there is too little consensus regarding the significance of postmodernism as a literary trend or movement in Germany to allow for the construction of a plausible narrative; secondly, because probably one of the most important cultural imperatives of postmodern writing is the rejection of precisely the type of conceptual packaging on which such literary-historical narratives rely. The alternative to the chronological tale that this essay provides is a series of four slices made at different levels of the global cultural phenomenon that postmodernism is. The first section considers some salient features of the social and cultural context of literary postmodernism. The second section attempts to delineate a postmodern style of thought. The third part of the essay discusses some of the major textual strategies employed by postmodern writers, while the concluding portion describes three texts that, although almost certainly unknown in this country, seem worthy of serious attention. For reasons of space, attempts have not been made to make explicit the many interconnections that join the four levels, but they hopefully will be obvious to the reader.

THE POSTMODERN SITUATION

Three features of the social and cultural environment in which writers live and work today are especially important for an understanding of postmodernism: (a) the institutional saturation of life; (b) the cybernetization and medialization of cultural communication; (c) the emergence as political forces of a number of groups that have traditionally been excluded from the political forum. To some degree, the sociological literature on postmodernism has taken note of these tendencies. Nevertheless, a brief account of them will be given here, if only to adumbrate the context in which postmodern texts are produced and received.

The institutional saturation of life simply means that the individual's patterns of activity are determined, in all realms of his/her experience, by a cluster of superpersonal and quasi-autonomous institutions.[1] In the domains of law and governance, this tendency produces what is called the welfare state (characterized by "overt intervention . . . in areas previously regarded as beyond the proper reach of state action") and the corporate state (characterized by "the gradual approximation of state and society, of the public and the private sphere."[2] Society is structured as a network of functionally differentiated but complexly interdependent organizations: institutions for the production and maintenance of knowledge (universities, disciplinary groups, research centers), institutions for the management of birth, health and death (hospitals, homes, asylums), self-maintaining economic institutions (corporations), and institutions charged with the socialization of the young (schools), not to speak of the myriad and semiindependent agencies of government. Within this network, questions of right dissolve into questions of procedure, and values are replaced by policies and regulations. The new roles of expert, manager, and therapist (doctors today are trained to treat the physico-psycho-social unit) assume increasing importance. Institutions are no longer bound to a particular set of meanings, nor do they refer to a sovereign institutionalizing subject (God, the People). Rather, they are open to constant revision according to regularized procedures; the process of institutionalization itself has become institutionalized.[3] One can see how social life in this context is experienced as paradoxical, at once regulated and groundless. For, although our lives are thoroughly administered, there exists no unique or ultimate institution, no center of authority that is not itself part of a larger system of interdependencies.[4] The institutional saturation of life leaves us both choked and confused.

Cybernetization and medialization are tendencies within the postmodern environment that immediately affect the writer's material and field of activity, but they also permeate the society as a whole. The emergence of a generalized theory of cybernetics (information theory) in the work of Norbert Wiener and others and the development of computer technology to its present advanced and ever-advancing state have brought about social, cultural, and intellectual transformations that have decisively altered the character of our lives.[5] Language—as code and information—now extends from the most elementary processes within the living cell to the most recondite forms of computation. This implies— and every postmodern writer must come to terms with the fact—that cultural communication is no longer organized around its traditional foci: the mutually defining concepts of the authorial subject and of the book as totality have lost their relevance. Knowledge is no longer a mapping of the world but a way of processing information,[6] and even money is only a single current within the universal flow of data.[7] Cybernetization has likewise engendered new patterns and problems in the areas of politics and governance as Daniel Bell especially has stressed.[8] There is good reason to take seriously Heidegger's characterization of our time as "the age of information."[9]

Similarly wide-reaching are the effects of medialization. Television, film, tape, phonograph, photograph, and so forth provide the culture with scene, sound, and spectacle in unprecedented density and scale. Herein lies, of course, a further reason for the demise of the book: it is simply no longer the privileged vehicle of the myths and meanings of the tribe.[10] Writing today is one sort of media production among others, and in many cases, such as the creation of political symbols, by no means the most important. This situation has produced many cooperative ventures between writers and other media specialists, especially filmmakers, as well as many hybrid careers. But it is also important to hold in mind another way that medialization influences postmodern writing: there is no writer of success today who is not to some degree produced by the media, whose work and personality are not images—both inflated and stereotypic—that circulate through television, radio, and the news.

The postmodern situation is characterized finally by new social and political conflicts involving what can be called outsider groups: women, the incarcerated, the "deviant," patients of all sorts. The environmentalist movement conforms to this paradigm as well since it is carried on in the name of an excluded "other" (nature). Also counted here are the teenage protests of the past few years, which are really part of a larger conflict that is taking place in the schools as well; and also the house occupations, which in Germany actually rose to the level of a national issue. Finally, we must recall in this context the conflicts within the Third World, which have often crystallized around instances of political, economic, or strategic colonization, and which, from Algeria to Vietnam and Palestine, have been a decisive factor in the formation of the contemporary European intellectual consciousness. Among sociologists, Touraine has particularly emphasized this new form of conflict as a component of the postmodern world, but it is Foucault who has provided us with the most acute interpretation of these developments.[11] In his view, they are conflicts that, first of all, "question the status of the individual," asserting on the one hand the individual's right to be different while on the other hand resisting those forces that work to atomize social life, to destroy the communal. Secondly, these new struggles often express themselves as oppositions to forms of domination that are linked with "knowledge, competence, and qualification," and that, of course, are of extreme importance where social life is institutionally saturated. Finally, these contemporary struggles are all concerned with a redefinition of our identity: "They are a refusal of those abstractions, of economic and ideological state violence, which ignore who we are individually, and also a refusal of a scientific or administrative inquisition which determines who one is." It is clear, I think, that Foucault's own prodigious research on the history of psychiatry, medicine, punishment, and sexuality is energized by these new forms of social conflict. But in this he is not a unique case: postmodern discourse in general vibrates with the voice of an Other which cannot entirely come to speech, indeed, which has traditionally been excluded from the sphere of cultural communication.

PHILOSOPHICAL ISSUES

There is no unified postmodern philosophy, and certainly not one that can be distinctly set off from modern philosophy. The terms "modern" and "postmodern" name neither philosophical schools, nor even coherent bodies of thought, and, when they are employed as if they were such names, it is usually a case of polemical self-definition rather than of reasoned appraisal. Avowed moderns and postmoderns, it seems, are always involved in a *querelle*, especially when they wish to determine what the true meaning of modernity or postmodernity might be. But even if these self-descriptions do not have a great deal of veridical value, they nevertheless do point to rifts and oppositions within the culture, and in this sense they can be taken as symptoms that betray issues of genuine substance and complexity. Indeed, the anxious shrillness with which they are pronounced makes a symptomatic reading seem especially warranted.

The case in point is a lecture by Juergen Habermas with the rather manichean title "Modernity versus Postmodernity." The lecture was first delivered in September 1980, on the occasion of Habermas' acceptance of the Adorno prize awarded him by the city of Frankfurt. It was subsequently published in the cultural pages of *Die Zeit*, West Germany's leading weekly newspaper.[12] These contextual factors help explain the rhetoric of the piece. Its public was in the first place the cultural and political elite of the city of Frankfurt, and then later the middle-brow readership of *Die Zeit*—in both cases an audience eager for oversimplifications. The occasion was a politico-symbolic ceremony involving homage to an honored father figure (Adorno) and celebration of the continuity and vitality of a tradition of thought. The tactics of the lecture conform exactly to the context. Habermas warns against a conservative alliance of postmodernists and premodernists and, in view of the threat that this alliance is said to pose, calls for a renewed commitment to the "project of modernity." Consensus, in other words, is generated through an act of exclusion. The portion of this polemic that is most important for our purposes identifies within the enemy camp a so-called Young Conservative faction, the proponents of a simple-minded irrationalism: "In France this line leads from Bataille via Foucault to Derrida."

Both the classification of Foucault and Derrida as "Young [they are of the same generation as Habermas] Conservatives" and the putative genealogy, which ignores so many important influences on the two thinkers, are such patent distortions that they provoke a very straightforward question: What motivated Habermas to submit this highly questionable statement to his public? A full answer to this question would have to touch on several factors, such as the crisis of the Social Democratic Party both in Frankfurt (Hessia) and in the nation as a whole, and an emerging institutional crisis within the universities. But the remark was prompted by philosophical issues, albeit different ones from the matter of irrationalism that Habermas explicitly mentions. The fact is that recent French thought has elaborated themes which problematize the philosophical position Habermas himself has come to represent over the last decade and a half. The symptomatic value of Habermas' simplistic juxtaposition, then, is that it indirectly points to important philosophical controversies. In this sense, by contrasting recent French philosophical (or paraphilosophical) writing with the work of Habermas, we can begin to perceive what might be called a postmodern style of thought.

Perhaps the most obvious point of contrast between Habermas and such French writers as Foucault, Derrida, Serres, and Lyotard concerns the theme of discourse. In both cases, this theme is at the center of the philosophical program, but in each case it is approached from a very different perspective. Habermas takes as his starting point the notion of an ideal communication situation that serves both as a criterion for evaluating concrete instances of discourse and as an Archimedean point from which to construct a social theory. Briefly put, this notion posits a universal norm of communicative action, a structure of symbol use in which the participants arrive at consensus without external constraint (emanating from institutions and structures of domination) and without internal constraint (emanating from a distortion of the communicative action itself).[13] It would be difficult to imagine a philosophical thesis more opposed to the views of the French writers listed above than this one. Whereas Habermas adheres to an ideal of transparent communication, the French investigate the opacities inherent in speech itself.[14] Whereas Habermas stresses the harmonious aspects of consensus, the French hold that consensus can only be established on the basis of acts of exclusion.[15] And whereas Habermas seeks in such notions as truth, truthfulness, and correctness criteria that, as it were, stand above language and give it its validity, the French interpret such notions as strategies for the control of speech and, through speech, of others.[16] Of course, the four writers mentioned all view language in very different ways; they by no means form a school. But the juxtaposition of their work with that of Habermas does reveal what is perhaps the most salient feature of the postmodern style of thought. All postmodern philosophers (if they can still be called that), *repudiate the dream of an innocent language*.

The second aspect of postmodern theorizing that our confrontation brings to light is what can be called the *rejection of the Great Narrative*. This is a theme that Lyotard has placed at the center of his suggestive study *The Postmodern Condition*, but it is also prominent in the work of the other thinkers considered here as representative of the postmodern style.[17] The narrative in question, of course, is the narrative of history, conceived as the story of a single logical-temporal movement that embraces and renders intelligible all individual histories. This framework of sense—for it is an interpretation that enables various events to be related one to another—arose in the last third of the eighteenth century with the development of global philosophies of history in the work of Kant, Herder, Condorcet, and finally Hegel.[18] Habermas understands his own work as a continuation of this historicophilosophical (*geschichtsphilosophisch*) discourse, as even his most recent publications show.[19] But in France, the narrative of history is viewed with extreme skepticism; it is seen as a ploy, an ideology, the very function of which is to deny the reality of history in order to celebrate such mythical heroes as Man, Reason, or Consciousness.

Continuous history is the indispensable correlative of the founding function of the subject: the guarantee that everything that has eluded him may be restored to him; the certainty that time will disperse nothing without restoring it in a reconstituted unity; the promise that one day the subject—in the form of historical consciousness—will once again be able to appropriate, to bring back under his sway, all those things that are kept at a distance by difference, and find in them what might be called his abode.[20]

In other words, what the classical philosophy of history from the Enlightenment to the present views as the ultimate horizon for all interpretations appears from the vantage point of postmodern thought as one way of making sense among others. It is a kind of myth that recounts the homecoming of a representative hero, according to Lyotard either a "hero of knowledge" or a "hero of liberty."[21] And like all myths, it serves to legitimate, and to protect from criticism, a specific set of cultural values. Whether these values are defined as the foundational concepts of the discourse of metaphysics since Plato, as in the case of Derrida,[22] or as the elements of the anthropological humanism that developed in the late eighteenth century, as in the case of Foucault and Lyotard,[23] matters little. The essential point is the shared rejection of the Great Narrative, a rejection that is by no means a flight from the historical world, but rather the first step toward comprehending our historicity without mythical distortion.

Both the philosophical (or perhaps antiphilosophical) themes identified thus far can be found in the work of Nietzsche, the most significant influence on the writers considered here. Of course, other figures such as Marx, Freud, Saussure, and Heidegger have been very influential as well, and their importance should not be diminished. But only in the case of Nietzsche can it be said that a certain creative reading of his works is constitutive of the postmodern style of thought. Again, comparison with Habermas can serve indirectly to highlight this stylistic feature insofar as his attitude toward Nietzsche exactly parallels his attitude toward his French contemporaries. In both he sees a reactionary embrace of the archaic and the mythical and consequently an "escape from the horizon of modernity."[24] This view is egregiously inaccurate in its interpretive claims, but it does confirm, in the manner of a litmus test, that postmodern theorizing is related in essential ways to Nietzsche's deeply problematic oeuvre. To give a precise account of this relationship would require many more pages than are available here, but one important factor should be emphasized. Rather than pointing out paths of "escape," Nietzsche's texts have opened up for such writers as Deleuze, Foucault, and Derrida fruitful domains of inquiry that, prior to their postmodern readings of Nietzsche, had been altogether ignored. For instance, Nietzsche's genealogical method—conceived, by the way, as an alternative to the totalizing schemata of history—has been adapted by Foucault in his analyses of such sociocultural phenomena as punishment, medical practices, and the organization of sexual behavior. For Deleuze, Nietzsche's texts suggest a new model for philosophical thought, an alternative both to dialectics and to positivism. And finally, Derrida has taken up both Nietzsche's critique of the governing metaphors of Western philosophy as well as his sovereign employment of literary strategies to fashion a hybrid philosophical-poetic form of discourse. Other Nietzschean themes are present in works by all the postmodern theoreticians: the stress on difference and repetition, the concept of the body as a plural and mobile form of identity, the suspicion of the official institutions of education, the resistance to the homogenizing tendencies at work in mass culture. In short, whatever else one thinks about postmodern theory, this much must be conceded: Derrida, Deleuze, and Foucault have removed Nietzsche's work from the great museum of world-views, in which for years it had been housed, and have rendered it vital and challenging for contemporary readers. This alone is an achievement of no mean measure.

THEMES AND STRATEGIES OF POSTMODERN WRITING

Postmodern writing is first of all just that: writing. Ordinarily our use and comprehension of language are conditioned by limiting aims and classifications. This is literature or fiction, we say, or a novel, a story, a poem; and now what I'm involved in is science, or social theory, or philosophy. The postmoderns seek to uncouple the use of language from these governing schemata in order to bring to the fore that which underlies all literary kinds: writing itself, conceived as an autonomous productive activity. To write so as to disclose the force and intricacies of writing—this is the strategy that defines the postmodern writer's intention toward language.[25] The work and the book, the traditional units of literary accomplishment, yield their priority to the text.[26]

There are two sorts of tactic employed to realize this project of absolute writing: a set of procedures designed to reveal the infinity of language and another to actualize language in its materiality. The first includes all the delimiting devices that writers of late have mobilized to transgress generic boundaries and to undo mechanisms of fictional closure. The idea is to create a text without finality or completion, one with which the reader can never be finished. Thus, stories fold back upon themselves and endings turn out to be beginnings, suggesting an endless recursivity; genre distinctions are blurred in order to prevent the text from being moored to a single communicative purpose; and again and again the act of writing itself is problematized, the narrator/writer's stance questioned, and the difference between metalanguage and object language eradicated, so that no secure, controlling position outside the text remains. Also important as regards the limitless nature of postmodern writing is the matter of intertextuality. The text acknowledges its links to a network of other texts, authored and anonymous, and at the same time offers itself as a text to be constantly transformed or rewritten by its readers. In this way the limiting singularity imposed by originality and authority is negated and the text is absorbed into an open-ended process of writing.

This infinity of language, however, must be seen in connection with the second feature noted here, the effort of writers to foreground the materiality of their products. The field of textuality within which postmodern literary production seeks to position itself is adamantly not a mental or spiritual realm. Just as Joseph Beuys makes sculpture out of spoilable substances such as animal fat in order to prevent his work from being perceived as an ideal or spiritual product, the postmodern writer seeks to make his language as palpable in all its material determinations as possible. In this sense, concrete poetry, often thought of as a negation of the literary, is continuous with other forms of postmodern writing; the concretists' concentration on the visual-typographical features of texts merely brings into extreme focus the general concern with materiality. Other writers draw different sorts of material features to the fore. Language appears as body and rhythm, as document, as a drift toward entropic noise, as field, and movement within that field. In this way, the text detaches itself from the authority and internality of the conscious subject, becoming other, at once autonomous and estranged. This is why, where there is a speaker in postmodernist texts, he/she often experiences his/her own language as objectified and enigmatic, an uncanny phantasm: "Whose voice, no one's, there is no one, there's a voice without a mouth, and somewhere a kind of hearing, . . . there is nothing but a voice murmuring a trace."[27]

The postmodern orientation toward language is interlaced with another set of concerns, which may be called the "problematics of power." Peter Handke's *Kaspar*, which dramatizes a subject's linguistic indoctrination into the role of responsible social agent, illustrates with remarkable intelligence how intricately entwined the two issues are. Not only for Handke, but for the postmodern writer generally, language embraces all the frames of activity, the institutional structures, norms and sanctions, the authorities, belief systems, and lines of legitimation, which sustain, and are sustained by, our speaking and writing. Postmodern aesthetic experimentation should be viewed as having an irreducible political dimension. It is inextricably bound up with a critique of domination.

In this sense, postmodern writing can be usefully read from the point of view of recent theoretical work on the nature of power.[28] A case in point is Oswald Wiener's neglected text, *Die Verbesserung von Mitteleuropa, Roman* (*The Improvement of Central Europe, Novel*, 1969). It is hard to imagine a text more fully committed to experimentalism than this one. Beginning with an index of names and concepts and concluding with a bibliography of some 1,200 entries, this melange of theory and fiction, aphorism, narrative and disquisition, parody and programmatic statement, in fact represents a kaleidoscopic but sustained meditation on the regularization of life by the state. The focal point of this dystopian vision is what Wiener calls the "bio-adapter," the learning and communication machine into which man is rapidly being transformed, the logical consequence of the state's program of therapeutic governance. Again and again, Wiener's rambling reflection brings him into proximity with Foucault:

the fact that ancient democracy found the jabbering Socrates dangerous testifies to an unusually fine sensibility—but his liquidation still wasn't rational: he should have been hospitalized, observed and cured with opium; or at least they should have cut open his corpse and investigated his brain. Modern democracy is so secure because it studies abnormality, declares abnormality an object of research."[29]

But perhaps the most remarkable example of this concern for the problematics of power is to be found in the work of Heiner Mueller, universally acknowledged as "the most important dramatist in the German language since the war.''[30] Mueller is one of the few German (not to say East German) writers who views his own work in terms of the concept of postmodernism, a concept that for him is inseparably tied up with the question of domination.[31] Both his experimental program and the dramatic works that seek to realize it fuse aesthetic and political elements into a single revolutionary gesture of agony and aspiration. Consider, for instance, the rhetoric of this passage from his New York statement on postmodernism:

As long as freedom is based on violence and the exercise of art on privilege, art works will show a tendency to be prisons, masterpieces the accomplices of power. The great texts of the century work toward the liquidation of their own autonomy, the product of their incest with private property, toward the expropriation and finally the disappearance of the author. The stable is the evanescent. What is in flight remains. . . . Two figures of poetry, in the hour of white heat melting to a single figure: Orpheus who sings beneath the plows, Daedalus in flight through the labyrinthian intestines of the minotaur.[32]

Similarly, Mueller's disruptive use of the theatrical code, which has produced scenes of remarkable intensity, is often most radical where power and exploitation are at issue. This is true, for example, of the intriguing play *Leben Gundlings*, which explores the Foucauldian theme of the interrelationship between absolutism, military organization, education, and the emergence of the modern state.[33] But Mueller is most suggestive when he turns to the imaginary of power, that is, the essential link between domination and phantasms of authority. No doubt the most memorable example of this is the penultimate scene of *Hamletmaschine*, in which gigantic busts of Marx, Lenin, and Mao are destroyed in a dramatic movement that combines extremes of parody and ritual seriousness.

To the movement toward an absolute writing and the critique of domination—two interrelated themes or characteristic orientations of postmodern texts—might be added a third major area of concern: the question of subjectivity. The term "subjectivity" has a different resonance in the European languages than in English, which inevitably assigns it a pejorative nuance. In French or German, it refers less to the limitations of personal perspective than to the sphere of the *pour soi*. The emphasis, in other words, falls on the uniqueness of an ontological dimension. The point here is that a salient feature of much postmodern writing is that this subjectivity has become problematic.

Paradigmatic for this tendency is Roland Barthes' text *A Lover's Discourse*. Here Barthes actually assumes the position of the speaking, desiring subject, but not—and this is decisive—in order to celebrate subjective autonomy or the uniqueness of emotional experience. On the contrary, the subject expresses and realizes itself only across a set of experienced figures that are themselves entirely general and repeatable. Subjectivity here is caught in a tension between the irreducibly personal quality of the pronoun "I," which Barthes employs throughout, and the impersonality of the alphabet, the order of which lends the text its principle of organization. Such tension and inner contradiction are in fact characteristic of the postmodern rendering of subjectivity. Thus, in *Rumor*, a novel by the most important of the so-called new subjectivist writers in Germany, Botho Strauss, the thematics and action are determined by two opposed semantic registers: the first having to do with the "institutional" (e.g., the research center for information studies, where the main character is employed), the second with what may be called the "creaturely vulnerability" of the human subject, its capacity for love, fear, and pain. Interestingly enough (and this too corresponds to an aspect of Barthes' text), special stress is placed on the bodily nature of this creatureliness. Thus, the phase of greatest contradiction, but at the same time greatest interpenetration of these two registers occurs in the hospital sequence, where the body is submitted, as it were, to a series of institutional incursions. Here too subjective identity becomes enigmatic: "In everything there is information and language, from the tiny bacterial cell to the most secret end of a dream, we are overfilled with microtexts, codes and alphabets, language everywhere and everywhere the rule of law and alien orders. Where in all this might there be room for an I?"[34]

The fissured subjectivity of postmodernism is unique to no genre; it is a field of uncertainty that can be approached through the novel, the story or novella, the diary, or the lyric. Exploration of this field produces compelling texts only so long as the subject in question is not simply given, but is in some sense tied up with an otherness that renders it problematic, threatened, elusive. This is the case, for instance, in the elaborate and uncanny dance of male and female identity in Mueller's *Hamletmaschine* as well as in the extremely fine works of Christa Wolf (*Nachdenken ueber Christa T.*, 1968; *Kindheitsmuster*, 1977), where the sense of alterity derives from the estrangement of the past. But perhaps the best illustration of this essential relation of the subject to an other (which, however, in some sense *is* the subject too) is provided by the demanding prose of Thomas Bernhard. In the text *Gehen* (1971), for example, his writing achieves an extraordinary synthesis of opposites. Every bend in the often elaborate syntax is in place, every attribution of indirect speech is accurate, but the repetitions are so obsessive, the tact so regular, the path of the narrative so circular, that the reader loses all sense of ground. Lacking the usual parsing signals of paragraph and chapter breaks, or for that matter even intonational changes, the text presents itself as a single, monotonous murmur, and yet the reader nevertheless suspects the presence of a mathematically rigorous principle of thematic and even lexical variation. This prose, at once lucid and delirious, fits the subject matter exactly. The point of the narrative is that the subject's everyday thoughts, if thought once again, if pursued in all their banal detail, become indistinguishable from madness.

THREE TEXTS

Hubert Fichte, *Versuch ueber die Pubertaet* (*Essay on Puberty*, 1974)

Hubert Fichte's writing derives its energy from a fundamental stylistic dissonance.[35] His texts occupy a border region between reflection and ecstatic transport, scientific neutrality and ritual participation. In this novel, which draws on adolescent experiences of learning and homosexuality in the theatre milieu of postwar Hamburg, the attitudinal incompatibility inherent in Fichte's writing and the remarkable effects it generates are forcefully in evidence. On the one hand, the text is sustained by an investigative will-to-analysis, the model for which is the autopsy or anatomical dissection; on the other hand, it exhibits a magical or incantory use of language in which words become fetishes, their repetition a hypnotic chant.

Fichte's theme in this novel, as in so many works produced during the seventies in Germany, is the problematics of subjectivity. Globally considered, the novel evinces a rough chronological coherence that winds through various adolescent rites of passage to a point of self-discovery, that Archimedian platform from which autobiographical writing becomes possible. In this regard, then, the text is held together by a fairly conventional macrostructure, the story of a writer's education in the manner of Proust (to whom there are innumerable allusions). And yet Fichte is adamantly concerned to prevent this emergent authorial self from attaining mastery over the past and its contingencies and opacities. Indeed, the insight that for him makes autobiographical writing possible has little to do with a coherent principle of retrospective interpretation. Fichte's is quite deliberately a method of contradiction: "Gradually there develops within me the freedom to write discrepancies, which I earlier . . . carefully erased; to register my defeats, not to smooth out the breaks, the contradictions, the incoherent elements, but to let disconnected parts remain next to one another, by means of two false and exaggerated statements to take a bearing on the facts." (304) The result of this procedure is that the overriding narrative structure can no longer hold together the individual segments of the text. The narrative account dissolves into a series of fragments: brief scenes, conversations, interjected associations, anecdotes, commentary on the action and reflections on the act of writing. At times these fragments form mere lists or litanies, in which the material and evocative qualities of individual words and names altogether disrupt the linkages of syntax and story.

Like the social theorists Oskar Negt and Alexander Kluge, Fichte writes in such a way as to render the "category of coherence" (*Kategorie des Zusammenhangs*) problematic.[36] The Great Narrative, be it history or the organic story of individual development, is viewed as a suspect myth, the legitimating ideology of European rationalism and its disciplines of knowledge. *Essay on Puberty* represents Fichte's most advanced novelistic attempt to dismantle that myth and to disclose through literary means an alternative conception of subjectivity. This is why he draws so heavily on the resources of the fragment, the inserted anecdote or reflection that presents the reader an unassimilable block of experience. The most notable instances of this are the two interviews with homosexuals that form the second and fourth parts of the text: first-person accounts of experiences and patterns of life, apparently taped and edited for fluent reading, which provide "alternate puberties" to that of the novel's central narrative line. No biographical connections join these lives to that of the authorial voice, nor to one another, for that matter; they are merely given in a kind of brute facticity and singularity, unprocessed by a unifying narrative consciousness.

All postmodern writing is concerned with the limits of consciousness and identity, but in Fichte's work this orientation takes a unique turn. He seeks out those extreme experiences where the controlling self dissolves and other forms of agency—the body, the group, the gods—assert themselves. Hence the remarkable intertwining, especially in this novel, of sexuality, violence, and ritual. And yet one must not confuse Fichte's endeavor with some sort of simplistic (and perhaps reactionary) irrationalism. The remarkable thing about his writing is the balance it holds between an analytic perspective (and language) and a perspective internal to these experiences themselves. *Essay on Puberty* is at once an ethnography of adolescence and an incantory reenactment of adolescent rites. The stylistic incompatibility at the core of Fichte's writing emerges out of a profoundly ethical project: the endeavor to allow the Other of reason to speak and simultaneously to maintain critical vigilance. Since the publication of *Essay* in 1974, this project has developed beyond the limits of the novelistic genre. With his enormous study of the syncretic Afro-American religions of the Caribbean region—a collaboration with the photographer Leonore Mau—Fichte has begun to develop an "ethnopoetics" that combines evocation with detailed empirical analyses and which constitutes one of the truly significant achievements of postmodern writing.[37]

Helmut Heissenbuettel, *Die goldene Kuppel des Comes Arbogast oder Lichtenberg in Hamburg. Fast eine einfache Geschichte (The Golden Cupola of Comes Arbogast or Lichtenberg in Hamburg. Almost a Simple Story,* 1979)

This text by Germany's most productive and consistently intellectual experimentalist is impossible to categorize, and this impossibility has to do with the word "almost" in the subtitle.[38] One could say with only slight exaggeration that the twenty-three chapters and one hundred or so pages that make up this text are designed solely to render this single word, which has also, by the way, caught Derrida's attention, uncanny and enigmatic.[39] The text is "almost" a dozen things without quite being any one: almost a simple narrative, and the narrative itself almost an odyssey (from Stuttgart to Hamburg) and almost a Dantesque descent (beginning in a "forest . . . in the middle of life's way" [35]); almost an essay on writing, on Heissenbuettel's own career of writing as well as on the writing of this very text; almost a psychoanalytic interpretation of dreams and images, a reflection on sexual obsessions; almost a commentary on a passage by Lacan. The text, as it were, tries on each of these classifications only to change costume almost immediately. The effect of this generic lability is a sense of continuous movement. The text frees itself from classificational constraints by remaining in perpetual transition. No other work manages with such subtlety and precision to demonstrate, or perform, the vagrancy of writing.

The generic vacillation is repeated as regards all aspects of the text. The narrative levels, for example, blend imperceptibly into one another as the text slides from a metareflection on narration/writing to the narration of the occasion of the writing to the story (almost a story) itself. Likewise, dream, description, memory, and abstract reflection are melded so that no categorization of degrees of reality can serve as a steady point of reference. But by far the most conspicuous instance of Heissenbuettel's art of perpetual transition is the flux of identities that moves back and forth among the proper names. Hubert Arbogast, the editor at Heissenbuettel's publishing house (Klett in Stuttgart), whose voice on the telephone urges work on the promised manuscript, merges with the Roman officer of the fourth century A.D., the companion ("comes") Arbogast, one of several Virgils for the author's descent. These eponymous figures, however, are joined by a host of other guides and voices that call forth things from the speaker/writer: a certain Eichendorff, one of Heissenbuettel's earlier creations; the eighteenth-century physicist and aphorist Lichtenberg, from whom three letters describing the city of Hamburg are included in the text; D'Alembert, who is both a historical figure (and contemporary of Lichtenberg); and a fictional character from Heissenbuettel's Project One, the novel *D'Alemberts Ende.* Other identities are merely suggested, as in the following: "D'Alembert's face is large, fleshy, heavy-cheeked and melancholy . . . Inventions too are only memories, he says hesitatingly. He is, in a certain way, my father." (95) Not merely the father, but also the poet-critic Max Kommerell, from whom the line about inventions and memories is borrowed and about whom Heissenbuettel has written, admiringly, elsewhere. In this text, then, no proper name rigidly designates, no individual identity holds firm.

One more instance of the elimination of fixed identities and positions that characterizes this text deserves special mention. The fourth-century cupola, hypothesized by art historians to have covered a structure recently unearthed in the city of Cologne and presumably built by the pagan Arbogast, reappears in the "shining, silver cupola . . . of the television tower" (80) that dominates the cityscape of Stuttgart. In both versions, archaic and ultramodern, the cupola is a mediator of the dreams and desires of the subject, a surface on which is inscribed the world of myth: "a sort of figural writing, bodily writing, hieroglyphic writing, structured according to a syntax entirely its own and expressing something that is otherwise inexpressible." (45) It is no accident, then, that the same cupola becomes the "white plaster ceiling" (96) of the writer's study, the blank screen onto which the author projects the ciphers of his dreams. The cupola is the "other dimension" of writing, the "interstitial space of the almost." (82)

What is it that generates this sliding from point to point within the writing, this meander that follows "the path of the subject"? (99) The answer to this question is not to be sought in the domain of positive entities, since Heissenbuettel's practice is to write works that relativize all fixed systems of reference. Rather, what lends the text its mysterious movement is a difference: a split, a gap, a divergence within the subject that both constitutes the subject as such and yet inevitably escapes its grasp. In a passage that alludes to Freud and Lacan, Heissenbuettel describes the matter in this way: "the break between perception and consciousness, . . . the split, the postponement also, in view of which the relationship between that which I perceive with my senses and that over which I have conscious mastery appears, according to the thesis, like a competition with changing and reversible roles." (77–78) It is this difference, this opening of an interstitial space, that is dramatized again and again in the individual scenes of the text. Hence the subject's voyeurism, his captivation by spectacles that are really enactments, in the register of castration and sexual identity, of the division within the subject himself. Through the opening of an eye is seen the opening of a window blind, through which is seen a woman lifting the edge of her dress to reveal the opening of her sex. The obsessive return to these scenes, however, only reveals the impossibility of knowing or exhaustively interpreting what is in fact being seen, or of seeing what in fact was never there. In this manner, Heissenbuettel's writing conveys "the experience of the fundamental and definitive hiddenness of the causal principle" (39). The "split, the snapping open" that sets into motion the series of displacements constitutive of the subject has the significance of "an absolute loss." (79) The golden cupola of writing is "at once palace and grave." (25)

Botho Strauss, *Paare, Passanten* (*Couples, Passers-by*, 1981)

It is revealing that Botho Strauss is the favorite writer of those young German literary critics and theoreticians who have been most influenced by contemporary French thought, for there is indeed a deep affinity between Strauss' writing and that of, say, Foucault or Derrida.[40] To take one example, the following set of assertions from *Paare, Passanten* echoes any number of French texts written over the past fifteen years: "Writing interprets the situation of lack. There is lack wherever the letter is. To desire things rendered absent, the body rendered absent, is the originary erotics of human language, which only achieves agreement via sense and symbol instead of by means of immediate stimuli. . . . " (102) One easily recognizes behind the lexical material out of which these sentences are fashioned the shadows of such French terms as *écriture, manque, désir*. Indeed, the German equivalents *Schreiben, Fehl, Begehren* have undergone in recent years a slight semantic displacement due to the exigencies of translating French theory. In any case, the claim that is being made regarding language: that it is marked by the nonpresence (at least as a possibility) not only of the things referred to but of the speaking subject as well, and that this fundamental nonpresence is the very lack that is constitutive of desire—this claim clearly has its roots in earth west of the Rhine. Of course, much the same can be said of the text by Heissenbuettel; and Fichte's borrowings are different only in that he draws directly on a group of writers themselves much admired by the postmodern theorists: Bataille, Leiris, Artaud. But in the case of Strauss one can argue for a more intimate relation to current French writing, a similarity of sensibility as well as ideas. This is why his writing possesses, in the context of German letters today, such a unique and intriguing physiognomy.

Paare, Passanten is a book of what—thinking of Nietzsche and the Adorno of *Minima Moralia*—one would have to call aphorisms: short blocks of prose, usually only a single paragraph and seldom more than two pages long, that develop a tightly circumscribed thematic point. Poetologically speaking, the best aphorisms are distinguished by two features: due to the imposed parsimoniousness of expression, an extreme precision of formulation, and, due to the narrow thematic focus, a strong capacity for *resonance*. By both these criteria, Strauss' writing ranks high; in fact, no contemporary writer in Germany can produce aphorisms of such quality. Also like Nietzsche and Adorno before him, or like Barthes in his last books, Strauss brings to his writing that paradoxical attitude without which aphorisms ring pretentious or flat: a will to theoretical penetration of the point at hand but at the same time a renunciation of any effort at theoretical totalization. Rather than seeking to integrate his individual insights into a conceptual whole, the aphorist develops each of them according to its unique and immanent rigor. This is a hazardous venture that can only be successful if the loss of theoretical coherence and generality is compensated by genuine aesthetic achievement. In *Paare, Passanten* this is clearly the case.

Throughout the six sections of the text, each of which bears a loosely thematic coherence, Strauss employs various discursive strategies: observation from outside, first-person narratives, conceptual explication or reinterpretation, fictions of several sorts, commentary on current events or trends. But whatever the particular form, the aphoristic thrust toward philosophical insight is evident in each. Thus, despite the very local and concrete nature of many of the passages, the reader will nevertheless discover themes familiar from other postmodern writing: the subject's entanglement in a network of orders, codes, discourses, and institutions; the body as the site of a plural identity; the collapse of the grand, encompassing systems of thought; the irrelevance of the book in an age of medial and computerized communication; the intricate and yet fragile coding of interpersonal relationships; suspicion of the official institutions of education, discipline, and therapy; a (paradoxical) commitment to the vocation of writing. And, as so often in postmodern writing, these themes are combined with a sense that we are living on the threshhold of a new (post) era:

Not "two cultures," but the pool, the total-today of consumer culture in the head of a human being; influxes of Ernst Juenger and The Clash, of fantasy novel and RAF, of the Black Messenger and the Ozu Retrospective; influxes that are superimposed on one another, split and traverse one another. A memory consisting of fissures, fragments, temperaments, missing connectors, areas of ignorance and the medial simulation of totality. This is how it looks "at the border of the archaic period of a future art," of a phase of renewal, which is characterized by the end of the predominance of writing and by the loss of figurative realism, a phase in which the forms of rational thought prepare themselves for a "return to a diffuse and multidimensional way of thinking." (118–119)

But the distinguishing feature of Strauss' writing is not a matter of thematics so much as of sensibility. This is not intended as an assertion about the author's person, of which I have no knowledge, but about the language he employs: about its selections and exclusions, the patterns of action and response it evinces, and also about the syntax, the diction, the tone. All of these factors combine to delineate for the reader the contours of a voice entirely unique in German literature today, a combination of vulnerability and ethical resoluteness, of a refined aestheticism and a remarkably penetrating critical intelligence. It is a voice that speaks from a deliberately chosen but nevertheless painful solitude, a voice that often conveys a sense of deep loss and desolation, but which on occasion also recalls the sheerly transient joy of song. As the aphorisms of *Paare, Passanten* reveal, this sensibility is not a given anterior to the text, but a significant complex that takes on body in what Strauss calls the *physis* of the writing itself. (102) Precisely this remarkable textual achievement—comparable only to that of Roland Barthes—lends the works of Botho Strauss their unrivalled keenness and authenticity as interpretations of our present (postmodern) condition.

NOTES

1. For an analysis of how these institutions function internally, see James March and Johan Olsen, *Ambiguity and Choice in Organizations* (Bergen, Oslo, Tromso: Universitetsforlaget, 1976).

2. Roberto Mangabeira Unger, *Law in Modern Society* (New York: The Free Press, 1976), p. 193.

3. See Niklas Luhmann, "Institutionalisierungs-Funktion und Mechanismus im sozialen System der Gesellschaft," in *Zur Theorie der Institutionen*, ed. Helmut Schelsky (Duesseldorf: Bertlesmann, 1970), pp. 27–41.

4. The phrase "administrated world" (*verwaltete Welt*), which I believe Horkheimer and Adorno first introduced as a characterization of modern social reality, has become a fixed syntagm in German by virtue of its aptness.

5. Norbert Wiener, *Cybernetics* (Cambridge, Mass.: MIT Press, 1948). For advances in the area of biology, see Heinz von Foerster, *Observing Systems* (Seaside, Calif.: Intersystems Publications, 1982).

6. See Fred I. Dretske, *Knowledge and the Flow of Information* (Cambridge, Mass.: MIT Press, 1981).

7. On this point, see Michael Serres, *The Parasite*, trans. Lawrence R. Schehr (Baltimore and London: Johns Hopkins University Press, 1982), p. 172.

8. Daniel Bell, "Teletext and Technology: New Networks of Knowledge and Information in Post-Industrial Society," *Encounter* 48 (1977).

9. Martin Heidegger, *Unterwegs zur Sprache* (Pfuellingen: Neske, 1959), p. 2.

10. Numbers make the point evident: from 1973 to 1979 Pink Floyd's album *The Dark Side of the Moon* sold eight million copies; during its first week, the film *Return of the Jedi* took in $45 million.

11. Michel Foucault, "The Subject and Power," *Critical Inquiry* 8 (1982): 777–96. The quotations from this article that follow are from pp. 780–81. See also Alain Touraine, *The Post-Industrial Society, Tomorrow's Social History: Classes, Conflicts, and Culture in the Programmed Society*, trans. Leonard F. X. Mayhew (New York: Random House, 1972).

12. The English translation is available in *New German Critique* 22 (1981): 3–14. The

same issue contains replies to Habermas by Anthony Giddens, Peter Buerger, and Andreas Huyssen.

13. See Juergen Habermas, "Vorbereitende Bemerkungen zu einer Theorie der kommunikativen Kompetenz," in J. H. Niklas Luhmann, *Theorie der Gesellschaft oder Sozialtechnologie—Was leistet die Systemforschung?* (Frankfurt a.M.: Suhrkamp, 1971), pp. 101–41.

14. See Jacques Derrida, *La Voix et la phenomene* (Paris: Presses Universitaires de France, 1972), p. 95.

15. See the motif of the "third man" in Serres' *The Parasite*.

16. See Michel Foucault, "The Discourse on Language," in *The Archaeology of Knowledge and the Discourse on Language*, trans. A. M. Sheridan Smith (New York: Harper Colophon, 1976), pp. 215–37.

17. Jean-Francois Lyotard, *La Condition postmoderne* (Paris: Minuit, 1979).

18. On the emergence of history as a "collective singular," see Reinhart Koselleck, "Historia magistra vitae," in *Natur und Geschichte*, ed. H. Braun and M. Riedel (Stuttgart: Metzler, 1967), pp. 196–219.

19. Juergen Habermas, "The Entwinement of Myth and Enlightenment: Re-Reading *Dialectic of Enlightenment*," *New German Critique* 26 (1982): 13–30.

20. Foucault, *The Archaeology of Knowledge*, p. 12.

21. Lyotard, *La Condition postmoderne*, chapter eight.

22. Jacques Derrida, *Of Grammatology*, trans. Gayatri Chakravorty Spivak (Baltimore and London: Johns Hopkins University Press, 1974), p. 10.

23. See the chapter entitled "The Anthropological Sleep" in Foucault's *The Order of Things* (New York: Vintage Books, 1973), pp. 340–43.

24. Habermas, "The Entwinement of Myth and Enlightenment," p. 29.

25. I borrow this term from Peter Szondi, *Celan-Studien* (Frankfurt a.M.: Suhrkamp, 1972), p. 18. Szondi himself took the term from Walter Benjamin.

26. See Roland Barthes, "From Work to Text," in *Image Music Text*, trans. Stephen Heath (New York: Hill & Wang, 1977).

27. Samuel Beckett, *Stories and Texts for Nothing* (New York: Grove Press, 1967), p. 137. Note that Foucault's "Discourse on Language" begins by quoting a similar passage from Beckett.

28. See Foucault, "The Subject and Power"; *The History of Sexuality*, trans. Robert Hurley (New York: Pantheon, 1978); Louis Marin, "Discourse of Power—Power of Discourse: Pascalian Notes," in *Philosophy in France Today*, ed. Alan Montefiore (Cambridge, London, New York: Cambridge University Press, 1983), pp. 155–74.

29. Oswald Wiener, *Die Verbesserung von Mitteleuropa, Roman* (Reinbek: Rowohlt, 1969).

30. Fritz J. Raddatz, *ZEIT-Gespraeche* (Frankfurt a.M.: Suhrkamp, 1978), 36.

31. "I cannot separate the question of postmodernism from politics. Periodization is colonial politics as long as history is not universal history, which presupposes equality of life-chances for everyone, but rather domination by elites through money or power." Heiner Mueller, "Der Schrecken ist die erste Erscheinung des Neuen. Zu einer Diskussion ueber Postmodernismus in New York," in *Rotwelsch* (Berlin: Merve, 1982), p. 95. Mueller's essay was originally written for the forum "The Question of Postmodernism" moderated by Ihab Hassan at the 93rd Annual Convention of the Modern Language Association, New York, December 27–30, 1978. An English translation of the essay is available in *New German Critique* 16 (1979): 55–57.

32. Ibid., pp. 97–98.

33. See esp. the scene "Die Schule der Nation" ("The School of the Nation"), in which the correlation between education, military organization, and absolutism is especially clear.

34. Botho Strauss, *Rumor* (Munich: Hanser, 1980), pp. 144–45.

35. Hubert Fichte, *Versuch ueber die Pubertaet* (Hamburg: Hoffman and Campe, 1974). Page references are given in parentheses following quotations.

36. See Alexander Kluge and Oskar Negt, *Geschichte und Eigensinn* (Frankfurt a.M.: Zweitausendeins, 1981). This text might well be considered the most significant postmodern theoretical work produced in Germany. Alexander Kluge also deserves mention in this context for his literary and film production.

37. See *Xango. (Die afroamerikanischen Religionen 1–11)* (Frankfurt a.M.: Fischer, 1976); *Petersilie. (Die afroamerikanischen Religionen 111–1V)* (Frankfurt a.M.: 1980).

38. Helmut Heissenbuettel, *Die goldene Kuppel des Comes Arbogast oder Lichtenberg in Hamburg. Fast eine einfache Geschichte* (Stuttgart: Klett, 1979). Page references to this text are given in parentheses following quotations.

39. See Jacques Derrida, "Limited Inc.," *Glyph* 2 (1977). Heissenbuettel's use of the term *Verschiebung* (delay, postponement, deferral) suggests the direct influence of Derrida (cf., his notion of *differance*).

40. Botho Strauss, *Paare, Passanten* (Munich: Hanser, 1981). Page references to this text are given in parentheses following the quotations.

BIBLIOGRAPHICAL ESSAY

This bibliography reflects the organization of the essay insofar as it concentrates on the literary scene in Germany, with some consideration of French thought. It is divided into two parts, the first dealing with the concept of postmodernism, the second with particular authors.

The standard bibliography for publications in the area of German literature, *Germanistik*, did not begin listing publications under the heading "postmodernism" until 1980. This belatedness is indicative of the fact that the notion of postmodernism has not served the same programmatic function in Europe as it has in the United States. Perhaps the decisive factor in bringing the term to general consciousness in Germany, and in Europe generally, was the 1980 Venice Biennale. For the first time in the history of the Biennale, architecture was designated an autonomous sector and the director, Paolo Portoghesi, suggested postmodernism as the special theme of the exhibition. (See *Architecture 1980*) But in the field of architecture postmodernism has a very specific meaning: the rejection of the severity of modernist architecture and a return to ornament, decoration, deliberate symbolism, and historical reminiscence. (See Jencks, 1977) Because of this local definition of the term, "postmodernism" has in many quarters come to connote conservatism and/or historicism. Such connotations were clearly an important influence on Habermas' interpretation discussed here. (Habermas, 1981) It must be stressed, however, that architectural postmodernism cannot be taken as a paradigm for postmodernism in literature and criticism. Indeed, a brief glance at developments in the plastic arts, in performance and other sorts of experimentation, indicates that architecture represents something of an anomaly. (See Brock, 1977, for a useful digest of artistic activities in Germany, and

Tisdall, 1979, for information regarding the single most important figure on the German art scene.)

American developments have also been important in determining the use of the term "postmodern" in Germany. One of the earliest uses (Hartung, 1971), for example, equates the term with the notion of American pop. Mueller's statement on postmodernism (Mueller, 1979) resulted from an invitation to participate in a special session on postmodernism at the 1978 Modern Language Association Convention and, however interesting his revolutionary interpretation of the term might be, it is fair to say that the selection of the term was motivated more by the circumstances of the invitation than by indigenous trends. (This may also be true of Kristeva's [1980] recent discussion of the concept.)

The existing bibliographies mirror this state of affairs exactly. To be sure, Hoffmann et al. (1977) list some items that are important for an understanding of the European scene (such as the indispensable Ehrmann, 1971), but in the main their entries apply to the discussion in the United States. The synoptic treatments of recent German developments, on the other hand, tend to avoid the notion of postmodernism altogether (Durzak, 1981; Luetzeler and Schwarz, 1980), no doubt because other terms—such as "new subjectivity"—have established themselves in the press, and subsequently in the scholarship, as the appropriate identificational labels for the major literary trends of the seventies.

In the absence of clear consensus on what the term "postmodernism" might mean when applied to German literature, then, the critic must select his/her own criteria. My tactic has been to make use of the sociological meaning of "postmodernism" as a point of departure, expanding on the basic definition of postmodern society as "knowledge-based society" (Holzner and Marx, 1979, 15) to include related factors that are especially important for an understanding of contemporary literature and criticism. Lyotard's excellent study moves in a similar direction, although he focuses almost exclusively on the question of legitimation. (See Lyotard, 1979) Another possible approach is to start from formal and generic features of postmodernist texts, as in the perceptive and intriguing discussions of French writing by Brooke-Rose (1981). The advantage of the sociological framework, however, is that it allows us to grasp important similarities between literature, criticism, and philosophy and to see how all these areas of cultural endeavor respond to common problems. The lines of influence that run between poststructuralist thought and recent German writing appear from this perspective as more than incidental; they express a genuine contemporaneity, a shared set of cultural pressures and meanings.

During the past ten years, the work of the French poststructuralists has become quite well known in this country through both translations and commentary. (The best bibliography on poststructuralist theory is that contained in Harari's anthology [1979]; the most perceptive and least sycophantic account of the philosophical issues is that of Descombes [1980].) Accordingly, a thorough review of the achievement of such writers as Barthes, Foucault, and Derrida has not been presented here, but rather some of the more interesting examples of German writing that evince a comparable response to the postmodern situation have been highlighted. In the main, these examples have been taken from the domain of literature. For other attempts to view recent German writing from the perspective of postmodernism, the reader is especially referred to the relevant special numbers of *Studies in Twentieth Century Literature* (1980, especially the excellent introductory article by Naegele) and *New German Critique* (1981). The adaptation of poststructuralist thought to literary criticism in Germany can be reviewed in the anthologies of Kittler (1980) and Kittler and Turk (1977); the most original statement in this regard is available in English as well (Kittler, 1981).

BIBLIOGRAPHY

Postmodernism

Architecture 1980. The Presence of the Past. Venice Biennale. New York: Rizzoli, 1980.

Beebe, Maurice. "Selected Bibliography on Theories of Modernism and Postmodernism." *Journal of Modern Literature* 3 (1974): 1080–84.

Bernhard, Hans Joachim. "Positionen und Tendenzen in der Literatur der BRD Mitte der siebziger Jahre." *Weimarer Beitraege* 23 (1977): 53–84.

Blau, Herbert. "*Off the Top of My Head*: Preface to a New Book of Questions about the Postmodern." *Sub-Stance* 25 (1980): 39–43.

Brock, Bazon. *Aesthetik als Vermittlung. Arbeitsbiographie eines Generalisten*. Edited by Karla Fohrbeck. Cologne: DuMont, 1977.

Brooke-Rose, Christine. "Exemplosions." *Genre* 4 (1981): 9–21.

———. *A Rhetoric of the Unreal: Studies in Narrative and Structure, especially of the Fantastic*. New York: Cambridge University Press, 1981.

Calinescu, Matei. "Avant-Garde, Neo-Avant-Garde, and Postmodernism." *Perspectives on the Avant-Garde*. Edited by Rudolf Kuenzli and Stephen Foster. Iowa City: University of Iowa Press, 1982.

———. *Faces of Modernity: Avant-Garde, Decadence, Kitsch*. Bloomington and London: Indiana University Press, 1977.

Descombes, Vincent. *Modern French Philosophy*. Cambridge, London, New York: Cambridge University Press, 1980.

Durzak, Manfred, ed. *Deutsche Gegenwartsliteratur. Ausgangspositionen und aktuelle Entscheidungen*. Stuttgart: Reclam, 1981.

Ehrmann, Jacques. "The Death of Literature." *New Literary History* 3 (1971): 31–48.

Garvin, Harry R., ed. *Romanticism, Modernism, Postmodernism*. Lewisburg, Pa.: Bucknell University Press, 1980.

Giddens, Anthony. "Modernism and Post-Modernism." *New German Critique* 22 (1981): 15–18.

Habermas, Juergen. "Modernity versus Postmodernity." *New German Critique* 22 (1981): 3–14.

Harari, Josue V., ed. *Textual Strategies. Perspectives in Post-Structuralist Criticism*. Ithaca, N.Y.: Cornell University Press, 1979.

Hartung, Harald. "Pop als ›postmoderne‹ Literatur. Die deutsche Szene: Brinkmann and andere." *Neue Rundschau* 82 (1971): 723–43.

Hassan, Ihab. *The Dismemberment of Orpheus: Toward a Postmodern Literature*. 2d ed. Madison: University of Wisconsin Press, 1982.

Hays, Michael. "Peter Handke and the End of the Modern." *Modern Drama* 23 (1981): 346–66.

Heise, Hans Juergen. "Das Dilemma der Postmoderne. Gegen eine Wegwerf-Lyrik." *Merkur* 34 (1980): 1004–11.

Hermand, Jost. "The 'Good New' and the 'Bad New': Metamorphoses of the Modernism Debate in the GDR since 1956." *New German Critique* 3 (1974): 73–92.

Hoffmann, Gerhard, Alfred Hornung, and Ruediger Kunow, " 'Modern,' 'Postmodern' and 'Contemporary' as Criteria for the Analysis of 20th Century Literature." *Amerikastudien/America Studies* 22 (1977): 19–46, bibliography 40–46.

Holzner, Burkart, and John H. Marx. *Knowledge Application. The Knowledge System in Society.* Boston, London, Sydney, Toronto: Allyn and Bacon, 1979.

Huyssen, Andreas. "The Search for Tradition: Avant-Garde and Post-Modernism in the 1970's." *New German Critique* 22 (1981): 23–40.

Jencks, Charles. *The Language of Post-Modern Architecture.* New York: Rizzoli, 1977.

Jenkins, Alan. "Outsoaring the Hob-Nailed Boot: Modern and Postmodern Poets." *Encounter* 57 (1981): 70–77.

Kavolis, Vyantes. "Notes on Post-Industrial Culture." *Arts in Society* 11 (1974).

———. "Post-Modern Man: Psycho-Cultural Responses to Social Trends." *Social Problems* 17 (1970): 435–39.

Kittler, Friedrich A., ed. *Austreibung des Geistes aus den Geisteswissenschaften.* Paderborn: Schoeningh, 1980.

———. "Forgetting." *Discourse* 3 (1981): 88–121.

Kittler, Friedrich A., and Horst Turk, eds. *Urszenen. Literaturwissenschaft als Diskursanalyse und Diskurskritik.* Frankfurt a.M.: Suhrkamp, 1977.

Koehler, Michael. " 'Postmodernismus': ein begriffsgeschichtlicher Ueberblick." *Amerikastudien/America Studies* 22 (1977): 8–18.

Kruezer, Helmut. "Zur Literatur der siebziger Jahre in der Bundesrepublik Deutschland." *Basis* 8 (1978): 7–32, 235–39.

Kristeva, Julia. "Postmodernism." *Romanticism, Modernism, Postmodernism.* Edited by Harry R. Garvin. Lewisburg, Pa.: Bucknell University Press, 1980.

Kutnik, Jerzy. "On the Modern Element in Modern Literature: A Post-Modern Stance." *Kwartalnik Neofilologiczny* 27 (1980): 385–96.

Lodge, David. *Modernism, Antimodernism and Postmodernism.* Birmingham: University of Birmingham, 1977.

Luetzeler, Paul Michael, and Egon Schwartz, eds. *Deutsche Literatur in der Bundesrepublik seit 1965.* Koenigstein: Athenaeum, 1980.

Lyotard, Jean-Francois. *La Condition postmoderne.* Paris: Minuit, 1979.

Mueller, Heiner. "Reflections on post-modernism." *New German Critique* 16 (1979): 55–57.

Naegele, Rainer. "Modernism and Post-Modernism: The Margins of Articulation." *Studies in Twentieth Century Literature* 5 (1980): 5–25.

New German Critique 22 (1981). Special issue on modernism/postmodernism.

Raulet, Gerard. "The Logic of Decomposition: German Poetry in the 1960's." *New German Critique* 21 (1980): 81–107.

Studies in Twentieth Century Literature 5/1 (1980). Special issue on modernism/postmodernism.

Tisdall, Caroline. *Joseph Beuys.* New York: Solomon R. Guggenheim Museum, 1979.

Touraine, Alain. *The Post-Industrial Society, Tomorrow's Social History: Classes, Conflicts, and Culture in the Programmed Society.* Translated by Leonard F. X. Mayhew. New York: Random House, 1972.

Wilde, Alan. *Horizons of Assent: Modernism, Postmodernism and the Ironic Imagination.* Baltimore and London: Johns Hopkins University Press, 1981.

Winter, Hans-Gerhard. "Von der Dokumentarliteratur zur neuen Subjektivitaet Anmerkungen zur westdeutschen Literatur der siebziger Jahre." *Seminar* 17 (1981): 95–113.

Authors

This bibliography lists texts in English translation by those authors mentioned in the essay, with the exception of Wiener and Fichte, neither of whom has as yet been translated. For more complete bibliographies of contemporary German writers see: *Kritisches Lexikon zur deutschsprachigen Gegenwartsliteratur (KLG)*. Edited by Heinz Ludwig Arnold. Munich: Edition Text und Kritik, 1978ff.

Bernhard, Thomas. *Correction*. Translated by Sophie Wilkins. New York: Knopf, 1979.

———. *The Force of Habit: A Comedy*. Translated by Neville and Stephen Plaice. London: Heinemann Educational, 1976.

———. *Gargoyles*. Translated by Richard Winston and Clara Winston. New York: Knopf, 1970.

———. *The Lime Works*. Translated by Sophie Wilkins. New York: Knopf, 1973.

———. *The President & Eve of Retirement: Two Plays*. Translated by Gitta Honegger. New York: Performing Arts Journal Publications, 1982.

Selections in: Schwebell, Gertrude C., ed. *Contemporary German Poetry: An Anthology*. Norfolk, Conn.: New Directions, 1964; Michael Hamburger, ed. *German Poetry: 1910–1975: An Anthology*. New York: Urizon Books, 1976.

Handke, Peter. *The Goalie's Anxiety at the Penalty Kick*. Translated by Michael Roloff. New York: Farrar, Straus and Giroux, 1972.

———. *The Innerworld of the Outerworld of the Innerworld*. Translated by Michael Roloff. New York: Seabury Press, 1974.

———. *Kaspar, and Other Plays*. Translated by Michael Roloff. New York: Farrar, Straus and Giroux, 1969.

———. *The Left-Handed Woman*. Translated by Ralph Manheim. New York: Farrar, Straus and Giroux, 1978.

———. *A Moment of True Feeling*. Translated by Ralph Manheim. New York: Farrar, Straus and Giroux, 1977.

———. *Offending the Audience. Self Accusation*. Translated by Michael Roloff. New York: Farrar, Straus and Giroux, 1969.

———. *The Ride across Lake Constance*. Translated by Michael Roloff. London: Methuen, 1973.

———. *Short Letter. Long Farewell*. Translated by Ralph Manheim. New York: Farrar, Straus and Giroux, 1974.

———. *A Sorrow beyond Dreams: A Life Story*. Translated by Ralph Manheim. New York: Farrar, Straus and Giroux, 1975.

———. *Three by Peter Handke*. Translated by Ralph Manheim and Michael Roloff. New York: Bard/Avon, 1977.

Selections in: Hamburger, *German Poetry: 1910–1975*.

Heissenbuettel, Helmut. *Texts*. Translated by Michael Hamburger. London: Calder and Boyars, 1977; Lawrence, Mass.: Merrimack Book Service, 1978.

Selections in: *New Young German Poets*. Translated by Jerome Rothenburg. San Francisco: City Lights, 1959; Schwebel, Gertrude C., ed. *Contemporary German Poetry: An Anthology*. Norfolk, Conn.: New Directions, 1964; Hamburger, Michael. *German Poetry: 1910–1975: An Anthology*. New York: Urizon Books,

1976; Russell, Charles, ed. *The Avant-Garde Today: An International Anthology.* Urbana: University of Illinois Press, 1981.

Mueller, Heiner. *Cement.* Translated by Helen Fehervary, Sue-Ellen Case, and Marc D. Silberman. Milwaukee: University of Wisconsin Press, 1978.

Strauss, Botho. *Big & Little.* Translated by Anne Cattaneo. New York: Farrar, Straus and Giroux, 1979.

———. *Devotion.* Translated by Sophie Wilkins. New York: Farrar, Straus and Giroux, 1979.

Wolf, Christa. *Divided Heaven.* Translated by Joan Becker. Berlin: Seven Seas Publications, 1965.

———. *A Model Childhood.* Translated by Ursule Molinaro and Hedwig Rappolt. New York: Farrar, Straus and Giroux, 1980.

———. *No Place on Earth.* Translated by Jan Van Heurck. New York: Farrar, Straus and Giroux, 1982.

———. *The Quest for Christa T.* Translated by Christopher Middleton. New York: Farrar, Straus and Giroux, 1970.

———. *The Reader and Writer: Essays, Sketches, Memories.* Translated by Joan Becker. New York: International, 1978.

Appendix II

Latin American Literature in the Postmodern Era

ALFRED J. MacADAM and FLORA H. SCHIMINOVICH

To understand contemporary Latin America, it is essential to understand that Latin America does not in fact exist. "Latin America" as an idea is a foreign (actually French) invention, a misnomer, since it excludes both the African and Amerindian components of the region's culture. Nevertheless, we will continue to use the term Latin America here as a shorthand reference that stands for the geographical zone that includes the Caribbean basin, Mexico, Central America, and South America. One distinction we must make in discussing the literature of the entire region is that between Brazil and the Spanish-speaking nations of the New World. This distinction is necessary because Brazil's literary history is so different from that of the Spanish-speaking nations. We shall first discuss the development of literature in Spanish America and then pass on to Brazil.

Modern Spanish American literature begins with the cultural movement called *Modernismo*, the transformation of Spanish American literature that makes possible both the avant-garde of the early decades of our century and the new writing of the Spanish American world.

The *modernista* period in Spanish America begins, roughly, in 1880 and ends around 1920. During that period, Spanish American writers consciously attempted to bring their literary language up to date by imitating foreign, mostly French literary models. Spanish American *modernismo* combines aspects of many European literary movements, from romanticism through Parnassianism to symbolism and has no connection with what in English is called "modernism."[1] The Spanish American "modernistas" were attracted by the French poetry of the period, which they saw as an antidote to the excessively empiricist worldview of positivism.

Latin American history over the past two decades has been a history of politically failed societies that have, despite internally and externally generated disasters, managed to produce a rich culture, one that has developed on the margin of official Western society. Cultural development is fundamentally different from economic or political development. Latin American economic independence is a fast-fading mirage, and the creation of Latin American governments that could account for past abuses and lead the people into a future brightened by traditional Western ideals (freedom of speech, life, liberty, the pursuit of happiness) remains only a hope. What we see in so many Latin American nations is an ironic relationship between governments and peoples, a paternalistic censoring of institutions that might threaten central authority. There are exceptions to this rule, of course, but somehow there is always a strongman lurking in the wings of Latin American history. The threat of outside intervention has always been a constant in Latin American history, although foreign powers have usually chosen economic and political coercion rather than direct military invasion. This subtler form of control reminds us that Latin America has always been a cultural colony, an intellectual dependency of Western civilization, although in recent years this situation has begun to change.

The idea that any nation in the West possesses cultural hegemony is either a chimera or a nostalgia. The idea so well expressed in the title of Walter Benjamin's essay, "Paris, Capital of the Nineteenth Century," is an anachronism today. As economic and political hegemony passed after World War II to the United States, so too passed some cultural hegemony. But not all. Unlike France in the nineteenth century, the United States does not concentrate its cultural, political, and economic centers in one place. That the United States is an influence on Latin America is undeniable, and that influence goes further than economics or politics. Latin America has been the avid reader of United States literature since the nineteenth century, when the French symbolists discovered Poe. Latin American intellectuals recognized the importance of our "hard-boiled" school (Dashiell Hammett, Raymond Chandler) long after they had been forgotten in the United States. And the influence of Hollywood on Latin American literature is immense. Writers as diverse as Carlos Fuentes, Mario Vargas Llosa, Manuel Puig, and Guillermo Cabrera Infante all readily admit the importance of American films on their writing, a "vulgar" influence they have transformed into "high art." Thus the influence of the United States, while diffuse and often a negative aspect, is immense in Latin America and is likely, despite politics, to remain so.

Paris in the latter twentieth century is again not the cultural center of the Western world as it was throughout the nineteenth century, but it still retains its prestige for Latin American writers. Like the modernistas of the last century, many Latin American writers and artists make their sentimental pilgrimage to Paris, some, like Julio Cortázar and Severo Sarduy, to become permanent residents. The fact that the most important literary magazine of the Spanish-speaking world during the late 1960s, *Mundo Nuevo*, had its offices in Paris, and that many Latin American intellectuals were associated with UNESCO or the Sorbonne also enhanced the image of Paris as a cultural center, at least for Latin America. But while Paris provides a space in which to locate a lost center, it certainly does not provide today the literary or artistic models that Latin Americans imitated in the nineteenth century.

The interplay between the two worlds—Paris and Buenos Aires—appears in several of Julio Cortázar's short stories and in his novel *Hopscotch* (1963) as well. The double setting allows Cortázar to write simultaneously on two levels. At the level of literary technique, he is able to juxtapose two different concepts of literary time. The Parisian world is crammed with various felt and learned histories, while the Buenos Aires world seems empty, a perpetual present. At the level of theme, he is able to study the problem, which is both Latin American and Argentine, of cultural identity. His characters must find their Latin American, Argentine, identity in Paris. This idea of expatriation as a means to gain perspective on one's homeland is important as well for authors such as the Cuban Alejo Carpentier and the Guatemalan Miguel Angel Asturias, who both sojourned in Paris during the avant-garde twenties and who returned with a fresh vision of Latin American culture and history.

This journey out enabled Latin American writers to see that they could no longer imitate, as did their literary fathers, the *modernistas*, the reigning masters in Paris. Latin

American literature became a trendsetter in its own right not by copying but by parodying European models. It has now returned to the former centers of Western culture their own writing, distorted and reshaped into something new. This is not a rejection of Western culture—parody always entails admiration—but it does involve an inversion, a declaration of cultural independence. And this labor involves not only the writers but their readers as well.

Wolfgang Iser and Hans Robert Jauss have recast traditional literary history to take into account the reader as not merely the consumer of literature but as producer of literary meaning.[2] Their efforts derive in part from their own cultural context. They seek to find a path between the Scylla of Marxist esthetics and the Charybdis of formalism. Each in his own way hopes to recover the historical impact of individual texts, either through a reconstruction of the readership or through a reading of the text that would concentrate on isolating the cues the text provides about how it wants to be read. This last idea, the more feasible of the two projects, is one of the more exciting contemporary critical ideas because it attempts to make the reader aware of the literary work of art as a multifaceted totality that includes instructions for use. This idea has also been enunciated by E. D. Hirsch in his discussion of "implied genres" in *Validity in Interpretation*, where he notes that being unaware of the text's signals about its generic identity leads to improper reading.[3]

Taking the reader, both the reader who was the novelist's or poet's original audience and the reader in the abstract sense of anyone who might be attuned to the text's suggestions about reading, into account makes us aware of the dynamic nature of literary history and of the many ironies inherent in the reading process. Jorge Luis Borges, the progenitor of modern Latin American literature, dramatizes this situation in his brilliant story "Pierre Menard, Author of the Quijote" (1939). Pierre Menard is a minor, provincial, late-symbolist poet and man of letters who one day decides to write (not rewrite!) Cervantes' *Don Quijote*. He reasons that his dim memory of the text corresponds to any writer's first thoughts about a new work and begins to compose. An untimely death prevents him from finishing, and all he leaves behind is chapters nine, thirty-eight, and a fragment of chapter twenty-two (all of Part I). The pious friend (who may well be the mischievous Menard himself) who writes this necrology points out that Menard's *Quijote* and Cervantes' *Quijote* are textually identical. Only their meanings are different. They have to be, since Cervantes was a late-Renaissance Spanish writer and Menard a French symbolist. Thus Borges spoofs the idea of literary meaning. If the text "belongs" to a particular period, then it can only have real meaning for an instant in history. What in fact happens is that each reader recreates the text and transforms it into something completely new.

Thus the meaning of a work varies infinitely, and its impact on a literary tradition is much more a matter of how it is received by a readership than the individual act a heroic author commits. That is, to have an impact a text must be assimilated by an audience (readers, spectators, listeners). And this matter of reception produces the ambiguities attendant on what we call the "meaning" of the text. Mikhail Bakhtin describes this situation in temporal terms:

Before us are two events—the event that is narrated in the work and the event of narration itself (we ourselves participate in the latter, as listeners or readers); these events take place in different times (which are marked by different durations as well) and in different places, but at the same time these two events are indissolubly united in a single but complex event that we might call the work in the totality of all its events, including the external material givenness of the work, and its text, and the world represented in the text, and the author-creator and the listener or reader; thus we perceive the fullness of the work in all its wholeness and indivisibility, but at the same time we understand the diversity of the elements that constitute it.[4]

Each reader, each reading, reconstitutes "the work in the totality of all its events," but each is different, and here we see that Wellek and Warren's "close unity" of Western civilization is a pious fiction. If we fill in Bakhtin's description of the reading process with names, if, for example, we imagine Ruben Dario, the outstanding figure of Spanish American poetry in the late nineteenth century, born in Nicaragua in 1867, reading Mallarmé, we wonder just what Bakhtin's "work in the totality of all its events" might be. Certainly it would be markedly different, although we wonder about the details, from that of Yeats (born in 1865) and Valery (born in 1871). To what extent is any reading of a text by someone not from the author's immediate historic, linguistic, and social context a parody? Here we might again recall Borges and his story about the Hispano-Arabic scholar Averroes trying to write a commentary on Aristotle's poetics without ever having seen a play or knowing what a theatre is.

We must expand the notion of parody to include not only those works an author deliberately creates but those brought into the world by the reader. The fear of incurring these involuntary parodies has always made Latin American writers sensitive to the differences between the cultures in which they live and the "other" culture, that of the metropolitan centers, real or imagined, of the Western world. In this they are different from their counterparts in the United States, at least in the twentieth century, who imagine the Anglo-American tradition to be self-sufficient. Latin American culture constantly reminds itself of its own insufficiency. This notion that the Latin American writer must have one foot firmly planted in local culture and the other in cosmopolitan culture has engendered in recent years a bizarre species of literary history. Ideologically inspired critics divide authors into those who mirror their reality faithfully and those who turn their backs on their reality. The latter group the critics define as "inauthentic" Latin American writers. This separation of the sheep from the goats has, sadly, created a hysteria that declares the writings of the late-nineteenth century *modernistas* (who renovated literary language in the Spanish-speaking world) to be of no value because those authors sold themselves to international capitalism; it also proclaims that Borges (despite the fact that every one of the books he published between 1923 and 1932 deals with Argentina) is no true Argentine and that the novelists of the 1960s wrote only for export and have little to do with their respective countries. To purge these writers from the Spanish American canon would mean, of course, to purge the best of Spanish American writing for purely ideological reasons.

Another result of the application of the reductive fictions of politics as a corrective to literature and literary history is the denial of the hybrid nature of Latin American culture, a fact once used to account for that culture's "belatedness" but that now serves as an index to its vitality. That vigor derives from misreading, both willful and accidental, from Latin America's parodic relationship with the Western tradition. Within Latin America itself, the enigma of that culture's true identity has spawned a polemic we can call "the Caliban controversy." The history of this polemic, which has been summarized by Emir Rodríguez Monegal, begins with the Uruguayan critic José Enrique Rodó, who attempted to formulate a myth that would restore Spanish America's self-esteem in the dark days after the Spanish American War of 1898, which not only signaled the end of Spain's empire in the New World but pointed out the power of the United States vis à vis the disorder of nineteenth-century Spanish America.[5] Rodó, more influenced by Ernest Renan's *Caliban* (1878) than by Shakespeare, wanted Latin Americans to identify their culture with the figure of Ariel, the airy spirit who for Rodó symbolized the refined and the ideal, and to associate the United States with Caliban, the materialistic, the utilitarian, and the ugly.

Rodó was fully aware that his 1900 essay *Ariel* was myth-making, but later generations of Spanish American writers have not treated him charitably, charging that he was blind to the realities of Latin America. The charge is unfair, but it does mark an important phenomenon, the inversion of Rodó's original myth, Latin America's identification of itself with Caliban, the cannibal, the exploited native of the island Prospero conquers. The idea that Caliban is the first mestizo in literature, the product of the union of Prospero with the witch Sycorax, is suggested in *The Tempest* (act v, scene 1, line 275), where Prospero ambiguously remarks about Caliban, "This thing of darkness I acknowledge mine." That Latin America is the result of cultural *mestizaje* is an undeniable fact, one that Latin Americans considered a handicap (Rodó's identification of Latin America with Ariel is symptomatic of his desire to emphasize the European heritage of Latin America and to forget its black and Indian heritage) at least until the Brazilian modernistas of the 1920s founded the *Revista de Antropofagia* (1928–29). They declared that their relationship to the West was and would be cannibalistic. They would ingest Western culture and make it into something new by fusing it with their own being.

The result is parody. Bakhtin describes the stages in literary production that lead to parody. He begins with "stylization," "an artistic representation of another's linguistic style, an artistic image of another's language." Parody is different from stylization because:

the intentions of the representing discourse are at odds with the intentions of the represented discourse; they fight against them, they depict a real world of objects not by using the represented language as a productive point of view, but rather by using it as an exposé to destroy the represented language. This is the nature of *parodic stylization.*[6]

If we were to use Bakhtin's notions of stylization and parody as an approach to Spanish American literary history, expanding it to include poetry as well as prose, we could say that the late nineteenth century and the early twentieth century (from 1880 to 1920), the period of Spanish American *modernismo*, was a time of stylization, while the period since 1920 has been marked by a tendency toward parody. If we understand *modernismo* as an attempt to bring the literary language of the Spanish-speaking world up to date by incorporating into it the literary languages of other nations, France especially, we see why it was a conscious effort at stylization and why it was bound to arouse xenophobic wrath. That *modernismo* entailed stylization does not automatically mean that it produced derivative or inferior literature—this would be a romantic prejudice, a privileging of originality above all other qualities—but it does mean that *modernismo* was more successful in certain areas, lyric for example, than it was in others (the novel would be the example in this case).

Even after 1920, the Spanish American novel was weak in comparison with the lyric, especially because of such strong poets as Pablo Neruda and Cesar Vallejo. There are many explanations for this narrative weakness, ranging from a dearth of novel-readers to the theory that the Hispanic genius expressed itself best in verse. There is probably some truth (or half-truth) in each of these ideas, but they ignore the nature of the novel actually being produced in Spanish America in the late nineteenth and early twentieth century. It too is a stylization, a use of someone else's literary style to represent (since it aspired to realism) Spanish American reality. The problem was that the devices of realism and naturalism were not suited to the re-creation of Spanish American reality. The result, with some exceptions, was a mass of well-intentioned but derivative texts, books whose models were all too clear.

In Brazil, however, the transition from stylization to parody took place during the period of Spanish American *modernismo*, and a radically different kind of prose fiction appeared. This emerged in the writings of Joaquim Maria Machado de Assis (1839– 1908), who inaugurated, with the publication of *As Memorias Postumas de Bras Cubas* (1880), the modern Latin American satiric novel. Flying in the face of realism, Machado chose fantasy and has his novel narrated by a dead man. This use of the fantastic together with his decision to reduce character to stereotype and his presentation of society as a madhouse without walls set him apart from his contemporaries, both in Brazil and in Spanish America. Why Machado should have written in this vein is one of the mysteries of literary history, but one to which literary history may provide at least a provisional solution. Machado as a reader seems to have found the English eighteenth-century novel, particularly *Tristram Shandy*, more congenial as material for stylization than, say, the novels of Flaubert. He turned to that satiric novel and found a structure he could adapt to a representation of Brazilian reality with more success than he would have had if he had attempted to rewrite *Madame Bovary* in Brazilian terms. This is not to say Flaubert did not influence Machado. He did, but not at the level of characterization and literary structure.

Bras Cubas is a stylization of Sterne used to create a caricature of nineteenth-century Brazilian life. Its style derives from eighteenth-century models and its structure certainly derives from *Tristram Shandy*. The English novelists of the nineteenth century, particularly Thackeray and Dickens, also show the lasting influence of eighteenth-century satire. We see it when Thackeray refers to his characters at the end of *Vanity Fair* as puppets and when Dickens uses transparently satiric names for his characters (Smallweed, Guppy). It was that same tendency toward social satire and caricature that attracted Machado and moved him away from the psychological realism of the French novel, and the mixture of fantasy (from the preternatural to the supernatural) and satiric stylization has become the hallmark of Latin American narrative in our century, a truly Calibanesque literature that stands the immediate tradition of realism on its head.

Why the mechanisms of realism were not suitable for the representation of Latin American life, why the novel took so long to develop in Latin America are problems for which literary history offers no real solutions. The transition from stylization to parody, our adaptation of Bakhtin's terms, which constitute no progression in his essay, is nothing more than an explanatory metaphor. It seeks to connect two phases of Latin American literary production while retaining the idea that this production is closely related to the way in which Latin American writers read the literature of the Western world. The phase of stylization views that outside literature as a source of models to imitate and acclimate to the Latin American milieu, while the phase of parody sees Western literary texts as raw material to be absorbed and transformed into something new, something quite strange, for both Latin American and non-Latin American readers. This is a clear inversion of the colonial economic system where, traditionally, the colonies supply the metropolis with raw material that the metropolis turns into manufactured goods and resells to the colonies.

The origin of this inversion, leaving aside the unique case of Machado de Assis, is history itself, the legacy of World War I and Oswald Spengler's seminal book *The Decline of the West* (1918). It was the spectacle of that war, which brought France, England, Germany, and Russia to the brink of disaster, together with Spengler's meditations on the life cycle of cultures that made Latin America momentarily turn its back on Europe and look for cultural inspiration within itself. The decline of Europe (the title of Spengler's book in the Russian translation) was an all-pervading axiom throughout the twenties and was circulated in Latin America by Ortega y Gasset's ironically titled magazine *Revista de Occidente*, which published Spengler. We see the results, both of the general idea of European decline and of Spengler's book, in the young Borges, who read Spengler in German and wrote about him frequently during the twenties and thirties. It was during those years that Borges sought to create an esthetic program that was non-European and consonant with what he thought best in Argentine life, the semi barbarous *criollo*.[7]

The totally Europeanized Borges of 1925 could never purge himself of a European culture that was part of his very essence, but his search for a native esthetics is symptomatic of Latin America's changing relationship with the West. Borges' search (the Borges of the twenties was a poet-essayist, not a writer of prose fiction) for a truly Argentine literary language was a means whereby he could declare his own independence from Europe and attack the Spanish American *modernistas*, particularly Ruben Dario, for being the apes of European decadence. Borges' rejection of Dario's stylization of Parnassian and symbolist poetry is an individual's move toward parody and is characteristic of the playful Latin American avant-garde of the early decades of this century.

In 1949, the Cuban writer Alejo Carpentier rather belatedly repeated the Spenglerian assault on Europe in his preface to *El reino de este mundo*. In that preface, Carpentier specifically rejects most of the modern literature of Europe, from the gothic novel to surrealism, on the grounds that it tries to create the marvelous through artificial means, that is, that it seeks to create supernatural effects for readers who do not believe in the supernatural.[8] The Americas, Carpentier argues, need no such artificiality because they are infused with a "real marvelous" ("real maravilloso"). However illusory an act of cultural self-assertion such as this one may appear—Carpentier's discovery of America's "real marvelous" is no more fanciful than Rodó's identification of Latin America with Ariel in 1900—they are necessary in the parodic phase of Latin American literature because they allow the writer to project an independent self-image, one that permits him to delineate his own literary space.

That space is made up of words, a style that identifies the individual writer by revealing both what he is and what he is not. But literary language in the parodic phase of Latin American literature comes into being as the result of the writer's ironic awareness of the dual nature of Latin American culture, its being a compound of local and external elements juxtaposed and made to clash. For Latin American prose fiction, which has eclipsed poetry since the sixties, this has resulted in a generalized hybridization. For Bakhtin, the idea of hybridization is essential to literary prose, especially the novel:

the novelistic hybrid is an *artistically organized system for bringing different languages in contact with one another*, a system having as its goal the illumination of one language by means of another, the carving-out of a living image of another language.[9]

For Latin American prose fiction, hybridization has meant that texts have become galleries of literary voices rather than transcriptions of reality. Following the esthetic lead of Borges, whose influence in Spanish America as artist, critic, and translator (of Virginia Woolf and William Faulkner, among others) has been immense, writers have come to the paradoxical conclusion that language is their only reality although, at the same time, that reality is illusory. That is, the Latin American novelist has become acutely aware of his own language in all its permutations: the spoken language (at all social and esthetic levels), written (at all social and esthetic levels), and the relation of that language to external languages, the spoken and written languages of the West. The result is a baroque intermingling of forms of discourse, a literary language that is simultaneously local and cosmopolitan, a reflection of specific times and places and a stylization.

For example, Cabrera Infante's *Three Trapped Tigers* makes considerable use of linguistic parody and wordplay. The novel is rife with puns and reflections on the nature of language. The basic metaphor at the center of *TTT* is the notion that esthetic (verbal) representation is betrayal. *TTT* is a symphony of betrayal in which photographers, whose mode of expression is visual, tell the stories of bolero singers or experts in punmanship, whose essence is the living voice. A bongo player tells the story of a singer whose physical beauty makes up for her lack of musical talent. The book examines as well the idea of translation, where one medium uses its languages to describe, ultimately to deform, another. Cabrera Infante's second novel, *Infante's Inferno*, has a rather different intention. Instead of chronicling the lives of characters who betray each other, it plunges a single character into a futile search for identity, one that ends when he realizes that the quest itself is an act of self-deception. In both works, melancholy is tempered by parody and wordplay.

Self-consciousness is one of the traits that typify the parodic literature of Latin America. In a sense it recalls Milton's attitude toward the Renaissance. Milton, an artist of baroque sensibility, feels obliged to include all the tropes, all devices, not only of the classical epics but of all the Renaissance epics in *Paradise Lost*. At the same time, he is impelled to show his knowledge of contemporary science. He feels a literary *horror vacui*, and the result is an intellectually overloaded text. The same is true for many Latin American writers. They know a great deal and require their readers to know at least as much. They seek to construct encyclopedic books, texts that are pedagogic as well as esthetic enterprises.

We may take as examples works like Gabriel García Márquez's *One Hundred Years of Solitude* (1967), Carlos Fuentes' *Terra Nostra* (1976), and Mario Vargas Llosa's *The War of the End of the World* (1983). These novels are compilations of myths, theories of art, literature, history, and forays into anthropology and sociology—all at the same time. They are encyclopedic narratives that call into question, because of their considerable learning, the very ideas of cognition and epistemology as well as the fundamental myths of Latin American culture. *One Hundred Years of Solitude* may in fact be called a Latin American death wish, since in it García Márquez chronicles the birth, growth, decay, and death of a Latin American community that constitutes a metaphor for Latin America itself.

Terra Nostra is an encyclopedic narrative that requires patient and devoted readers. It deals with all the myths of the Spanish and Spanish American world as a simultaneity, so that while the novel opens in what may well be a Paris of the future, it moves easily into the Spain of Philip II in order to study the relationship between Don Quijote, Don Juan, and the go-between Celestina. Mario Vargas Llosa is also fascinated by historical problems. His *The War of the End of the World* is both a historical novel and a parody of the historical novel. Vargas Llosa tells in that huge novel that Latin American history is incomprehensible if we use the framework of Western historiography, that we can only understand it fully in the context of a fiction. Vargas Llosa emphasizes the fictionality, the impossibility of the events he describes (which are historical) by narrating them in such a way that they are all jumbled together. Instead of the chronological development of conventional historical novels, the events of *The War of the End of the World* all seem to occur simultaneously. The text appears to negate ideas of order and progress, leaving the reader continually *in* medias res.

Another writer deeply concerned with Latin American life, with those banal or trivial aspects of it that cannot become history, but which yet constitute reality is Manuel Puig. His parody of the traditional novel derives from his rewriting of such popular forms as serial, soap operas, and sentimental movies. His characters often derive their sense of human relationships from popular music (tangos or boleros) and are therefore obsessed with romantic and sentimental dreams. *Betrayed by Rita Hayworth* (1968), *Heartbreak Tango* (1970), and *The Buenos Aires Affair* (1973) exemplify Puig's parodistic borrowing from popular culture. A later fiction, *The Kiss of the Spider Woman* is a political novel, but one in which the characters use popular movies to project and relive their fantasies while in prison.

José Donoso's novels play with the possibilities of meaning and form in a self-conscious way. In *The Obscene Bird of Night* (1969), the conventional distinction between art and artist disappears and the narrative itself is a monstrous creator, incapable of doing anything except narrating, creating stories in its own grotesque image. *A House in the Country* shares some of the phantasmagoric writing of *The Obscene Bird*, but at the same time it is a mystery story. The reader is invited to determine for himself just what is real and unreal in the narrative, what is historical and what is invented. It is a malignant sort of pastoral, a visit to a country house that is, like a detective novel, a setting outside of time and yet within it.

The most significant development of the past decade has been a Renaissance of Latin American women's fiction. And foremost among Latin American women writers is the Brazilian Clarice Lispector. Her first novel, *Perto do Coraçao Selvagem* (1944), already anticipates the dazzling poetic imagination she displays in *Agua Viva* (1973). Her career was a long one, and her recognition was slow in coming. French feminist critics use her writings as a model of feminine writing, especially with regard to the idea of the inscription of the female body and female differences in language and writing. Lispector's parodic stance involves a constant play with language. In her novels she destroys and re-creates the meaning of words, inverts traditional metaphoric associations, and draws her imagery from antithetical sources. Lispector's fictive world is preponderantly female, but her writings point to the possibility of a language that resists fixity and binary (male-female) oppositions. Hers is a language in the process of being reinvented.

Two other writers typify contemporary trends in contemporary Latin American women's literature. Luisa Valenzuela's novel *El gato eficaz* (1972) also deals with language and wit to play with traditional concepts of women and myth. In her novel, the cats are linguistic reactions that undergo metamorphosis and are treated as scapegoats. Valenzuela's humor has a directly social target. She wants to change her world through writing. Elena Poniatowska's writings seek to reconcile language and experience (instead of pointing to their differences, as Valenzuela does) in order to create an image of Mexican culture. Her favorite devices are humor and fantasy, which she uses to awaken the reader's consciousness and to oblige the reader to question social conventions. In her novel *Hasta no verte Jesus mío* (1969), she records the anecdotes of a working-class woman (a real person), from the time of the Mexican Revolution (1910–20) until today. This woman, like the rest of Poniatowska's female characters, refuses to submit to male-dominated society. Poniatowska herself mirrors that rebellious attitude by parodying the idea of mimesis or literary realism. She challenges a literature that represses the feminine and she seeks to open new paths of communication between the sexes.

Parody has enabled Latin American literature to find its own space in the Western world. It is the means by which a culture is able to express both its social concerns and its aesthetic dilemmas. It has given a literary voice to groups and subjects hitherto excluded from Latin American literature, which has succeeded in making its presence known throughout the world. Those who feel the need for a regeneration of Western literature may well find it in Latin America. The voice of the repressed is now returning, not to condemn the rest of us, but to teach us its valuable lessons.

NOTES

1. Octavio Paz, *Children of the Mire* (Cambridge, Mass.: Harvard University Press, 1974): "Toward 1880 the literary movement called modernismo appeared in Spanish America. Let me clarify my terms: Spanish American modernismo is, to a certain extent, the equivalent of French Parnassianism and Symbolism, and so has no connection with what in English is called 'modernism.' Modernism refers to the literary and artistic movements that began in the second decade of the twentieth century; as used by North American and English critics, it is what in France and the Hispanic countries we call vanguardia, the avant-garde.'' (pp. 88–89)

2. Wolfgang Iser, *The Act of Reading: A Theory of Aesthetic Response* (Baltimore: Johns Hopkins University Press, 1978); Hans Robert Jauss, "Literary History as a Challenge to Literary Theory," *New Literary History* 11 (Autumn 1970): 7–37.

3. E. D. Hirsch, *Validity in Interpretation* (New Haven, Conn.: Yale University Press, 1971), pp. 78–79.

4. M. M. Bakhtin, *The Dialogic Imagination: Four Essays*, ed. Michael Holquist (Austin: University of Texas Press, 1981), p. 255.

5. Emir Rodríguez Monegal, "The Metamorphoses of Caliban," *Diacritics* (September 1977): 7–83.

6. Bakhtin, *The Dialogic Imagination*, pp. 362, 364.

7. Alfred MacAdam, "Borges the *criollo*: 1923–1932," *Review* 28 (January-April 1981): 65–68.

8. We refer to the essay "De lo real maravilloso americano," first published as a preface to *El reino de este mundo* and later, in an expanded form, included in the collection of essays *Tientos y differencias* (1964). For a description of Spengler's influence on Alejo Carpentier, see: Roberto Gonzalez Echevarria, *The Pilgrim at Home* (Ithaca, N.Y.: Cornell University Press, 1983). A more detailed analysis of the influence of Spengler on Carpentier, including a description of the French Spenglerian Pierre Mabille appears in: Irlemar Chiampi, *O Realismo Maravilhoso: Forma e Ideologia no Romance Hispano-Americano* (São Paulo: Editora Perspectiva, 1980), esp. pp. 31–39.

9. Bakhtin, *The Dialogic Imagination*, p. 361.

ANNOTATED BIBLIOGRAPHY

Bacarisse, Salvador, ed. *Contemporary Latin American Fiction*. Edinburgh: Scottish Academic Press, 1980. A selection of essays about Carpentier, Roa Bastos, García Márquez, Fuentes, Sabato, Onetti, and José Donoso.

Brotherston, Gordon. *The Emergence of the Latin American Novel*. Cambridge: Cambridge University Press, 1977. Analytical studies of contemporary Latin American novels representative of their time, authors, and countries. Carpentier, Onetti, Rulfo, Cortázar, Vargas Llosa, and García Márquez are among the authors studied.

Donoso, José. *The Boom in Spanish American Literature. A Personal History*. Translated by Gregory Kolovakos. New York: Columbia University Press, 1977. A personal account of the boom by one of its writers.

Gallagher, D. P. *Modern Latin American Literature*. London: Oxford University Press, 1973. Examines the motivating concepts, complex structures, and distinctive language and imagery of Jorge Luis Borges, García Márquez, Neruda, Cabrera Infante, Vallejo, Vargas Llosa, and Octavio Paz and places their works in the context of both current trends and the traditions of Latin American letters.

MacAdam, Alfred J. *Modern Latin American Narratives*. Chicago: University of Chicago Press, 1977. The book links the developments in Contemporary Latin American literature to a unifying narrative theory. The essays focus on writings by Machado de Assis, Bioy Casares, J. Cortázar, Donoso, García Márquez, and Lezama Lima, among others.

Meyer, Doris, and Margarite Fernandez Olmos, eds. *Contemporary Women Authors of Latin America, New Translations*. New York: Brooklyn College Press, 1983. Translations in three genres: poetry, theatre, and narrative. Rosario Castellanos, Cristina Peri Rosi, and Alejandra Pizarnik are among the authors translated.

————. eds. *Contemporary Women Authors of Latin America. Introductory Essays*. New York: Brooklyn College Press, 1983. Seven essays about contemporary Latin American female writers like Maria Luisa Bombal, Rosario Ferré, and Agueda Pizarro, among others.

Miller, Yvette, and Charles Tatum. *Latin American Women Writers: Yesterday and Today*. Pittsburgh: Latin American Literary Review, 1977. Proceedings from the Conference of Women Writers from Latin America held in 1975 at Carnegie Mellon University. The essays study several contemporary Latin American female writers and serve as an important point of departure for feminist studies in Latin American literature.

Paz, Octavio. *Children of the Mire*. Cambridge, Mass.: Harvard University Press, 1974. An analysis of the modern poetic movement and its contradictory relationships with what we call "the modern." The book discusses the crisis of the idea of the modern in literature and the arts and the end of the avant-garde movement toward the second half of our century.

Rodríguez Monegal, Emir. *The Borzoi Anthology of Latin American Literature*. Vol. 2. *The Twentieth Century*. New York: Alfred A. Knopf, 1977. Selected and edited with introductions by Emir Rodríguez Monegal, the book presents a varied selection of Latin American contemporary authors (including Brazilian) and a complete rereading for the poststructuralist era. Emphasis on the poetic avant-garde, Borges, Cortázar, Donoso, Carlos Fuentes, García Márquez, and other important figures.

The most important magazines devoted to the study of contemporary Latin American writers are *Revista Iberoamericana*, published by the University of Pittsburgh, and *Latin America Literary Review*, published by the same university. *World Literature Today* (formerly *Books Abroad*) is published by the University of Oklahoma and has several issues devoted to the study of Latin American authors. *Review* is published by the Center for Interamerican Relations, *Hispamérica* is published by the University of Maryland. *Latin American Fiction Today* is a selection of volumes from the symposiums that took place at Montclair State College in New Jersey. Published by Hispamérica and edited by Rose S. Minc, the volumes include essays about the most important figures in Latin American fiction. For studies of individual authors it is necessary to consult the selected bibliographies which appear in the magazines already mentioned and other selected information sources.

Chronology: 1960–84

Disciplines		World and National Events
	1960	
Architecture	Philip Johnson, New Harmony Church, New Harmony, Ind.	Sit-ins begin when blacks are refused service at lunch counters in the South
Art	Claes Oldenburg, *Snapshots from the City* show	Launching of first U.S. weather satellite
	Frank Stella, First individual show at Leo Castelli Gallery	
	Sixteen Americans exhibition at MOMA	Adolph Eichmann captured
	George Maciunas, Fluxus Manifesto	American U-2 reconnaissance plane shot down over Soviet territory
	Jasper Johns, *Painted Bronze*	
Dance	Simone Forti, *See Saw*; *Rollers*	Independence proclaimed for former Belgian Congo
Literature	John Barth, *The Sot Weed Factor*	
	Leslie Fiedler, *Love and Death in the American Novel*	John Fitzgerald Kennedy elected thirty-fifth president
	Isaac Bashevis Singer, *The Magician of Lublin*	
	John Updike, *Rabbit Run*	Death of Clark Gable (b. 1901)
	Deaths of Albert Camus (b. 1913), Boris Pasternak (b. 1890), Richard Wright (b. 1908)	
Music	Lukas Foss, *Time Cycle*	
Theatre	Eugene Ionesco, *Rhinoceros*	
	Edward Albee, *The Sandbox*	

Disciplines		World and National Events

1961

Architecture	Jane Jacobs, *The Death and Life of Great American Cities*	Peace Corps established
		Bay of Pigs invasion
Art	Clement Greenberg, *Art and Culture*	Alan Shepard becomes first American in space
	Morris Louis, *Alfa Delta, Sigma*	
Dance	Simone Forti, "Five Dance Constructions + Some Other Things"	$700 million program for fallout shelters proposed by Office of Emergency Planning
	Yvonne Ranier, *Three Satie Spoons*; *The Bells*	Deaths of Ty Cobb (b. 1886), Dag Hammarskjold (b. 1905)
Film	Bruce Conner, *Cosmic Ray*	
	Ken Jacobs, *The Death of P'town*	Nonaligned nations meet in Belgrade, Yugoslavia
Literature	John Hawkes, *The Lime Twig*	
	Joseph Heller, *Catch-22*	
	Bernard Malamud, *A New Life*	
	Claude Lévi-Strauss, *Tristes Tropiques*	
	Isaac Bashevis Singer, *The Spinoza of Market Street*	
	Deaths of Ernest Hemingway (b. 1899), James Thurber (b. 1894)	
Music	Withold Lutoslawski, *Venetian Games*	
	John Cage, *Silence*, Variations II	
Photography	Harry Callahan, *The Multiple Image*	
Theatre	Edward Albee, *The American Dream*; *The Death of Bessie Smith*	
	Harold Pinter, *The Collection*	
	Samuel Beckett, *Happy Days*	

1962

Architecture	Robert Venturi, Vanna Venturi House, Chestnut Hill, Penn.	John Glenn becomes first American to orbit the earth
	Le Corbusier, Parliament Building, Chandigarh, India	Seattle World's Fair opens with theme "Man in the Space Age"
	Eero Saarinen, TWA Terminal, Kennedy International Airport, New York	Supreme Court in *Baker* v. *Carr* rules against discriminatory apportionment of seats in state

Disciplines	World and National Events

Art

Andy Warhol, *One Hundred Campbell's Soup Cans*
Sidney Janis opens New Realists show which launches pop art
Roy Lichtenstein, *Blam*

legislature; in *Engel* v. *Vitale* Court rules against reading prayer in public school

Dance

First concert by Judson Dance Theater and weekly workshops through 1964
Yvonne Ranier, *Three Seascapes*; *Ordinary Dance*
Trisha Brown, *Trillium*

Telstar communications satellite launched

James Watson and Francis Crick win Nobel Prize for discovering configuration of DNA molecule

Film

Robert Breer, *Horse Over Teakettle*
Ken Jacobs, *Blonde Cobra*

James Meredith becomes first black enrolled in University of Mississippi

Literature

Jorge Luis Borges, *Ficciones*
Vladimir Nabokov, *Pale Fire*
Philip Roth, *Letting Go*
Kurt Vonnegut, *Mother Night*
John Steinbeck awarded Nobel Prize

Cuban missile crisis

Deaths of Eleanor Roosevelt (b. 1884); Marilyn Monroe (b. 1926)

Music

John Cage, *O'O''*
Earle Brown, *Novara*
First publication of *Perspectives of New Music*

Theatre

Edward Albee, *Who's Afraid of Virginia Woolf?*; *The Zoo Story*
Peter Brook joins Royal Shakespeare Company
Ellen Stewart opens La Mama Theatre

1963

Architecture

James Stirling, Engineering Building Leicester, England
Mies van der Rohe, National Gallery, Berlin

Supreme Court in *Gideon* v. *Wainwright* rules indigent defendants must be offered free legal counsel

Art

Roy Lichtenstein, *Torpedo . . . Los!*, *Okay Hot Shot, Okay*
Andy Warhol, Marilyn Monroe Diptych
Nam June Paik shows video art at Galerie Parnass, Wuppertal, West Germany
George Segal, *Cinema*
Ed Ruscha, *Standard Station, Amarillo, Texas*

Martin Luther King, Jr., leads demonstrations in Alabama

Project Mercury completed with Gordon Cooper's twenty-two orbits around the earth

Nuclear test ban treaty signed by United States, Great Britain, and Soviet Union

Disciplines

Dance Judson Dance Theater, Concerts
#3–13
Judith Dunn, *Acapulco*,
"Motorcycle"
Yvonne Ranier, *Terrain*; *Room
Service* (with Charles Ross)
Robert Rauschenberg, *Pelican*
Beverly Schmidt, *Blossoms*
Trisha Brown, *Lightfall*
Lucinda Childs, *Pastime*

Film Andy Warhol, *Tarzan and Jane
Regained . . . Sort of*; *Haircut*
Jack Smith, *Flaming Creatures*

Literature Bernard Malamud, *Idiots First*
Bruce J. Friedman, *Stern*
Joyce Carol Oates, *By the North
Gate*
Thomas Pynchon, *V*
John Updike, *The Centaur*
Deaths of Robert Frost (b. 1874),
Van Wyck Brooks (b. 1886),
Aldous Huxley (b. 1894)

Music Lukas Foss, *Echoi*
Death of Paul Hindemith (b. 1895)

Theatre Joseph Chaikin founds Open
Theatre
Living Theatre stages Kenneth
Brown's *The Brig*
Death of Clifford Odets (b. 1906)

World and National Events

Regime of South Vietnam President
Ngo Dinh Diem overthrown
following protests including self-
immolation of Buddhist monks

President Kennedy assassinated;
Lyndon Baines Johnson sworn in as
thirty-sixth president

Death of Pope John XXIII (Angelo
Roncalli, b. 1881)

1964

Architecture Gordon Bunshaft, Bieneke Library,
New Haven, Conn.
Minoru Yamasaki, Consolidated
Gas Building, Detroit

Art Post-Painterly Abstraction show
opens at Los Angeles County
Museum
New York State Pavilion at world's
fair decorated by pop artists
Robert Rauschenberg, First American
to win grand prize at Venice
Biennale
Frank Stella, *Ifafa II*, *Quathlamba*

Civil Rights Act establishes Equal
Opportunity Commission

Senate passes Tonkin Gulf
resolution

Lyndon Baines Johnson defeats
Barry Goldwater for presidency

Disciplines		World and National Events

Dance

Lucinda Childs, *Street Dance*,
  Carnation
Deborah Hay, *Victory 14*
Elaine Summers, *Fantastic Gardens*
Kenneth King, *cup/saucer/two
  dancers/radio*

Film

Robert Breer, *First Fight*
Kenneth Anger, *Scorpio Rising*
Stan VanDerBeek, *Breathdeath*
Stan Brakhage, *Dog Star Man*
Andy Warhol, *Empire, Eat, Henry
  Geldzahler*

Literature

Samuel Beckett, *How It Is*
Saul Bellow, *Herzog*
Donald Barthelme, *Come Back, Dr.
  Caligari*
Thomas Berger, *Little Big Man*
Jerome Charyn, *Once Upon a
  Droshky*
John Cheever, *The Wapshot
  Scandal*
Stanley Elkin, *Boswell*
Bruce J. Friedman, *A Mother's
  Kisses*
John Hawkes, *Second Skin*
Marshall McLuhan, *The Gutenberg
  Galaxy*
Charles Simmons, *Powdered Eggs*

Music

Milton Babbitt, *Philomel*
La Monte Young, *The Tortoise, His
  Dreams and Journeys*
Karlheinz Stockhausen,
  Mikrophonie I
Terry Riley, *In C*

Photography

Harry Callahan, *Photographs*
John Szarkowski, *The
  Photographer's Eye* (Exhibition
  at MOMA)

Theatre

Peter Brook stages Peter Weiss'
  Marat/Sade
Sam Shepard, *Cowboys, The Rock
  Garden*
The Living Theatre moves to
  Europe after difficulties wth
  Internal Revenue
Edward Albee, *Tiny Alice*

Disciplines		World and National Events

1965

Architecture	Louis Kahn, Jonas Salk Institute, La Jolla, Calif.	President Johnson announces "Great Society" goals
	Philip Johnson, New York State Theatre, Lincoln Center, New York	Martin Luther King, Jr., leads protest marches in Alabama
	Charles Moore (with D. Lyndon), Sea Ranch, Calif.	United States sends troops to Dominican Republic
	Death of Le Corbusier (Charles Edward Jeanneret, b. 1887)	
Art	James Rosenquist, *The F-111*	Medicare, Voting Rights Acts signed into law
	Three American Painters: Noland, Olitski, Stella (exhibition at Fogg Art Museum, catalog introduction by Michael Fried)	Race riots erupt in Watts area of Los Angeles
	National Endowment for the Arts established	Massive power failure causes blackout in Northeast
	Jules Olitski, *Prince Patutsky Command*	
	Joseph Kosuth, *One and Three Chairs*	Deaths of Winston Churchill (b. 1874), Adlai Stevenson (b. 1900)
Dance	Trisha Brown, *Motor*	
	Robert Morris, *Waterman Switch*	
	Twyla Tharp, *Tank Dive*	
Film	Bruce Baillie, *Quixote*	
	Stan Brakhage, *Metaphors on Vision*	
Literature	Richard Brautigan, *A Confederate General From Big Sur*	
	Michel Foucault, *Madness and Civilization*	
	Norman Mailer, *An American Dream*	
	Kurt Vonnegut, *God Bless You Mr. Rosewater*	
	Death of T. S. Eliot (b. 1885)	
Music	George Crumb, *Eleven Echoes of Autumn*	
	George Rochberg, *Contra mortem et tempus*	
Photography	Aaron Siskind, *Aaron Siskind: Photographer*	
	Edward Weston, *Edward Weston: The Flame of Recognition* (edited by Nancy Newhall)	

Disciplines		World and National Events
Theatre	Harold Pinter, *The Homecoming* Sam Shepard, *Chicago* Living Theatre stages *Frankenstein*	

1966

Architecture	Charles Moore, Moore House, New Haven, Conn. Paul Rudolph, Art and Architecture Building, New Haven, Conn. Aldo Rossi, *L'Architettura della Citta* Robert Venturi, Guild House, Philadelphia, *Complexity and Contradiction in Architecture*	President of General Motors admits company investigated Ralph Nader, whose book *Unsafe at Any Speed* was critical of automobile industry Supreme Court in *Miranda* v. *State of Arizona* rules police may not interrogate suspects until informing them of their rights
Art	Sol LeWitt, *Serial Project No. 1* Primary Structures exhibition opens at The Jewish Museum Death of Hans Hofmann (b. 1880)	Death of Walt Disney (b. 1901)
Dance	Meredith Monk, *16 Millimeter Earrings* Rudy Perez, *Countdown* Twyla Tharp, *Re-Moves* Nine Evenings, Theater and Technology	
Film	Peter Kubelka, *Our Trip to Africa* Tony Conrad, *The Flicker* Andy Warhol, *The Velvet Underground, Chelsea Girls*	
Literature	Robert Coover, *The Origin of the Brunists* Joseph McElroy, *A Smuggler's Bible* Stanley Elkin, *Criers and Kibbitzers, Kibbitzers and Criers* Northrop Frye, *Anatomy of Criticism* Thomas Pynchon, *The Crying of Lot 49* Lionel Trilling, *Beyond Culture*	
Music	Steve Reich, *It's Gonna Rain, Come Out*	
Photography	John Szarkowski, *The Photographer's Eye* *Contemporary Photographers: Toward a Social Landscape*, edited by Nathan Lyons	

Disciplines   ## World and National Events

Theatre   Edward Albee, *A Delicate Balance*
                   Jean Genet, *The Screens*
                   Peter Handke, *Offending the*
                       Audience, Prophesy, Self
                       Accusation
                   Open Theatre stages Megan Terry's
                       Viet Rock at La Mama and Jean-
                       Claude van Itallie's America
                       Hurrah, Interview, and *Motel*

1967

Architecture   Michael Graves, Hanselmann   Race riots in Newark and Detroit
                   House, Ft. Wayne, Ind.   among the worst that break out
                                                       across the country

Art   Alfred Leslie, *Alfred Leslie*
                   Sol LeWitt "Paragraphs on   Thurgood Marshall becomes first
                       Conceptual Art"   black associate justice of the
                   Death of Ad Reinhardt (b. 1913)   Supreme Court
                   David Hockney, *A Bigger Splash*
                                                       Apollo program to reach the moon
Dance   Simone Forti, *Faces Tunes, Cloths* begins with liftoff of Saturn 5
                   Deborah Hay, *Group I*   rocket
                   Steve Paxton, *Satisfying Lover*
                                                       U.S. population reaches 200 million

Film   Michael Snow, *Wavelengths*
                   Peter Gidal, *Room (Double Take)*   Israel defeats combined Arab armies
                                                       in Six Day War

Literature   Donald Barthelme, *Snow White*
                   Roland Barthes, *Writing Degree*   Biafra declares independence from
                       Zero   Nigeria
                   Richard Brautigan, *Trout Fishing in*
                       America, In Watermelon Sugar
                   Jerry Bumpus, *Anaconda*
                   Jerome Charyn, *Going to Jerusalem*
                   William Gass, *Omensetter's Luck*
                   Norman Mailer, *Why Are We in*
                       Vietnam?
                   Philip Roth, *When She Was Good*

Music   Lukas Foss, *Baroque Variations*
                   Steve Reich, *Slow Motion Sound*

Photography   New Documents exhibit at MOMA
                   Paul Caponigro, *Paul Caponigro*

Theatre   Sam Shepard, *La Turista*
                   Tom Stoppard, *Rosencrantz and*
                       Guildenstern Are Dead

1968

Architecture   I. M. Pei, Everson Museum,   Viet Cong launch "Tet" offensive
                   Syracuse, N.Y.

Disciplines	World and National Events
	Louis Kahn, Medical Research Building, Philadelphia James Stirling, Cambridge University History Faculty, Cambridge, England	U.S.S. *Pueblo* Navy intelligence ship captured by North Korean navy Senator Eugene McCarthy wins 42 percent of vote in New Hampshire Democratic presidential primary
Art	Wayne Thiebaud, *Girl With Blue Shoes* Art for Peace exhibition at Paula Cooper Gallery, containing Sol LeWitt's first wall drawings Richard Serra, *Prop*	Democratic Convention in Chicago marked by violence
Dance	Lucinda Childs *Untitled Trio* William Dunas, *Gap* Simone Forti, *Sleepwalkers* Yvonne Ranier, *The Mind Is a Muscle* Trisha Brown, *Planes*	George Wallace runs for president on third party ticket with General Curtis LeMay as running mate Russia and Warsaw Pact allies invade Czechoslovakia
Film	Paul Sharts, *N.O.T.H.I.N.G.*	Supreme Court approves merger of Pennsylvania and N.Y. Central Railroads
Literature	John Barth, *Lost in the Funhouse* Donald Barthelme, *Unspeakable Practices, Unnatural Acts* Jonathan Baumbach, *What Comes Next* Italo Calvino, *Cosmicomics* Robert Coover, *The Universal Baseball Association, J. Henry Waugh, Prop.* Willliam Gass, *In the Heart of the Heart of the Country, Willie Masters' Lonesome Wife* Steve Katz, *The Exaggerations of Peter Prince* Norman Mailer, *The Armies of the Night* John Updike, *Couples*	Richard M. Nixon elected thirty-seventh president France becomes fifth thermoculear power Assassinations of Robert Kennedy (b. 1925), Martin Luther King, Jr. (b. 1929)
Music	George Rochberg, *Tableaux* Karlheinz Stockhausen, *Stimmung* David Del Tredici, *Pop Pourri* Steve Reich, ''Music as a Gradual Process''	
Photography	Robert Heinecken, *Are You Real?*	
Theatre	Peter Brook stages *The Tempest* for Theatre des Nations Jerzy Grotkowski stages *Apocalypsis cum Figuris*	

Disciplines   World and National Events

Peter Handke, *Kaspar*
Living Theatre stages *Mysteries—
    and Smaller Pieces*
Open Theater stages *The Serpent*
Richard Schechner organizes The
    Performance Group, stages
    Dionysus in '69

1969

| Architecture | Michael Graves, Benacerraf House, Princeton, N.J. | Warren Burger becomes Chief Justice of Supreme Court |

Architecture   Michael Graves, Benacerraf House,   Warren Burger becomes Chief
                      Princeton, N.J.   Justice of Supreme Court
                  Robert A. M. Stern, *New
                      Dimensions in American*   Apollo II space mission lands first
                      Architecture   man on the moon
                  Robert Venturi, Lieb House, Long
                      Beach, N.J.   More than 300,000 attend music
                  Deaths of Walter Gropius (b.   festival at Woodstock, N.Y.
                      1883), Ludwig Mies van der
                      Rohe (b. 1886)   Sharon Tate murdered by cult led
                                                            by Charles Manson
Art   Carl Andre, *Lead Piece*
                  Anti-Illusion: Procedures/Materials   Trial of Chicago Eight begins
                      exhibition at Whitney Museum
                  Christo, *Wrapped Coast*, Little   Department of Health, Education
                      Bay, Sidney, Australia   and Welfare bans use of cyclamates
                  Claes Oldenburg, *Lipstick on   as artificial sweetener
                      Catepillar Tracks*, erected at Yale
                      University; *Giant Icebag*   Death of Dwight D. Eisenhower (b.
                                                            1890)
Dance   Trisha Brown, *Man Walking Down
                      the Side of the Building*
                  Meredith Monk, *Juice*
                  Kei Takei, *Light, Part I*

Film   Stan Brakhage, *The Machine of
                      Eden*
                  Ken Jacobs, *Tom, Tom, the Piper's
                      Son*
                  P. Adams Sitney, "Structural
                      Film"
                  Michael Snow, ←———▶
                  Andy Warhol, *Blue Movie*

Literature   Italo Calvino, *T Zero*
                  Robert Coover, *Pricksongs and
                      Descants*
                  John Cheever, *Bullet Park*
                  Joseph McElroy, *Hind's Kidnap*
                  Vladimir Nabokov, *Ada*
                  Philip Roth, *Portnoy's Complaint*

Disciplines   World and National Events

Ishmael Reed, *Yellow Back Radio
  Broke Down*
Kurt Vonnegut, *Slaughterhouse Five*
Rudolph Wurlitzer, *Nog*
Ronald Sukenick, *The Death of the
  Novel and Other Stories*
Joyce Carol Oates, *them*
Samuel Beckett awarded Nobel Prize

Photography   Danny Lyon, *The Destruction of
                       Lower Manhattan*
                     Minor White, *Mirrors, Messages,
                       Manifestations*
                     Garry Winogrand, *The Animals*

Theatre   Samuel Beckett, *Breath*
                     Open Theatre stages *Terminal*

1970

Architecture   Ceasar Pelli, Pacific Design Center,   U.S. troops invade Cambodia
                       Los Angeles, Calif.
                                                               National Guard fires on students at
Art   Richard Estes, *Drugstore*   Kent State University
                     Richard Diebenkorn, *Ocean Park
                       #36*   Senate repeals Tonkin Gulf
                     Robert Smithson, *Spiral Jetty*   resolution
                     Donald Judd, Untitled (Anodized
                       Aluminum, 8 boxes)   Angela Davis arrested in connection
                     Mark Rothko suicide (b. 1903)   with black militant killing of
                     Death of Barnett Newman (b. 1905)   California judge

Dance   Grand Union, Improvisational   Trials begin for soldiers accused of
                       Performances (through 1976)   Mylai massacre
                     Yvonne Ranier, *Continuous
                       Project—Altered Daily*   Environmental Protection Agency
                     Gus Solomons, Jr., *cat#ccs70–10/*   established
                       13NSSR-gsj9M
                                                               Deaths of Charles de Gaulle (b.
Film   Hollis Framton, *Zorn's Lemma*   1890), Gamal Abdel Nasser (b.
                     Ernie Gehr, *Serene Velocity*   1918)
                     Anthology Film Archives founded

Literature   Donald Barthelme, *City Life*
                     Saul Bellow, *Mr. Sammler's Planet*
                     Thomas Berger, *Vital Parts*
                     Richard Brautigan, *Rommel Drives
                       On Deep Into Egypt*
                     Jorge Luis Borges, *The Aleph and
                       Other Stories*
                     William Gass, *Fiction and the
                       Figures of Life*

Disciplines   World and National Events

Steve Katz, *Creamy and Delicious*
Joyce Carol Oates, *The Wheel of
  Love*
Gilbert Sorrentino, *Steelwork*
Eugene Wildman, *Montezuma's
  Ball*
Rudolph Wurlitzer, *Flats*
John Updike, *Bech: A Book*
Death of John Dos Passos (b. 1896)

Music   George Crumb, *Black Angels,
                     Echoes of Time and the River,
                     Ancient Voices of Children*
                   Karlheinz Stockhausen, *Mantra*

Photography   Lee Friedlander, *Self Portrait*
                   Ralph Eugene Meatyard, *Ralph
                     Eugene Meatyard*
                   Duane Michals, *Sequences*
                   Jerry Uelsmann, *Jerry Uelsmann*
                   Minor White, *Being Without Clothes*

Theatre   Peter Brook stages *A Midsummer
                     Night's Dream*

1971

Architecture   Peter Eiseman, House III (for   Supreme Court in *Swann* v.
                     Robert Miller), Lakeville, Conn.   *Charlotte-Mecklenburg Board of
                   James Stirling, Florey Building,   Education* approves school busing
                     Oxford, England
                   Robert Venturi, Brant House,   William Calley convicted of Mylai
                     Greenwich, Conn.   massacre
                   Gordon Bunshaft, LBJ Library,
                     Austin, Tex.   Post Office Department replaced by
                                                         U.S. Postal Service
Dance   Trisha Brown, *Accumulation, Roof
                     Piece*   Voting age lowered from twenty-
                   Meredith Monk, *Vessel*   one to eighteen by twenty-sixth
                   Twyla Tharp, *Eight Jelly Rolls*   Amendment

Film   Hollis Framton, *nostalgia*   Inmate take-over of Attica prison
                   Michael Snow, *La Region Central*   quelled after four days
                   George Landow, *Remedial Reading
                     Comprehension*   Mariner 9 orbits Mars

Literature   Richard Brautigan, *Revenge of the   President Nixon imposes ninety-day
                     Lawn, The Abortion: An   freeze on wages and prices
                     Historical Romance 1966*
                   Italo Calvino, *The Watcher and   Death of Louis Armstrong (b. 1900)
                     Other Stories*
                   Jerome Charyn, *Eisenhower, My
                     Eisenhower*

Disciplines

World and National Events

Don DeLillo, *Americana*
Stanley Elkin, *The Dick Gibson
  Show*
Raymond Federman, *Double or
  Nothing*
John Hawkes, *The Blood Oranges*
Ihab Hassan, *The Dismemberment
  of Orpheus*
Claude Lévi-Strauss, *Mythologiques*
Bernard Malamud, *The Tenants*
Cynthia Ozick, *The Pagan Rabbi
  and Other Stories*
Marshall McLuhan, *Understanding
  Media*
Philip Roth, *Our Gang*
Gilbert Sorrentino, *Imaginative
  Qualities of Actual Things*

Music

Steve Reich, *Drumming*
John Cage, *Sixty-Two Mesostics re
  Merce Cunningham*
Donald Martino, Seven Pious Pieces
Karlheinz Stockhausen, *Sternklang*
Stuart Sherman, *Here and There*
Elliott Carter, String Quartet No. 3
Death of Igor Stravinski (b. 1882)

Photography

Danny Lyon, *Conversations with
  the Dead*
Stephen Shore, *The City*

Theatre

Peter Handke, *The Ride Across
  Lake Constance*

1972

Architecture

Peter Eisenman House VI (Frank
  House), Cornwall, Conn.
Louis Kahn, Kimbell Museum, Ft.
  Worth, Tex.
Michael Graves, Snyderman House,
  Ft. Wayne, Ind.
Dynamiting of Pruitt-Igoe Housing
  Project (Designed by Minoru
  Yamasaki 1955)
Robert Venturi, Denise Scott-
  Brown, Steven Izenour, *Learning
  from Las Vegas*

Art

Lucy Lippard, Six Years: The
  Dematerialization of the Art
  Object
Robert Cottingham, *Roxy*

President Nixon visits Mainland
China

Dow Jones average passes 1,000

President Nixon orders mining of
Haiphong harbor

Alabama Governor George Wallace
shot

Hafez al Assad elected president of
Syria

New York Times begins publication
of Pentagon Papers tracing U.S.
involvement in Vietnam

Disciplines		World and National Events
Dance	Laura Dean, *Circle Dance* David Gordon, *The Matter* Deborah Hay, *Circle Dances* Steve Paxton and others, Contact Improvisation (ongoing)	Watergate break-in conspirators indicted Supreme Court invalidates death penalty
Film	Yvonne Rainer, *Lives of Performers* Jonas Mekas, *Movie Journal*	Peoples Republic of China admitted to United Nations, Nationalist China expelled
Literature	John Barth, *Chimera* Roland Barthes, *Mythologies* Jorge Luis Borges, *Dr. Brodie's Report* Don DeLillo, *End Zone* Jerome Charyn, *The Tar Baby* Michel Foucault, *An Archaeology of Knowledge* Steve Katz, *Saw* Joyce Carol Oates, *Marriages and Infidelities* Ishmael Reed, *Mumbo Jumbo* Gerald Rosen, *Blues for a Dying Nation* Isaac Bashevis Singer, *Enemies* Rudolph Wurlitzer *Quake* Death of Georg Lukacs (b. 1885)	Senate ratifies Strategic Arms Limitation Treaty SALT I Bobby Fischer becomes first American chess champion Richard M. Nixon wins reelection, defeating George McGovern Swimmer Mark Spitz becomes first person to win seven gold medals at Olympics Widespread introduction of natural cereals by commercial firms Deaths of Harry S. Truman (b.
Music	Arthur Berger, Trio for Guitar, Violin and Piano	1884), Nikita Khrushchev (b. 1894)
Photography	Diane Arbus, *Diane Arbus* (text edited from tape recordings of a series of classes) Robert Frank, *The Lines of My Hand*	
Theatre	Richard Foreman's First Manifesto of the Theatre Sam Shepard, *The Tooth of Crime*	

1973

Architecture	Richard Meier, Douglas House, Harbor Springs, Mich. I. M. Pei, John Hancock Tower, Boston, Mass. (Henry Cobb designer) Jørn Utzon, Sidney Opera House, Sidney, Australia	Supreme Court in *Roe* v. *Wade* rules states may not restrict right of woman to have an abortion during first three months of pregnancy United States and North Vietnam sign cease-fire
Art	Richard Diebenkorn, Ocean Park, No. 67	Presidential assistants Haldeman and Erlichman along with

Disciplines

	Chuck Close, *Richard*
	Deaths of Pablo Picasso (b. 1881),
	Robert Smithson (b. 1938)
Dance	Lucinda Childs, *Calico Mingling, Particular Reel*
	Laura Dean, *Walking Dancing, Changing Pattern Steady Pulse, Spinning Dance*
	Douglas Dunn, *Time Out*
	Robert Wilson, *The Life and Times of Joseph Stalin*
	Batya Zamir, *Off the Wall*
Film	Peter Gidal, *Room Film 1973*
Literature	Donald Barthelme, *Sadness*
	Don DeLillo, *Great Jones Street*
	Stanley Elkin, *Searches and Seizures*
	Steve Katz, *Cheyenne River Wild Track*
	Gilbert Sorrentino, *Splendide Hotel*
	Isaac Bashevis Singer, *A Crown of Feathers*
	Ronald Sukenick, *Out*
	Thomas Pynchon, *Gravity's Rainbow*
	Kurt Vonnegut, *Breakfast of Champions*
Music	Steve Reich, Music for Mallet Instruments, Voices, and Organ
Photography	Michael Lesy, *Wisconsin Death Trip*
	Death of Edward Steichen (b. 1879)
Theatre	Beckett, *Not I*
	Open Theatre disbands

World and National Events

president's counsel John Dean resign. Archibald Cox appointed special prosecutor. Subsequently, Cox is fired in "Saturday Night Massacre"

Launching of space station begins Skylab program

Existence of presidential tapes revealed

Henry Kissinger named secretary of state

Vice President Spiro Agnew resigns, succeeded by Gerald R. Ford

Syria and Egypt attack Israel beginning "Yom Kippur" war

OPEC initiates oil embargo causing energy crisis in United States

Juan Peron elected president of Argentina

Death of Lyndon Baines Johnson (b. 1908)

1974

Architecture	Michael Graves, Claghorn House, Princeton, N.J.
	Charles Moore, Kresge College, University of California, Santa Cruz; Burns House, Santa Monica Canyon, Los Angeles, Calif.
	Death of Louis Kahn (b. 1901)

Patricia Hearst kidnapped

Richard Nixon resigns presidency, succeeded by Vice President Gerald R. Ford, who grants him full pardon

Violence erupts in Boston as a result of court ordered busing

Disciplines		World and National Events
Dance	Simone Forti, *Crawling, Handbook in Motion* David Gordon, *Chair, Alternatives 1 through 5, Spilled Milk Variations* Yvonne Ranier, *Work 1961–73* Douglas Dunn, *101, Octopus*	India explodes first nuclear device Turkey invades Cyprus after overthrow of Archbishop Makarios as president Dow Jones drops below 700
Film	Malcolm LeGrice, *Dejeuner Sur L'Herbe, After Manet, Giorgione* Laura Mulvey and Peter Wollen, *Penthesilea* P. Adams Sitney, *Visionary Film*	Death of Juan Peron (b. 1859), succeeded as president by his wife Evita Deaths of Earl Warren (b. 1891), Jack Benny (b. 1894)
Literature	Walter Abish, *The Alphabetical Africa* Italo Calvino, *Invisible Cities* Richard Brautigan, *The Hawkline Monster* Jonathan Baumbach, *Reruns* John Hawkes, *Death, Sleep, and the Traveler* Joseph Heller, *Something Happened* Joyce Carol Oates, *The Goddess and Other Women* Grace Paley, *Enormous Changes at the Last Minute* Joseph McElroy, *Lookout Cartridge* Ishmael Reed, *The Last Days of Louisiana Red* Philip Roth, *My Life as a Man* Fiction Collective founded as an authors cooperative publishing venture	
Music	George Crumb, *Music for a Summer Evening* Donald Martino, *Notturno* Steve Reich, *Writings About Music* Elliott Carter, Duo for Violin and Piano	
Photography	William Eggleston, *14 Pictures* Les Krims, *Making Chicken Soup* Minor White, *Celebrations* (with Jonathan Green)	
Theatre	Peter Handke, *They Are Dying Out* Sam Shepard, *Geography of a Horse Dreamer* Tom Stoppard, *Travesties*	

Disciplines   ## World and National Events

1975

Architecture	Robert Venturi, Tucker House, Mt. Kisco, N.Y. Architecture of the Ecole des Beaux Arts exhibition at MOMA Stanley Tigerman, Hot Dog House, Harvard, Ill.	Watergate conspirators Mitchell, Haldeman, Erlichman convicted U.S. car manufacturers offer rebates on new car purchases New York City averts default with aid from teacher's union
Art	Jules Olitski, *Jehovah Cover-2*	
Dance	Laura Dean, *Drumming* Douglas Dunn, *Gestures in Red* Kenneth King, *Battery* David Gordon, *Times Four* *The Drama Review* postmodern dance issue (T-65)	Patricia Hearst arrested by FBI United States ends military involvement in Vietnam. Saigon renamed Ho Chi Minh City United States recaptures freighter *Mayaguez* from Cambodia
Film	George Landow, *New Improved Institutional Quality*	Jimmy Hoffa reported missing
Literature	Donald Barthelme, *The Dead Father* Thomas Berger, *Sneaky People* Walter Abish, *Minds Meet* Jerry Bumpus, *Things in Place* Jerome Charyn, *Blue Eyes* William Gaddis, *J.R.* Joyce Carol Oates, *The Hungry Ghosts* Isaac Bashevis Singer, *Passions* Ishmael Reed, *Flight to Canada* Raymond Federman, *Surfiction: Fiction Now and Tomorrow* Saul Bellow wins Pulitzer Prize for *Humboldt's Gift* Death of Lionel Trilling (b. 1905) Heinrich Böll awarded Nobel Prize	Deaths of Francisco Franco (b. 1892), Haile Selassie (b. 1892), Chang Kai-shek (b. 1887)
Photography	Les Krims, *Fictcryptokrimsographs* Jerry Uelsmann, *Jerry N. Uelsmann: Silver Meditations* New Topographics Exhibition at International Museum of Photography, George Eastman House	
Theatre	The Performing Garage stages Brecht's *Mother Courage*	

Disciplines	World and National Events

1976

| Architecture | Richard Rogers and Renzo Piano, Pompidou Center, Paris | Concorde begins regular flights |

Aldo Rossi, Gallaratese Housing, Milan, Italy

Israel rescues hostages at Entebbe Airport in Uganda

Robert Venturi, Franklin Court, Philadelphia

United States observes bicentennial arrival of tall ships

Death of Alvar Aalto (b. 1898)

Art

Susan Rothberg, *Butterfly*

Viking I space probe lands on Mars

Claes Oldenburg, *Clothespin*

Sol LeWitt, *Lines to Points on a Grid*

Deaths of Martin Heidegger (b. 1889), Mao Tse-tung (b. 1893)

Jennifer Bartlett, *Falcon Avenue, Seaside Walk, Dwight Street, Jarvis Street, Green Street*

Jimmy Carter elected president, defeating Gerald R. Ford

Dance

Lucinda Childs, Choreography for *Einstein on the Beach* (opera by Robert Wilson and Philip Glass)

Meredith Monk, *Quarry*

Kenneth King, *RAdeoA.C.tiv(ID)ty* (1976–78)

Jim Self, *Scraping Bottoms*

Wendy Perron, *The Daily Mirror*

Film

Yvonne Rainer, *Kristina Talking Pictures*

Pat O'Neill, *Saugus Series*

Peter Gidal, *Structural Film Anthology*

Literature

Richard Brautigan, *Sombrero Fallout*

Ann Beattie, *Chilly Scenes of Winter*

Renata Adler, *Speedboat*

Raymond Carver, *Will You Please Be Quiet, Please?*

Jerome Charyn, *Marilyn the Wild*

Don DeLillo, *Ratner's Star*

Stanley Elkin, *The Franchiser*

Raymond Federman, *Take It Or Leave It*

Cynthia Ozick, *Bloodshed & Three Novellas*

Death of Raymond Queneau (b. 1903)

Saul Bellow awarded Nobel Prize

Disciplines   ## World and National Events

Music   John Cage, *Apartment House 1776,*
                 Branches
                 Elliott Carter, A Symphony of
                 Three Orchestras
                 Philip Glass, *Einstein on the Beach*
                 David Del Tredici, *Final Alice*

Photography   Ansel Adams, *Photographs of the*
                 Southwest
                 Harry Callahan, *Callahan,* edited
                 by John Szarkowski
                 Lee Friedlander, *The American*
                 Monument
                 Emmet Gowin, *Emmet Gowin:*
                 Photographs
                 Aaron Siskind, Photographs 1966–
                 75, introduction by Thomas B.
                 Hess, *Places,* introduction by
                 Thomas B. Hess
                 Death of Minor White (b. 1908)

Theatre   Sam Shepard, *Angel City*
                 David Mamet, *Sexual Perversity in*
                 Chicago, Duck Variations

1977

Architecture   Michael Graves, Fargo Moorhead   Trans-Alaska pipeline opens
                 Cultural Center Project, Plocek
                 House, Warren, N.J.   Menachem Begin becomes Israel's
                 Charles Jencks, *The Language of*   sixth prime minister. Anwar Sadat
                 Post-Modern Architecture   addresses Israeli Knesset
                 Edward L. Barnes, IBM Building, N.Y.
                                                        Massive power failure causes
Art   Jennifer Bartlett, *2 Priory Walk*   blackout of New York City
                 Carl Andre, *Trabum*
                 Richard Estes, *Ansonia*
                 Philip Guston, *Cabal*
Dance   Trisha Brown, *Line Up*
                 Deborah Hay, *The Grand Dance*
                 Kenneth King, *Video Dances*
                 Steve Paxton, *Backwater: Twosome*
                 (with David Moss, ongoing)
                 Dana Reitz, *Journey: Moves 1*
                 through 7

Film   Laura Mulvey and Peter Wollen,
                 Riddles of the Sphinx
                 Malcolm LeGrice, *Abstract Film*
                 and Beyond

Disciplines   World and National Events

Stuart Sherman's first films *Globes,*
Scotty and Stuart
Deaths of Charlie Chaplin (b.
1889), Roberto Rossellini (b.
1906).

Literature   Roland Barthes, *Image Music Text*
(translated by Stephen Heath)
Thomas Berger, *Who is Teddy*
Villanova?
Richard Brautigan, *Dreaming of*
Babylon
Italo Calvino, *The Castle of*
Crossed Destinies
Jerome Charyn, *The Franklin Scare*
John Cheever, *Falconer*
Robert Coover, *The Public Burning*
Don DeLillo, *Players*
Steve Katz, *Moving Parts*
Philip Roth, *The Professor of*
Desire

Music   Pauline Oliveros, *Rose Moon*
Milton Babbitt, *Playing for Time*
John Cage, *Inlets*
Donald Martino, Triple Concerto
First publication of *Soundings*

Photography   Ansel Adams, *The Portfolio of*
Ansel Adams
William Eggleston, *Election Eve*
Duane Michals, *Real Dreams*
Susan Sontag, *On Photography*
Garry Winogrand, *Public Relations*

Theatre   Sam Shepard, *Suicide in B Flat*
David Mamet, *American Buffalo*

1978

Architecture   Michael Graves, Schulman House,   Agreement between Israel and
Princeton, N.J.   Egypt reached at Camp David
I. M. Pei and Partners, East
Building Addition to National   Trading of 63.5 million shares sets
Gallery, Washington, D.C.   record on N.Y. stock exchange
Charles Moore, Piazza d'Italia,
New Orleans   Panama Canal Treaty approved
Stanley Tigerman, Animal Crackers
House, Highland Park, Ill.   Members of People's Temple
Deaths of Edward Durrell Stone (b.   commit suicide at Jonestown
1902), Charles Eames (b. 1907)   Commune in Guyana

Disciplines

World and National Events

Art
    Carl Andre, *Equivalent VIII*
    Chuck Close, *Phil/Fingerprint II*
    Elizabeth Murray, *Children Meeting*
    Frank Stella, *Indian Birds*
    Death of Giorgio de Chirico (b. 1888)
    "New Image Painting" show at Whitney Museum

Aldo Moro murdered by Red Brigade terrorists in Italy

Supreme Court declares Allan Bakke victim of reverse discrimination

First "test-tube" baby born in England

Dance
    Trisha Brown, *Water Motor, Splang*
    Lucinda Childs, *Katema*
    David Gordon, *Not Necessarily Recognizable Objectives, What Happened*
    Andy de Groat, *Get Wreck*
    Mary Overlie, *Painter's Dream*

Death of Pope John Paul I (Albino Luciani, b. 1912), Karol Wojtyla of Poland elected John Paul II

Film
    Michelle Citron, *Daughter Rite*
    Ericka Beckman, *We Imitate; We Break Up*
    The New Cinema opens on New York's East Side

Literature
    Jerome Charyn, *Secret Isaac*
    Don DeLillo, *Running Dog*
    Ann Beattie, *Secrets and Surprises*
    Charles Simmons, *Wrinkles*
    Isaac Bashevis Singer wins Nobel Prize
    Death of James Gould Cozzens (b.1903)

Music
    Steve Reich, Octet, Music for a Large Ensemble

Photography
    William Eggleston, *Troubled Waters*
    Lee Friedlander, *Photographs*
    John Szarkowski, Mirrors and Windows Exhibit at MOMA

Theatre
    David Mamet, *The Water Engine*
    Harold Pinter, *Betrayal*
    Sam Shepard, *Buried Child*

1979

Architecture
    Buildings for Best Products exhibition at MOMA
    Stanley Tigerman, Marion House, Lisle, Ill.
    Richard Meier, Atheneum, New Harmony, Ind.

Margaret Thatcher becomes first woman prime minister of Great Britain

SALT II Treaty signed

Disciplines

Art

Susan Rothenberg, *Pontiac, Tattoo*
Robert Ryman, *Carrier*
Frank Stella, *Kastura*

Dance

Trisha Brown, *Glacial Decoy*
Lucinda Childs, *Dance*
Laura Dean, *Music*
Bill T. Jones and Arnie Zane, *Hand
Dance, Monkey Run*
Susan Rethorst, *Long Sleepless
Afternoons*

Film

Scott and Beth B., *The Black Box*
Su Friedrich, *Cool Hands, Warm
Heart*
Malcolm LeGrice, *Emily—Third
Party Speculation*
Sally Potter, *Thriller*

Literature

John Barth, *Letters*
Jonathan Baumbach, *Chez Charlotte
and Emily, The Return of Service*
Thomas Berger, *Arthur Rex*
Jerry Bumpus, *The Worms Are
Singing*
Raymond Federman, *The Voice in
the Closet*
John Hawkes, *The Passion Artist*
Joseph Heller, *Good as Gold*
Kenneth Gangemi, *The Volcanoes
of Puebla*
Gerald Graff, *Literature Against
Itself*
Clarence Major, *Emergency Exit*
Bernard Malamud, *Dubin's Lives*
Philip Roth, *The Ghost Writer*
Ronald Sukenick, *Long Talking Bad
Conditions Blues*
Kurt Vonnegut, *Jailbird*

Music

Pauline Oliveros, *El Rilicario de los
Animales*
Steve Reich, Variations for Winds,
Strings, and Keyboards

Theatre

Richard Foreman's Environmental
Theatre closes
Richard Schechner stages bricolage
production of Genet's *The
Balcony*

World and National Events

Gold price hits $528 an ounce

Congress agrees to loan guarantees
for Chrysler Corporation

Disciplines	World and National Events

The Drama Review publishes issue on autoperformance (including coverage of work by Jack Smith, Spalding Gray, Jeff Weiss)

1980

Architecture	Robert A. M. Stern, Points of View, Mt. Desert, Maine	Prime lending rate hits 21.5 percent
	Stanley Tigerman, Anti-Cruelty Society Building, Chicago, Ill.	Polish workers strike at Gdansk shipyards
	The Presence of the Past: First Exhibition of Architecture Venice Biennale	Unmanned Voyager I flies past Saturn
	Walter Netsch, Art Museum, Oxford, Ohio	John Lennon shot to death (b. 1940)
	Charles Moore, Rodes House, Los Angeles, Calif.	
		Death of Aleksei Kosygin (b. 1904)
Art	Julian Schnabel, *St. Francis in Ecstasy*	
	Gary Stephan, *Sator, Arepo, Tenet, Opera, Rotas*	
	Death of Oskar Kokoschka (b. 1886)	
Dance	Sally Banes, *Terpsichore in Sneakers: Post-Modern Dance*	
	Johanna Boyce, *Out of the Ordinary*	
	Douglas Dunn, *Pulcinella*	
	Molissa Fenley, *Energizer*	
	Charles Moulton, *Thought Movement Motor*	
	Jim Self, *Marking Time, Domestic Interlude, Silent Partner*	
Film	Manuel DeLanda, *Raw Nerves*	
	McCall, Tyndall, Pajaczkowska, Weinstock, *Sigmund Freud's Dora*	
	Yvonne Rainer, *Journeys from Berlin/1971*	
Literature	Walter Abish, *How German Is It*	
	Thomas Berger, *Neighbors*	
	Ann Beattie, *Falling in Place*	
	Richard Brautigan, *The Tokyo Montana Express*	
	Ihab Hassan, *The Right Promethean Fire*	

Disciplines

World and National Events

Gerald Rosen, *Dr. Ebenezer's Book
and Liquor Store*
Gilbert Sorrentino, *Aberration of
Starlight*
Deaths of Jean Paul Sartre (b.
1905), Roland Barthes (b. 1915)

Music
Leonard Bernstein, *Touches*
Philip Glass, *Modern Love Waltz*
Steve Reich, *My Name Is:
Ensemble Portrait*
George Rochberg, *Slow Fires of
Autumn*, Sonata for Harp, Viola
and Piano
Joseph Schwantner, *Wind, Willow,
Whispers . . .*

Photography
Harry Callahan, *Water's Edge,
Harry Callahan: Color*
Robert Heinecken, *Robert
Heinecken, He/She*
Paul Outerbridge, Jr., *Paul
Outerbridge, Jr.: Photographs*
Joel Meyerowitz, *St. Louis and the
Arch*
Garry Winogrand, *Stock
Photographs: The Fort Worth Fat
Stock Show and Rodeo*
John Szarkowski, *American
Landscapes*
Sandy Skoglund, "Revenge of the
Goldfish"

Theatre
Mabou Mines stages JoAnne
Akalaitis' *Dead End Kids*
Sam Shepard, *True West*

1981

Architecture
Gwathmey/Siegel, Viereck House,
Long Island, N.Y.; Taft House,
Cincinnati, Ohio
Death of Marcel Breuer (b. 1902)

Sandra Day O'Conner becomes first
woman appointed to Supreme Court

U.S. debt reaches $1 trillion

Art
Jennifer Bartlett, *Swimmer Lost at
Night* (for Tom Hess)
Jonathan Borofsky, *Self Portrait at
2,719,997*
Sandro Chia, *The Idleness of
Sisyphus*
Neil Jenney, *Sino-Spring*

Anwar Sadat assassinated (b. 1918)

Martial law declared in Poland

Death of Jacques Lacan (b. 1901)

Disciplines

World and National Events

Elizabeth Murray, *Painter's Progress*
Robert Mangold, *Three Red X
Within X*
Philip Pearlstein, *Two Models in
Bamboo Chairs with Mirror*
David Salle, *A Long Life*
Julian Schnabel, *Pre History:
Glory, Honor, Privilege, and
Poverty*

Turkish terrorist attempts
assassination of Pope John Paul II

Dance

Karole Armitage, *Drastic
Classicism*
Johanna Boyce, *Incidents (in
coming of age)*
Yoshiko Chum, *Champing at the
Bit*
Judy Padow, *Complex Desires*
Wendy Perron, *Dancing to Good
Bands . . . As Revealing Self
Portraits*

Film

Su Friedrich, *Gently Down the
Stream*
Michael Snow, *Presents*
Leslie Thornton, *Jennifer, Where
Are You?*

Literature

Thomas Berger, *Reinhart's Women*
Jerry Bumpus, *Special Offer*
Jacques Derrida, *Dissemination*
Tony Morrison, *Tar Baby*
Philip Roth, *Zuckerman Unbound*
Philip Stevick, *Alternate Pleasures*
Gilbert Sorrentino, *Crystal Vision*
Kurt Vonnegut, *Palm Sunday*

Music

Lukas Foss, Night Music for Brass
Quintet and Orchestra
Philip Glass *The Photographer*
Stuart Glazer, *Dialogue*
Gordon Jacob, Concerto No. 2 for
Flute and String Orchestra
George Rochberg, Trio

Photography

Sally Eauclaire, *The New Color
Photography*
Lee Friedlander, *Flowers and Trees*
Danny Lyon, *Pictures from the New
World*

Disciplines		World and National Events

1982

Architecture	Michael Graves, Portland Municipal Building, Portland, Oreg. Peter Eisenman, *House X*	First permanent artificial heart transplant
Art	Jonathan Borofsky, *Five Hammering Men* Sandro Chia, *Melancholic Encampment* Elizabeth Murray, *Sentimental Education* Susan Rothenberg, *Endless*	Argentina seizes Falkland Islands, surrenders to British forces after brief war Braniff Airlines, Manville Corporation file for bankruptcy; De Lorean Motors of Belfast placed in receivership
Dance	Molissa Fenley, *Eureka* Kenneth King, *Bridge/S-C-A-N (Dance Motor)* Jim Self, *Lookout, Phenix City Story* Judson Dance Theatre 1962–66, exhibition and dance reconstructions organized by Bennington College Judson Project Black postmodern dance series at Danspace	House votes to initial production funds for MX missile program Equal Rights Amendment fails to gain ratification by three-fourths states Seven persons in Chicago die from cyanide found in Extra-Strength Tylenol capsules Israel invades southern Lebanon
Film	Laura Mulvey and Peter Wollen, *Amy!* Scott and Beth B., *Vortex* Michael Snow, *So Is This*	U.S. Marines part of multinational force sent to guard evacuation of Palestinian forces from Beirut
Literature	John Barth, *Sabbatical* Jonathan Baumbach, *My Father More or Less* Ann Beattie, *The Burning House* Richard Brautigan, *So the Wind Won't Blow it All Away* John Cheever, *Oh What a Paradise It Seems* Jerome Charyn, *Donna Maria* Stanely Elkin, *George Mills* Raymond Federman, *The Twofold Vibration* John Hawkes, *Virginie: Her Two Lives* Bernard Malamud, *God's Grace* Joyce Carol Oates, *A Bloodsmoor Romance* Cynthia Ozick, *Levitation: Five Fictions*	Lebanese Christian militia massacre Palestinians at Sabra and Shatila refugee camps Yuri Andropov elected to head Soviet Union

Disciplines   World and National Events

Music

George Crumb, *Gnomic* (Variations
    for piano)
Elliott Carter, *Night Fantasies*
John Harbison, Variations for
    Clarinet, Violin, and Piano
Ned Rorem, *After Long Silence:*
    Voice, Oboe, Strings
Steve Reich, *Tehillim*
Death of Carl Orff (b. 1895)

Photography

Lee Friedlander, *Factory Valleys*
Stephen Shore, *Uncommon Places*

Theatre

Death of Peter Weiss (b. 1916)

1983

Architecture

John Burgee, Philip Johnson, PPG
    Place, Pittsburgh, Penn.
Hardy, Holzman, Pfeiffer, WCCO-
    TV, Minneapolis, Minn.
Michael Graves, San Juan
    Capistrano Library, San Juan
    Capistrano, Calif.
Richard Meier, High Museum,
    Atlanta, Ga.
Venturi, Rauch, and Scott Brown,
    Gurdon Wu Dining Hall,
    Princeton, N.J.

United States along with
detachments from six Caribbean
nations invade Grenada

South Korean commercial airliner
shot down over Soviet territory

Terrorist attack kills 241 marines in
Beirut

U.S. District Court approves
divestiture of twenty-two Bell
system companies from AT&T

Art

Roy Lichtenstein, *Green Street
    Mural*
Elizabeth Murray, *Sail Baby, More
    Than You Know*
Susan Rothenberg, *Falling Rock, The
    Monk*
David Salle, *The Cruelty of the
    Father, Brother Animal*
Julian Schnabel, *The King,
    Chinkzee*
Lauri Simmons, *The Acropolis*
Judy Rifka, *On Acropolis III,
    Valley of the Queens*

Dance

Timothy Buckley, *Out of the Blue,
    Barn Fever*
Ishmael Houston-Jones and Fred
    Holland, *Babble: First
    Impressions of the White Man*
Pooh Kay and Elisabeth Ross,
    Sticks on the Move (cinedance)

Disciplines   World and National Events

Wendy Perron, *Child Judge/Party
   Crasher/Stiff Tricks, Bad Day,
   Tin Quiz, Toy Eyes*
School for Movement Research
   Studies Project

Film   Erica Beckman, *You the Better*
                        Leslie Thornton, *Adynata*
                        Slava Tsukerman, *Liquid Sky*

Literature   Renata Adler, *Pitch Dark*
                        Thomas Berger, *The Feud*
                        Raymond Carver, *Cathedral*
                        Jerome Charyn, *Pinocchio's Nose*
                        Cynthia Ozick, *The Cannibal
                           Galaxy*
                        Philip Roth, *The Anatomy Lesson*
                        William Golding wins Nobel Prize

Music   Milton Babbitt, Canonical Forms
                        Elliott Carter, Changes for Solo
                           Guitar
                        Gordon Jacob, *Mercy and Truth are
                           Met*
                        Ulysses Kay, *Chariots:* Orchestral
                           Rhapsody
                        George Rochberg, *Between Two
                           Worlds:* Five Images for Flute
                           and Piano

Photography   Joel Meyerowitz, *Wild Flowers*
                        Stephen Shore, *The Gardens at
                           Giverny*

Theatre   David Mamet, *Glengarry, Glen
                           Ross*
                        Sam Shepard, *A Fool for Love*
                        Tom Stoppard, *The Real Thing*
                        Alan Schneider stages Beckett's
                           Ohio Impromptu Catastrophe,
                           What Where
                        Death of Tennessee Williams (b.
                           1911)

1984

Architecture   Philip Johnson, AT&T Building,   Death of Yuri Andropov (b. 1915),
                           New York   succeeded by Konstantin Chernenko
                        James Stirling, Neue Staatsgalerie,
                           Stuttgart, Germany   Geraldine Ferraro becomes first
                                                                   woman nominated for vice
Art   Elizabeth Murray, *Can You Hear Me?*   presidency by a major party

Disciplines

"An International Survey of Recent
Paintng and Sculpture" exhibit at
MOMA
"Five Painters in New York" (John
Torreano, Gary Stephan, Brad
Davis, Bill Jensen, Elizabeth
Murray) show at Whitney
Museum

Dance
Pina Bausch and the Wuppertaler
Tanztheater perform in the United
States
Sankai Juku, Japanese Butoh group
perform in the United States
Death of George Balanchine (b.
1904)

Film
Alex Cox, *Repo Man*
Stuart Sherman, *Portrait of
Benedicte Pesle, Mr. Ashley
Proposes* (Portrait of George)
Death of Francois Truffaut (b.
1932)

Literature
Saul Bellow, *Him With His Foot in
His Mouth*
Joseph Heller, *God Knows*
Joyce Carol Oates, *Mysteries of
Winterthurn*
Mario Vargas Llosa, *The War of
the End of the World*
Deaths of John Cheever (b. 1912),
Julio Cortázar (b. 1915), Michel
Foucault (b. 1927), Richard
Brautigan (b. 1935)

Music
Leonard Bernstein, *Halil*, a
Nocturne for Solo Flute, with
Piccolo, Alto Flute, Percussion,
Harp, and Strings
Aaron Copland, Proclamation for
Piano
George Rochberg, Quartet for Piano
and Strings
Joseph Schwantner, *Magabunda:
Four poems of Agueda Pizaro*
William Schuman, *Judith:
Choreographic Poem for
Orchestra, Night Journey*
Steve Reich, *The Desert Music*
Philip Glass, *Akhnaten*

World and National Events

Ronald W. Reagan reelected to
presidency, defeating Walter
Mondale

Indira Gandhi assassinated (b.
1917)

Death toll exceeds 1,600 in poison
gas leak at Union Carbide plant in
Bhopal, India

Disciplines   World and National Events

Theatre   Arthur Kopit, *The End of the World*
                   Peter Brook stages *Carmen* at
                       Vivian Beaumont Theatre
                   David Rabe, *Hurlyburly*
                   Alan Schneider stages Beckett's
                       Rockaby and *Footfalls* at Samuel
                       Beckett Theatre

Name and Title Index

Subject Index

About the Contributors

Sally Banes is senior critic for *Dance Magazine*, performance art critic for the *Village Voice*, and editor of *Dance Research Journal*. She is the author of *Terpsichore in Sneakers: Post-Modern Dance* and *Democracy's Body: Judson Dance Theater 1962–64*. A past president of the Dance Critics Association, she was dance editor of the *Soho Weekly News* and a contributing editor to *Dance Scope* and *Performing Arts Journal*. A Guggenheim Fellow for 1983–84, she currently teaches dance history and criticism at the State University of New York, College at Purchase.

Stanley J. Bowman lives in upstate New York and is Associate Professor and Chairperson of the Department of Art at Cornell University. After receiving an MFA in 1973 from the University of New Mexico, he joined the Cornell faculty to teach and establish a new program in photography. Over the last fifteen years, he has had numerous individual and group exhibitions of his photography, both in the United States and abroad, including the San Francisco Museum of Modern Art, the O.K. Harris Gallery in New York City, the Chicago Arts Institute, and Studio 666 in Paris. In addition to the San Francisco Museum of Modern Art, he also has work in the collections of the Erie Art Museum, the Museum of New Mexico, and the Bibliotheque Nationale in Paris.

Noël Carroll presently teaches philosophy at Wesleyan University. He holds a Ph.D. in Cinema from New York University and a Ph.D. in Philosophy from the University of Illinois. He has taught film at New York University, the State University of New York at Buffalo, and Columbia University and philosophy at Temple University. From 1977 to 1980, he regularly covered avant-garde film for the *Soho Weekly News* and has written four documentaries on the avant-garde for WNET. He is an editor of *Millennium Film Journal* and a contributor to *Dance Magazine* and has published widely in the fields of philosophical aesthetics, film, theatre, dance, and painting.

Garry E. Clarke is Professor of Music and Chairman of the Department of Music at Washington College. A composer and pianist, he holds degrees from Cornell College and Yale University. His book, *Essays on American Music*, is number sixty-two in the Greenwood Press Contributions in American History Series.

Alfred J. MacAdam is Professor of Latin American Literature at Barnard College and Columbia University. He is the author of *Modern Latin American Narrative* and currently editor of *Review Magazine*.

Mary McLeod is an Assistant Professor in the Graduate School of Architecture and Planning at Columbia University. She has worked as a designer and draftsman at Marcel Breuer and Associates, I. M. Pei and Partners, and with Michael Graves and conducted design reviews at Princeton, Harvard, and Syracuse universities. She has published widely in art and architectural journals and participated in lecture series and symposia at Columbia University and at the Institute for Architecture and Urban Studies.

John T. Paoletti is a professor in the history of art at Wesleyan University. He has held numerous fellowships and grants, among them a Kress Foundation Grant at Yale University and a Dartmouth Faculty Fellowship and has had visiting appointments at Yale University and Smith College. He has published articles in *Art Bulletin*, *Apollo*, *Arts Magazine*, and the *Encyclopaedia Britannica* and has been guest curator at the Wesleyan University Art Gallery at the Wadsworth Atheneum and at the Yale Center for British Art.

Flora H. Schiminovich is an instructor at Barnard College. She has written on Macedonio Fernandez and Manuel Puig and published widely on several other modern Latin American writers.

June Schleuter is Associate Professor of English at Lafayette College. She is the author of *Metafictional Characters in Modern Drama* and *The Plays and Novels of Peter Handke* and, with her husband Paul Schleuter, has edited *The English Novel: Twentieth Century Criticism*. In 1978–79, she held a Fulbright Lectureship in West Germany and is currently at work on a study of Arthur Miller.

Philip Stevick is Professor of English at Temple University. He is the author of *Alternative Pleasures: Postrealist Fiction* and the *Tradition and the Chapter in Fiction: Theories of Narrative Division* and has assembled two pivotal anthologies: *The Theory of the Novel* and *Anti-Story: An Anthology of Experimental Fiction*. He has also edited an edition of Richardson's *Clarissa*. His articles and reviews have appeared in *University of Toronto Quarterly*, *Western Humanities Review*, *Novel*, and *Criticism*, in addition to many other journals.

Stanley Trachtenberg is Professor of American literature at Texas Christian University. Formerly a senior trade editor at Macmillan and at Crown Publishing companies, he has written and lectured on subjects ranging from film technique and Freud's *Jokes and Their Relation to the Unconscious* to curriculum development. He has edited a collection of critical essays on Saul Bellow's fiction and a two-volume history of American humor. In 1968–69 he was a Fulbright Lecturer at the University of Bergen in Norway. His fiction, reviews, and essays have appeared in the *Yale Review, Kenyon Review, Michigan Quarterly*, the *Antioch Review, Commentary*, and in the *Dallas Times Herald*, the *Los Angeles Times*, and the *New York Times*.

David E. Wellbery is Associate Professor of German Studies at Stanford University. He has published *Lessing's "Laocoon": Semiotics and Aesthetics in the Age of Reason* and (with Klaus Weimar) *Goethe's "Harzreise im Winter": Eine Deutungskontroverse*. He is the editor of *Stanford Literature Review*.

About the Editor

STANLEY TRACHTENBERG is Professor of English at Texas Christian University. His earlier works include *Critical Essays on Saul Bellow, American Humor 1800–1950, Dictionary of Literary Biography*, and articles in the *Journal of Narrative Technique, Yale Review*, and *Modern Fiction Studies*, among others.